# Let's Get Pickled!

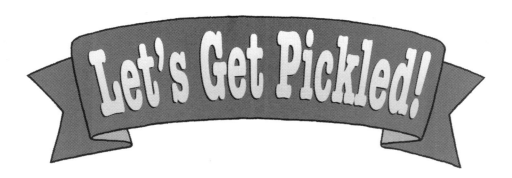

**Also by Brian Crane**

*Still Pickled After All These Years*

# Let's Get Pickled!

*A Pickles Collection by Brian Crane*

**Andrews McMeel
Publishing, LLC**

Kansas City

**Pickles** is syndicated by the Washington Post Writers Group.

**Let's Get Pickled!** copyright © 2006 by Brian Crane. All rights reserved. Printed in the United States of America. No part of this book may be used or reproduced in any manner whatsoever without written permission except in the case of reprints in the context of reviews. For information, write Andrews McMeel Publishing, LLC, an Andrews McMeel Universal company, 4520 Main Street, Kansas City, Missouri 64111.

08 09 10  BBG  10 9 8 7 6 5 4 3 2

ISBN-13: 978-0-7407-6192-8
ISBN-10: 0-7407-6192-7

Library of Congress Control Number: 2006926006

www.andrewsmcmeel.com

───── **ATTENTION: SCHOOLS AND BUSINESSES** ─────

Andrews McMeel books are available at quantity discounts with bulk purchase for educational, business, or sales promotional use. For information, please write to: Special Sales Department, Andrews McMeel Publishing, LLC, 4520 Main Street, Kansas City, Missouri 64111.

**For Diana,**
**beloved wife, biggest fan, most trusted critic,**
**and occasional inspiration for Opal.**
**I couldn't have done it without you.**

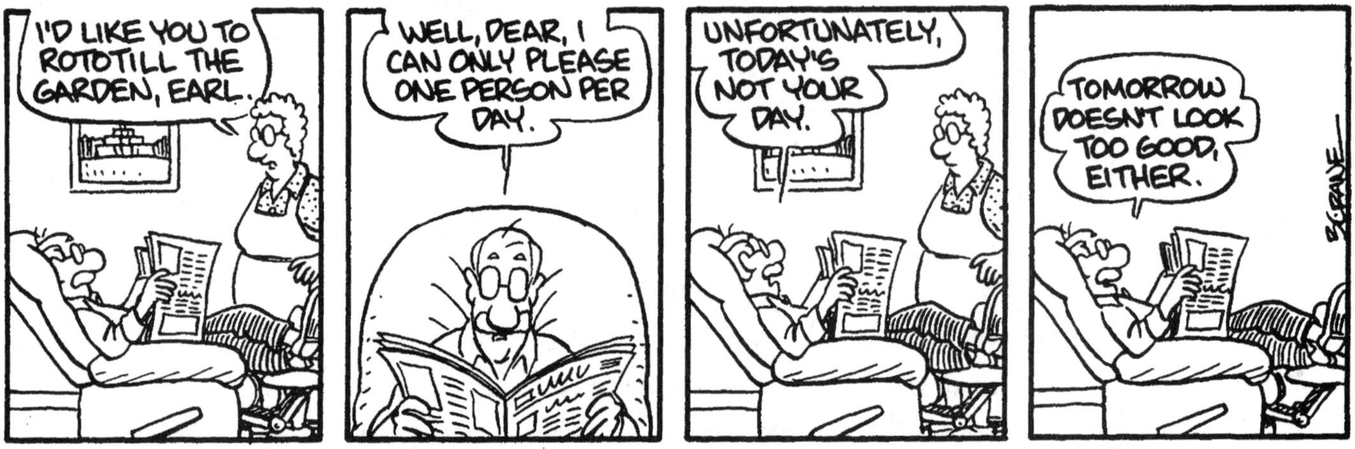
I'D LIKE YOU TO ROTOTILL THE GARDEN, EARL.
WELL, DEAR, I CAN ONLY PLEASE ONE PERSON PER DAY.
UNFORTUNATELY, TODAY'S NOT YOUR DAY.
TOMORROW DOESN'T LOOK TOO GOOD, EITHER.

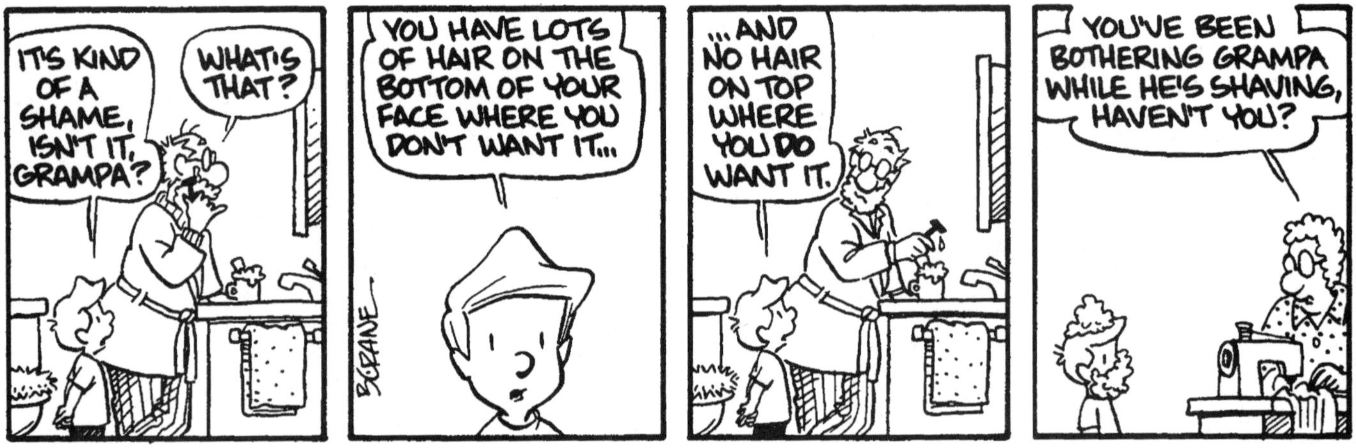
IT'S KIND OF A SHAME, ISN'T IT, GRAMPA?
WHAT'S THAT?
YOU HAVE LOTS OF HAIR ON THE BOTTOM OF YOUR FACE WHERE YOU DON'T WANT IT...
...AND NO HAIR ON TOP WHERE YOU DO WANT IT.
YOU'VE BEEN BOTHERING GRAMPA WHILE HE'S SHAVING, HAVEN'T YOU?

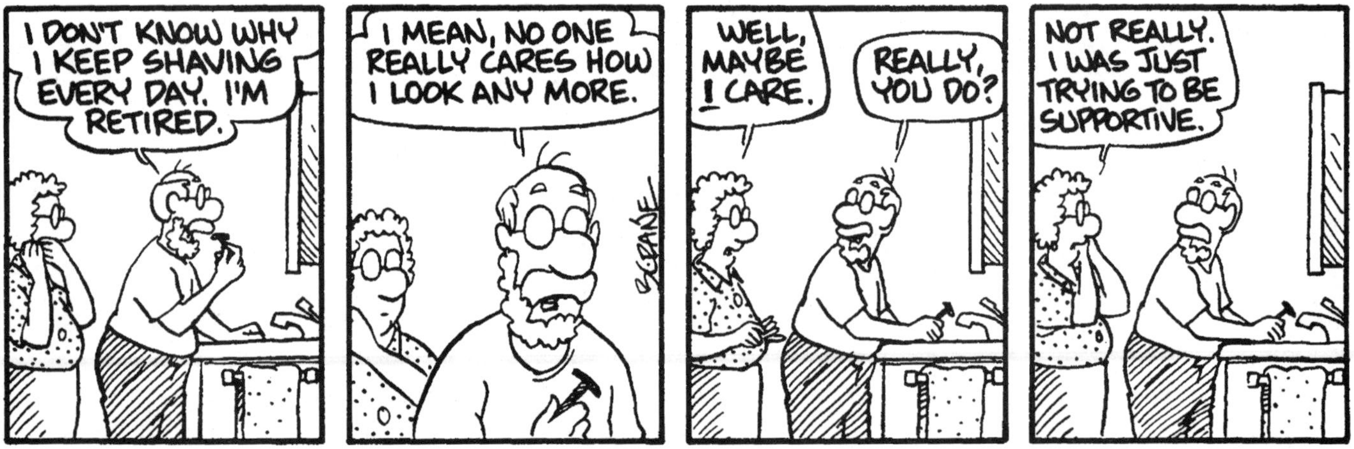
I DON'T KNOW WHY I KEEP SHAVING EVERY DAY. I'M RETIRED.
I MEAN, NO ONE REALLY CARES HOW I LOOK ANY MORE.
WELL, MAYBE I CARE.
REALLY, YOU DO?
NOT REALLY. I WAS JUST TRYING TO BE SUPPORTIVE.

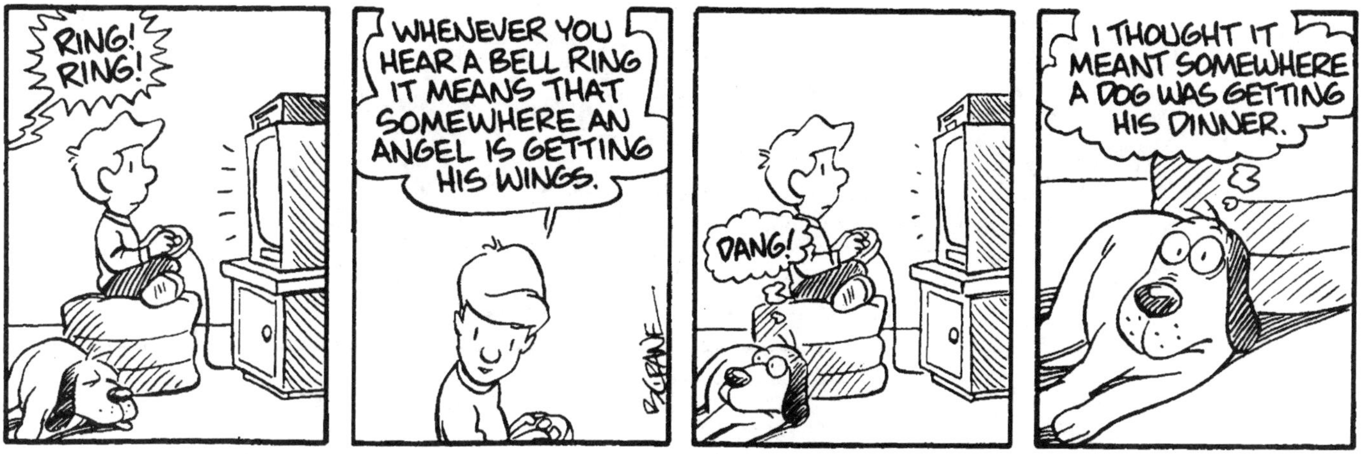
RING! RING!
WHENEVER YOU HEAR A BELL RING IT MEANS THAT SOMEWHERE AN ANGEL IS GETTING HIS WINGS.
DANG!
I THOUGHT IT MEANT SOMEWHERE A DOG WAS GETTING HIS DINNER.

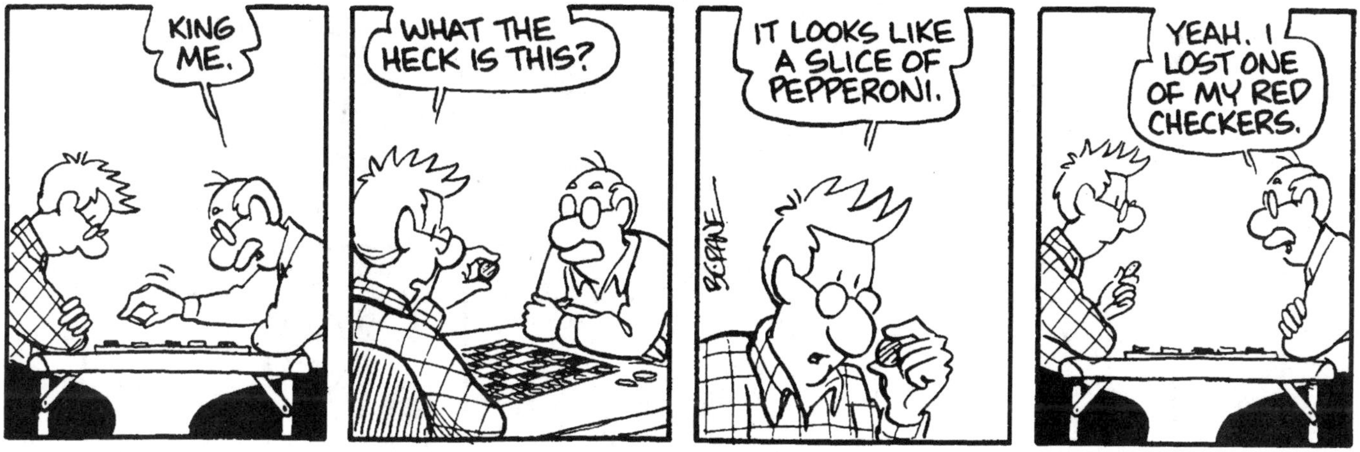
KING ME.
WHAT THE HECK IS THIS?
IT LOOKS LIKE A SLICE OF PEPPERONI.
YEAH. I LOST ONE OF MY RED CHECKERS.

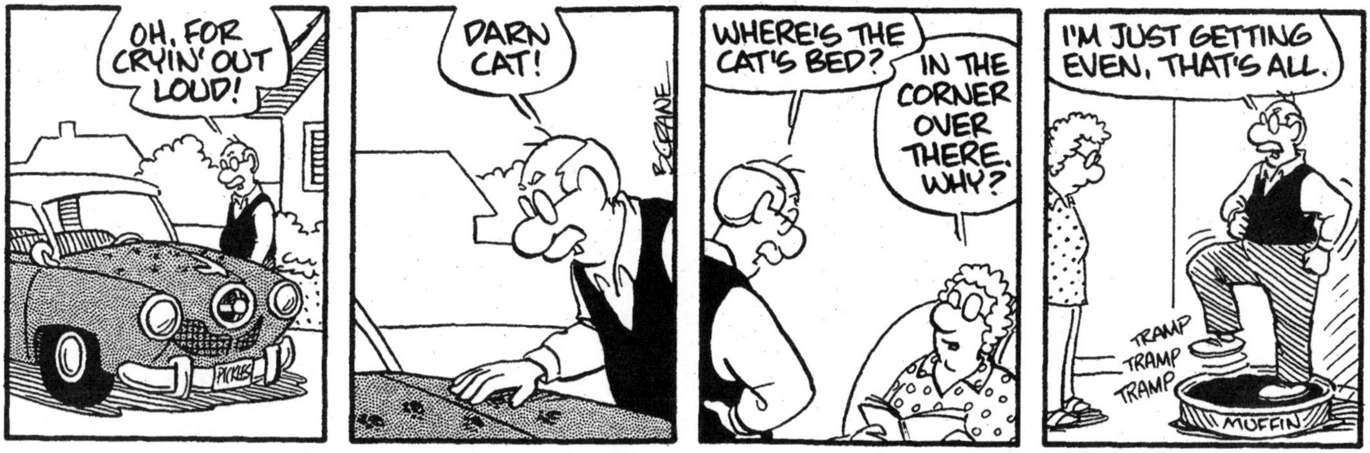
OH, FOR CRYIN' OUT LOUD!
PICKLES
DARN CAT!
WHERE'S THE CAT'S BED?
IN THE CORNER OVER THERE. WHY?
I'M JUST GETTING EVEN, THAT'S ALL.
TRAMP TRAMP TRAMP
MUFFIN

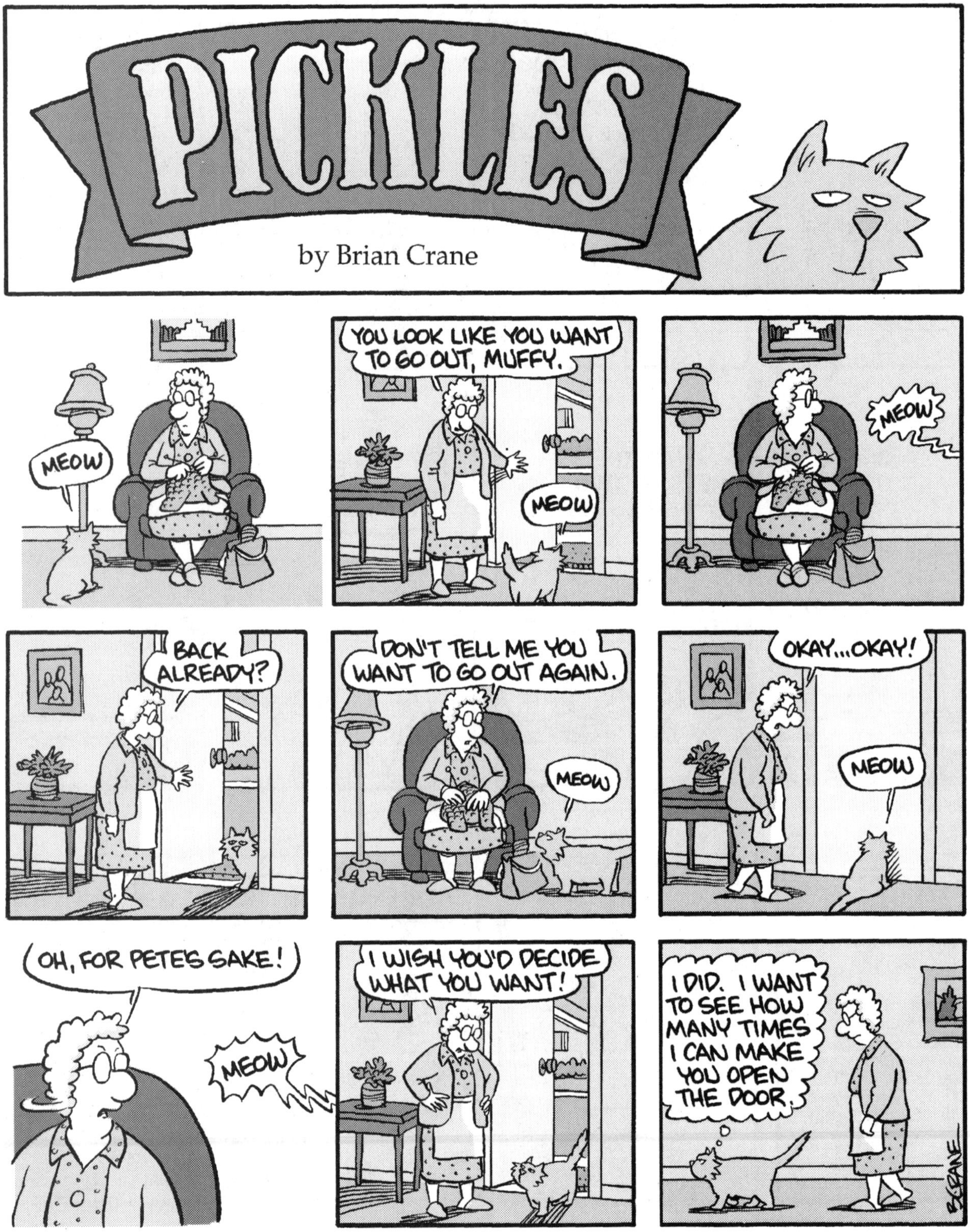
PICKLES
by Brian Crane
MEOW
YOU LOOK LIKE YOU WANT TO GO OUT, MUFFY.
MEOW
MEOW
BACK ALREADY?
DON'T TELL ME YOU WANT TO GO OUT AGAIN.
MEOW
OKAY...OKAY!
MEOW
OH, FOR PETE'S SAKE!
MEOW
I WISH YOU'D DECIDE WHAT YOU WANT!
I DID. I WANT TO SEE HOW MANY TIMES I CAN MAKE YOU OPEN THE DOOR.

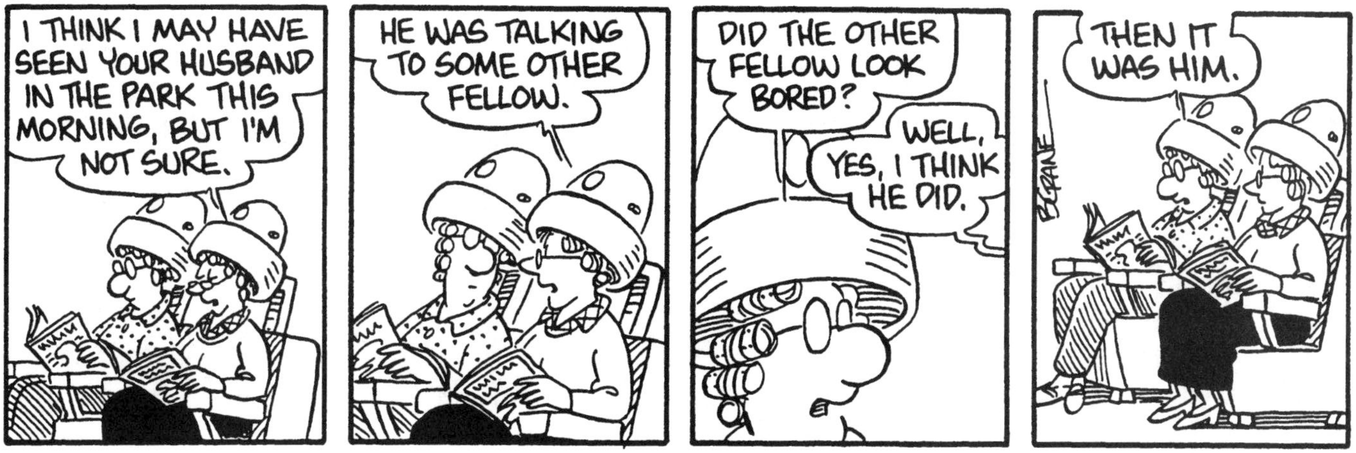
I THINK I MAY HAVE SEEN YOUR HUSBAND IN THE PARK THIS MORNING, BUT I'M NOT SURE.
HE WAS TALKING TO SOME OTHER FELLOW.
DID THE OTHER FELLOW LOOK BORED?
WELL, YES, I THINK HE DID.
THEN IT WAS HIM.

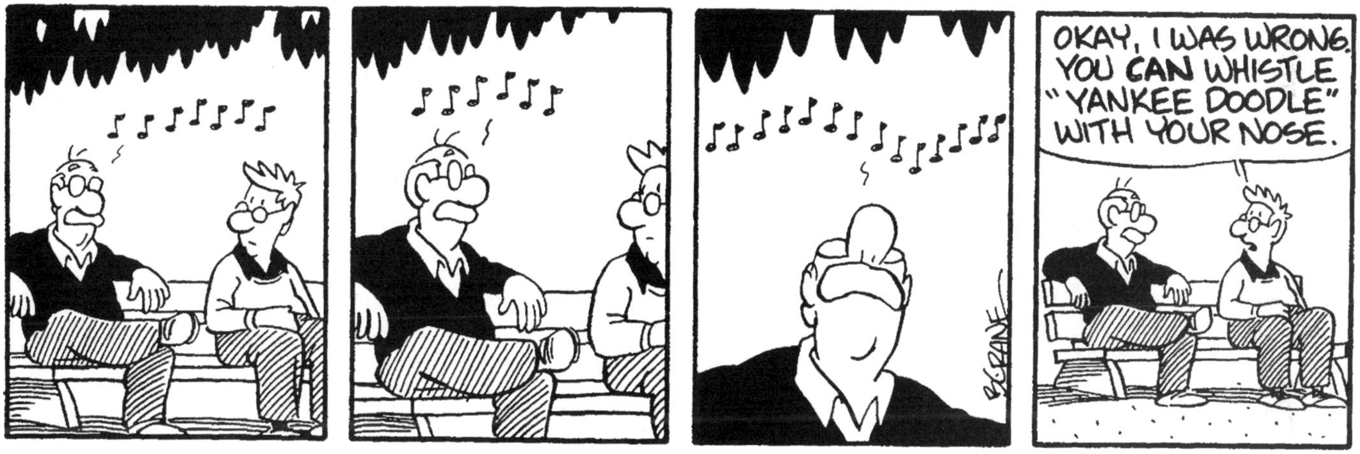
OKAY, I WAS WRONG. YOU CAN WHISTLE "YANKEE DOODLE" WITH YOUR NOSE.

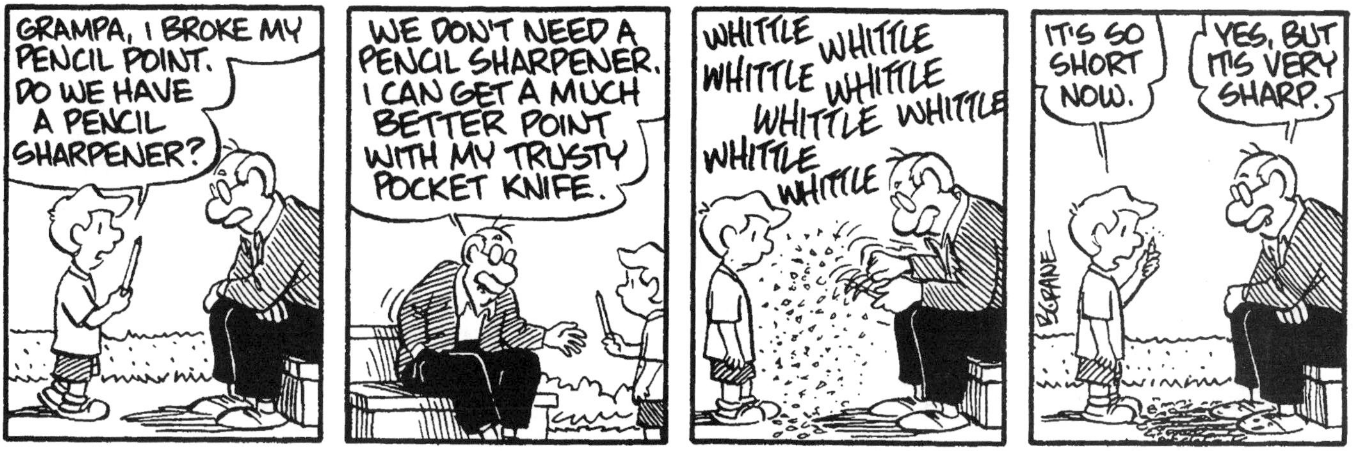
GRAMPA, I BROKE MY PENCIL POINT. DO WE HAVE A PENCIL SHARPENER?
WE DON'T NEED A PENCIL SHARPENER. I CAN GET A MUCH BETTER POINT WITH MY TRUSTY POCKET KNIFE.
WHITTLE WHITTLE WHITTLE WHITTLE WHITTLE WHITTLE WHITTLE WHITTLE
IT'S SO SHORT NOW.
YES, BUT IT'S VERY SHARP.

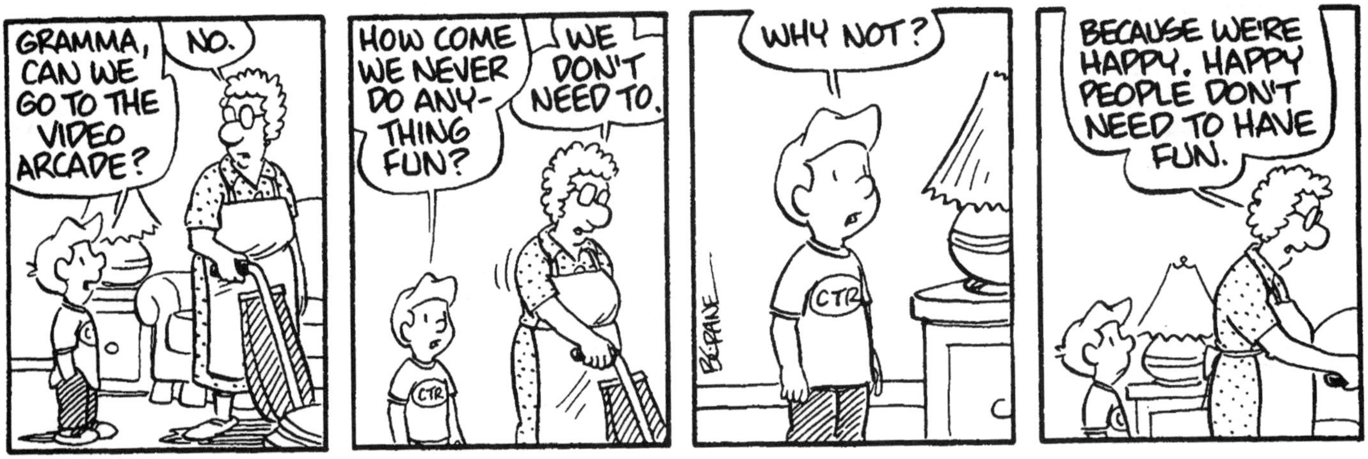
GRAMMA, CAN WE GO TO THE VIDEO ARCADE?
NO.
HOW COME WE NEVER DO ANY-THING FUN?
WE DON'T NEED TO.
WHY NOT?
BECAUSE WE'RE HAPPY. HAPPY PEOPLE DON'T NEED TO HAVE FUN.

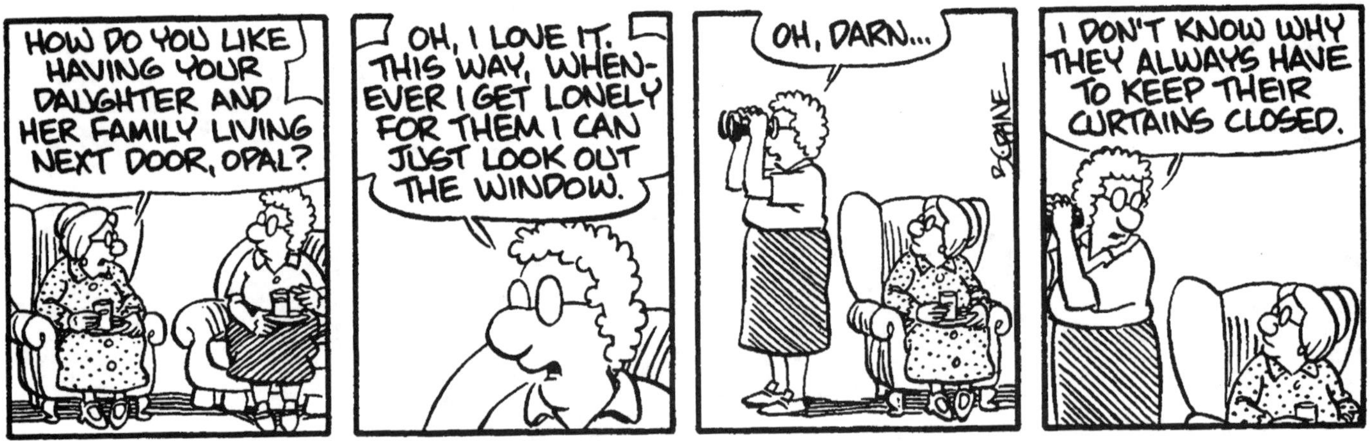
HOW DO YOU LIKE HAVING YOUR DAUGHTER AND HER FAMILY LIVING NEXT DOOR, OPAL?
OH, I LOVE IT. THIS WAY, WHEN-EVER I GET LONELY FOR THEM I CAN JUST LOOK OUT THE WINDOW.
OH, DARN...
I DON'T KNOW WHY THEY ALWAYS HAVE TO KEEP THEIR CURTAINS CLOSED.

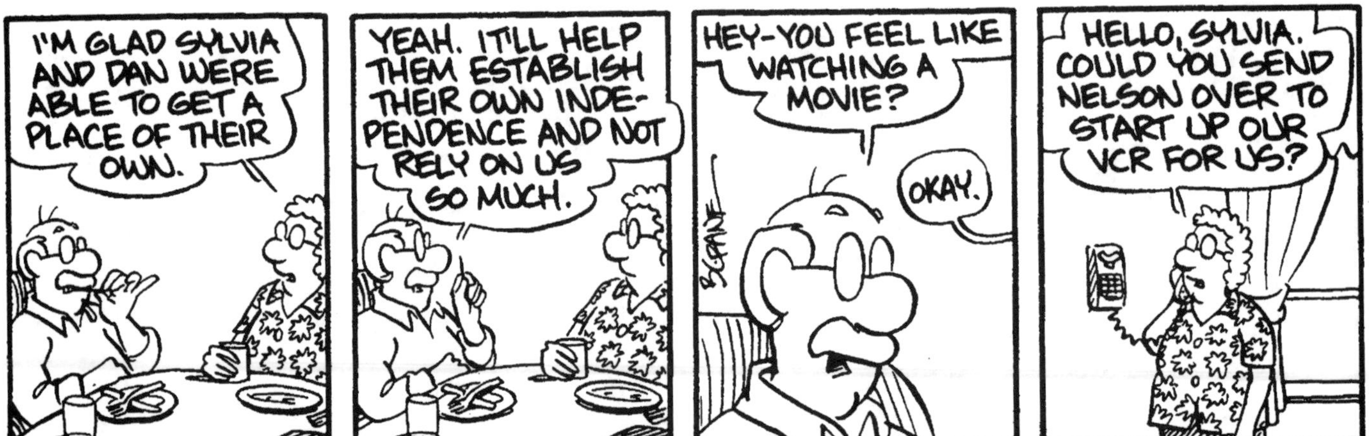
I'M GLAD SYLVIA AND DAN WERE ABLE TO GET A PLACE OF THEIR OWN.
YEAH. IT'LL HELP THEM ESTABLISH THEIR OWN INDE-PENDENCE AND NOT RELY ON US SO MUCH.
HEY-YOU FEEL LIKE WATCHING A MOVIE?
OKAY.
HELLO, SYLVIA. COULD YOU SEND NELSON OVER TO START UP OUR VCR FOR US?

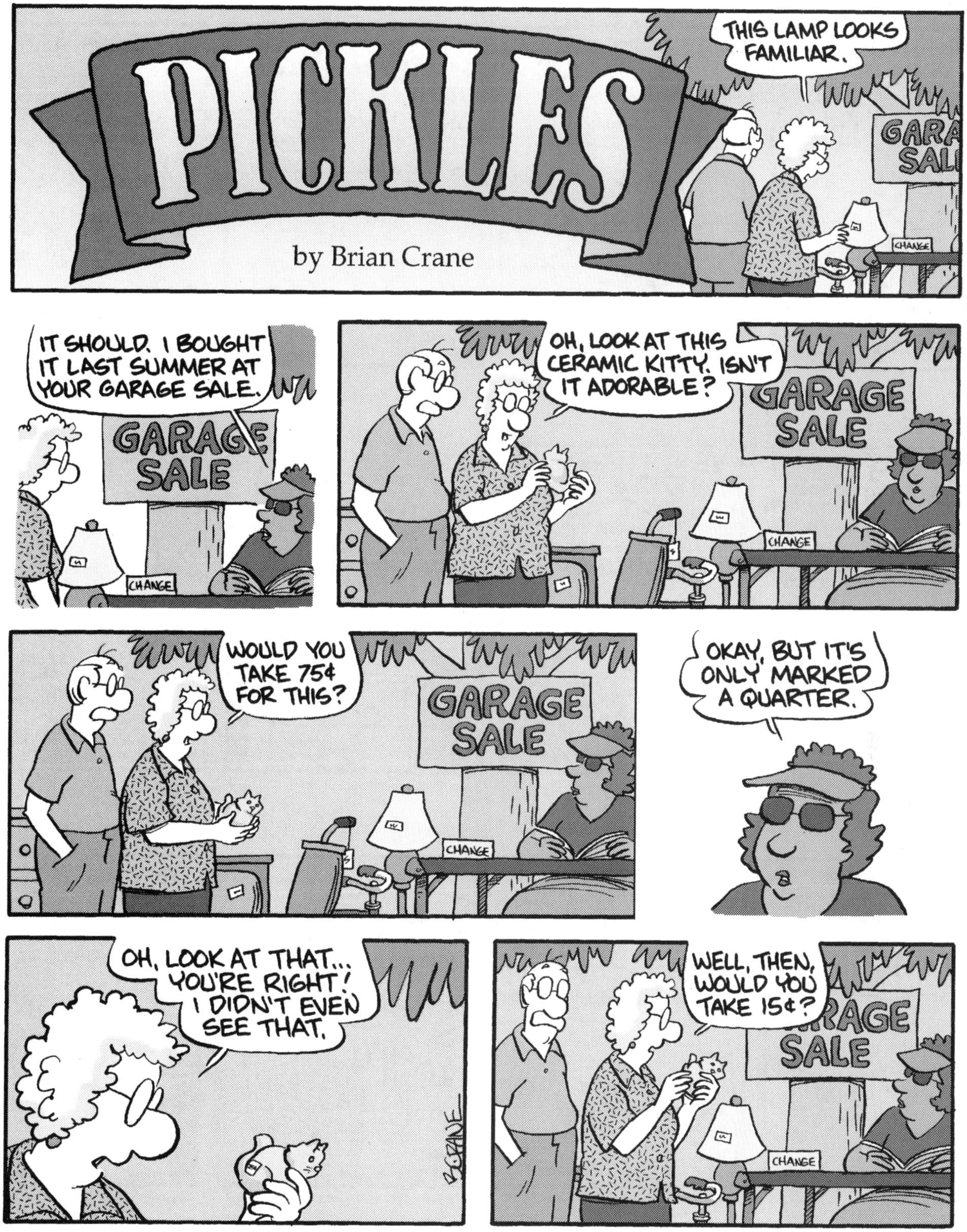
PICKLES
by Brian Crane
THIS LAMP LOOKS FAMILIAR.
GARAGE SALE
IT SHOULD. I BOUGHT IT LAST SUMMER AT YOUR GARAGE SALE.
OH, LOOK AT THIS CERAMIC KITTY. ISN'T IT ADORABLE?
WOULD YOU TAKE 75¢ FOR THIS?
OKAY, BUT IT'S ONLY MARKED A QUARTER.
OH, LOOK AT THAT... YOU'RE RIGHT! I DIDN'T EVEN SEE THAT.
WELL, THEN, WOULD YOU TAKE 15¢?
CHANGE
B. CRANE

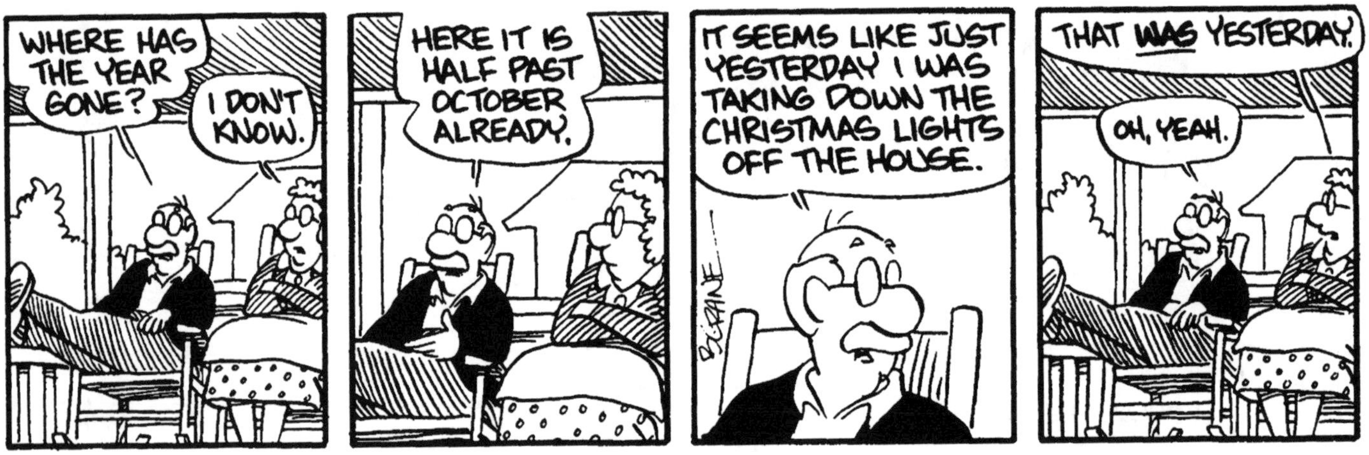
WHERE HAS THE YEAR GONE?
I DON'T KNOW.
HERE IT IS HALF PAST OCTOBER ALREADY.
IT SEEMS LIKE JUST YESTERDAY I WAS TAKING DOWN THE CHRISTMAS LIGHTS OFF THE HOUSE.
THAT WAS YESTERDAY.
OH, YEAH.

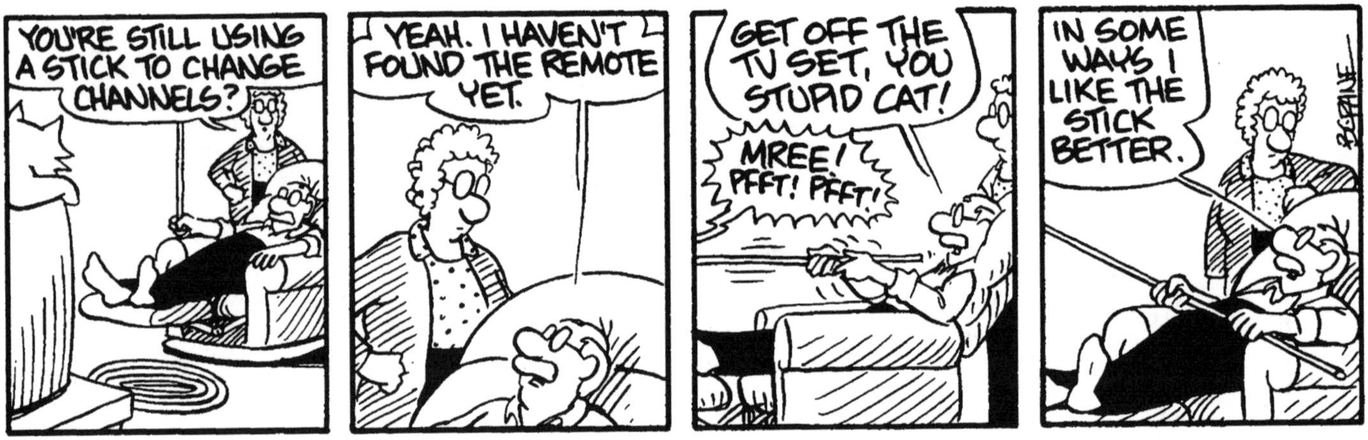
YOU'RE STILL USING A STICK TO CHANGE CHANNELS?
YEAH. I HAVEN'T FOUND THE REMOTE YET.
GET OFF THE TV SET, YOU STUPID CAT!
MREE! PFFT! PFFT!
IN SOME WAYS I LIKE THE STICK BETTER.

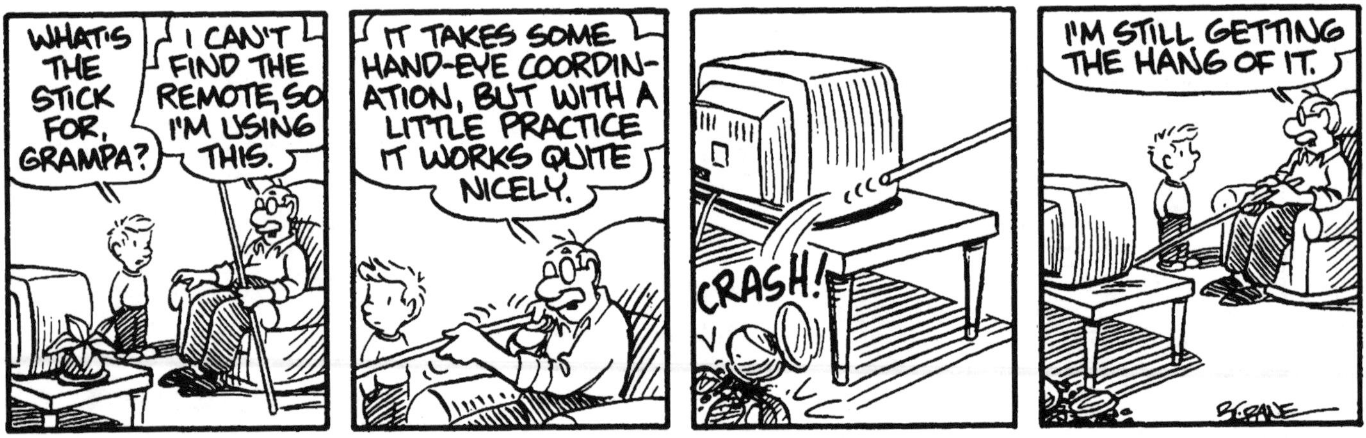
WHAT'S THE STICK FOR, GRAMPA?
I CAN'T FIND THE REMOTE, SO I'M USING THIS.
IT TAKES SOME HAND-EYE COORDINATION, BUT WITH A LITTLE PRACTICE IT WORKS QUITE NICELY.
CRASH!
I'M STILL GETTING THE HANG OF IT.

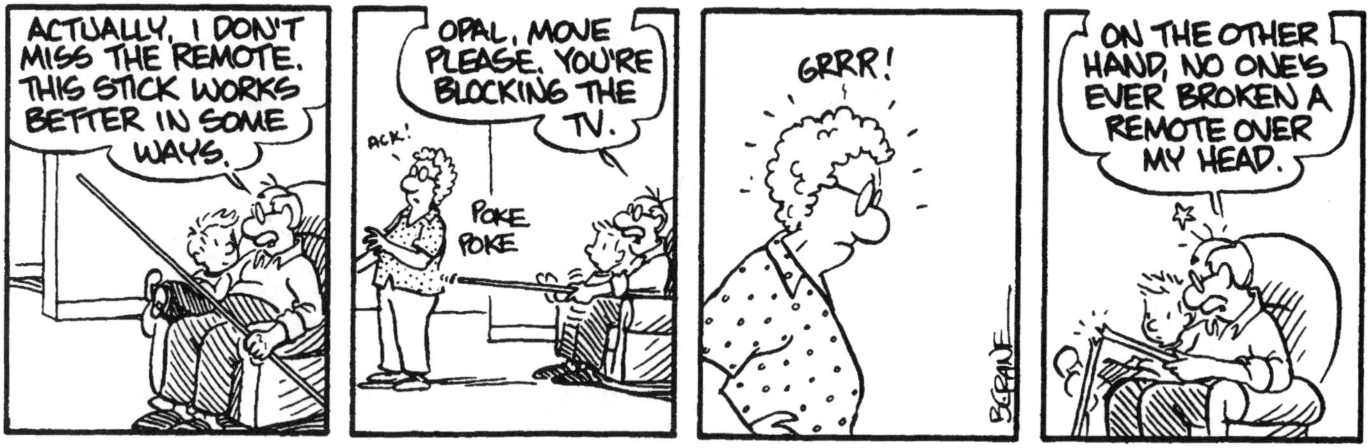
ACTUALLY, I DON'T MISS THE REMOTE. THIS STICK WORKS BETTER IN SOME WAYS.
OPAL, MOVE PLEASE. YOU'RE BLOCKING THE TV.
ACK!
POKE POKE
GRRR!
ON THE OTHER HAND, NO ONE'S EVER BROKEN A REMOTE OVER MY HEAD.

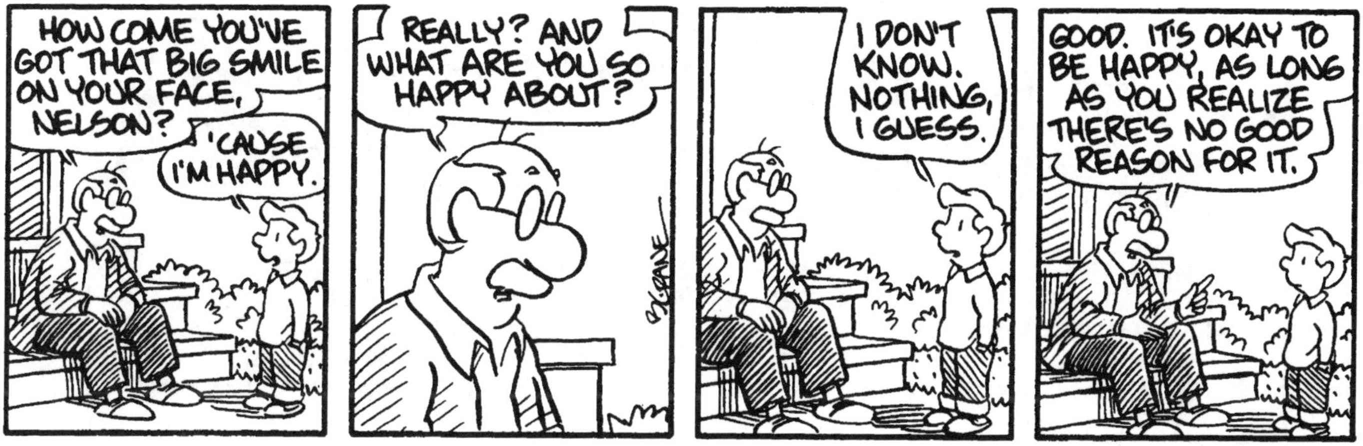
HOW COME YOU'VE GOT THAT BIG SMILE ON YOUR FACE, NELSON?
'CAUSE I'M HAPPY.
REALLY? AND WHAT ARE YOU SO HAPPY ABOUT?
I DON'T KNOW. NOTHING, I GUESS.
GOOD. IT'S OKAY TO BE HAPPY, AS LONG AS YOU REALIZE THERE'S NO GOOD REASON FOR IT.

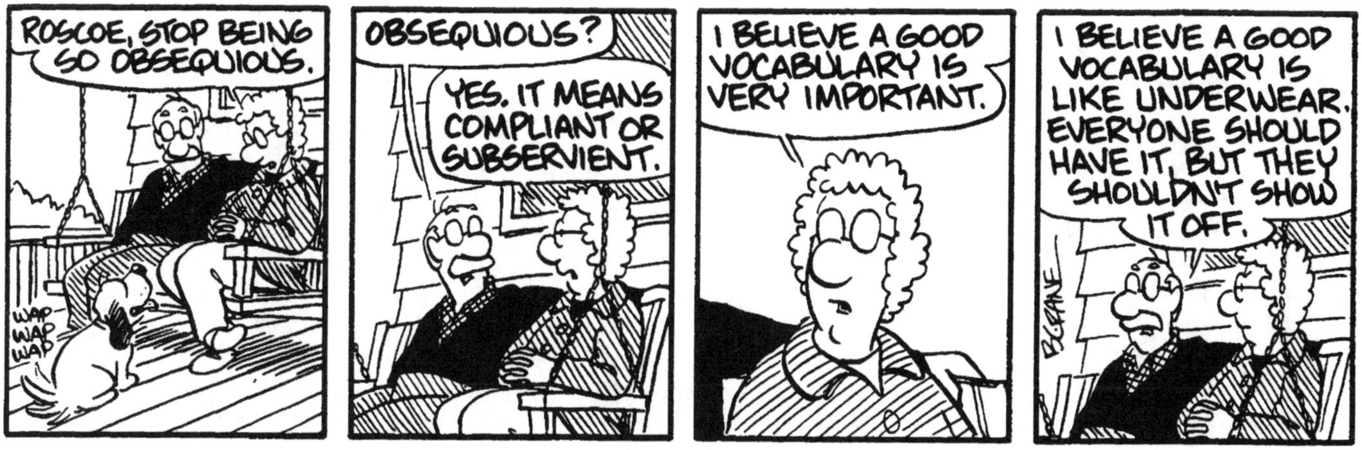
ROSCOE, STOP BEING SO OBSEQUIOUS.
WAP WAP WAP
OBSEQUIOUS?
YES. IT MEANS COMPLIANT OR SUBSERVIENT.
I BELIEVE A GOOD VOCABULARY IS VERY IMPORTANT.
I BELIEVE A GOOD VOCABULARY IS LIKE UNDERWEAR. EVERYONE SHOULD HAVE IT, BUT THEY SHOULDN'T SHOW IT OFF.

# PICKLES

by Brian Crane

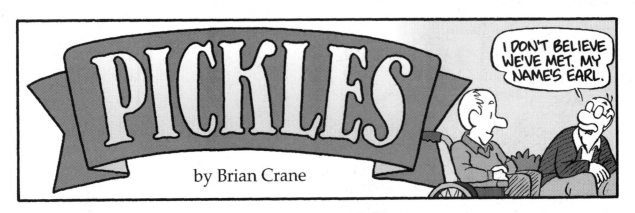

**I DON'T BELIEVE WE'VE MET. MY NAME'S EARL.**

**I'M BOB, AND THIS IS MY FRIEND BUDDY.**

**NICE LOOKIN' DOG. WHAT'S THAT THING ON HIS BACK?**

**THAT'S TO SHOW THAT HE'S NOT JUST A DOG. HE'S A "CANINE COMPANION".**

**HE'S BEEN SPECIALLY TRAINED TO HELP ME WITH MY DAILY TASKS.**

**REALLY? WHAT KINDS OF THINGS CAN HE DO?**

**OH, LOTS OF THINGS. BUDDY CAN OPEN DOORS, PICK THINGS UP OFF THE FLOOR AND GIVE THEM TO ME...**

**...TURN LIGHTS ON AND OFF, OPEN DRAWERS, GET THINGS OUT OF THE REFRIGERATOR FOR ME, HELP ME WITH SALES TRANSACTIONS AT THE STORE...**

**WOW! THAT'S INCREDIBLE.**

**THIS IS MY DOG, ROSCOE. I'M TRYING TO TRAIN HIM TO STOP GETTING HIS HEAD STUCK IN THINGS.**

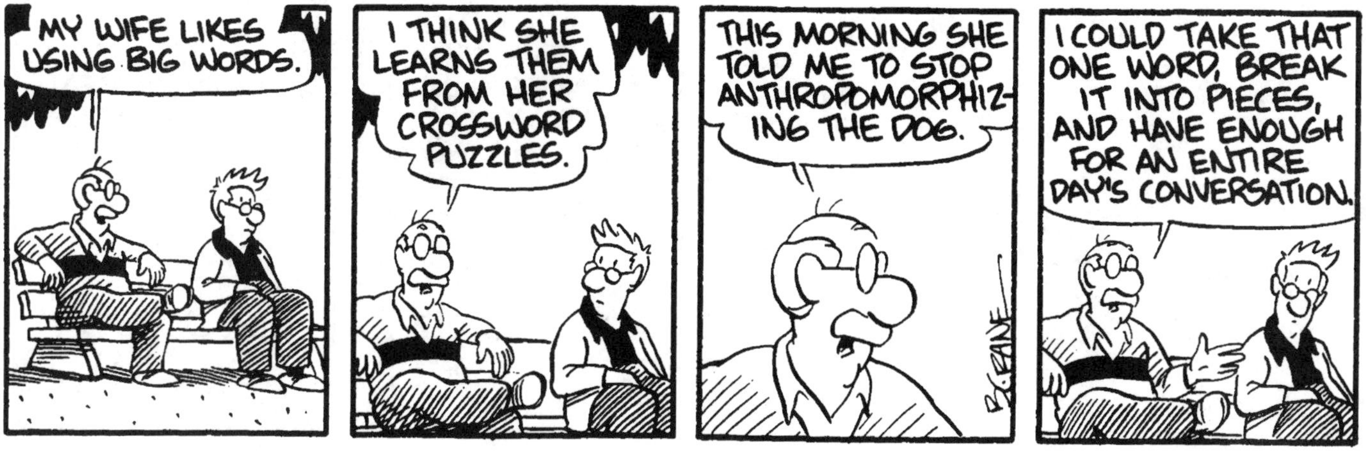
MY WIFE LIKES USING BIG WORDS.
I THINK SHE LEARNS THEM FROM HER CROSSWORD PUZZLES.
THIS MORNING SHE TOLD ME TO STOP ANTHROPOMORPHIZ-ING THE DOG.
I COULD TAKE THAT ONE WORD, BREAK IT INTO PIECES, AND HAVE ENOUGH FOR AN ENTIRE DAY'S CONVERSATION.

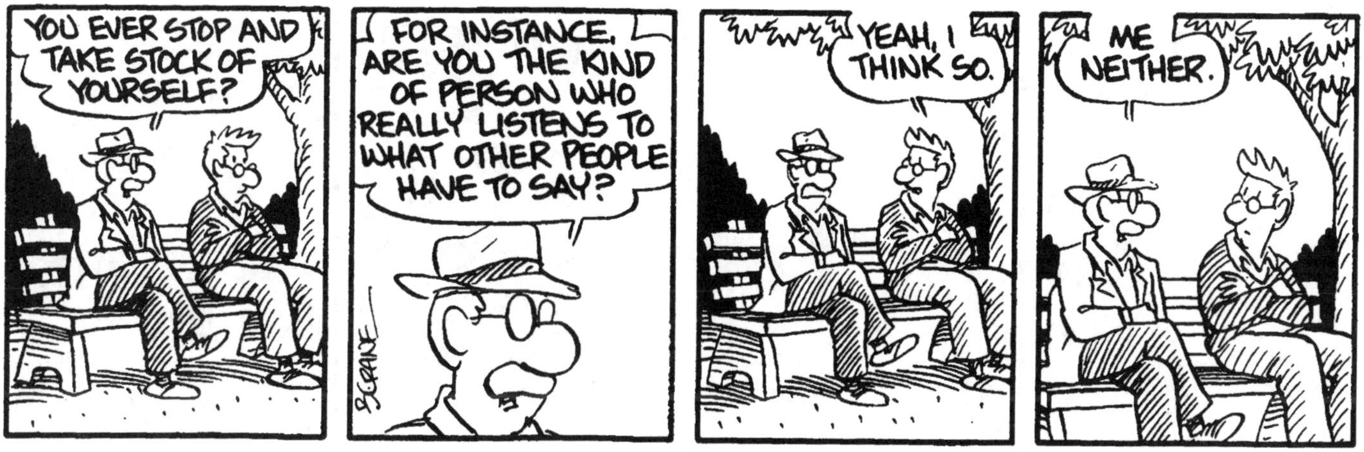
YOU EVER STOP AND TAKE STOCK OF YOURSELF?
FOR INSTANCE, ARE YOU THE KIND OF PERSON WHO REALLY LISTENS TO WHAT OTHER PEOPLE HAVE TO SAY?
YEAH, I THINK SO.
ME NEITHER.

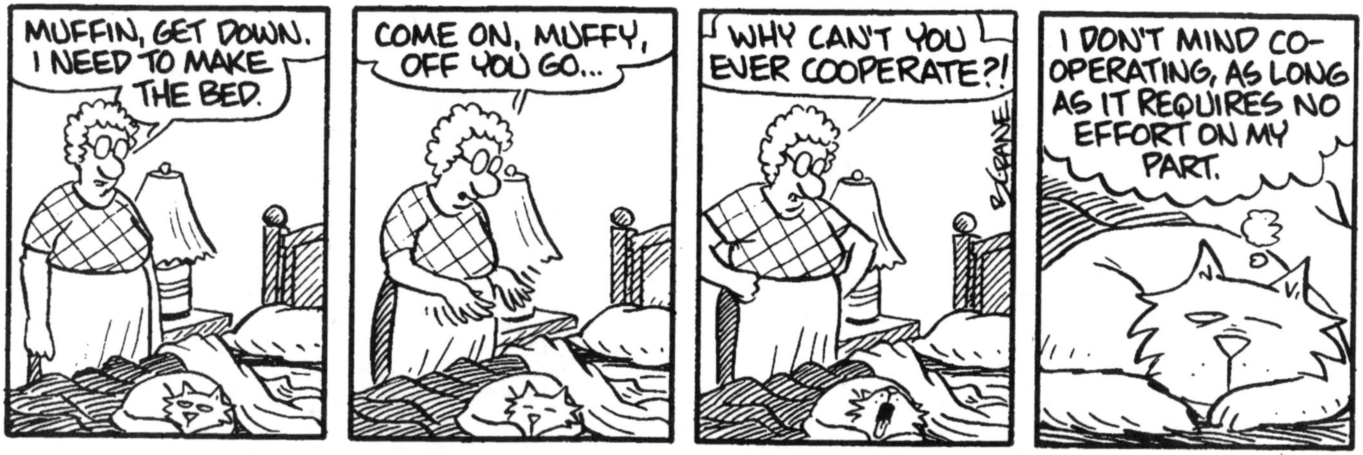
MUFFIN, GET DOWN. I NEED TO MAKE THE BED.
COME ON, MUFFY, OFF YOU GO...
WHY CAN'T YOU EVER COOPERATE?!
I DON'T MIND CO-OPERATING, AS LONG AS IT REQUIRES NO EFFORT ON MY PART.

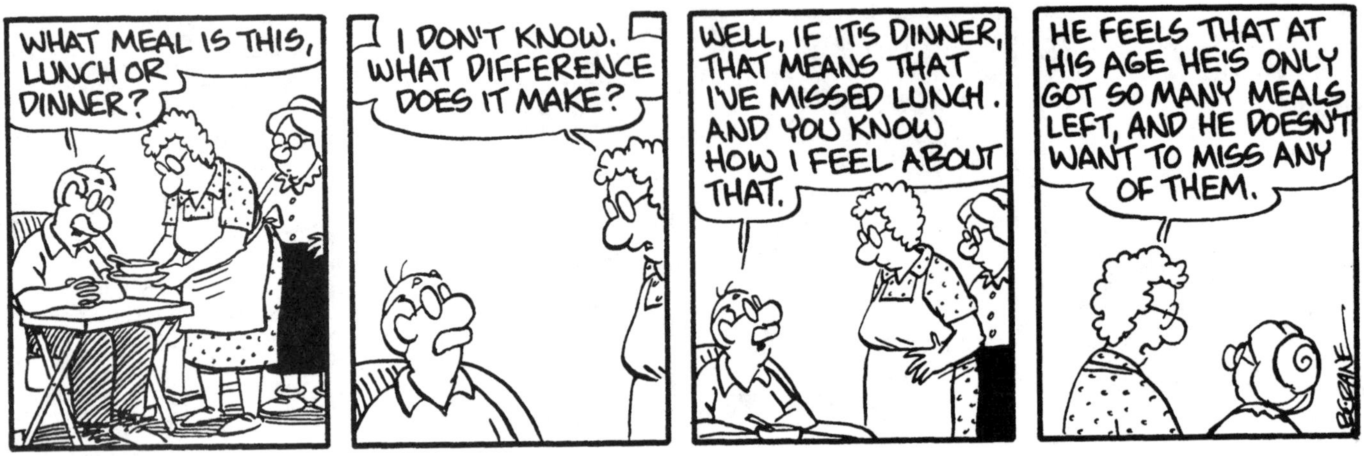
WHAT MEAL IS THIS, LUNCH OR DINNER?
I DON'T KNOW. WHAT DIFFERENCE DOES IT MAKE?
WELL, IF IT'S DINNER, THAT MEANS THAT I'VE MISSED LUNCH. AND YOU KNOW HOW I FEEL ABOUT THAT.
HE FEELS THAT AT HIS AGE HE'S ONLY GOT SO MANY MEALS LEFT, AND HE DOESN'T WANT TO MISS ANY OF THEM.

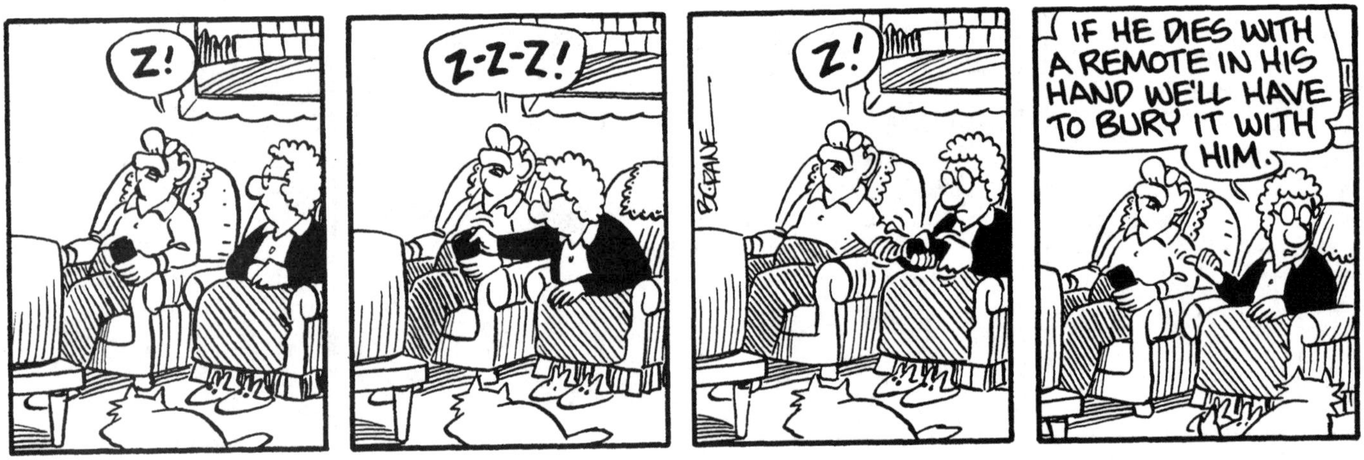
Z!
Z-Z-Z!
Z!
IF HE DIES WITH A REMOTE IN HIS HAND WE'LL HAVE TO BURY IT WITH HIM.

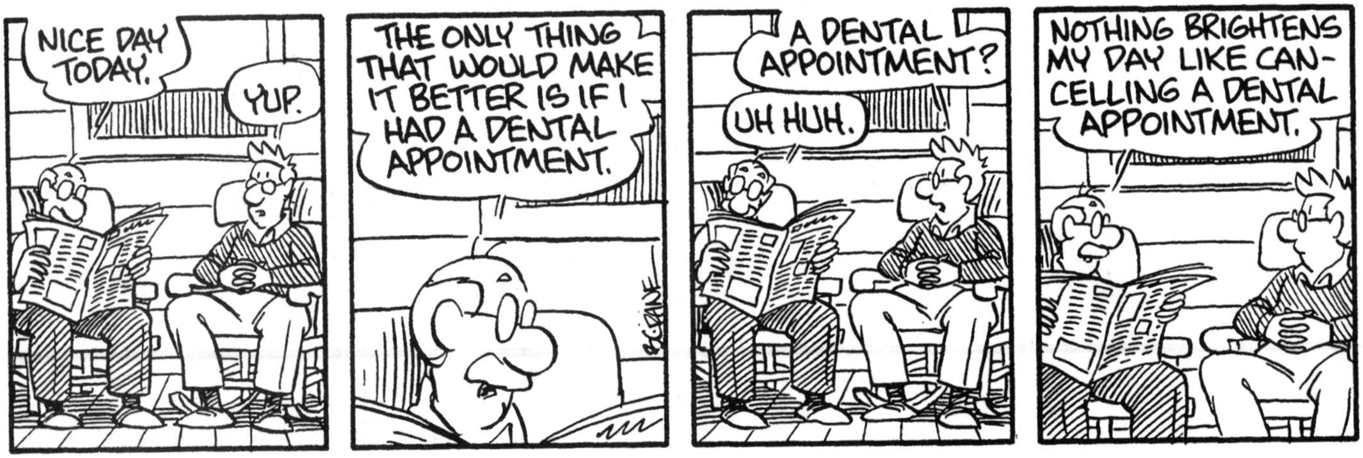
NICE DAY TODAY.
YUP.
THE ONLY THING THAT WOULD MAKE IT BETTER IS IF I HAD A DENTAL APPOINTMENT.
A DENTAL APPOINTMENT?
UH HUH.
NOTHING BRIGHTENS MY DAY LIKE CANCELLING A DENTAL APPOINTMENT.

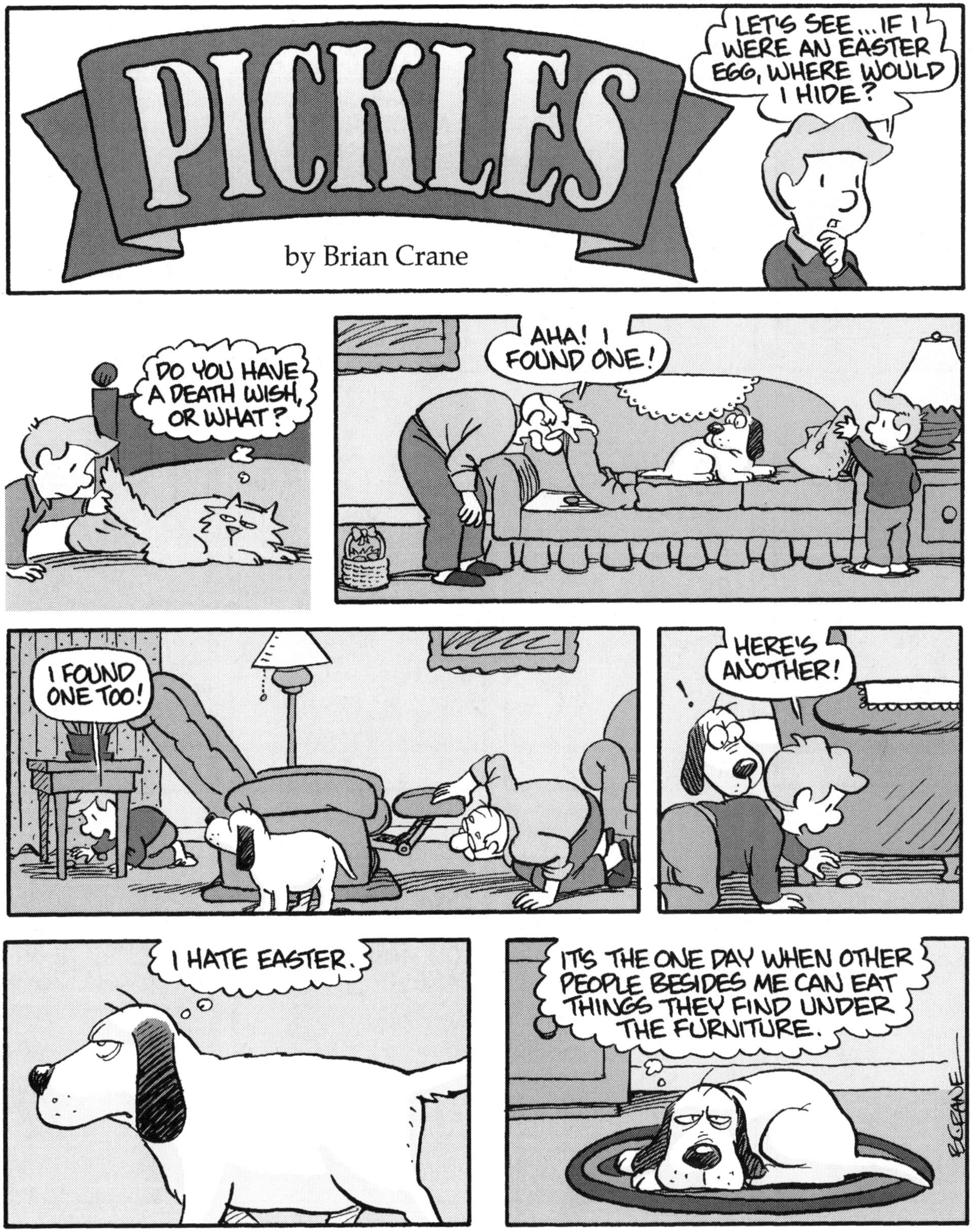
PICKLES
by Brian Crane
LET'S SEE... IF I WERE AN EASTER EGG, WHERE WOULD I HIDE?
DO YOU HAVE A DEATH WISH, OR WHAT?
AHA! I FOUND ONE!
I FOUND ONE TOO!
HERE'S ANOTHER!
!
I HATE EASTER.
IT'S THE ONE DAY WHEN OTHER PEOPLE BESIDES ME CAN EAT THINGS THEY FIND UNDER THE FURNITURE.
B. CRANE

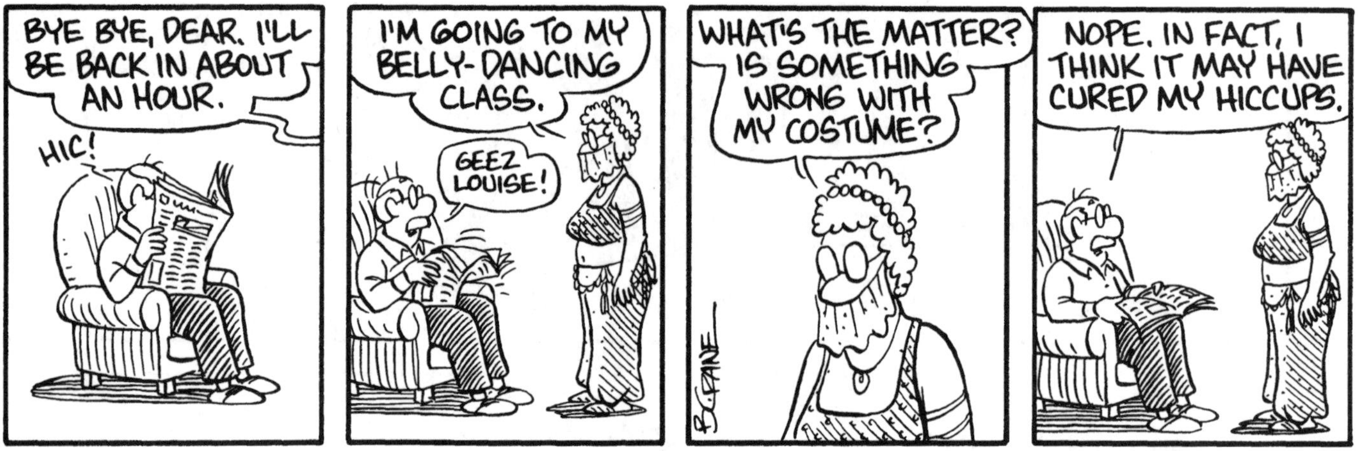
BYE BYE, DEAR. I'LL BE BACK IN ABOUT AN HOUR.
HIC!
I'M GOING TO MY BELLY-DANCING CLASS.
GEEZ LOUISE!
WHAT'S THE MATTER? IS SOMETHING WRONG WITH MY COSTUME?
NOPE. IN FACT, I THINK IT MAY HAVE CURED MY HICCUPS.

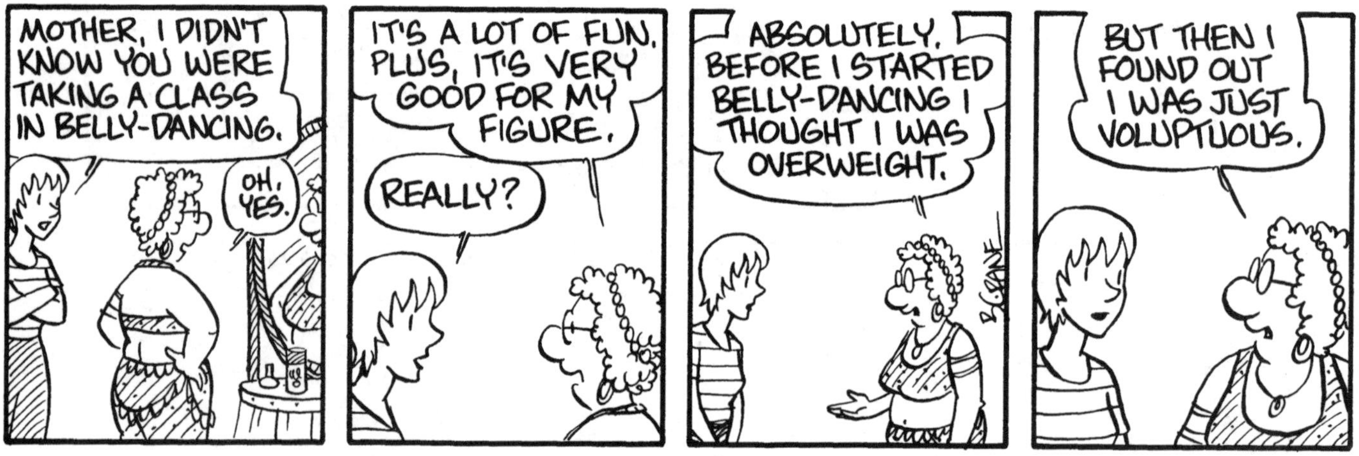
MOTHER, I DIDN'T KNOW YOU WERE TAKING A CLASS IN BELLY-DANCING.
OH, YES.
IT'S A LOT OF FUN. PLUS, IT'S VERY GOOD FOR MY FIGURE.
REALLY?
ABSOLUTELY. BEFORE I STARTED BELLY-DANCING I THOUGHT I WAS OVERWEIGHT.
BUT THEN I FOUND OUT I WAS JUST VOLUPTUOUS.

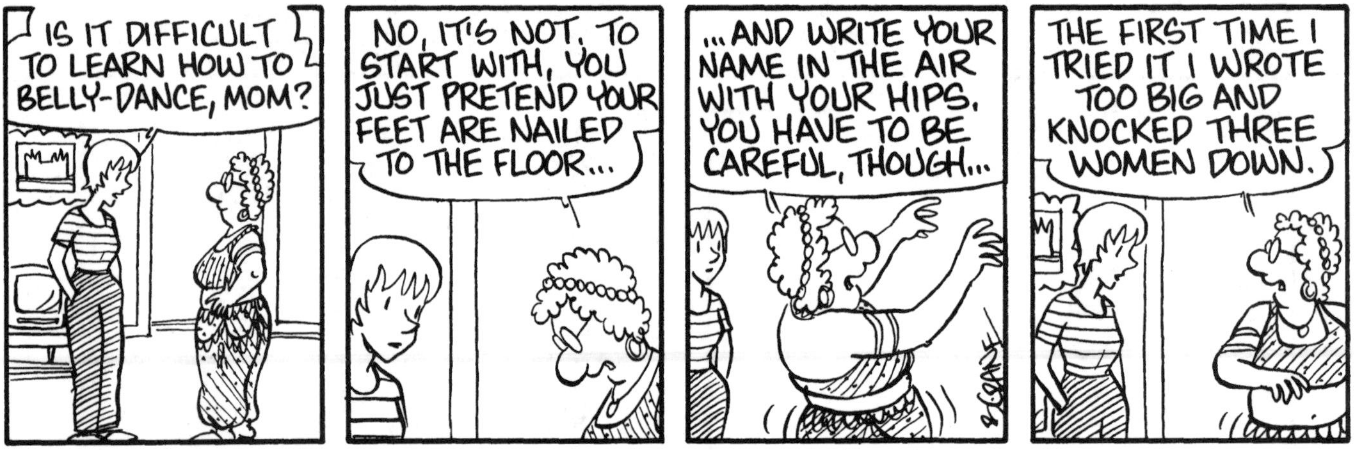
IS IT DIFFICULT TO LEARN HOW TO BELLY-DANCE, MOM?
NO, IT'S NOT. TO START WITH, YOU JUST PRETEND YOUR FEET ARE NAILED TO THE FLOOR...
...AND WRITE YOUR NAME IN THE AIR WITH YOUR HIPS. YOU HAVE TO BE CAREFUL, THOUGH...
THE FIRST TIME I TRIED IT I WROTE TOO BIG AND KNOCKED THREE WOMEN DOWN.

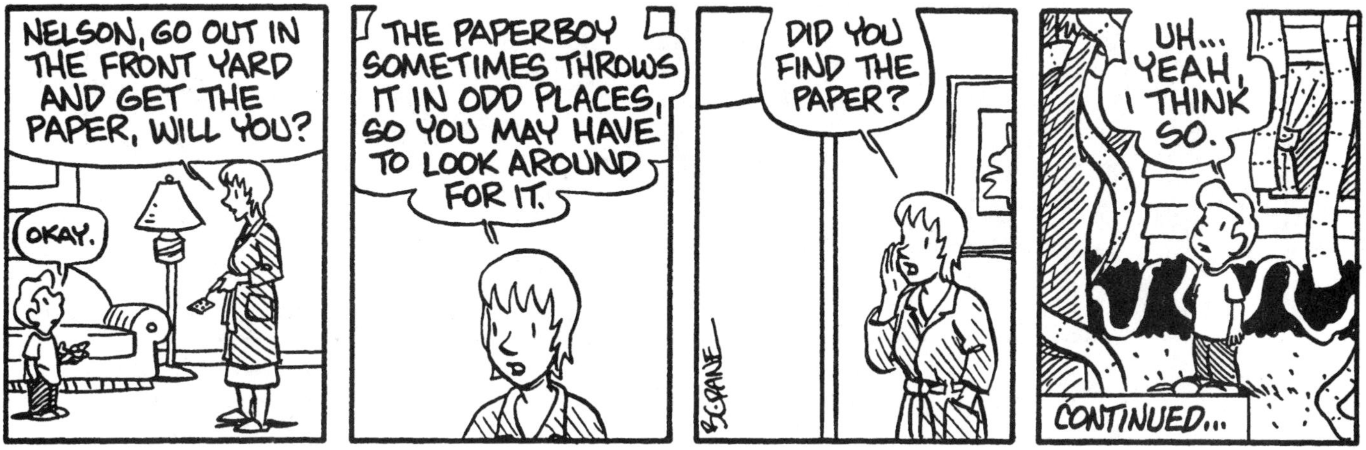
NELSON, GO OUT IN THE FRONT YARD AND GET THE PAPER, WILL YOU?
OKAY.
THE PAPERBOY SOMETIMES THROWS IT IN ODD PLACES, SO YOU MAY HAVE TO LOOK AROUND FOR IT.
DID YOU FIND THE PAPER?
UH... YEAH, I THINK SO.
CONTINUED...

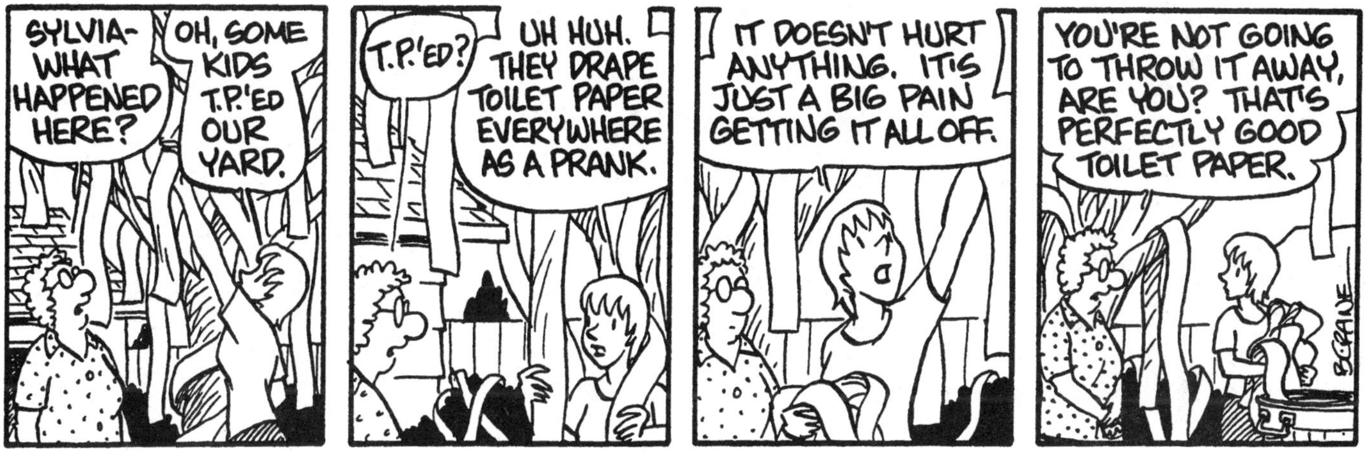
SYLVIA- WHAT HAPPENED HERE?
OH, SOME KIDS T.P.'ED OUR YARD.
T.P.'ED?
UH HUH. THEY DRAPE TOILET PAPER EVERYWHERE AS A PRANK.
IT DOESN'T HURT ANYTHING. IT'S JUST A BIG PAIN GETTING IT ALL OFF.
YOU'RE NOT GOING TO THROW IT AWAY, ARE YOU? THAT'S PERFECTLY GOOD TOILET PAPER.

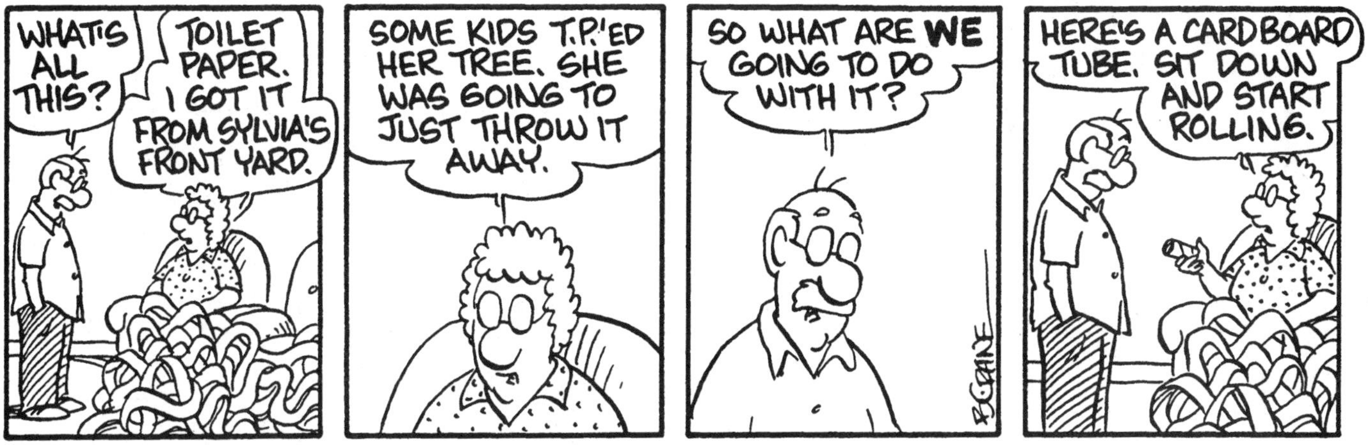
WHAT'S ALL THIS?
TOILET PAPER. I GOT IT FROM SYLVIA'S FRONT YARD.
SOME KIDS T.P.'ED HER TREE. SHE WAS GOING TO JUST THROW IT AWAY.
SO WHAT ARE WE GOING TO DO WITH IT?
HERE'S A CARDBOARD TUBE. SIT DOWN AND START ROLLING.

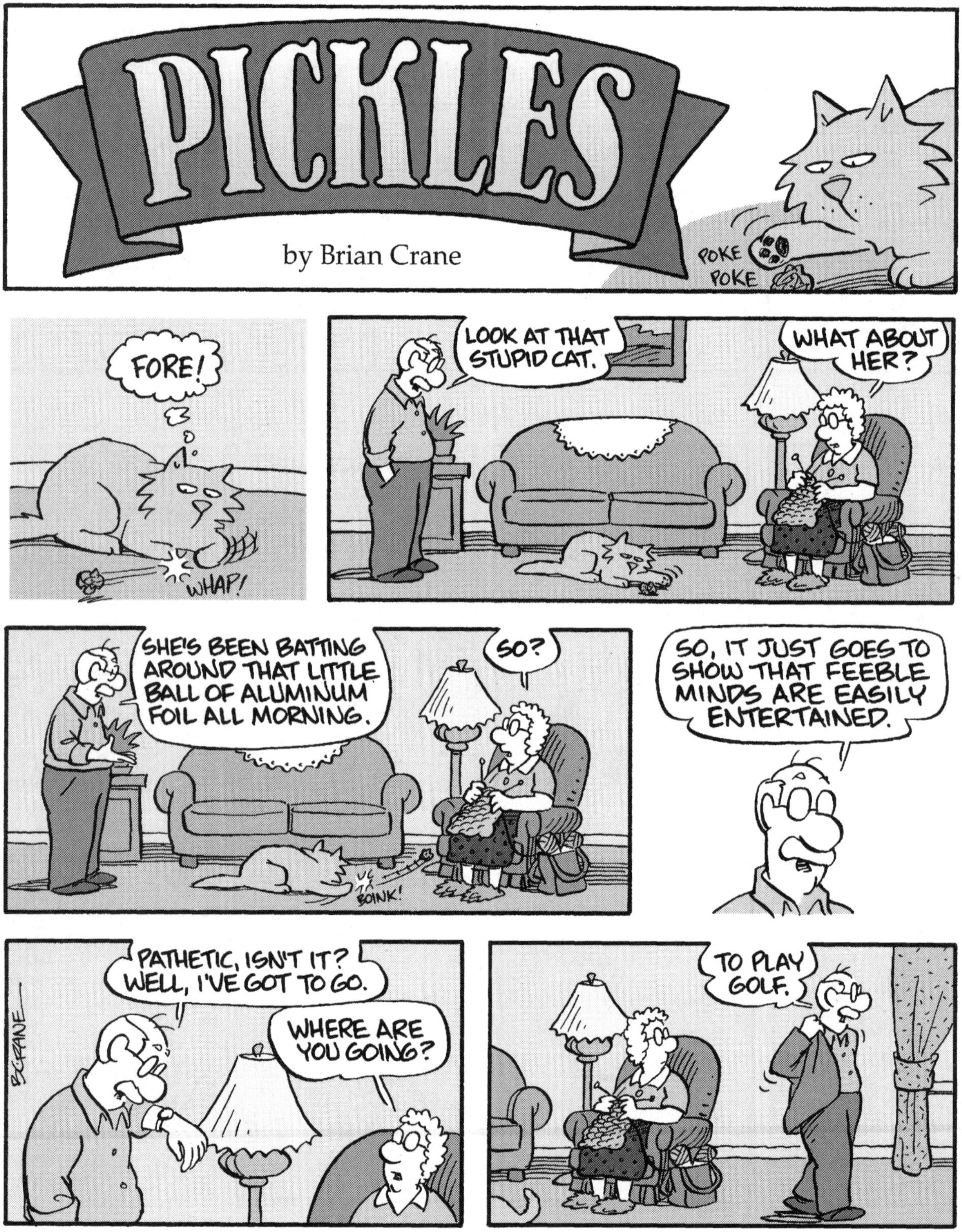
PICKLES
by Brian Crane
POKE
POKE
FORE!
WHAP!
LOOK AT THAT STUPID CAT.
WHAT ABOUT HER?
SHE'S BEEN BATTING AROUND THAT LITTLE BALL OF ALUMINUM FOIL ALL MORNING.
SO?
BOINK!
SO, IT JUST GOES TO SHOW THAT FEEBLE MINDS ARE EASILY ENTERTAINED.
PATHETIC, ISN'T IT? WELL, I'VE GOT TO GO.
WHERE ARE YOU GOING?
B. CRANE
TO PLAY GOLF.

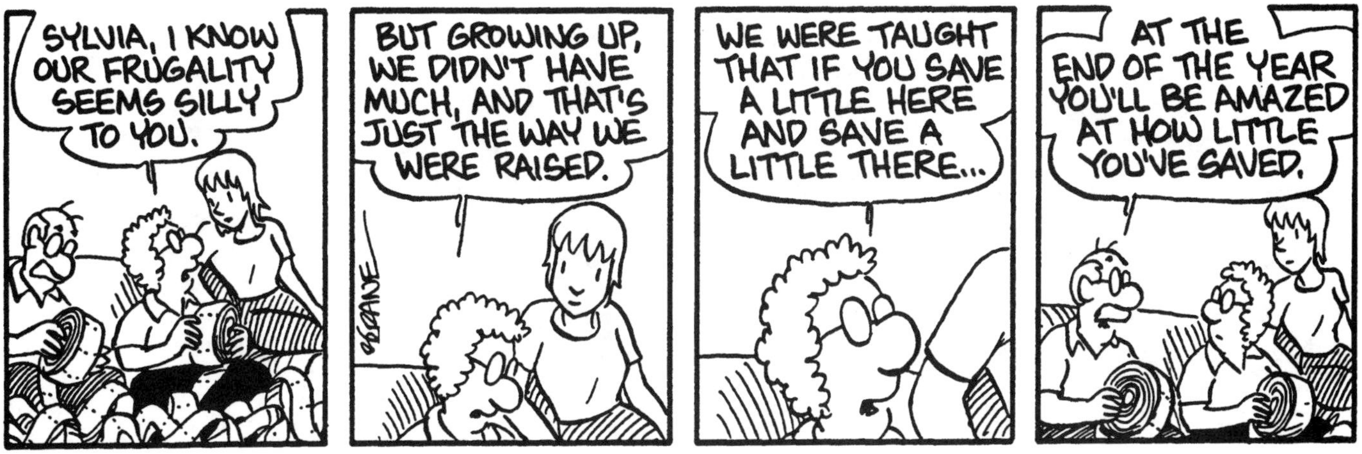
SYLVIA, I KNOW OUR FRUGALITY SEEMS SILLY TO YOU.
BUT GROWING UP, WE DIDN'T HAVE MUCH, AND THAT'S JUST THE WAY WE WERE RAISED.
WE WERE TAUGHT THAT IF YOU SAVE A LITTLE HERE AND SAVE A LITTLE THERE...
AT THE END OF THE YEAR YOU'LL BE AMAZED AT HOW LITTLE YOU'VE SAVED.

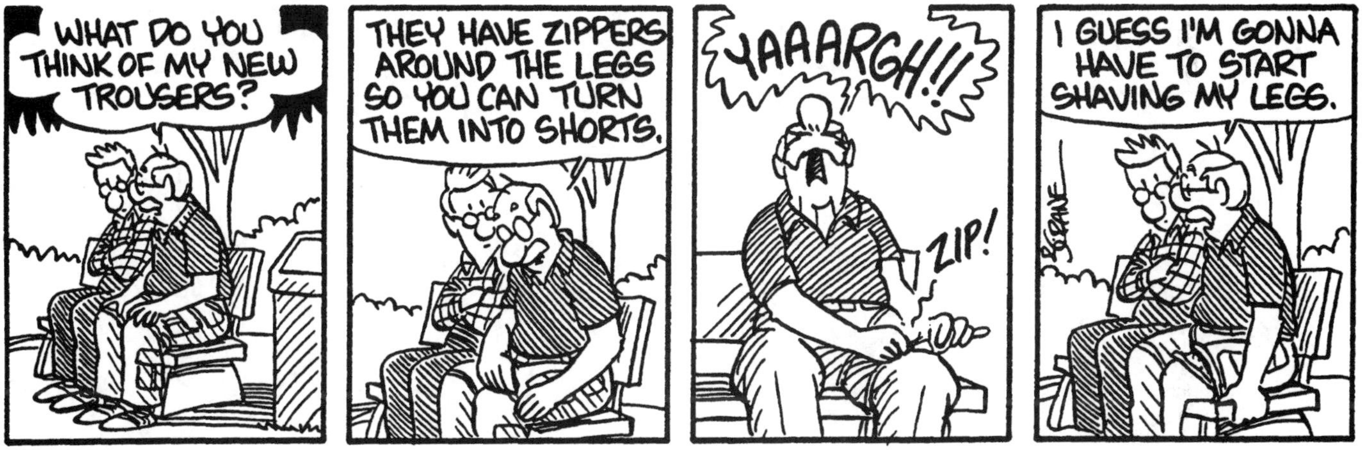
WHAT DO YOU THINK OF MY NEW TROUSERS?
THEY HAVE ZIPPERS AROUND THE LEGS SO YOU CAN TURN THEM INTO SHORTS.
YAAARGH!!!
ZIP!
I GUESS I'M GONNA HAVE TO START SHAVING MY LEGS.

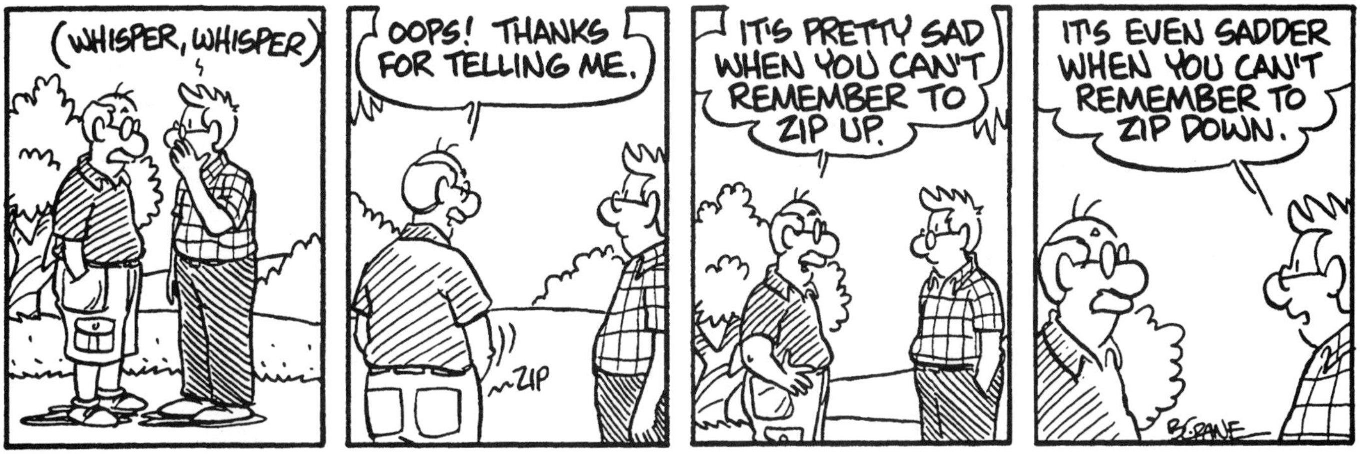
(WHISPER, WHISPER)
OOPS! THANKS FOR TELLING ME.
ZIP
IT'S PRETTY SAD WHEN YOU CAN'T REMEMBER TO ZIP UP.
IT'S EVEN SADDER WHEN YOU CAN'T REMEMBER TO ZIP DOWN.

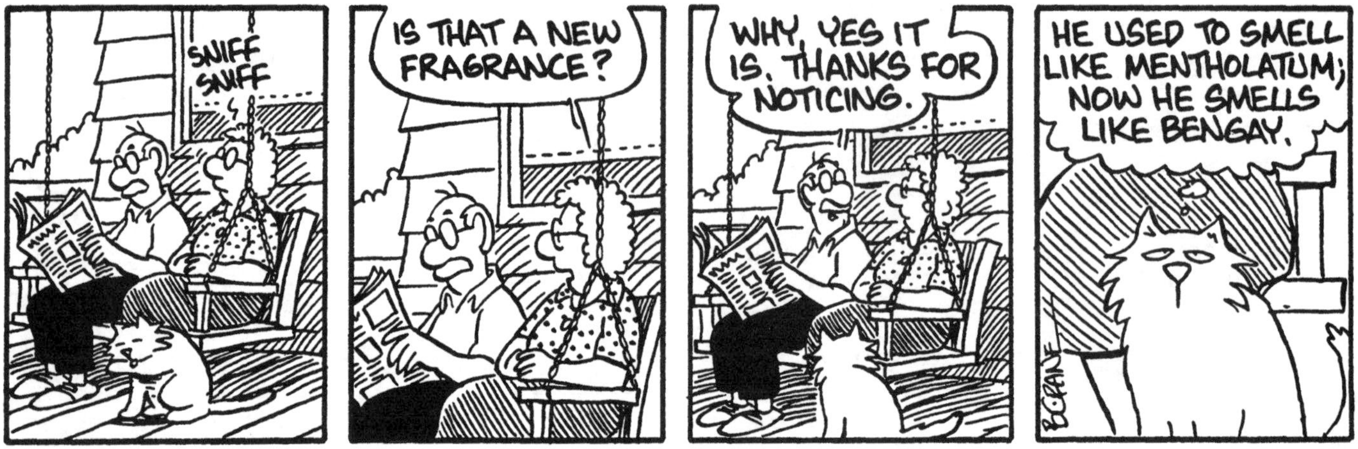
SNIFF SNIFF
IS THAT A NEW FRAGRANCE?
WHY, YES IT IS. THANKS FOR NOTICING.
HE USED TO SMELL LIKE MENTHOLATUM; NOW HE SMELLS LIKE BENGAY.
B. CRANE

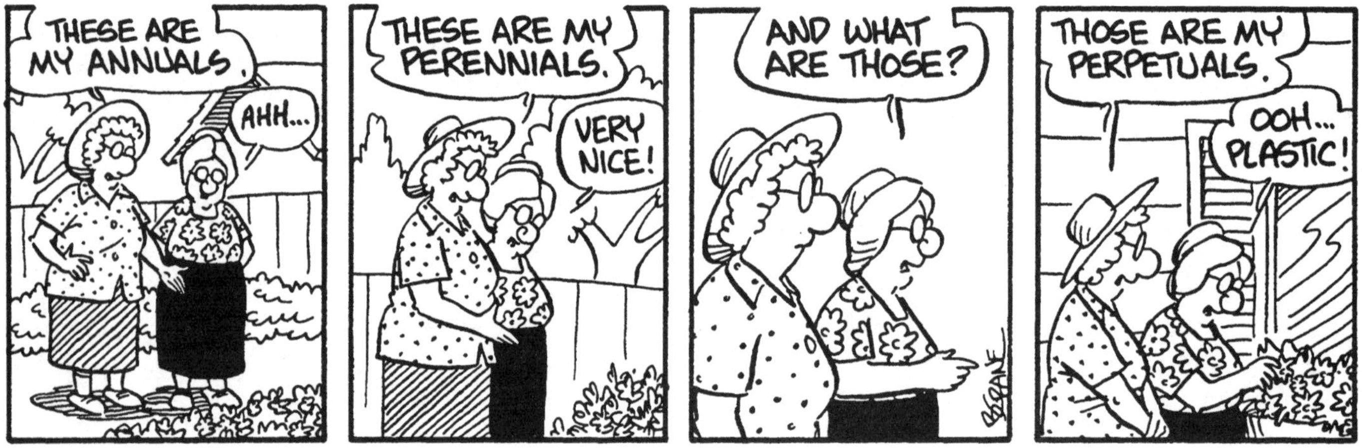
THESE ARE MY ANNUALS.
AHH...
THESE ARE MY PERENNIALS.
VERY NICE!
AND WHAT ARE THOSE?
B. CRANE
THOSE ARE MY PERPETUALS.
OOH... PLASTIC!

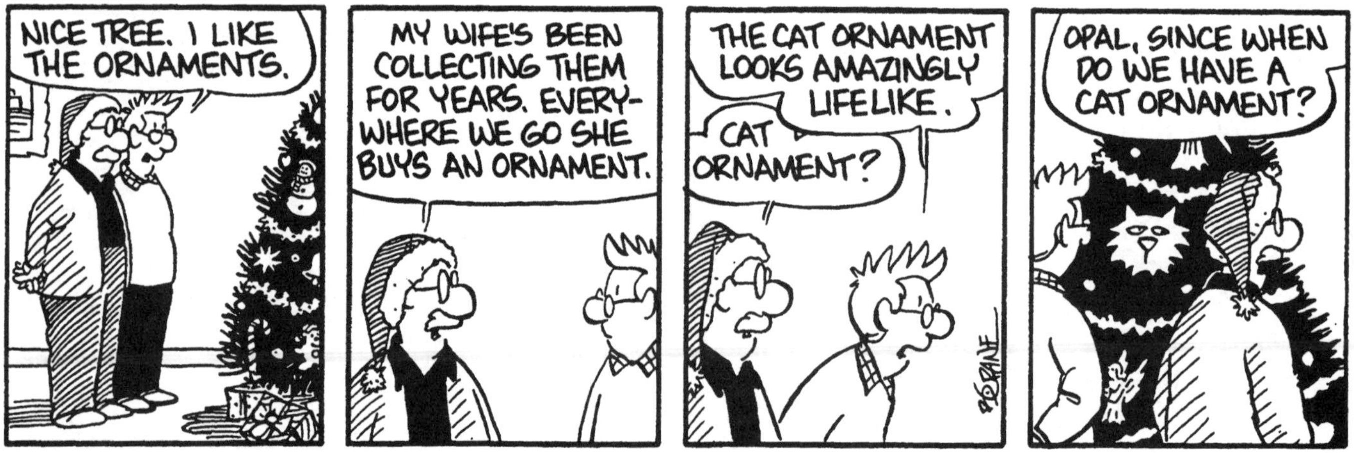
NICE TREE. I LIKE THE ORNAMENTS.
MY WIFE'S BEEN COLLECTING THEM FOR YEARS. EVERY-WHERE WE GO SHE BUYS AN ORNAMENT.
THE CAT ORNAMENT LOOKS AMAZINGLY LIFELIKE.
CAT ORNAMENT?
B. CRANE
OPAL, SINCE WHEN DO WE HAVE A CAT ORNAMENT?

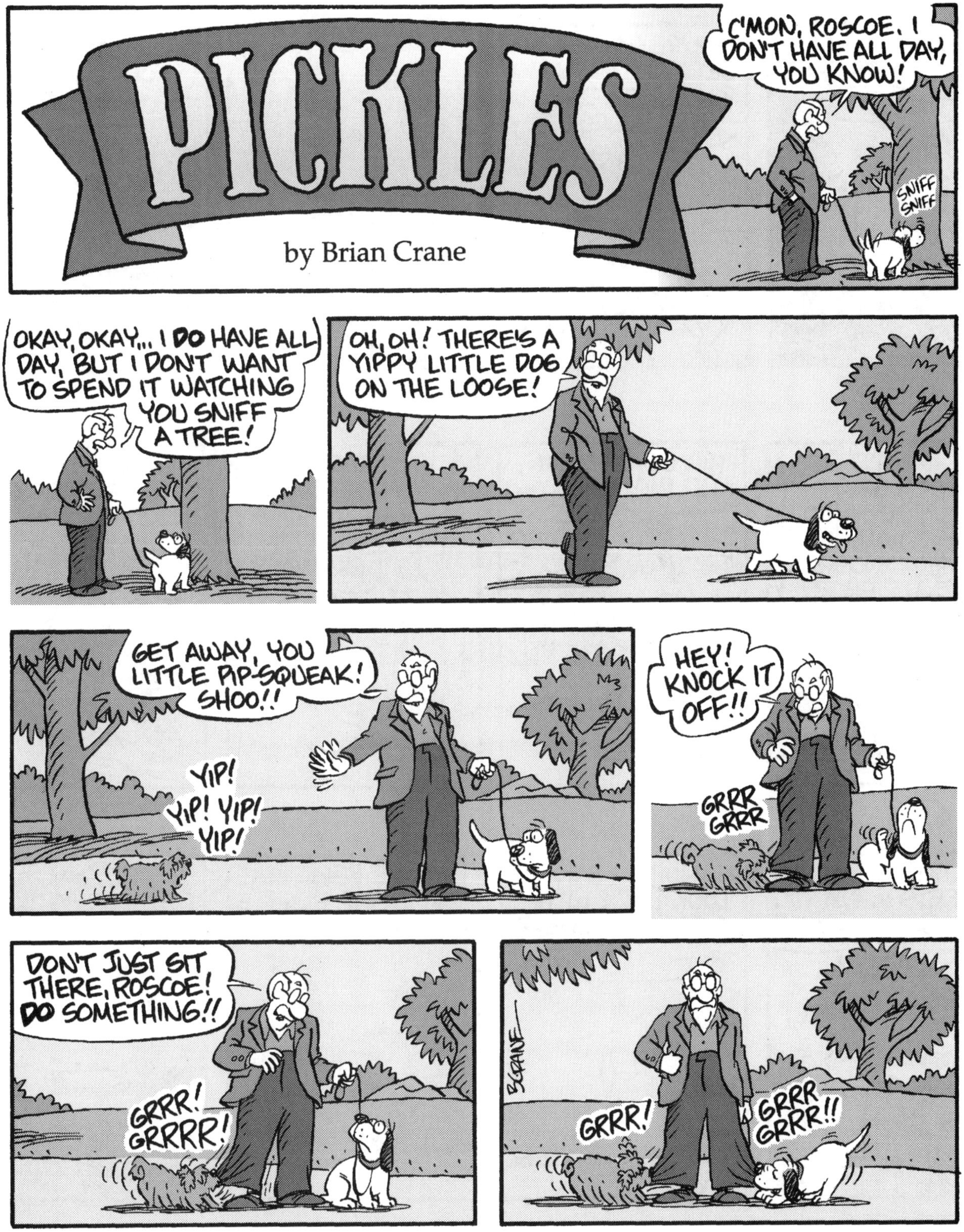
PICKLES
by Brian Crane
C'MON, ROSCOE. I DON'T HAVE ALL DAY, YOU KNOW!
SNIFF SNIFF
OKAY, OKAY... I DO HAVE ALL DAY, BUT I DON'T WANT TO SPEND IT WATCHING YOU SNIFF A TREE!
OH, OH! THERE'S A YIPPY LITTLE DOG ON THE LOOSE!
GET AWAY, YOU LITTLE PIP-SQUEAK! SHOO!!
YIP! YIP! YIP! YIP!
HEY! KNOCK IT OFF!!
GRRR GRRR
DON'T JUST SIT THERE, ROSCOE! DO SOMETHING!!
GRRR! GRRRR!
GRRR!
GRRR GRRR!!
B.CRANE

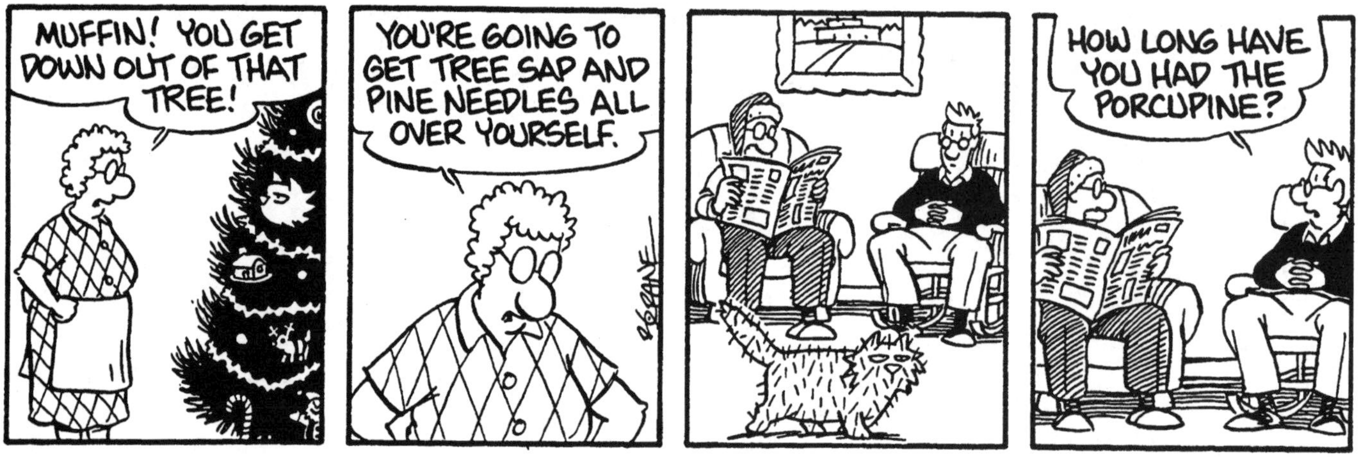
MUFFIN! YOU GET DOWN OUT OF THAT TREE!
YOU'RE GOING TO GET TREE SAP AND PINE NEEDLES ALL OVER YOURSELF.
HOW LONG HAVE YOU HAD THE PORCUPINE?

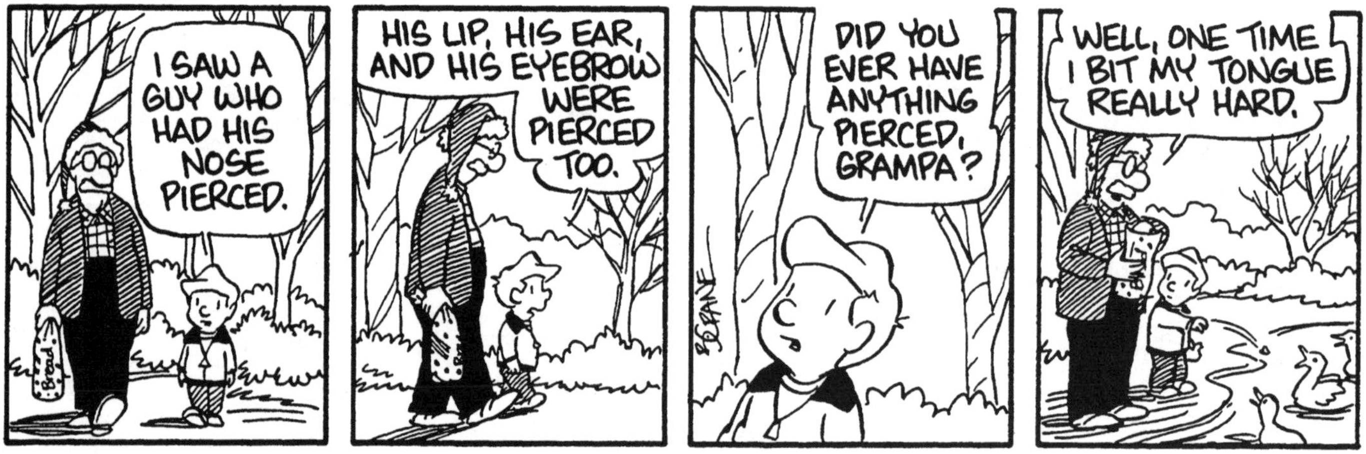
I SAW A GUY WHO HAD HIS NOSE PIERCED.
HIS LIP, HIS EAR, AND HIS EYEBROW WERE PIERCED TOO.
DID YOU EVER HAVE ANYTHING PIERCED, GRAMPA?
WELL, ONE TIME I BIT MY TONGUE REALLY HARD.

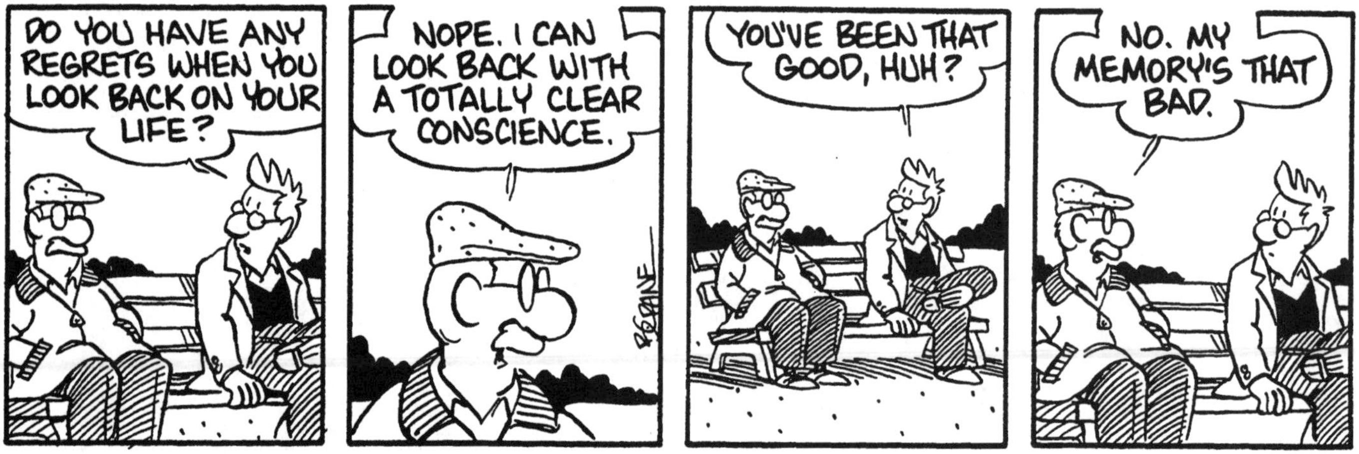
DO YOU HAVE ANY REGRETS WHEN YOU LOOK BACK ON YOUR LIFE?
NOPE. I CAN LOOK BACK WITH A TOTALLY CLEAR CONSCIENCE.
YOU'VE BEEN THAT GOOD, HUH?
NO. MY MEMORY'S THAT BAD.

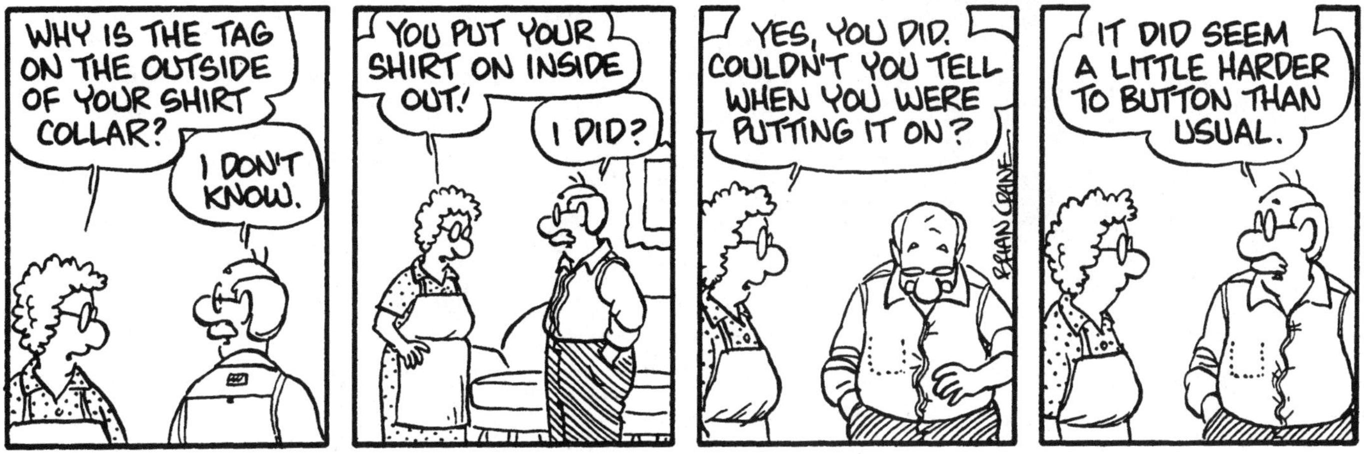
WHY IS THE TAG ON THE OUTSIDE OF YOUR SHIRT COLLAR?
I DON'T KNOW.
YOU PUT YOUR SHIRT ON INSIDE OUT!
I DID?
YES, YOU DID. COULDN'T YOU TELL WHEN YOU WERE PUTTING IT ON?
BRIAN CRANE
IT DID SEEM A LITTLE HARDER TO BUTTON THAN USUAL.

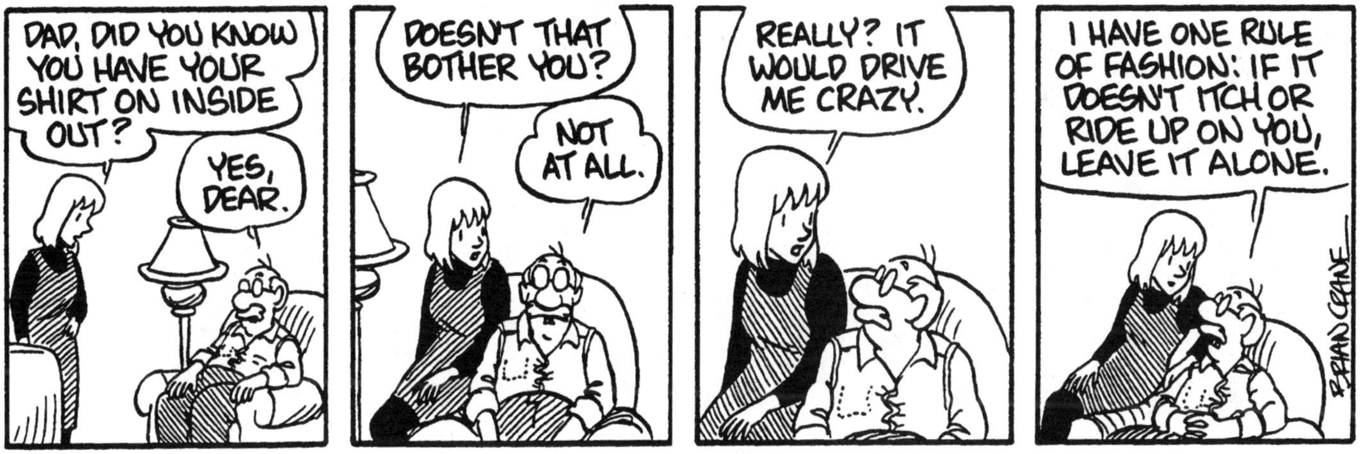
DAD, DID YOU KNOW YOU HAVE YOUR SHIRT ON INSIDE OUT?
YES, DEAR.
DOESN'T THAT BOTHER YOU?
NOT AT ALL.
REALLY? IT WOULD DRIVE ME CRAZY.
I HAVE ONE RULE OF FASHION: IF IT DOESN'T ITCH OR RIDE UP ON YOU, LEAVE IT ALONE.
BRIAN CRANE

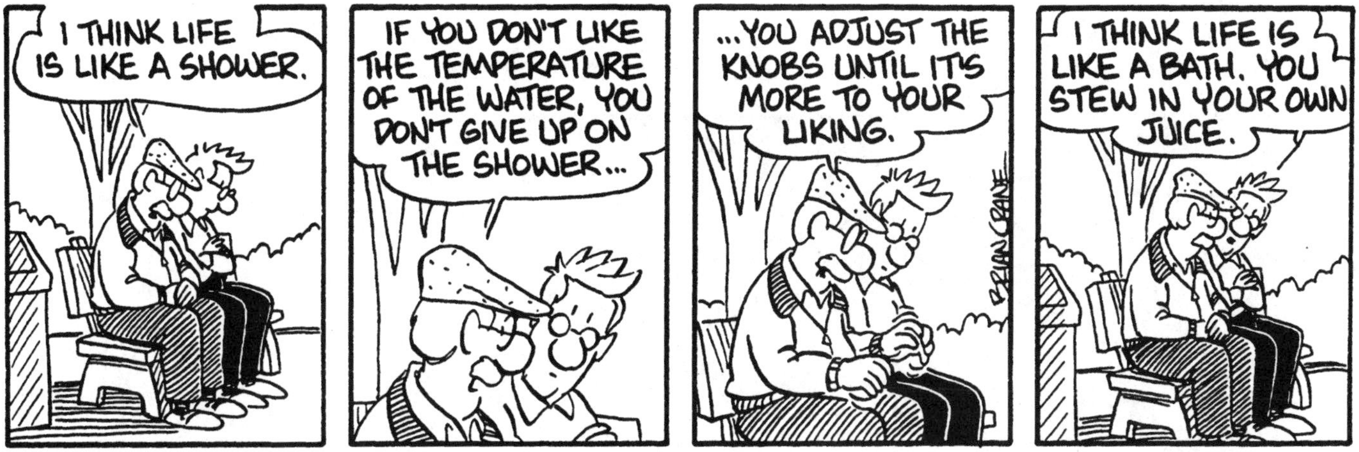
I THINK LIFE IS LIKE A SHOWER.
IF YOU DON'T LIKE THE TEMPERATURE OF THE WATER, YOU DON'T GIVE UP ON THE SHOWER...
...YOU ADJUST THE KNOBS UNTIL IT'S MORE TO YOUR LIKING.
BRIAN CRANE
I THINK LIFE IS LIKE A BATH. YOU STEW IN YOUR OWN JUICE.

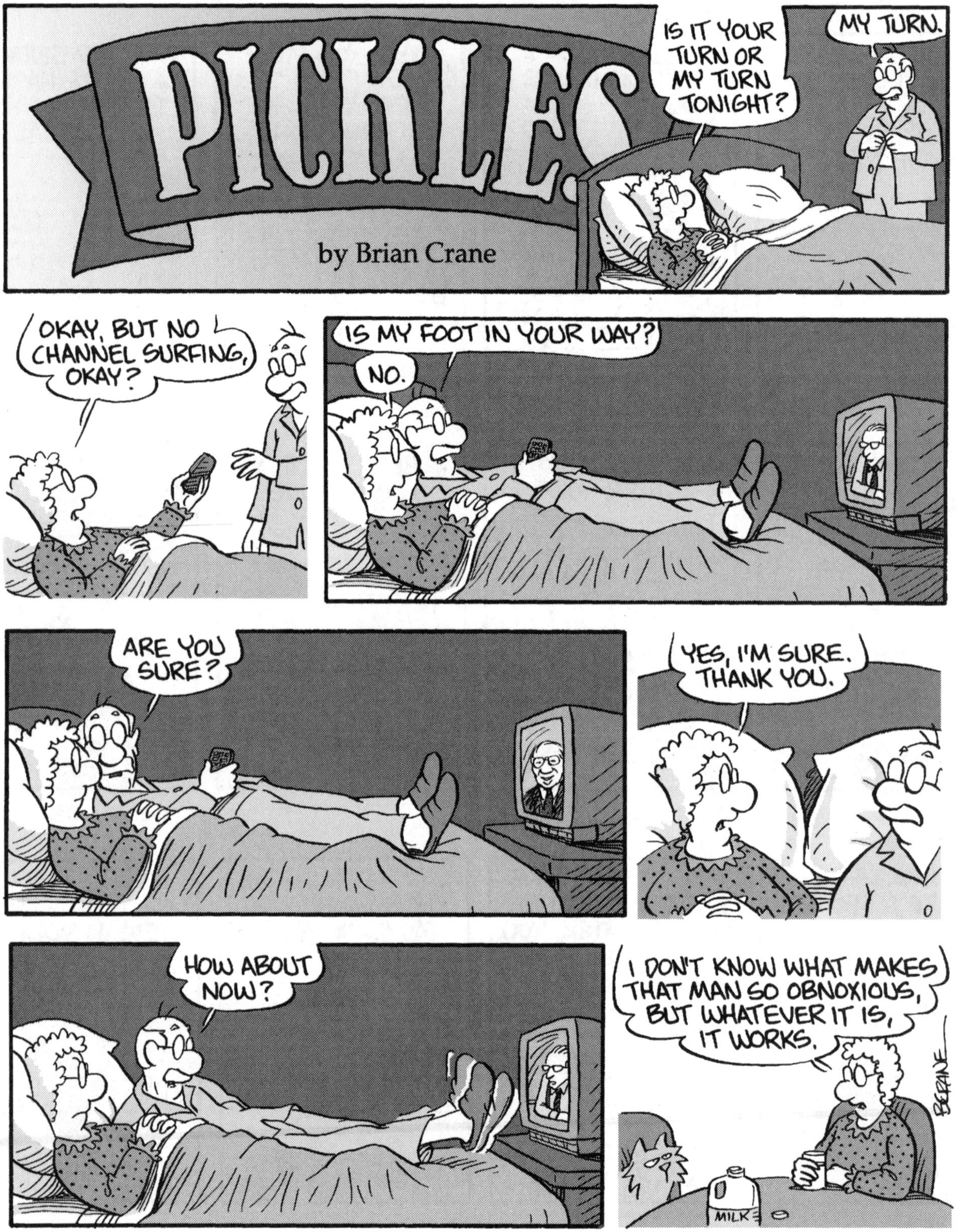
PICKLES
by Brian Crane
IS IT YOUR TURN OR MY TURN TONIGHT?
MY TURN.
OKAY, BUT NO CHANNEL SURFING, OKAY?
IS MY FOOT IN YOUR WAY?
NO.
ARE YOU SURE?
YES, I'M SURE. THANK YOU.
HOW ABOUT NOW?
I DON'T KNOW WHAT MAKES THAT MAN SO OBNOXIOUS, BUT WHATEVER IT IS, IT WORKS.
CRANE
MILK

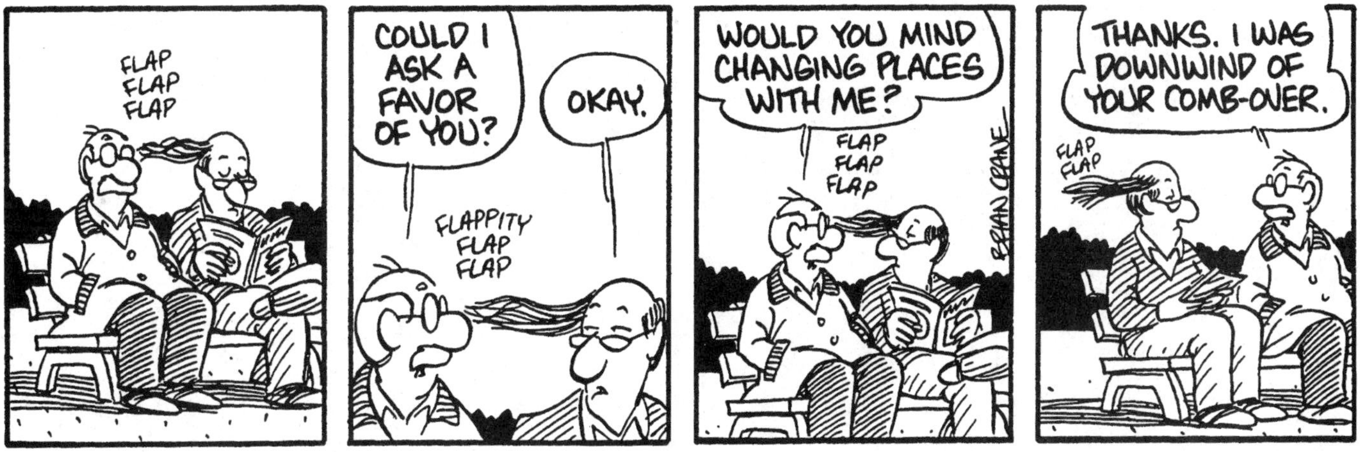
FLAP FLAP FLAP
COULD I ASK A FAVOR OF YOU?
OKAY.
FLAPPITY FLAP FLAP
WOULD YOU MIND CHANGING PLACES WITH ME?
FLAP FLAP FLAP
BRIAN CRANE
FLAP FLAP
THANKS. I WAS DOWNWIND OF YOUR COMB-OVER.

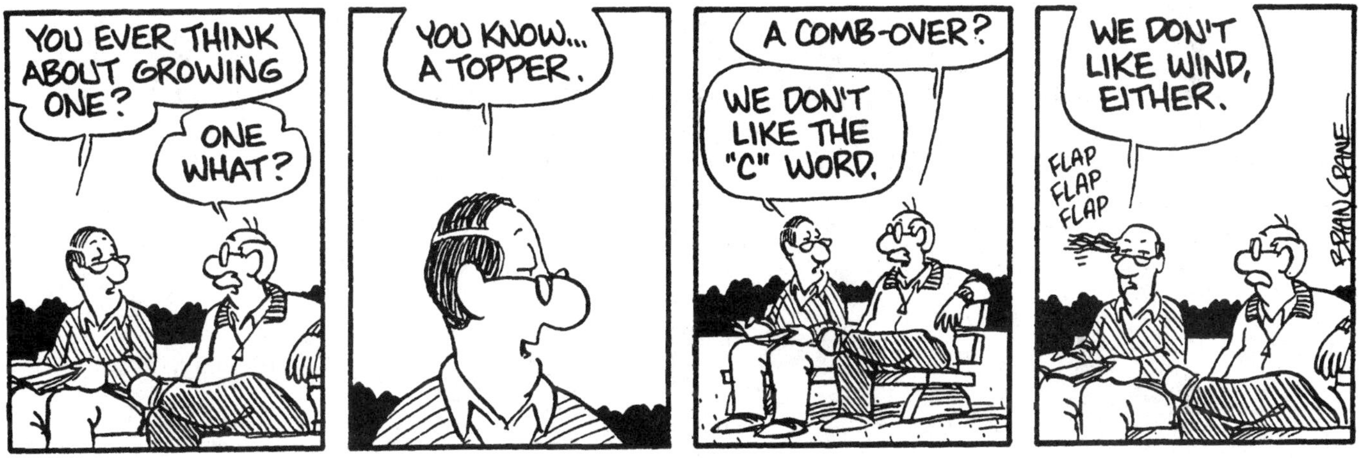
YOU EVER THINK ABOUT GROWING ONE?
ONE WHAT?
YOU KNOW... A TOPPER.
A COMB-OVER?
WE DON'T LIKE THE "C" WORD.
WE DON'T LIKE WIND, EITHER.
FLAP FLAP FLAP
BRIAN CRANE

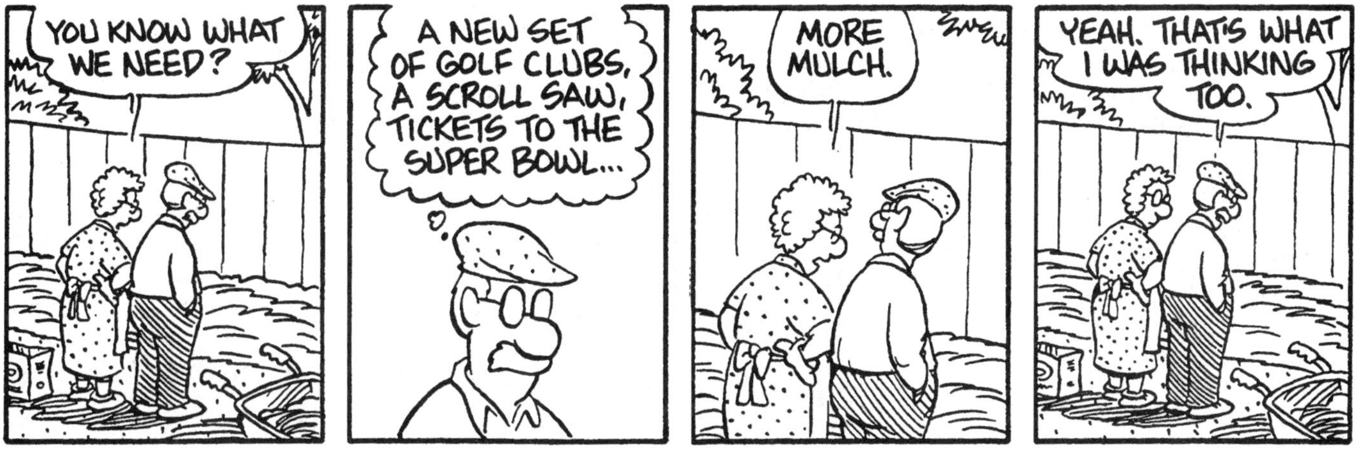
YOU KNOW WHAT WE NEED?
A NEW SET OF GOLF CLUBS, A SCROLL SAW, TICKETS TO THE SUPER BOWL...
MORE MULCH.
YEAH. THAT'S WHAT I WAS THINKING TOO.

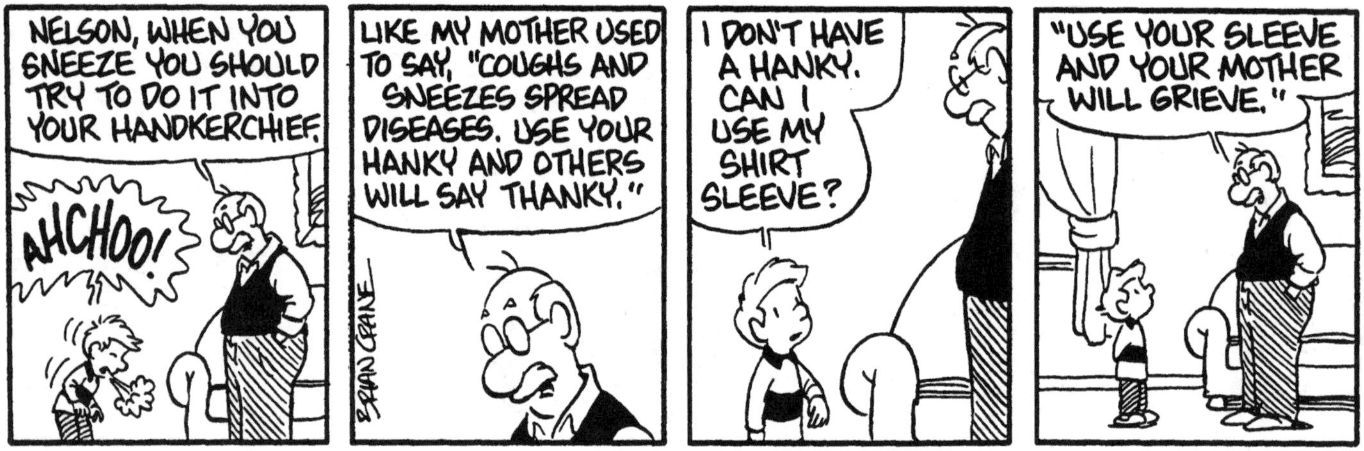
NELSON, WHEN YOU SNEEZE YOU SHOULD TRY TO DO IT INTO YOUR HANDKERCHIEF.
AHCHOO!
LIKE MY MOTHER USED TO SAY, "COUGHS AND SNEEZES SPREAD DISEASES. USE YOUR HANKY AND OTHERS WILL SAY THANKY."
BRIAN CRANE
I DON'T HAVE A HANKY. CAN I USE MY SHIRT SLEEVE?
"USE YOUR SLEEVE AND YOUR MOTHER WILL GRIEVE."

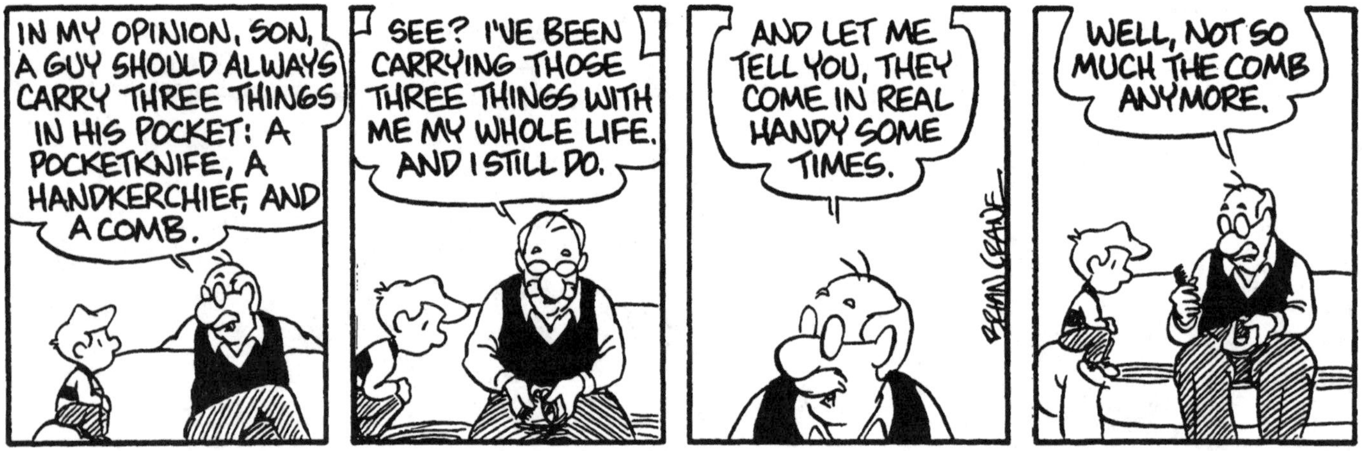
IN MY OPINION, SON, A GUY SHOULD ALWAYS CARRY THREE THINGS IN HIS POCKET: A POCKETKNIFE, A HANDKERCHIEF, AND A COMB.
SEE? I'VE BEEN CARRYING THOSE THREE THINGS WITH ME MY WHOLE LIFE. AND I STILL DO.
AND LET ME TELL YOU, THEY COME IN REAL HANDY SOME TIMES.
BRIAN CRANE
WELL, NOT SO MUCH THE COMB ANYMORE.

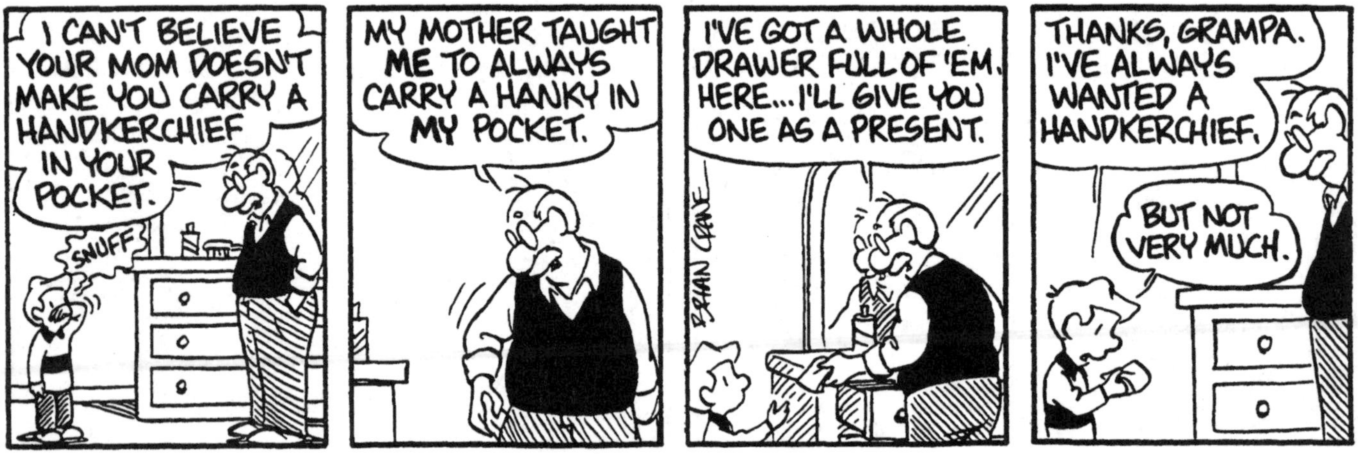
I CAN'T BELIEVE YOUR MOM DOESN'T MAKE YOU CARRY A HANDKERCHIEF IN YOUR POCKET.
SNUFF
MY MOTHER TAUGHT ME TO ALWAYS CARRY A HANKY IN MY POCKET.
I'VE GOT A WHOLE DRAWER FULL OF 'EM. HERE...I'LL GIVE YOU ONE AS A PRESENT.
BRIAN CRANE
THANKS, GRAMPA. I'VE ALWAYS WANTED A HANDKERCHIEF.
BUT NOT VERY MUCH.

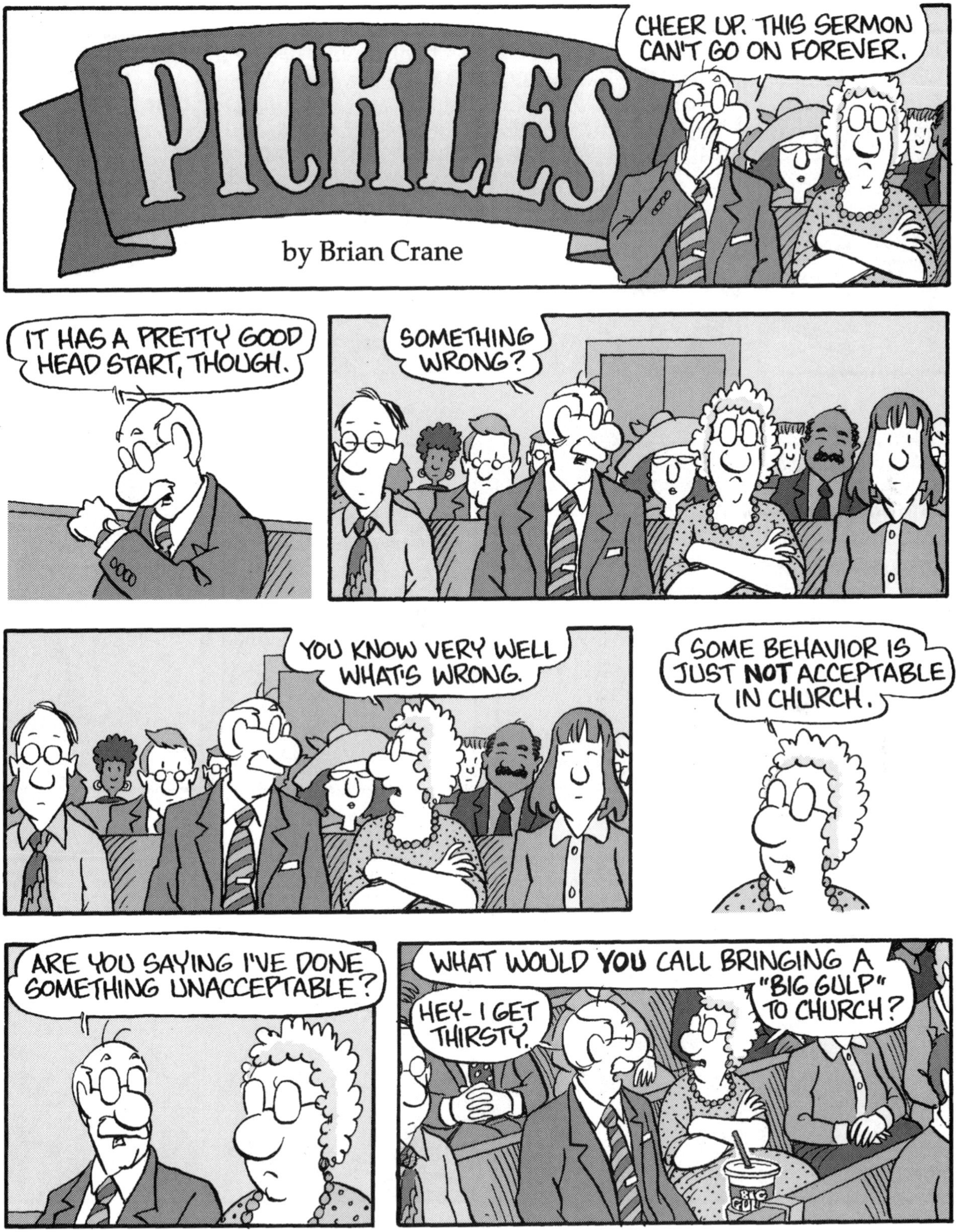
PICKLES
by Brian Crane
CHEER UP. THIS SERMON CAN'T GO ON FOREVER.
IT HAS A PRETTY GOOD HEAD START, THOUGH.
SOMETHING WRONG?
YOU KNOW VERY WELL WHAT'S WRONG.
SOME BEHAVIOR IS JUST **NOT** ACCEPTABLE IN CHURCH.
ARE YOU SAYING I'VE DONE SOMETHING UNACCEPTABLE?
WHAT WOULD **YOU** CALL BRINGING A "BIG GULP" TO CHURCH?
HEY- I GET THIRSTY.

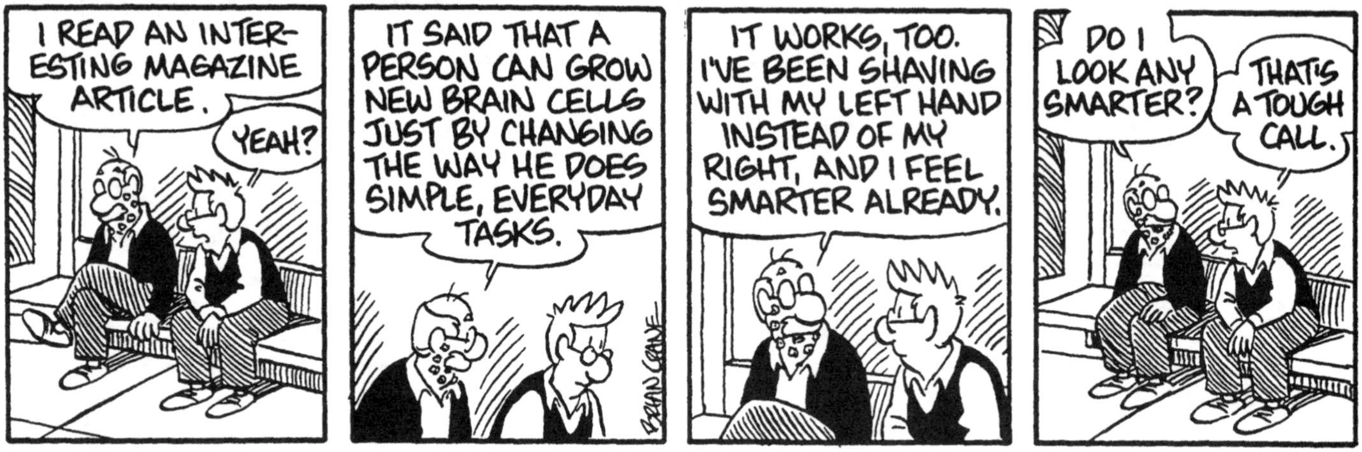
I READ AN INTERESTING MAGAZINE ARTICLE.
YEAH?
IT SAID THAT A PERSON CAN GROW NEW BRAIN CELLS JUST BY CHANGING THE WAY HE DOES SIMPLE, EVERYDAY TASKS.
IT WORKS, TOO. I'VE BEEN SHAVING WITH MY LEFT HAND INSTEAD OF MY RIGHT, AND I FEEL SMARTER ALREADY.
DO I LOOK ANY SMARTER?
THAT'S A TOUGH CALL.

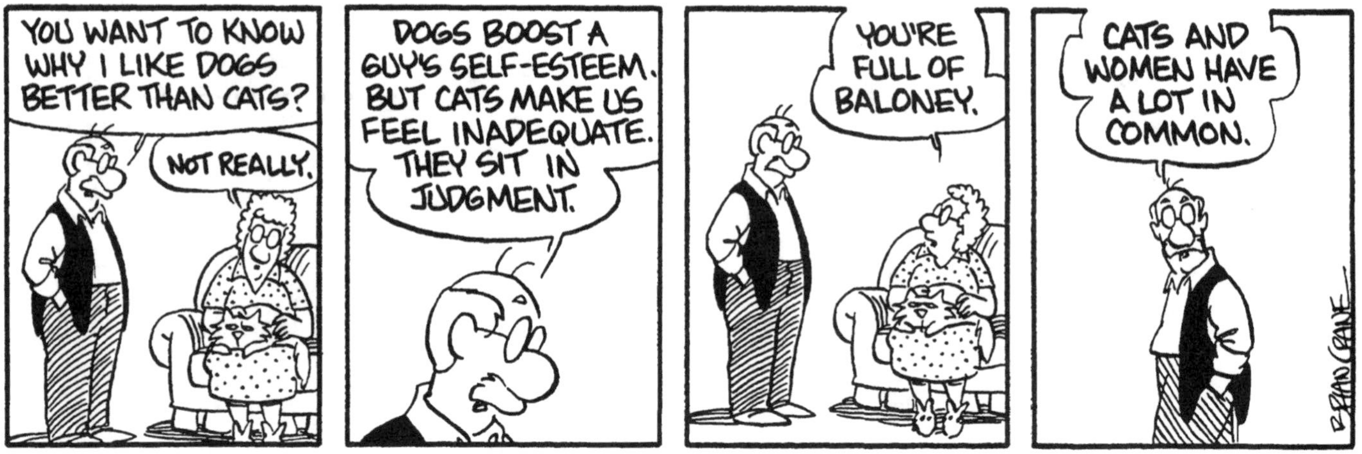
YOU WANT TO KNOW WHY I LIKE DOGS BETTER THAN CATS?
NOT REALLY.
DOGS BOOST A GUY'S SELF-ESTEEM. BUT CATS MAKE US FEEL INADEQUATE. THEY SIT IN JUDGMENT.
YOU'RE FULL OF BALONEY.
CATS AND WOMEN HAVE A LOT IN COMMON.

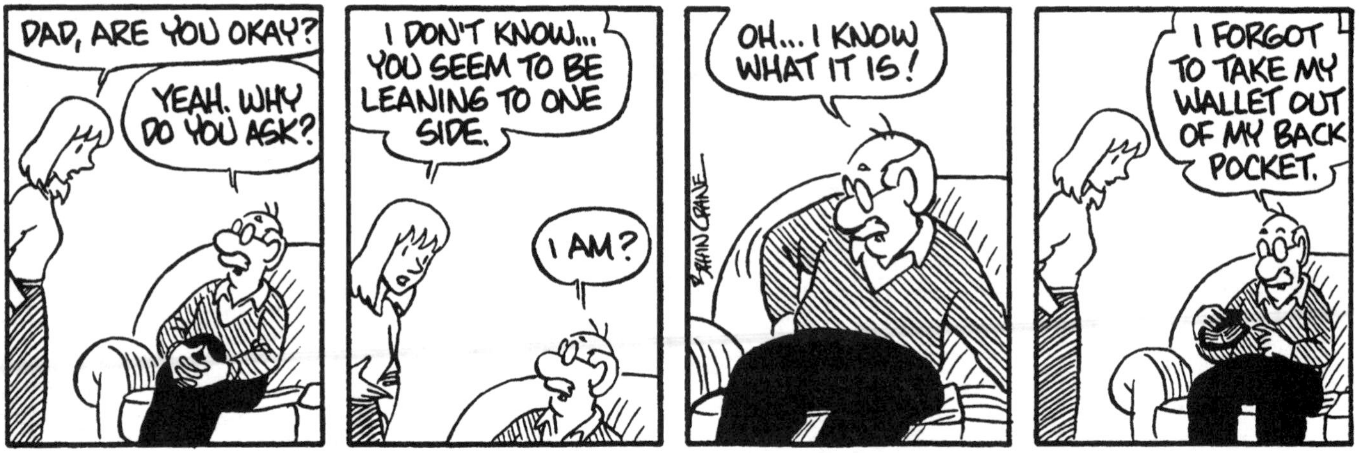
DAD, ARE YOU OKAY?
YEAH. WHY DO YOU ASK?
I DON'T KNOW... YOU SEEM TO BE LEANING TO ONE SIDE.
I AM?
OH... I KNOW WHAT IT IS!
I FORGOT TO TAKE MY WALLET OUT OF MY BACK POCKET.

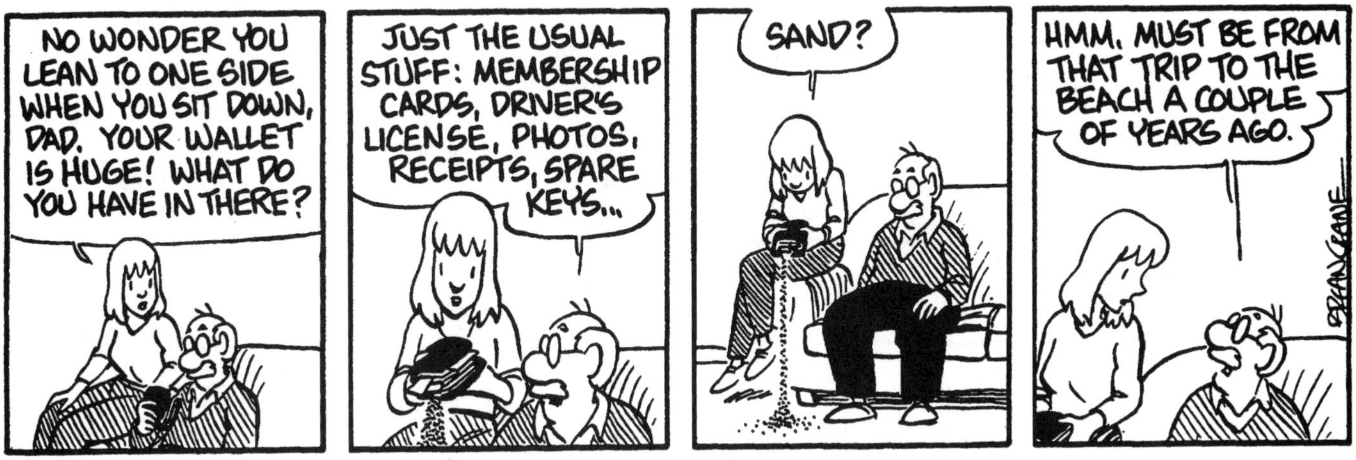
NO WONDER YOU LEAN TO ONE SIDE WHEN YOU SIT DOWN, DAD. YOUR WALLET IS HUGE! WHAT DO YOU HAVE IN THERE?
JUST THE USUAL STUFF: MEMBERSHIP CARDS, DRIVER'S LICENSE, PHOTOS, RECEIPTS, SPARE KEYS...
SAND?
HMM. MUST BE FROM THAT TRIP TO THE BEACH A COUPLE OF YEARS AGO.
BRIAN CRANE

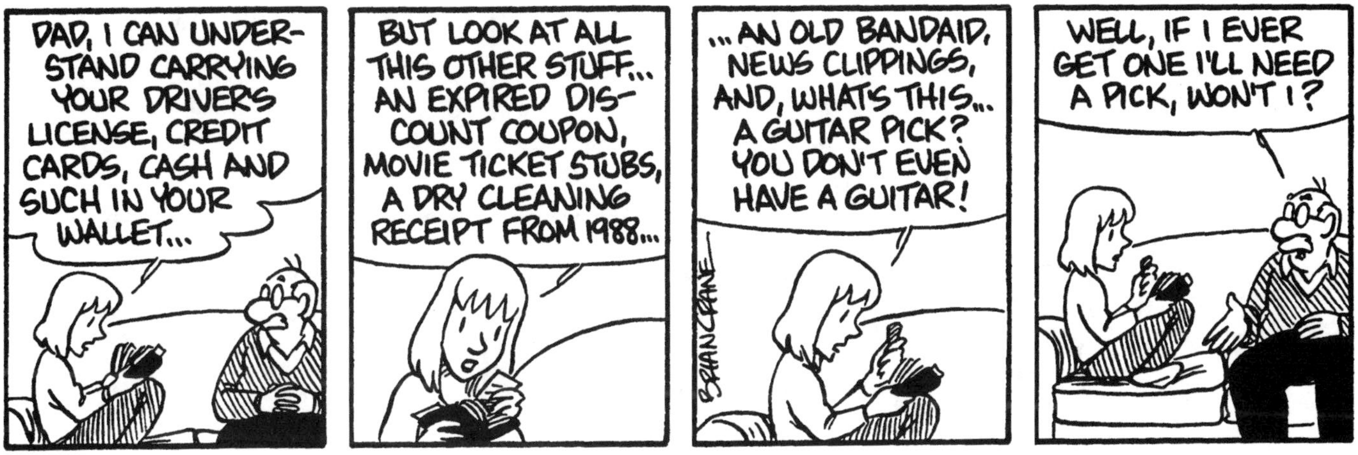
DAD, I CAN UNDERSTAND CARRYING YOUR DRIVER'S LICENSE, CREDIT CARDS, CASH AND SUCH IN YOUR WALLET...
BUT LOOK AT ALL THIS OTHER STUFF... AN EXPIRED DISCOUNT COUPON, MOVIE TICKET STUBS, A DRY CLEANING RECEIPT FROM 1988...
...AN OLD BANDAID, NEWS CLIPPINGS, AND, WHAT'S THIS... A GUITAR PICK? YOU DON'T EVEN HAVE A GUITAR!
BRIAN CRANE
WELL, IF I EVER GET ONE I'LL NEED A PICK, WON'T I?

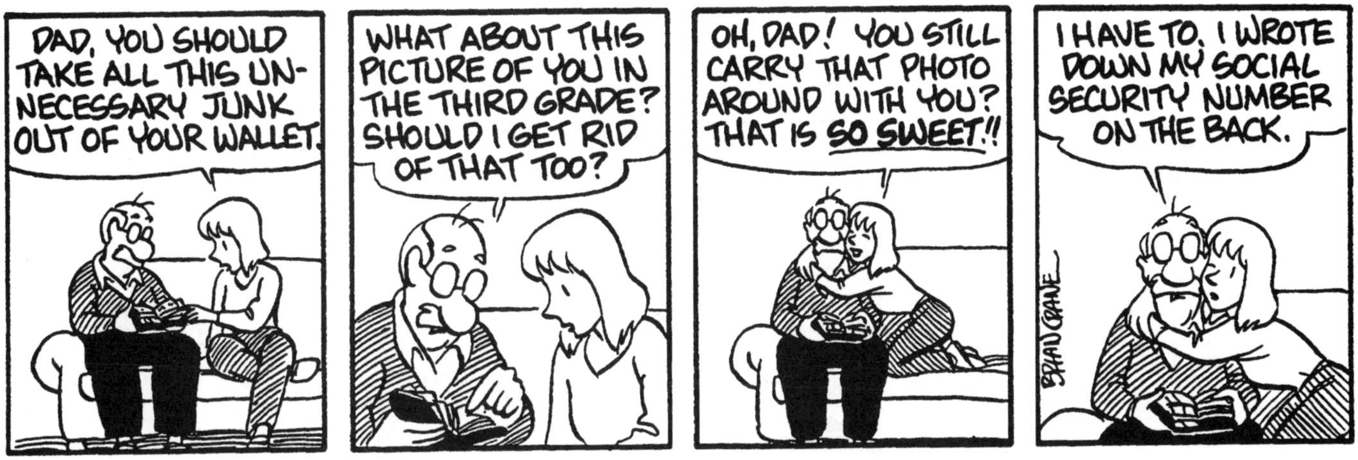
DAD, YOU SHOULD TAKE ALL THIS UNNECESSARY JUNK OUT OF YOUR WALLET.
WHAT ABOUT THIS PICTURE OF YOU IN THE THIRD GRADE? SHOULD I GET RID OF THAT TOO?
OH, DAD! YOU STILL CARRY THAT PHOTO AROUND WITH YOU? THAT IS SO SWEET!!
BRIAN CRANE
I HAVE TO. I WROTE DOWN MY SOCIAL SECURITY NUMBER ON THE BACK.

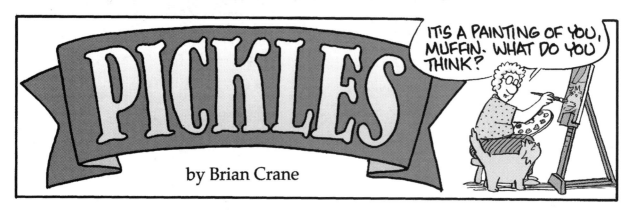

# PICKLES

by Brian Crane

IT'S A PAINTING OF YOU, MUFFIN. WHAT DO YOU THINK?

I THINK THE HUMANE SOCIETY SHOULD TAKE AWAY YOUR BRUSHES.

EARL, COME HERE AND LOOK AT THIS.

I PAINTED THIS PICTURE TO COVER UP THAT HOLE IN THE WALL.

WHAT HOLE?

OH, YOU REMEMBER... YOU WERE TRYING TO SWAT A FLY AND YOU COULDN'T FIND A SWATTER...

...SO YOU USED A HAMMER INSTEAD.

OH... THAT HOLE.

ANYWAY, WHAT DO YOU THINK OF THE PAINTING?

I DON'T KNOW. COULD I SEE THE HOLE AGAIN?

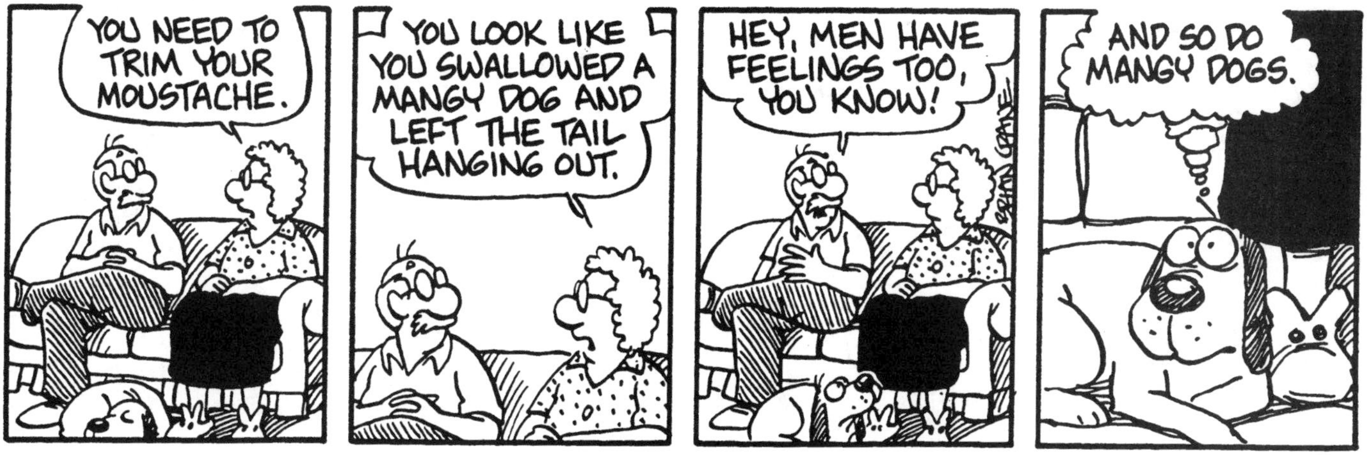
YOU NEED TO TRIM YOUR MOUSTACHE.
YOU LOOK LIKE YOU SWALLOWED A MANGY DOG AND LEFT THE TAIL HANGING OUT.
HEY, MEN HAVE FEELINGS TOO, YOU KNOW!
BRIAN CRANE
AND SO DO MANGY DOGS.

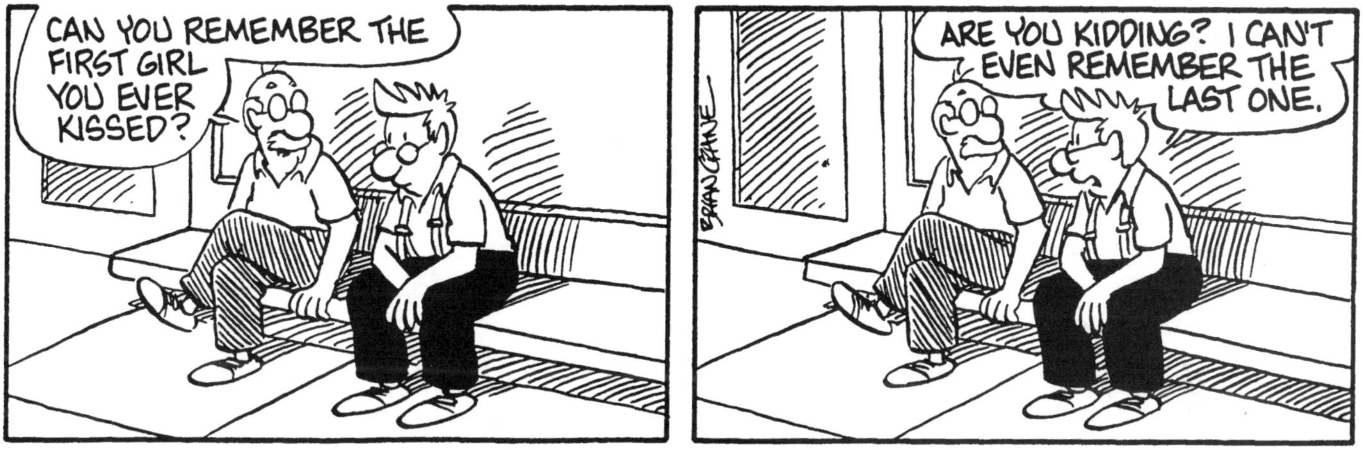
CAN YOU REMEMBER THE FIRST GIRL YOU EVER KISSED?
BRIAN CRANE
ARE YOU KIDDING? I CAN'T EVEN REMEMBER THE LAST ONE.

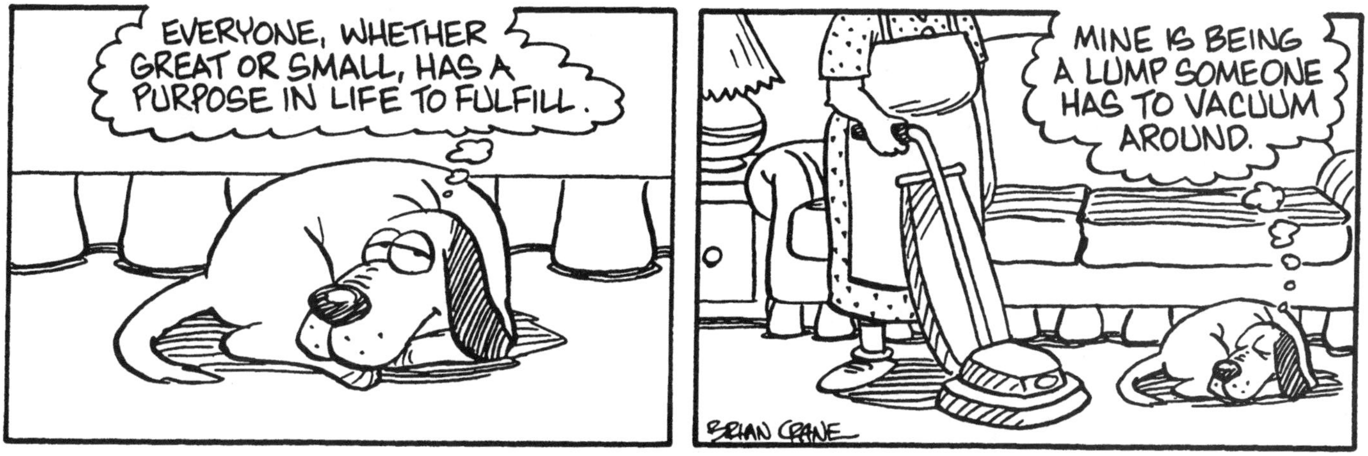
EVERYONE, WHETHER GREAT OR SMALL, HAS A PURPOSE IN LIFE TO FULFILL.
MINE IS BEING A LUMP SOMEONE HAS TO VACUUM AROUND.
BRIAN CRANE

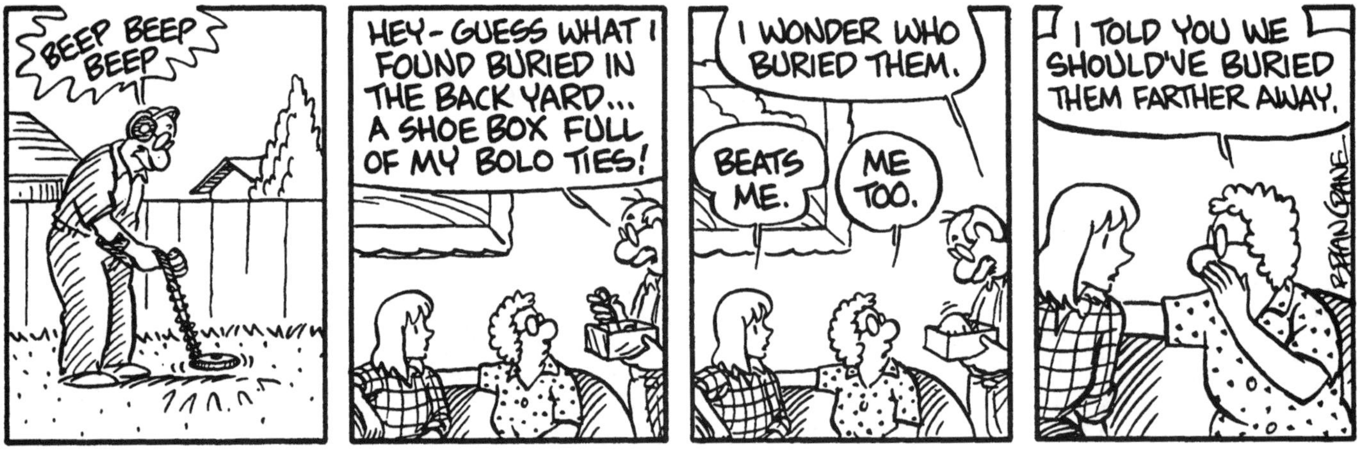
BEEP BEEP BEEP
HEY- GUESS WHAT I FOUND BURIED IN THE BACK YARD... A SHOE BOX FULL OF MY BOLO TIES!
I WONDER WHO BURIED THEM.
BEATS ME.
ME TOO.
I TOLD YOU WE SHOULD'VE BURIED THEM FARTHER AWAY.

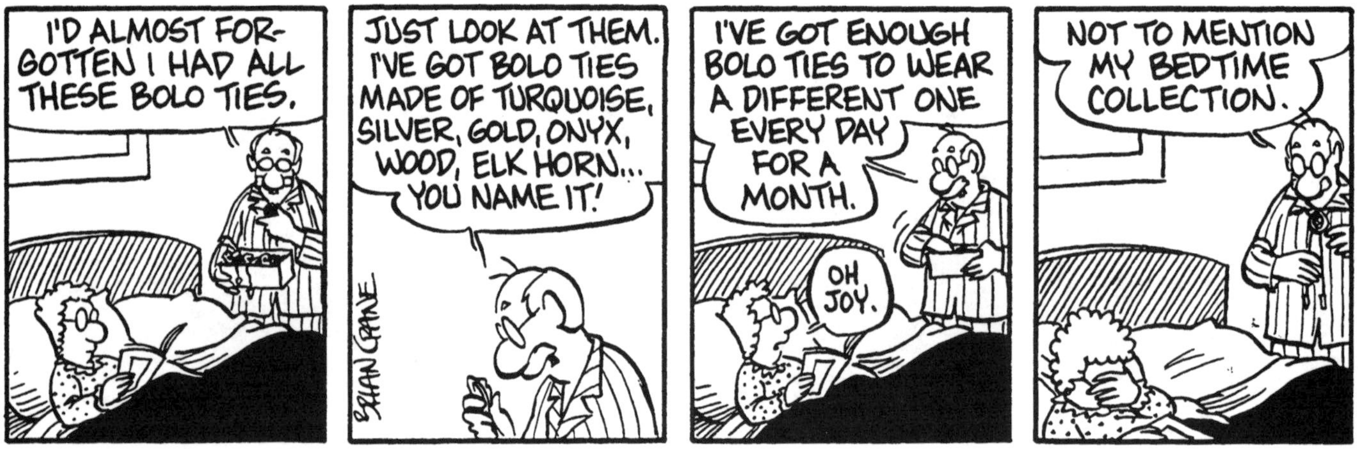
I'D ALMOST FORGOTTEN I HAD ALL THESE BOLO TIES.
JUST LOOK AT THEM. I'VE GOT BOLO TIES MADE OF TURQUOISE, SILVER, GOLD, ONYX, WOOD, ELK HORN... YOU NAME IT!
I'VE GOT ENOUGH BOLO TIES TO WEAR A DIFFERENT ONE EVERY DAY FOR A MONTH.
OH JOY.
NOT TO MENTION MY BEDTIME COLLECTION.

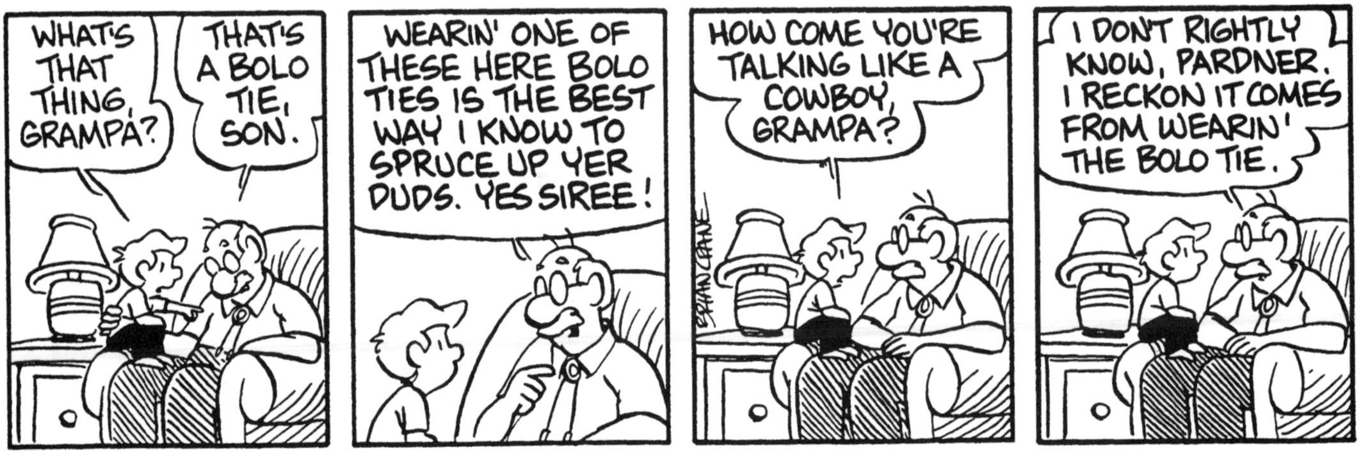
WHAT'S THAT THING, GRAMPA?
THAT'S A BOLO TIE, SON.
WEARIN' ONE OF THESE HERE BOLO TIES IS THE BEST WAY I KNOW TO SPRUCE UP YER DUDS. YES SIREE!
HOW COME YOU'RE TALKING LIKE A COWBOY, GRAMPA?
I DON'T RIGHTLY KNOW, PARDNER. I RECKON IT COMES FROM WEARIN' THE BOLO TIE.

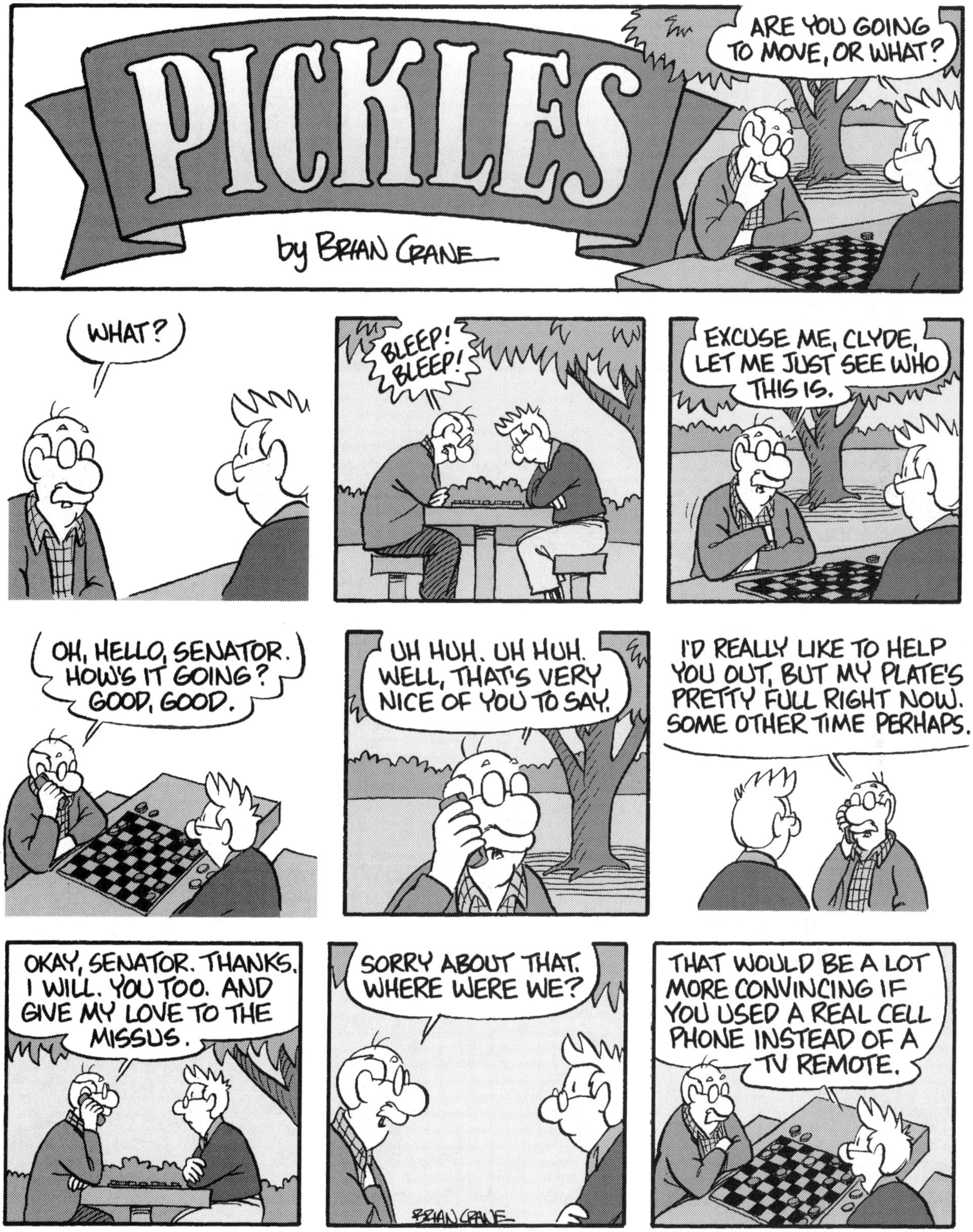
PICKLES
by BRIAN CRANE
ARE YOU GOING TO MOVE, OR WHAT?
WHAT?
BLEEP! BLEEP!
EXCUSE ME, CLYDE, LET ME JUST SEE WHO THIS IS.
OH, HELLO, SENATOR. HOW'S IT GOING? GOOD, GOOD.
UH HUH. UH HUH. WELL, THAT'S VERY NICE OF YOU TO SAY.
I'D REALLY LIKE TO HELP YOU OUT, BUT MY PLATE'S PRETTY FULL RIGHT NOW. SOME OTHER TIME PERHAPS.
OKAY, SENATOR. THANKS. I WILL. YOU TOO. AND GIVE MY LOVE TO THE MISSUS.
SORRY ABOUT THAT. WHERE WERE WE?
BRIAN CRANE
THAT WOULD BE A LOT MORE CONVINCING IF YOU USED A REAL CELL PHONE INSTEAD OF A TV REMOTE.

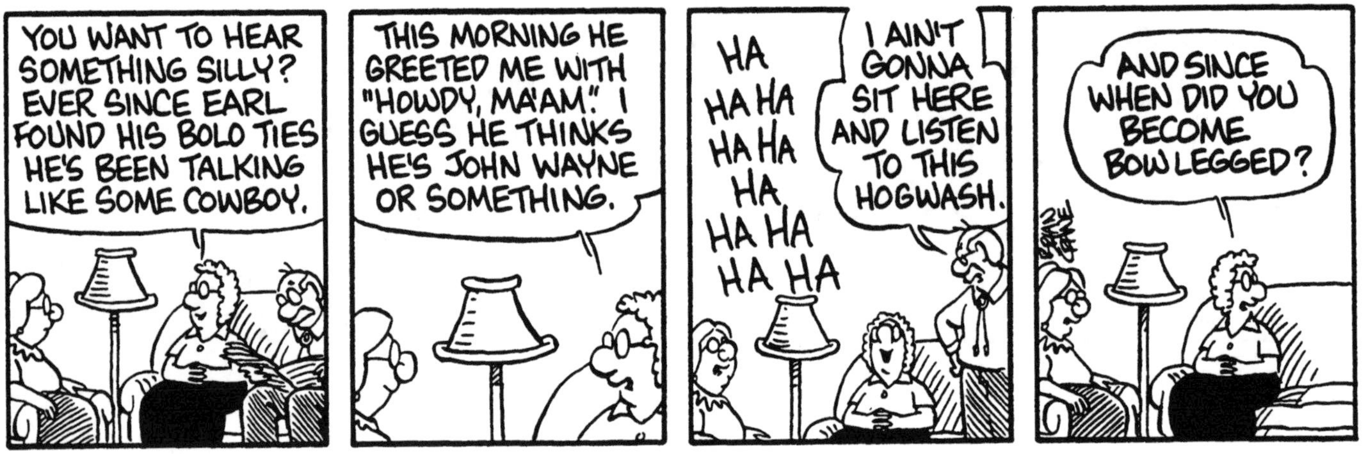
YOU WANT TO HEAR SOMETHING SILLY? EVER SINCE EARL FOUND HIS BOLO TIES HE'S BEEN TALKING LIKE SOME COWBOY.
THIS MORNING HE GREETED ME WITH "HOWDY, MA'AM." I GUESS HE THINKS HE'S JOHN WAYNE OR SOMETHING.
HA HA HA HA HA HA HA HA HA HA HA
I AIN'T GONNA SIT HERE AND LISTEN TO THIS HOGWASH.
AND SINCE WHEN DID YOU BECOME BOWLEGGED?

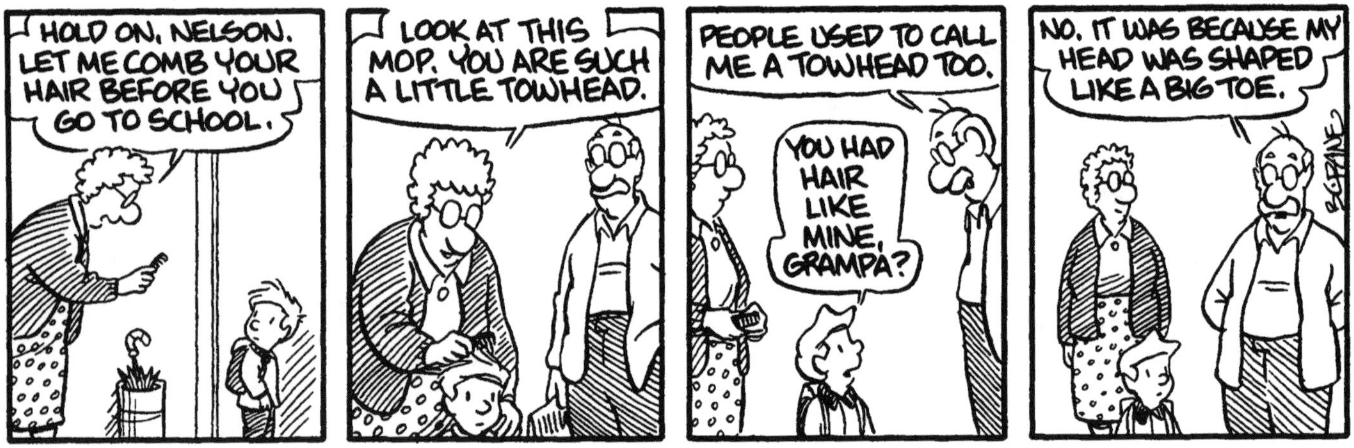
HOLD ON, NELSON. LET ME COMB YOUR HAIR BEFORE YOU GO TO SCHOOL.
LOOK AT THIS MOP. YOU ARE SUCH A LITTLE TOWHEAD.
PEOPLE USED TO CALL ME A TOWHEAD TOO.
YOU HAD HAIR LIKE MINE, GRAMPA?
NO. IT WAS BECAUSE MY HEAD WAS SHAPED LIKE A BIG TOE.

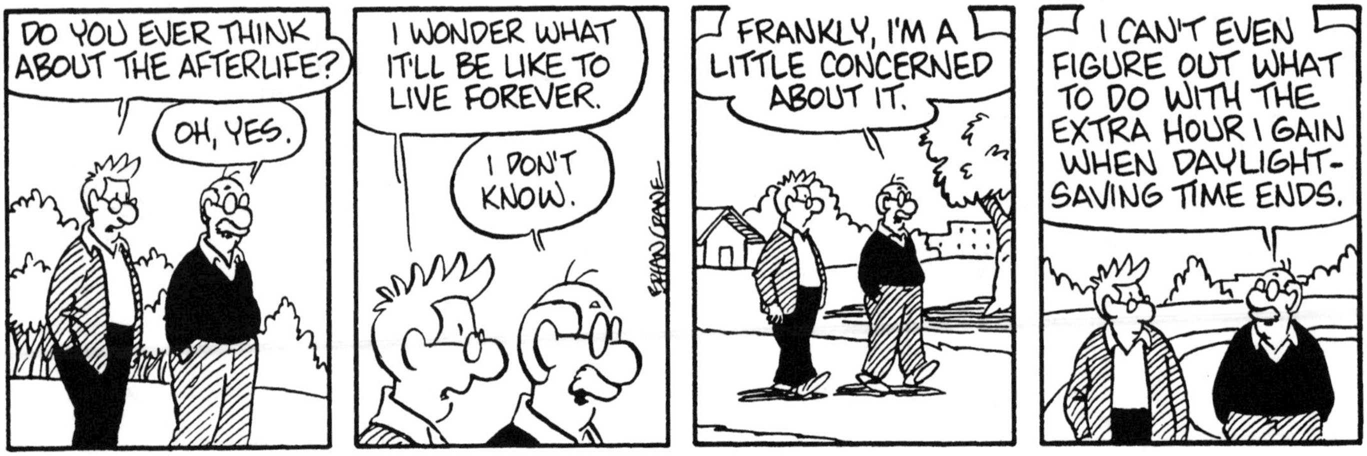
DO YOU EVER THINK ABOUT THE AFTERLIFE?
OH, YES.
I WONDER WHAT IT'LL BE LIKE TO LIVE FOREVER.
I DON'T KNOW.
FRANKLY, I'M A LITTLE CONCERNED ABOUT IT.
I CAN'T EVEN FIGURE OUT WHAT TO DO WITH THE EXTRA HOUR I GAIN WHEN DAYLIGHT-SAVING TIME ENDS.

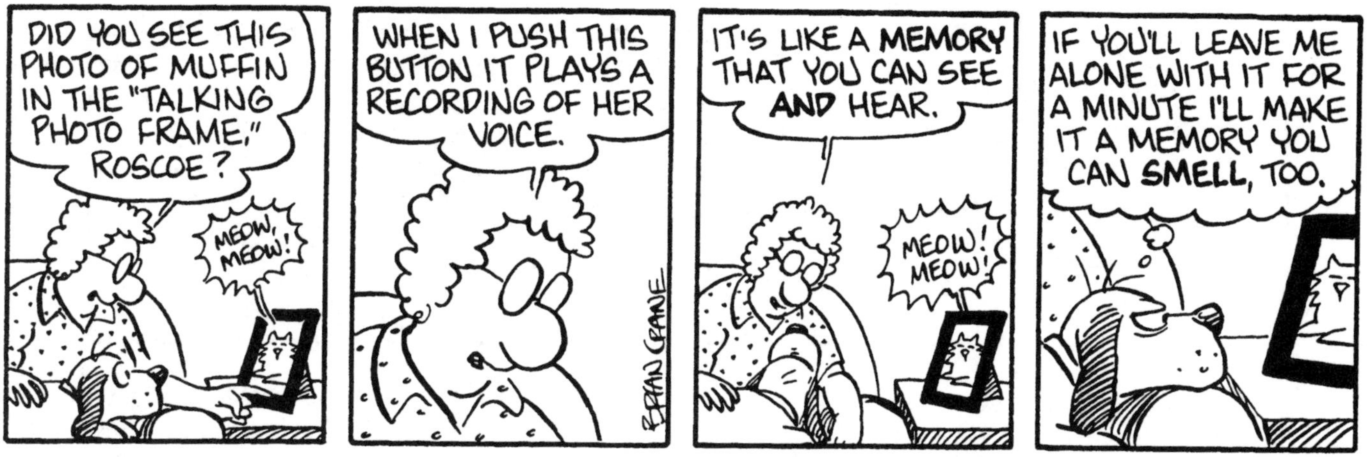
DID YOU SEE THIS PHOTO OF MUFFIN IN THE "TALKING PHOTO FRAME," ROSCOE?
MEOW, MEOW!
WHEN I PUSH THIS BUTTON IT PLAYS A RECORDING OF HER VOICE.
IT'S LIKE A **MEMORY** THAT YOU CAN SEE **AND** HEAR.
MEOW! MEOW!
IF YOU'LL LEAVE ME ALONE WITH IT FOR A MINUTE I'LL MAKE IT A MEMORY YOU CAN **SMELL**, TOO.

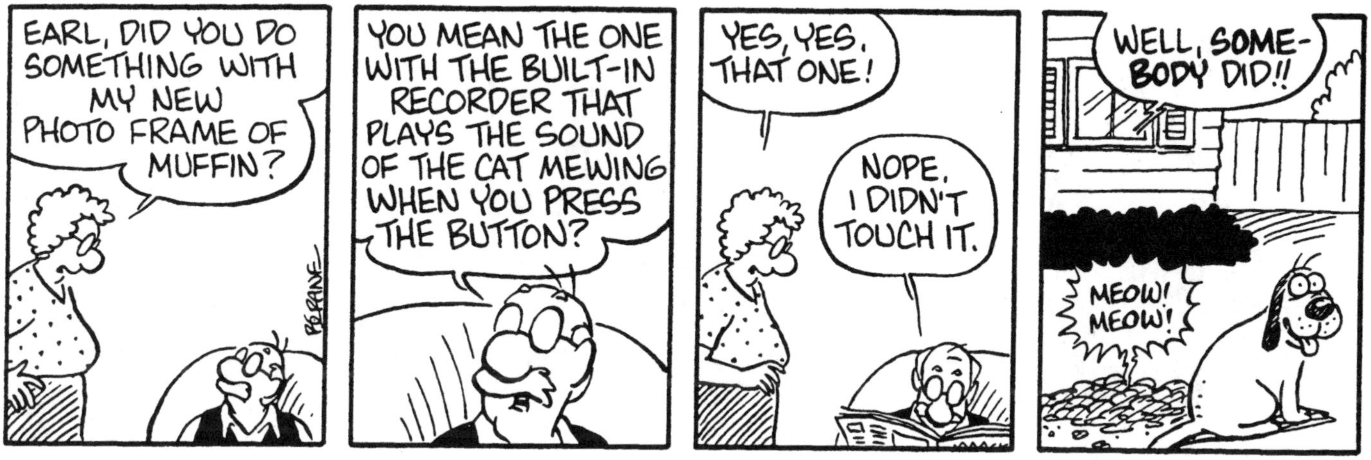
EARL, DID YOU DO SOMETHING WITH MY NEW PHOTO FRAME OF MUFFIN?
YOU MEAN THE ONE WITH THE BUILT-IN RECORDER THAT PLAYS THE SOUND OF THE CAT MEWING WHEN YOU PRESS THE BUTTON?
YES, YES, THAT ONE!
NOPE, I DIDN'T TOUCH IT.
WELL, **SOMEBODY** DID!!
MEOW! MEOW!

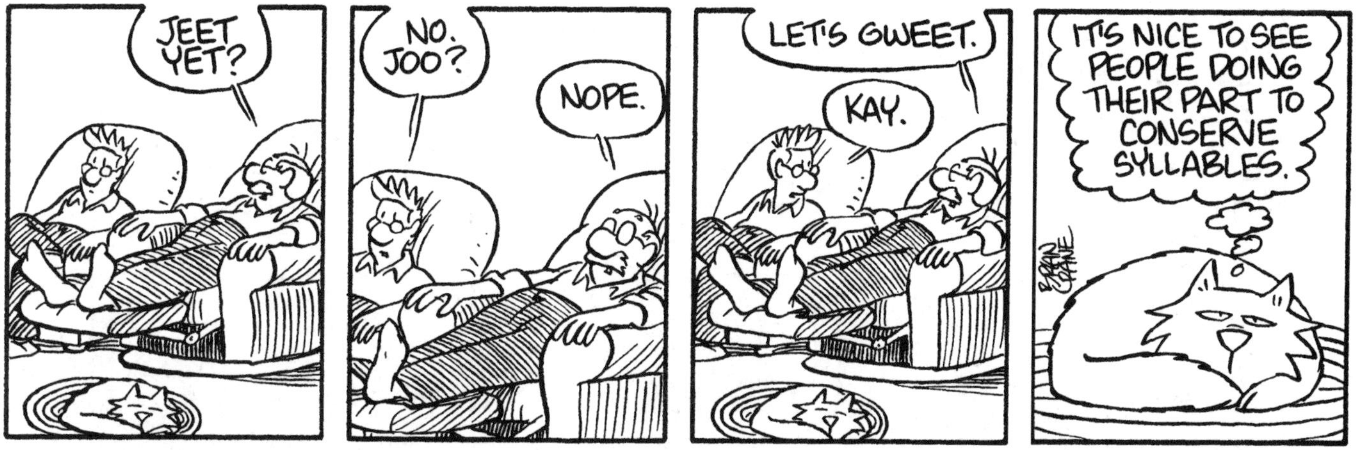
JEET YET?
NO. JOO?
NOPE.
LET'S GWEET.
KAY.
IT'S NICE TO SEE PEOPLE DOING THEIR PART TO CONSERVE SYLLABLES.

**PICKLES** by Brian Crane

"I'VE GOTTA GO. I WANT TO GO TO THE CLINIC TODAY. THEY'RE GIVING FREE IMMUNIZATIONS."

"I THOUGHT YOU HATED SHOTS."

"I DO, BUT HEY—THEY'RE FREE!"

"GET YOUR SHOES ON, EARL. THEY'RE GIVING FREE IMMUNIZATIONS TO SENIOR CITIZENS AT THE CLINIC TODAY."

"IMMUNIZATIONS? I DON'T NEED ANY IMMUNIZATIONS. I HAD 'EM ALL WHEN I WAS A KID."

"WELL, THEY NEED TO BE UPDATED. AS WE GET OLDER OUR IMMUNE SYSTEMS GET WEAKER."

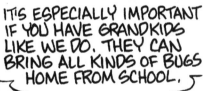

"IT'S ESPECIALLY IMPORTANT IF YOU HAVE GRANDKIDS LIKE WE DO. THEY CAN BRING ALL KINDS OF BUGS HOME FROM SCHOOL."

"OKAY! I'LL GO."

"EXCUSE ME. WHERE ARE YOU GIVING THE FREE IMMUNIZATIONS?"

"IN THE BASEMENT."

"FORGET IT! I TAKE MY SHOTS IN THE ARM OR NOT AT ALL."

"PAT PAT"

**Panel 1:** I GOT ME SOME NEW "WRAPAROUND" SUNGLASSES.

**Panel 2:** THEY CALL THEM THAT BECAUSE THEY WRAP AROUND YOUR REGULAR GLASSES.

**Panel 3:** THEY MAKE ME LOOK PRETTY COOL, DON'T THEY?

**Panel 4:** IF BY "COOL" YOU MEAN "DORKY", THEN YES, THEY MAKE YOU LOOK VERY COOL.

**Panel 5:** I SEE YOU'VE GOT NEW SUNGLASSES, EARL. ARE THEY PRESCRIPTION?

NOPE.

**Panel 6:** PRESCRIPTION BI-FOCAL SUNGLASSES CAN COST A BUNDLE. AND THEY DON'T EVEN PROTECT THE SIDES OF YOUR EYES FROM UV RAYS.

**Panel 7:** THESE DO BECAUSE THEY FIT RIGHT OVER MY REGULAR GLASSES, AND... THEY ONLY COST $6.95.

**Panel 8:** THE FACT THAT THEY MAKE ME LOOK SO GROOVY IS JUST A BONUS.

**Panel 9:** THAT WOMAN OVER THERE IS GIVING ME THE EYE.

**Panel 10:** THE LADIES CAN'T RESIST A MAN IN COOL SHADES AND A SNAZZY HAT. LOOK... SHE'S COMIN' OVER!

**Panel 11:** HOWDY, MA'AM.

**Panel 12:** ! CLINK CLINK

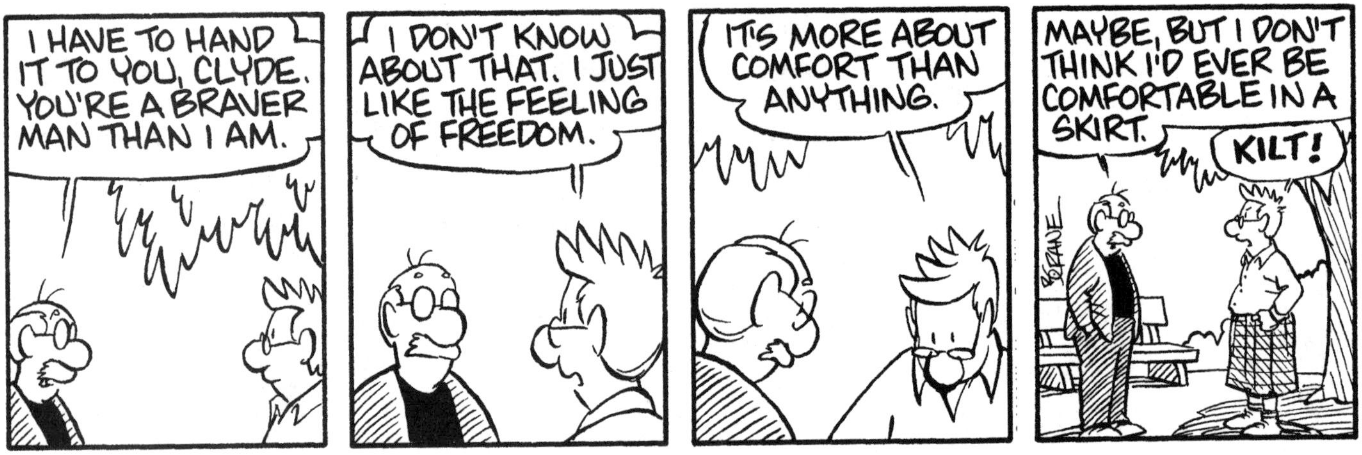
I HAVE TO HAND IT TO YOU, CLYDE. YOU'RE A BRAVER MAN THAN I AM.
I DON'T KNOW ABOUT THAT. I JUST LIKE THE FEELING OF FREEDOM.
IT'S MORE ABOUT COMFORT THAN ANYTHING.
MAYBE, BUT I DON'T THINK I'D EVER BE COMFORTABLE IN A SKIRT.
KILT!

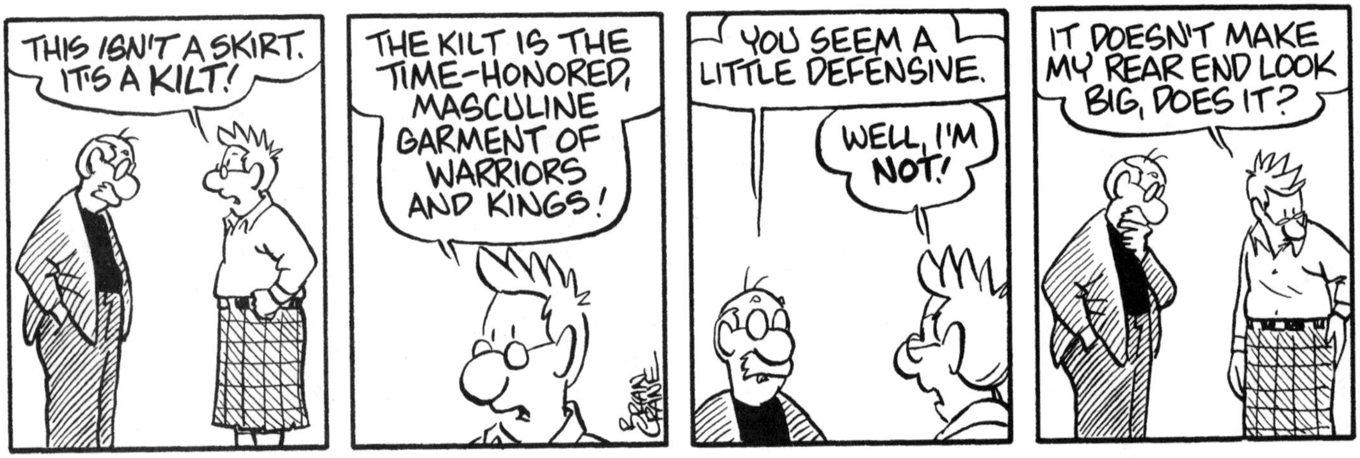
THIS ISN'T A SKIRT. IT'S A KILT!
THE KILT IS THE TIME-HONORED, MASCULINE GARMENT OF WARRIORS AND KINGS!
YOU SEEM A LITTLE DEFENSIVE.
WELL, I'M NOT!
IT DOESN'T MAKE MY REAR END LOOK BIG, DOES IT?

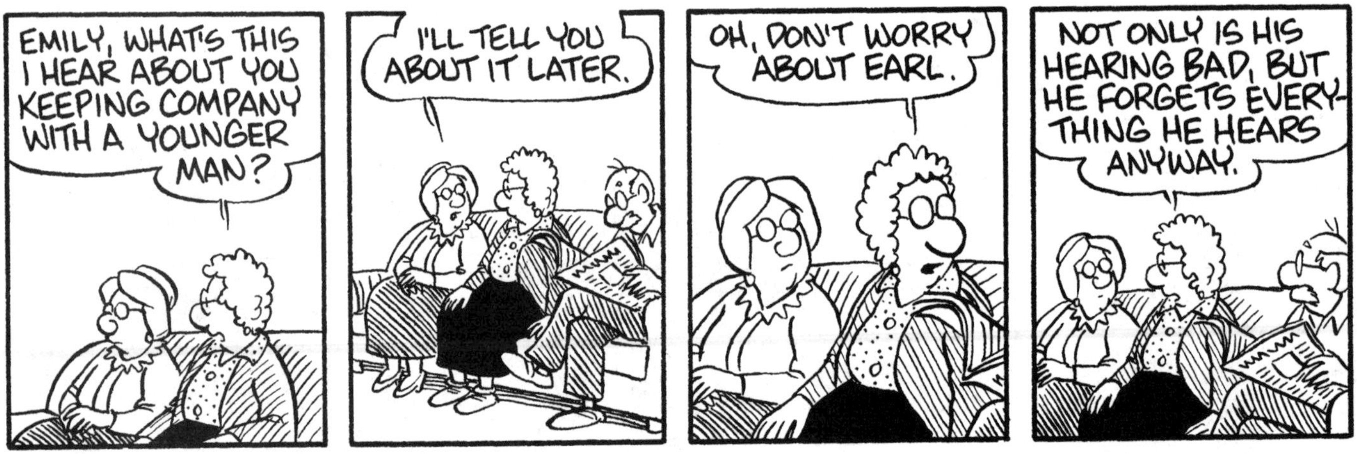
EMILY, WHAT'S THIS I HEAR ABOUT YOU KEEPING COMPANY WITH A YOUNGER MAN?
I'LL TELL YOU ABOUT IT LATER.
OH, DON'T WORRY ABOUT EARL.
NOT ONLY IS HIS HEARING BAD, BUT HE FORGETS EVERYTHING HE HEARS ANYWAY.

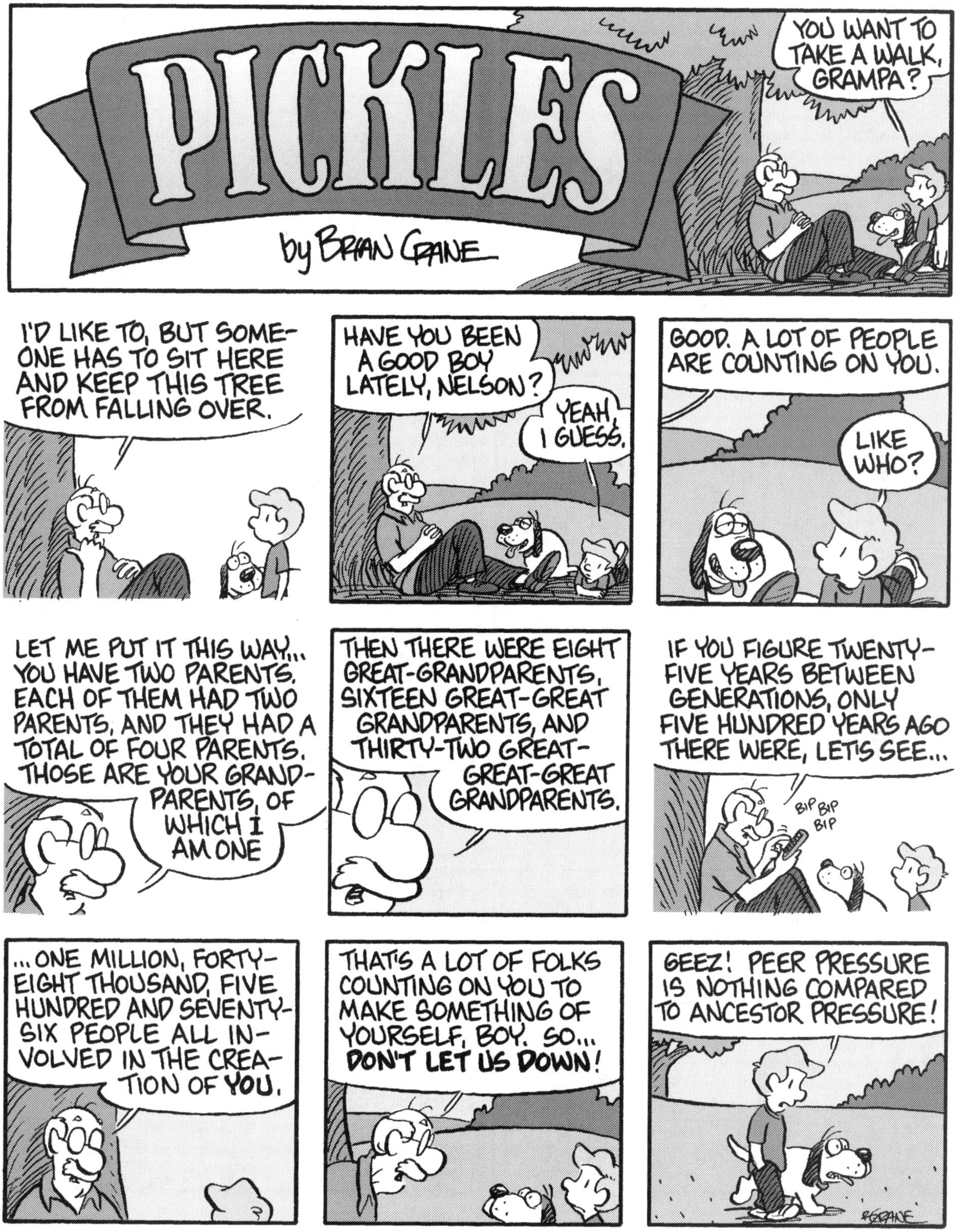
PICKLES
by BRIAN CRANE
YOU WANT TO TAKE A WALK, GRAMPA?
I'D LIKE TO, BUT SOMEONE HAS TO SIT HERE AND KEEP THIS TREE FROM FALLING OVER.
HAVE YOU BEEN A GOOD BOY LATELY, NELSON?
YEAH, I GUESS.
GOOD. A LOT OF PEOPLE ARE COUNTING ON YOU.
LIKE WHO?
LET ME PUT IT THIS WAY... YOU HAVE TWO PARENTS. EACH OF THEM HAD TWO PARENTS, AND THEY HAD A TOTAL OF FOUR PARENTS. THOSE ARE YOUR GRANDPARENTS, OF WHICH I AM ONE
THEN THERE WERE EIGHT GREAT-GRANDPARENTS, SIXTEEN GREAT-GREAT GRANDPARENTS, AND THIRTY-TWO GREAT-GREAT-GREAT GRANDPARENTS.
IF YOU FIGURE TWENTY-FIVE YEARS BETWEEN GENERATIONS, ONLY FIVE HUNDRED YEARS AGO THERE WERE, LET'S SEE...
BIP BIP BIP
...ONE MILLION, FORTY-EIGHT THOUSAND, FIVE HUNDRED AND SEVENTY-SIX PEOPLE ALL INVOLVED IN THE CREATION OF **YOU**.
THAT'S A LOT OF FOLKS COUNTING ON YOU TO MAKE SOMETHING OF YOURSELF, BOY. SO... **DON'T LET US DOWN**!
GEEZ! PEER PRESSURE IS NOTHING COMPARED TO ANCESTOR PRESSURE!
B CRANE

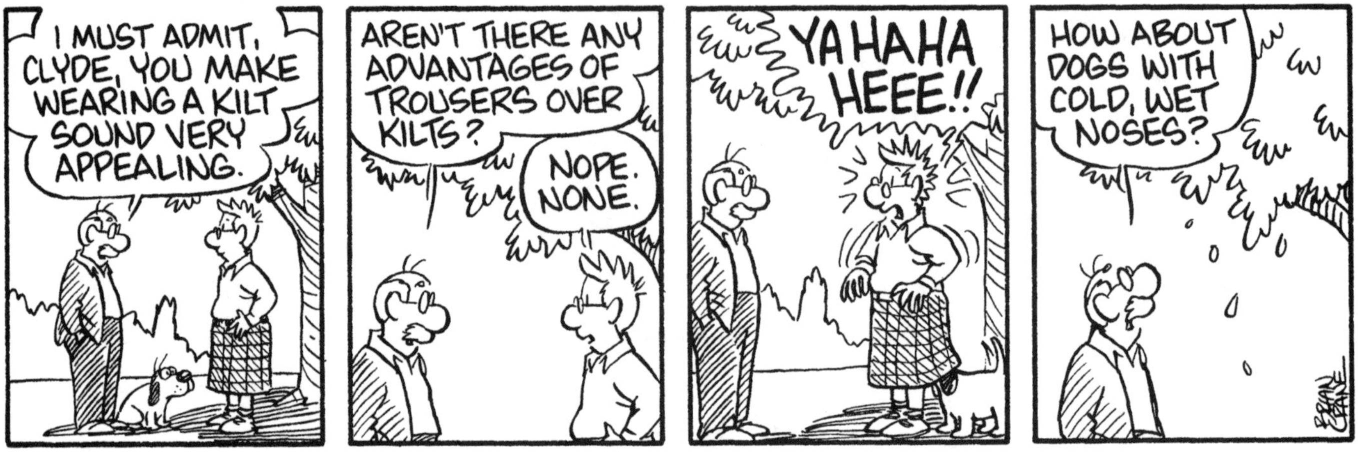
I MUST ADMIT, CLYDE, YOU MAKE WEARING A KILT SOUND VERY APPEALING.
AREN'T THERE ANY ADVANTAGES OF TROUSERS OVER KILTS?
NOPE. NONE.
YA HA HA HEEE!!
HOW ABOUT DOGS WITH COLD, WET NOSES?

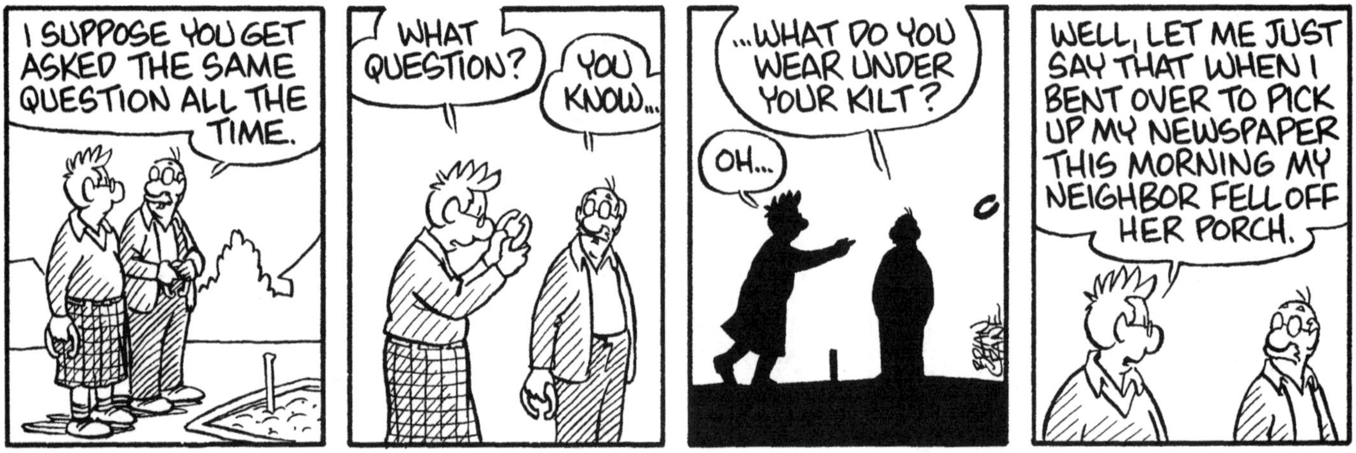
I SUPPOSE YOU GET ASKED THE SAME QUESTION ALL THE TIME.
WHAT QUESTION?
YOU KNOW...
...WHAT DO YOU WEAR UNDER YOUR KILT?
OH...
WELL, LET ME JUST SAY THAT WHEN I BENT OVER TO PICK UP MY NEWSPAPER THIS MORNING MY NEIGHBOR FELL OFF HER PORCH.

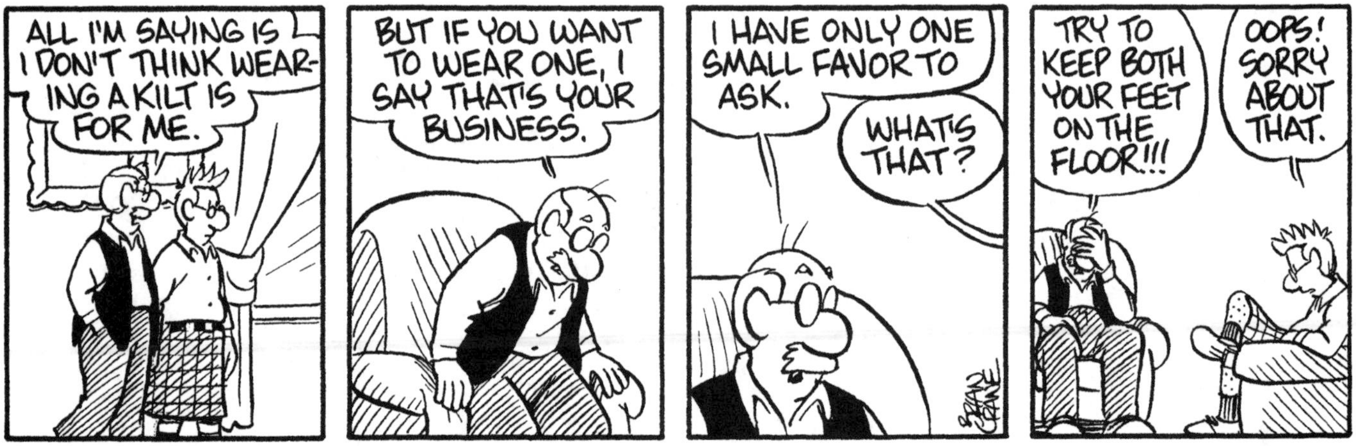
ALL I'M SAYING IS I DON'T THINK WEAR-ING A KILT IS FOR ME.
BUT IF YOU WANT TO WEAR ONE, I SAY THAT'S YOUR BUSINESS.
I HAVE ONLY ONE SMALL FAVOR TO ASK.
WHAT'S THAT?
TRY TO KEEP BOTH YOUR FEET ON THE FLOOR!!!
OOPS! SORRY ABOUT THAT.

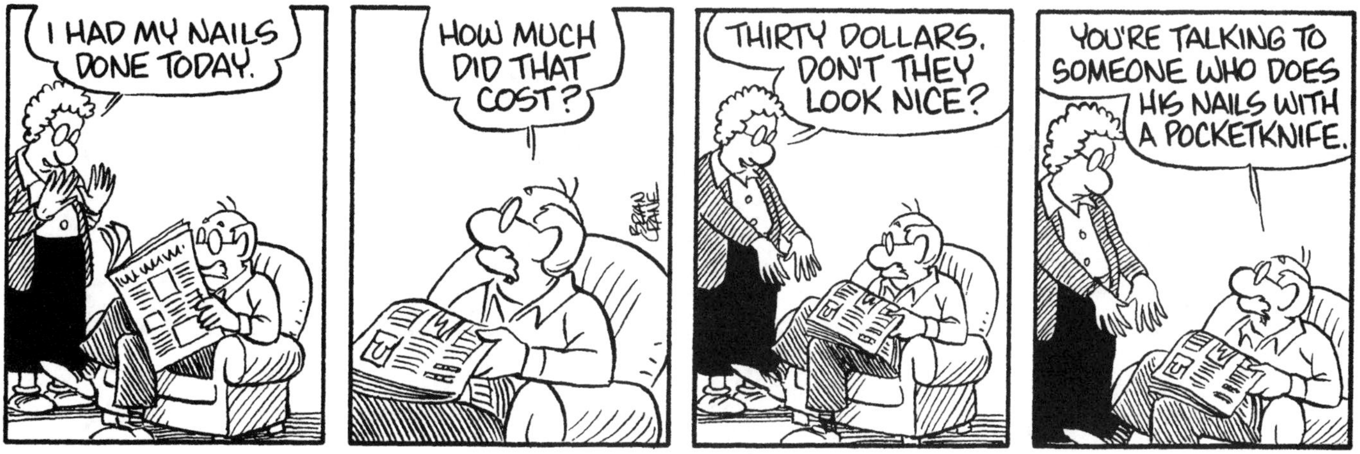
I HAD MY NAILS DONE TODAY.
HOW MUCH DID THAT COST?
THIRTY DOLLARS. DON'T THEY LOOK NICE?
YOU'RE TALKING TO SOMEONE WHO DOES HIS NAILS WITH A POCKETKNIFE.

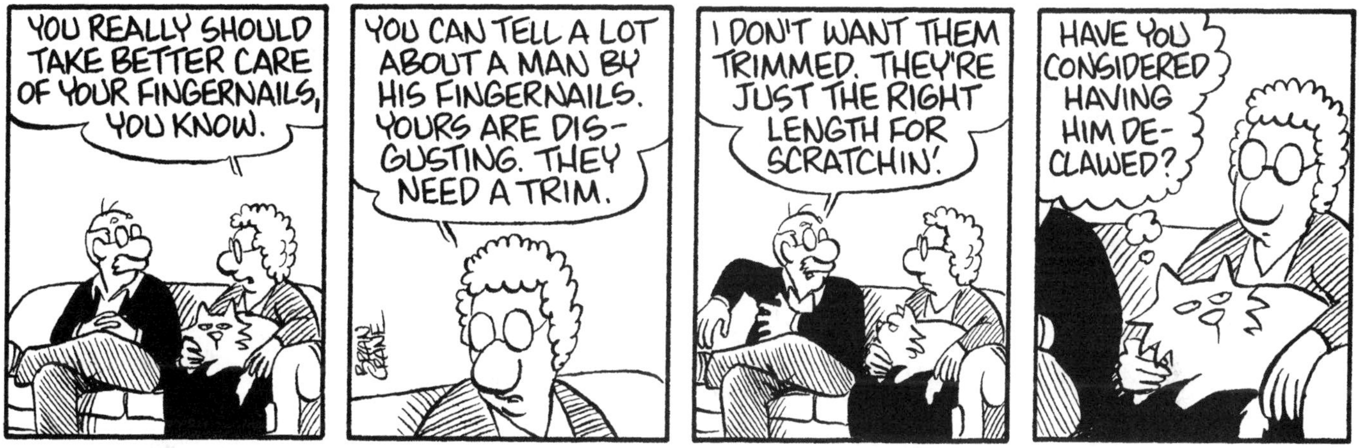
YOU REALLY SHOULD TAKE BETTER CARE OF YOUR FINGERNAILS, YOU KNOW.
YOU CAN TELL A LOT ABOUT A MAN BY HIS FINGERNAILS. YOURS ARE DIS-GUSTING. THEY NEED A TRIM.
I DON'T WANT THEM TRIMMED. THEY'RE JUST THE RIGHT LENGTH FOR SCRATCHIN'.
HAVE YOU CONSIDERED HAVING HIM DE-CLAWED?

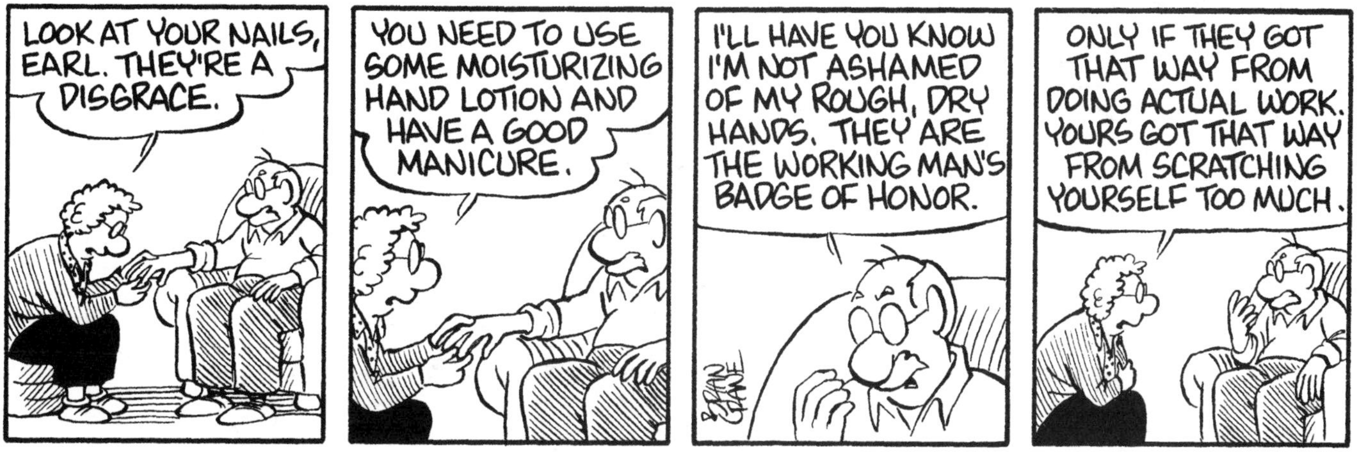
LOOK AT YOUR NAILS, EARL. THEY'RE A DISGRACE.
YOU NEED TO USE SOME MOISTURIZING HAND LOTION AND HAVE A GOOD MANICURE.
I'LL HAVE YOU KNOW I'M NOT ASHAMED OF MY ROUGH, DRY HANDS. THEY ARE THE WORKING MAN'S BADGE OF HONOR.
ONLY IF THEY GOT THAT WAY FROM DOING ACTUAL WORK. YOURS GOT THAT WAY FROM SCRATCHING YOURSELF TOO MUCH.

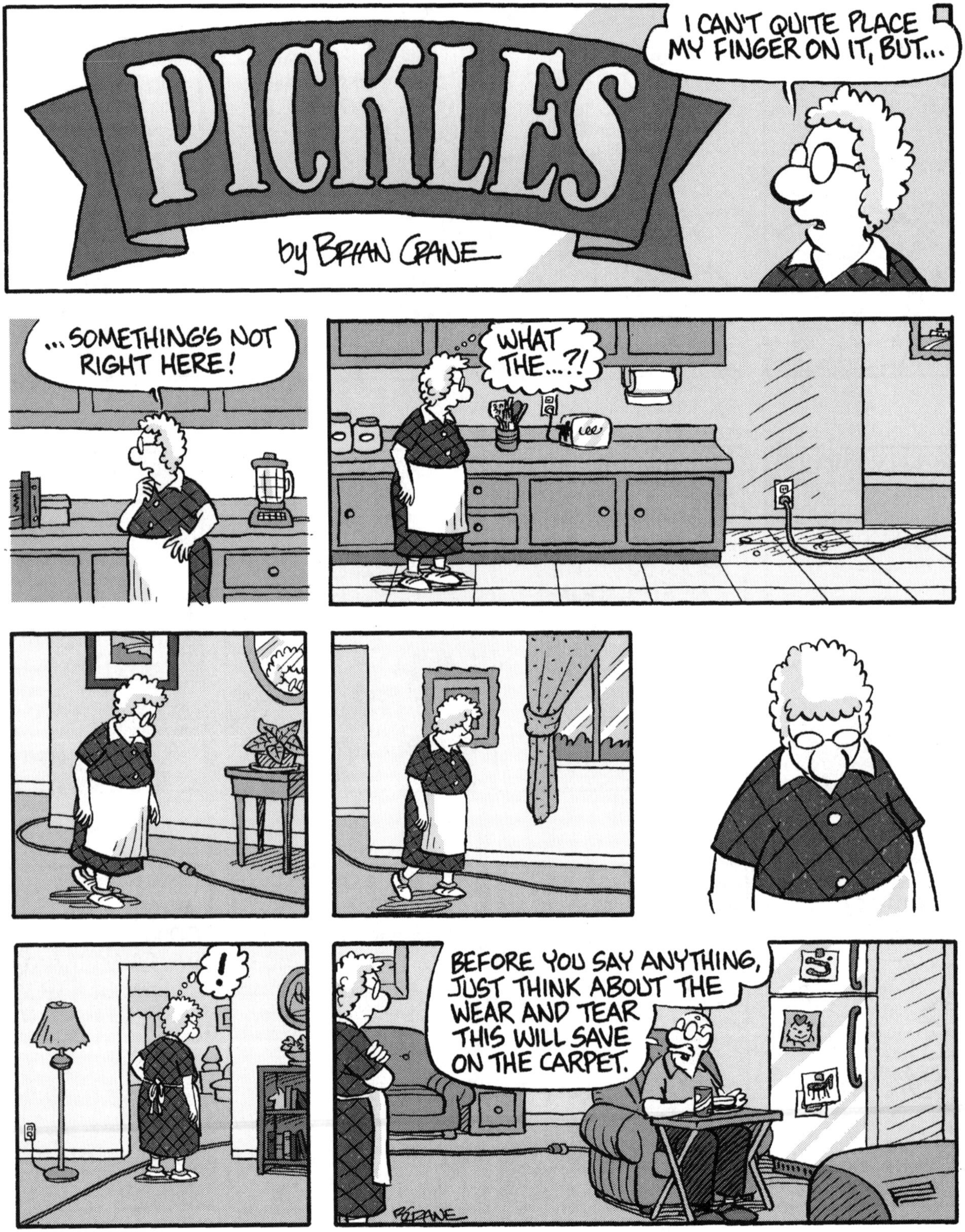
PICKLES
by BRIAN CRANE
I CAN'T QUITE PLACE MY FINGER ON IT, BUT...
...SOMETHING'S NOT RIGHT HERE!
WHAT THE...?!
!
BEFORE YOU SAY ANYTHING, JUST THINK ABOUT THE WEAR AND TEAR THIS WILL SAVE ON THE CARPET.
CRANE

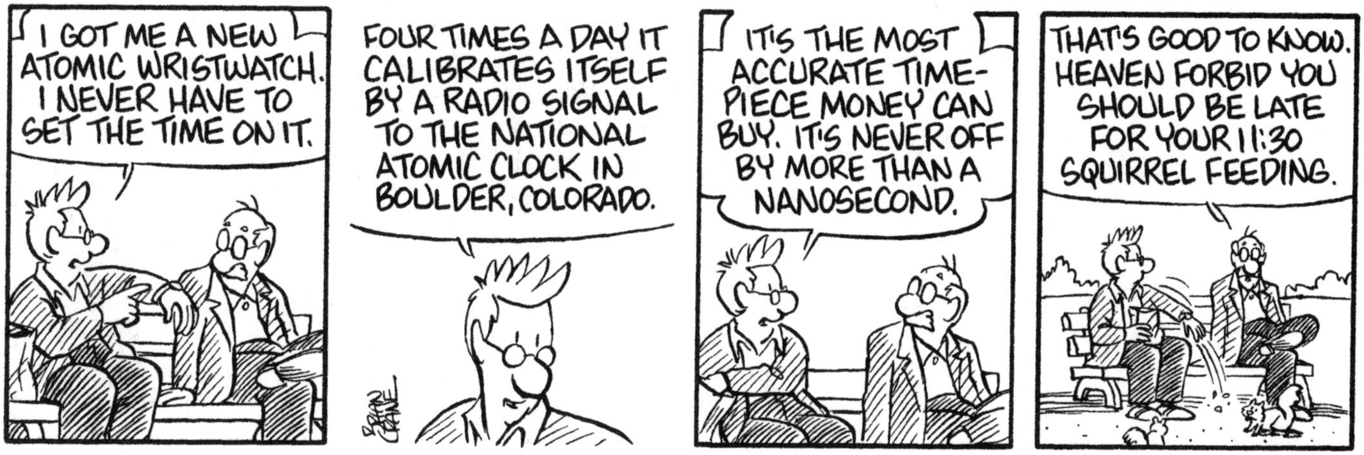
I GOT ME A NEW ATOMIC WRISTWATCH. I NEVER HAVE TO SET THE TIME ON IT.
FOUR TIMES A DAY IT CALIBRATES ITSELF BY A RADIO SIGNAL TO THE NATIONAL ATOMIC CLOCK IN BOULDER, COLORADO.
IT'S THE MOST ACCURATE TIME-PIECE MONEY CAN BUY. IT'S NEVER OFF BY MORE THAN A NANOSECOND.
THAT'S GOOD TO KNOW. HEAVEN FORBID YOU SHOULD BE LATE FOR YOUR 11:30 SQUIRREL FEEDING.

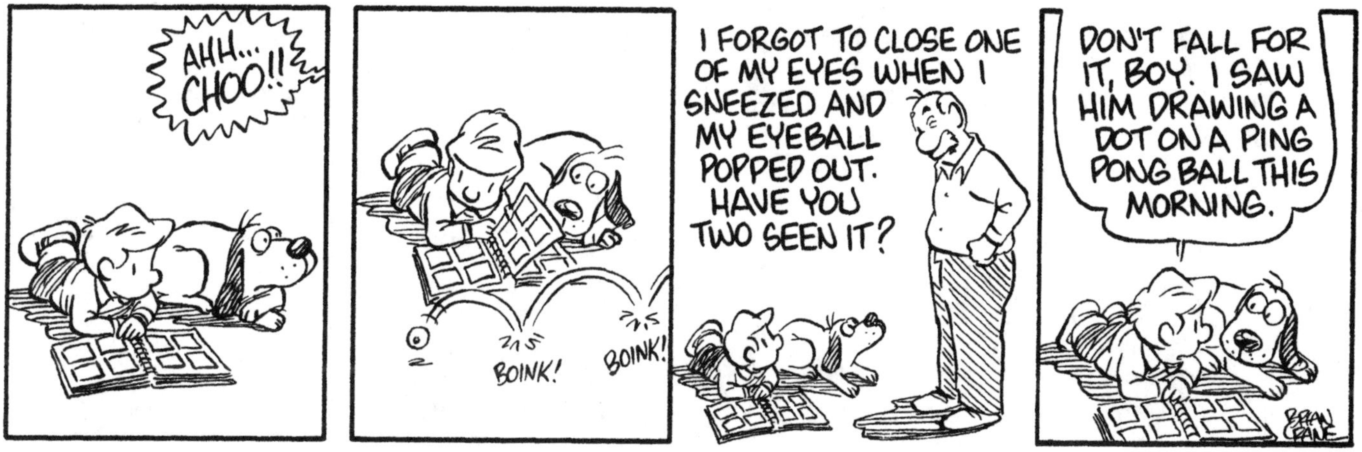
AHH... CHOO!!
BOINK!
BOINK!
I FORGOT TO CLOSE ONE OF MY EYES WHEN I SNEEZED AND MY EYEBALL POPPED OUT. HAVE YOU TWO SEEN IT?
DON'T FALL FOR IT, BOY. I SAW HIM DRAWING A DOT ON A PING PONG BALL THIS MORNING.

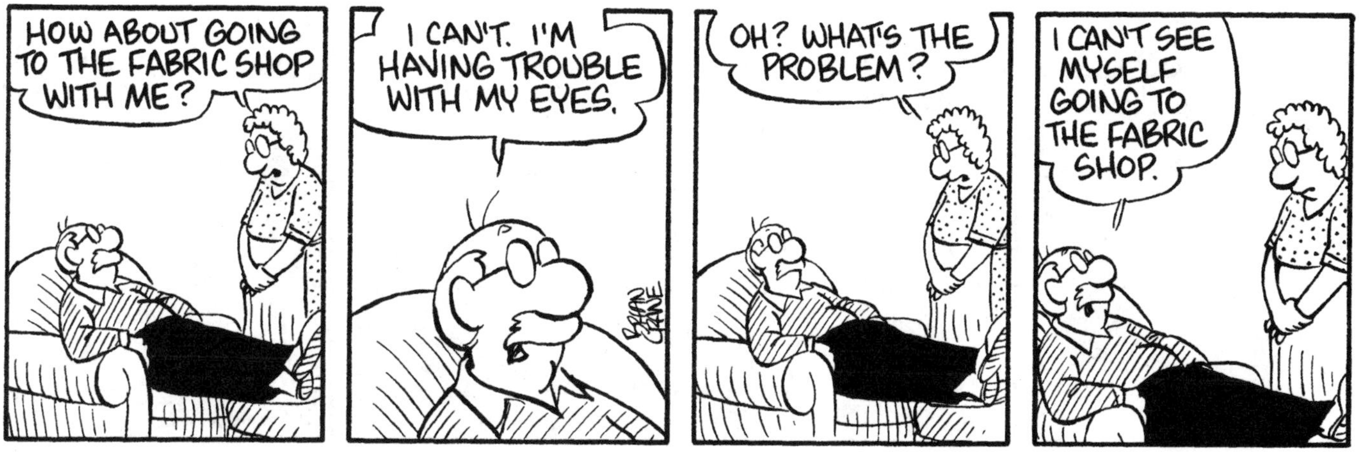
HOW ABOUT GOING TO THE FABRIC SHOP WITH ME?
I CAN'T. I'M HAVING TROUBLE WITH MY EYES.
OH? WHAT'S THE PROBLEM?
I CAN'T SEE MYSELF GOING TO THE FABRIC SHOP.

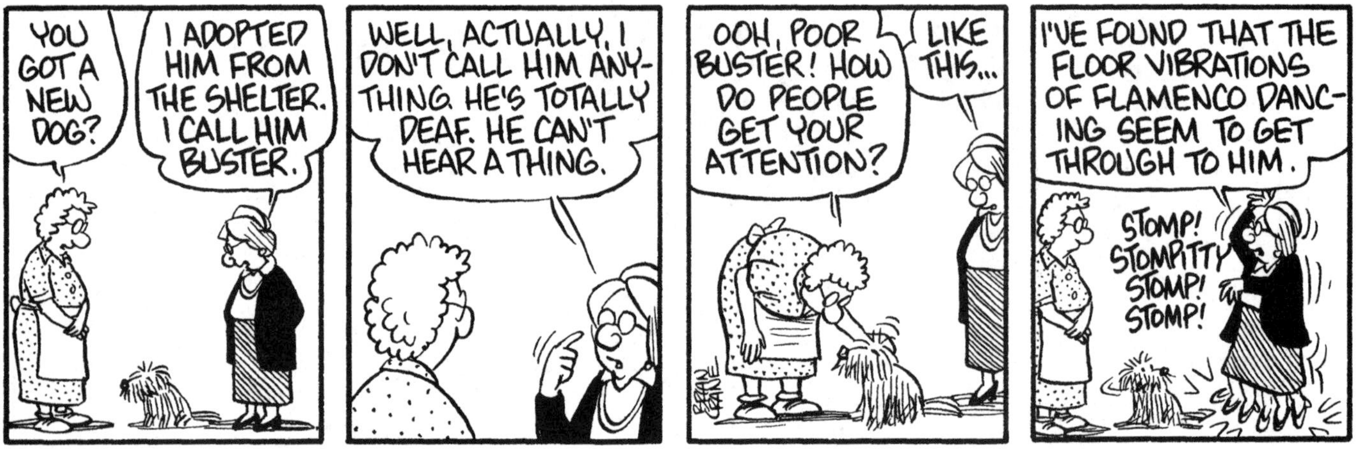
YOU GOT A NEW DOG?
I ADOPTED HIM FROM THE SHELTER. I CALL HIM BUSTER.
WELL, ACTUALLY, I DON'T CALL HIM ANYTHING. HE'S TOTALLY DEAF. HE CAN'T HEAR A THING.
OOH, POOR BUSTER! HOW DO PEOPLE GET YOUR ATTENTION?
LIKE THIS...
I'VE FOUND THAT THE FLOOR VIBRATIONS OF FLAMENCO DANCING SEEM TO GET THROUGH TO HIM.
STOMP! STOMPITTY STOMP! STOMP!

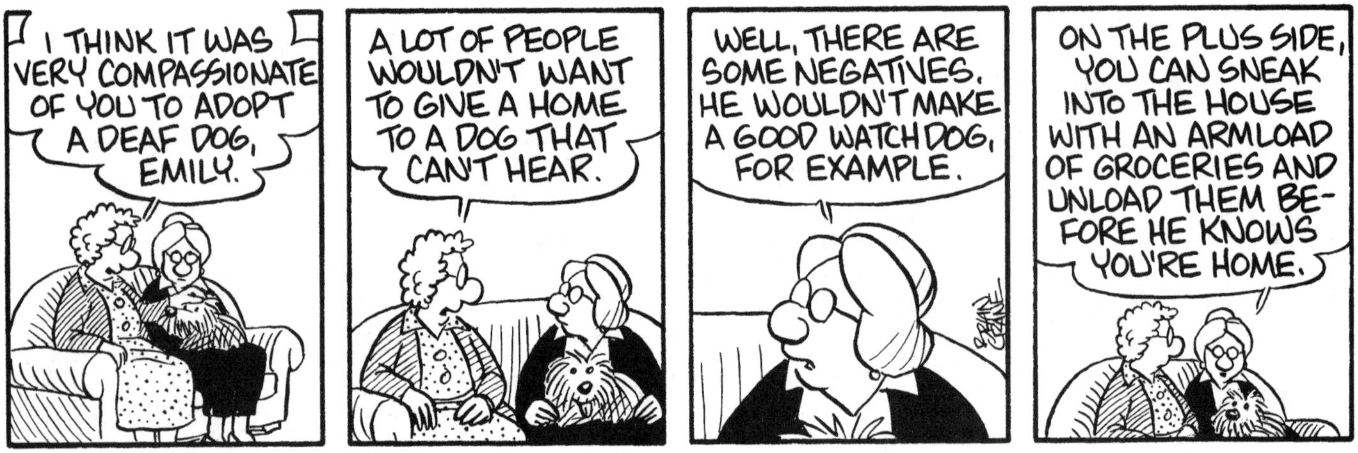
I THINK IT WAS VERY COMPASSIONATE OF YOU TO ADOPT A DEAF DOG, EMILY.
A LOT OF PEOPLE WOULDN'T WANT TO GIVE A HOME TO A DOG THAT CAN'T HEAR.
WELL, THERE ARE SOME NEGATIVES. HE WOULDN'T MAKE A GOOD WATCHDOG, FOR EXAMPLE.
ON THE PLUS SIDE, YOU CAN SNEAK INTO THE HOUSE WITH AN ARMLOAD OF GROCERIES AND UNLOAD THEM BEFORE HE KNOWS YOU'RE HOME.

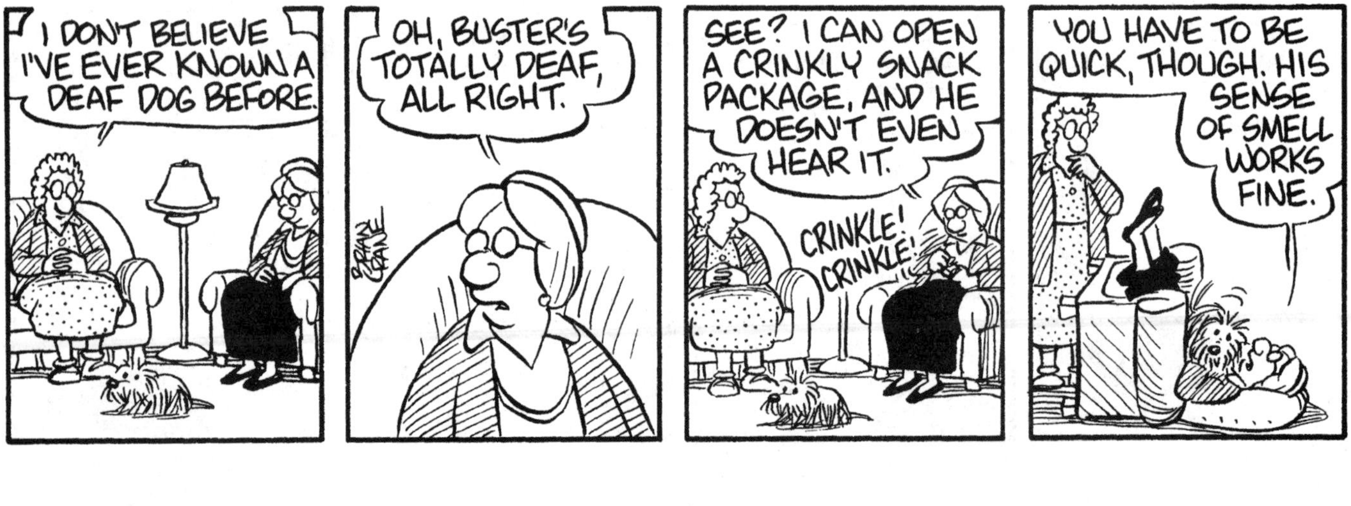
I DON'T BELIEVE I'VE EVER KNOWN A DEAF DOG BEFORE.
OH, BUSTER'S TOTALLY DEAF, ALL RIGHT.
SEE? I CAN OPEN A CRINKLY SNACK PACKAGE, AND HE DOESN'T EVEN HEAR IT.
CRINKLE! CRINKLE!
YOU HAVE TO BE QUICK, THOUGH. HIS SENSE OF SMELL WORKS FINE.

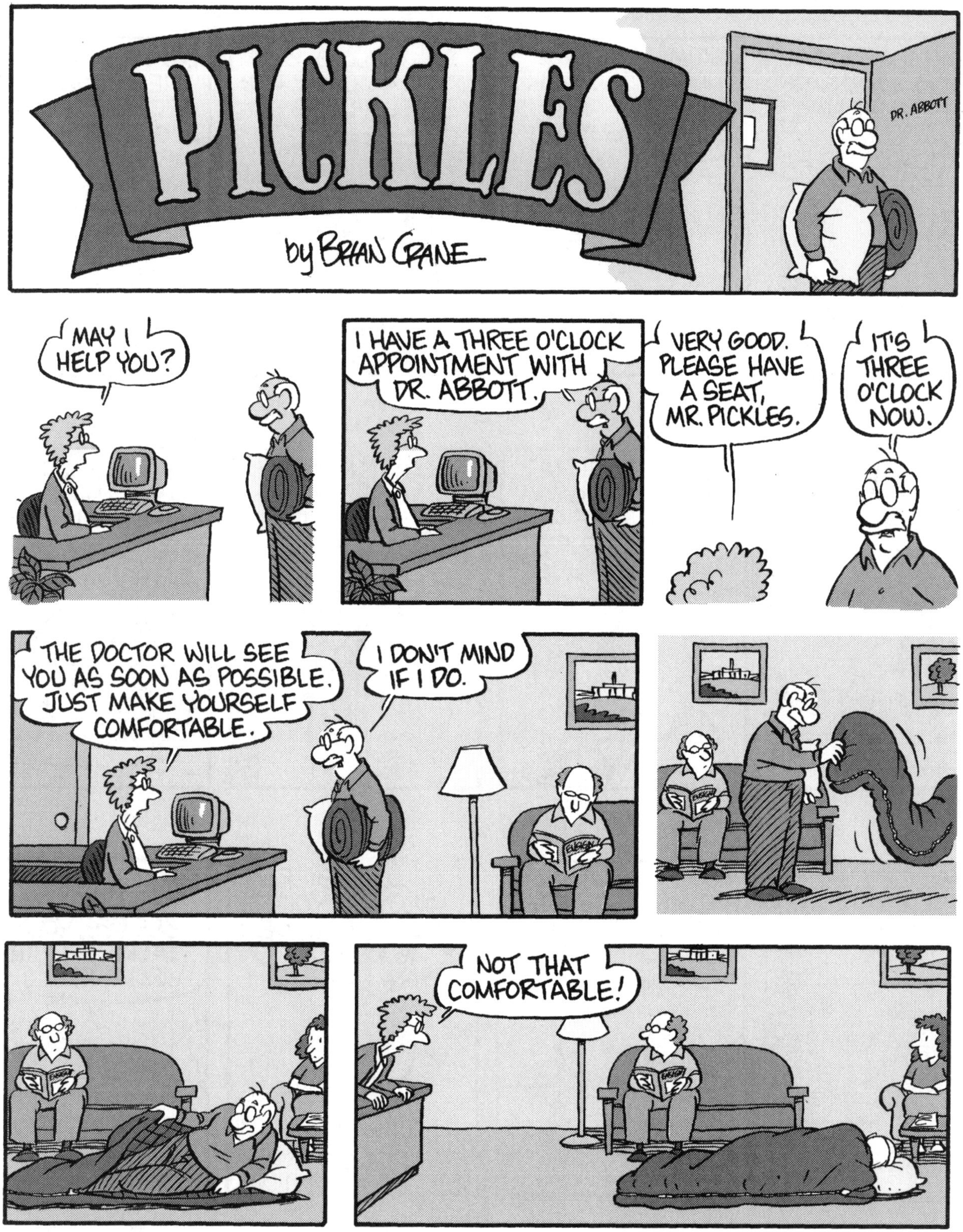
PICKLES
by BRIAN CRANE
DR. ABBOTT
MAY I HELP YOU?
I HAVE A THREE O'CLOCK APPOINTMENT WITH DR. ABBOTT.
VERY GOOD. PLEASE HAVE A SEAT, MR. PICKLES.
IT'S THREE O'CLOCK NOW.
THE DOCTOR WILL SEE YOU AS SOON AS POSSIBLE. JUST MAKE YOURSELF COMFORTABLE.
I DON'T MIND IF I DO.
NOT THAT COMFORTABLE!

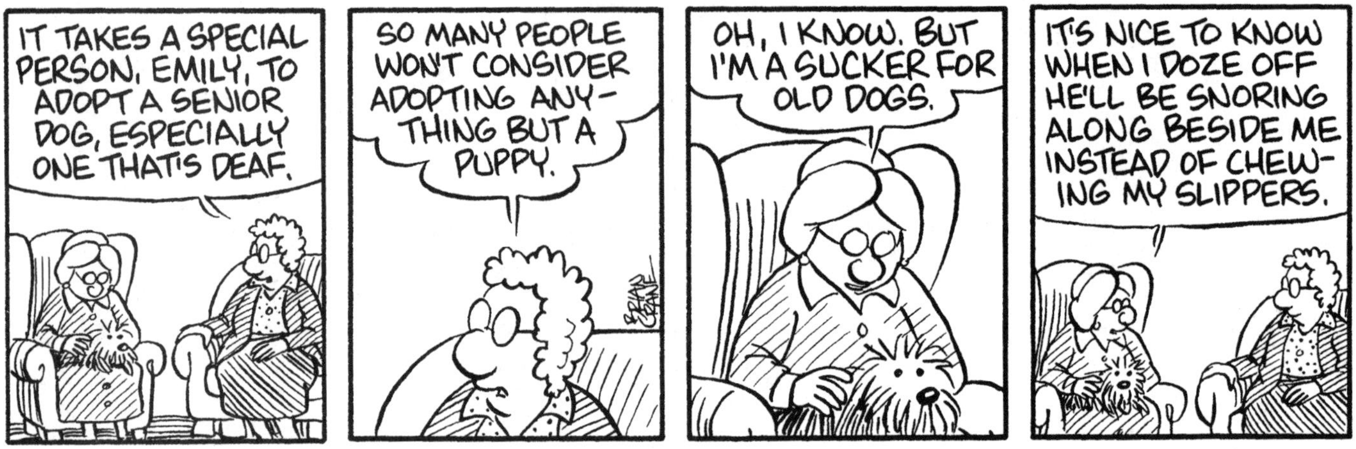
IT TAKES A SPECIAL PERSON, EMILY, TO ADOPT A SENIOR DOG, ESPECIALLY ONE THAT'S DEAF.
SO MANY PEOPLE WON'T CONSIDER ADOPTING ANY-THING BUT A PUPPY.
OH, I KNOW. BUT I'M A SUCKER FOR OLD DOGS.
IT'S NICE TO KNOW WHEN I DOZE OFF HE'LL BE SNORING ALONG BESIDE ME INSTEAD OF CHEW-ING MY SLIPPERS.

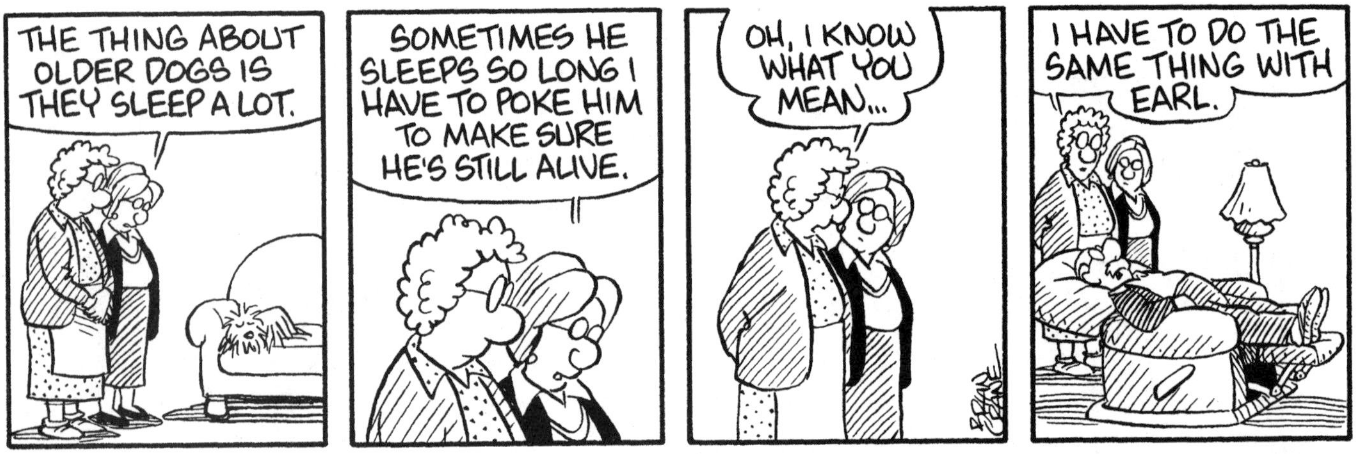
THE THING ABOUT OLDER DOGS IS THEY SLEEP A LOT.
SOMETIMES HE SLEEPS SO LONG I HAVE TO POKE HIM TO MAKE SURE HE'S STILL ALIVE.
OH, I KNOW WHAT YOU MEAN...
I HAVE TO DO THE SAME THING WITH EARL.

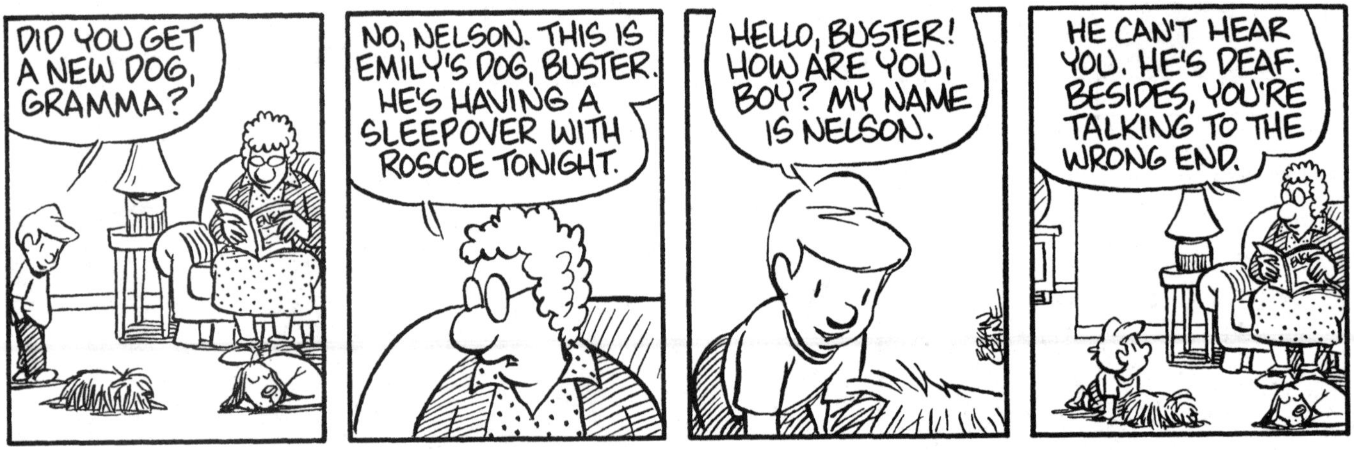
DID YOU GET A NEW DOG, GRAMMA?
NO, NELSON. THIS IS EMILY'S DOG, BUSTER. HE'S HAVING A SLEEPOVER WITH ROSCOE TONIGHT.
HELLO, BUSTER! HOW ARE YOU, BOY? MY NAME IS NELSON.
HE CAN'T HEAR YOU. HE'S DEAF. BESIDES, YOU'RE TALKING TO THE WRONG END.

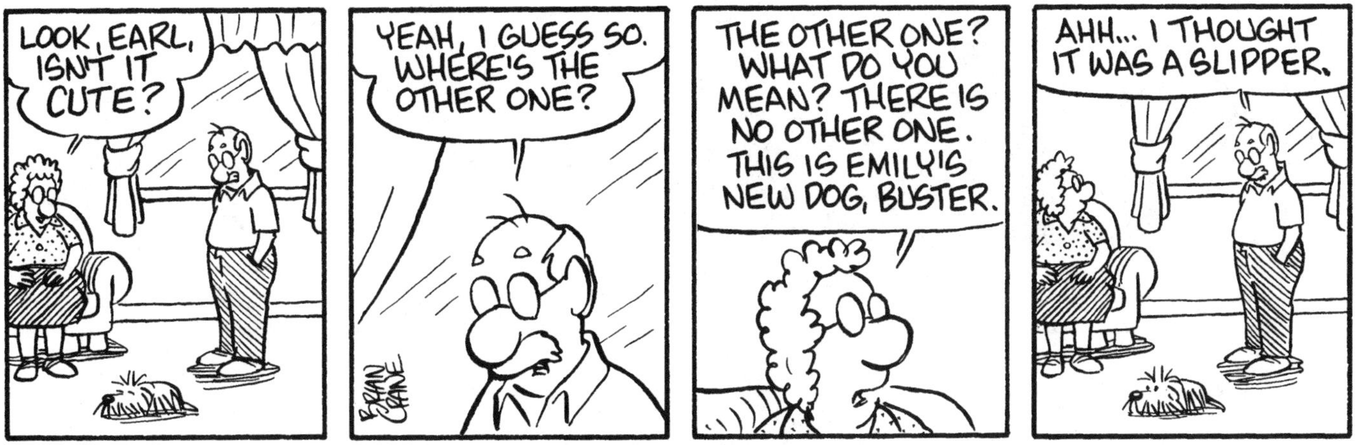
LOOK, EARL, ISN'T IT CUTE?
YEAH, I GUESS SO. WHERE'S THE OTHER ONE?
THE OTHER ONE? WHAT DO YOU MEAN? THERE IS NO OTHER ONE. THIS IS EMILY'S NEW DOG, BUSTER.
AHH... I THOUGHT IT WAS A SLIPPER.

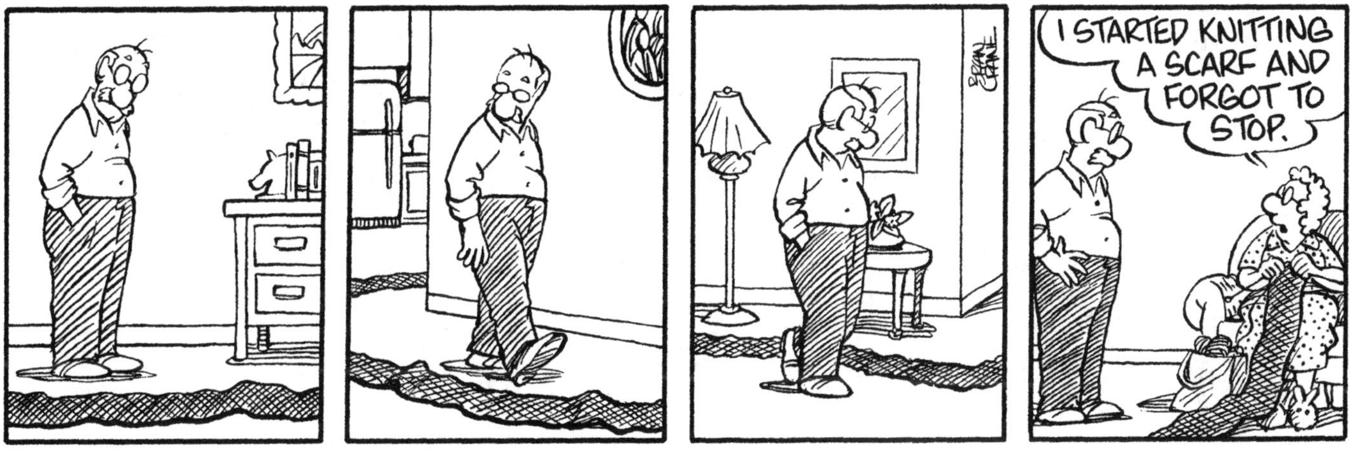
I STARTED KNITTING A SCARF AND FORGOT TO STOP.

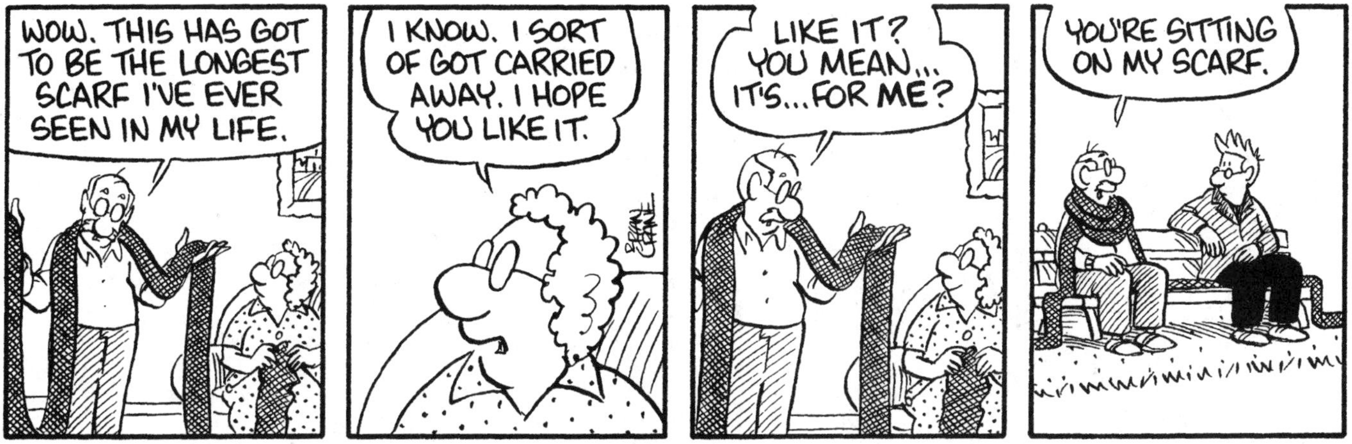
WOW. THIS HAS GOT TO BE THE LONGEST SCARF I'VE EVER SEEN IN MY LIFE.
I KNOW. I SORT OF GOT CARRIED AWAY. I HOPE YOU LIKE IT.
LIKE IT? YOU MEAN... IT'S...FOR ME?
YOU'RE SITTING ON MY SCARF.

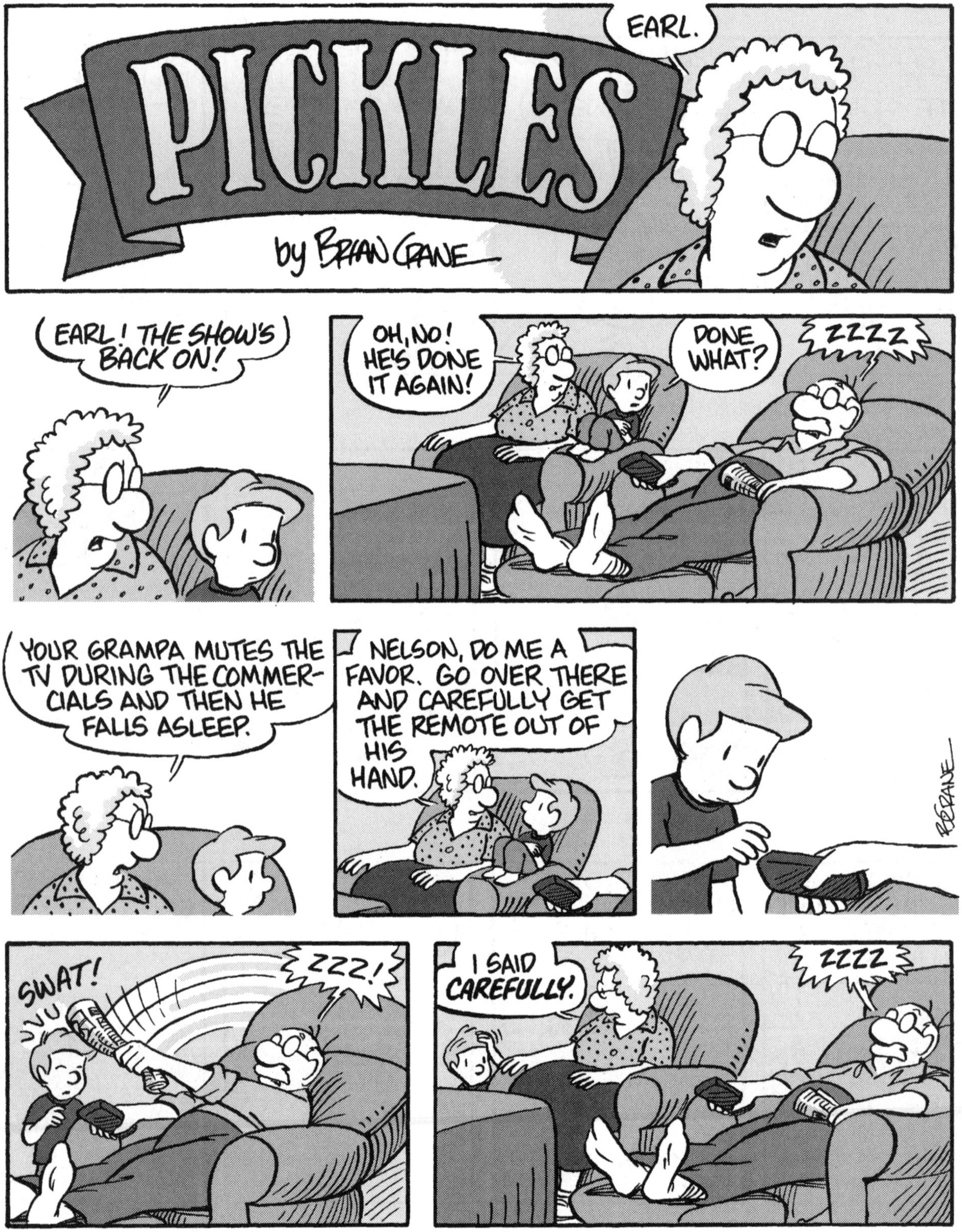
PICKLES
by BRIAN CRANE
EARL.
EARL! THE SHOW'S BACK ON!
OH, NO! HE'S DONE IT AGAIN!
DONE WHAT?
ZZZZ
YOUR GRAMPA MUTES THE TV DURING THE COMMERCIALS AND THEN HE FALLS ASLEEP.
NELSON, DO ME A FAVOR. GO OVER THERE AND CAREFULLY GET THE REMOTE OUT OF HIS HAND.
SWAT!
ZZZ!
I SAID **CAREFULLY.**
ZZZZ

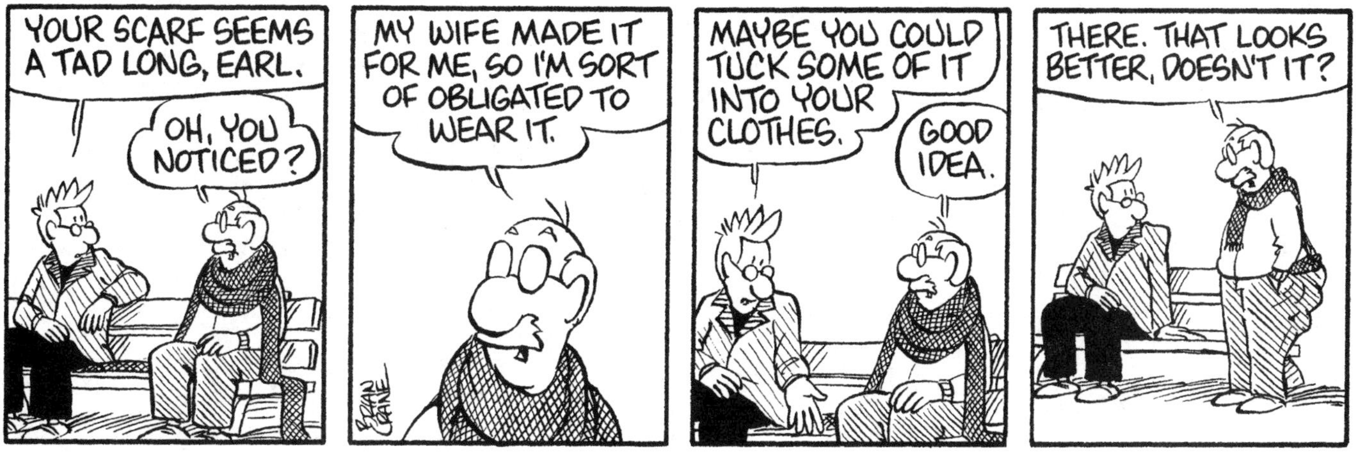
YOUR SCARF SEEMS A TAD LONG, EARL.
OH, YOU NOTICED?
MY WIFE MADE IT FOR ME, SO I'M SORT OF OBLIGATED TO WEAR IT.
MAYBE YOU COULD TUCK SOME OF IT INTO YOUR CLOTHES.
GOOD IDEA.
THERE. THAT LOOKS BETTER, DOESN'T IT?

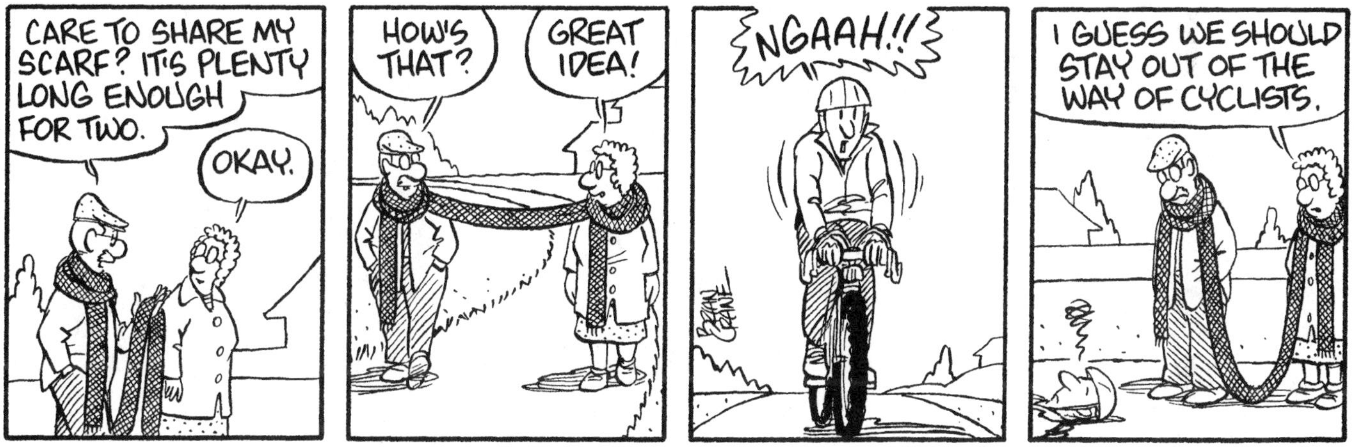
CARE TO SHARE MY SCARF? IT'S PLENTY LONG ENOUGH FOR TWO.
OKAY.
HOW'S THAT?
GREAT IDEA!
NGAAH!!
I GUESS WE SHOULD STAY OUT OF THE WAY OF CYCLISTS.

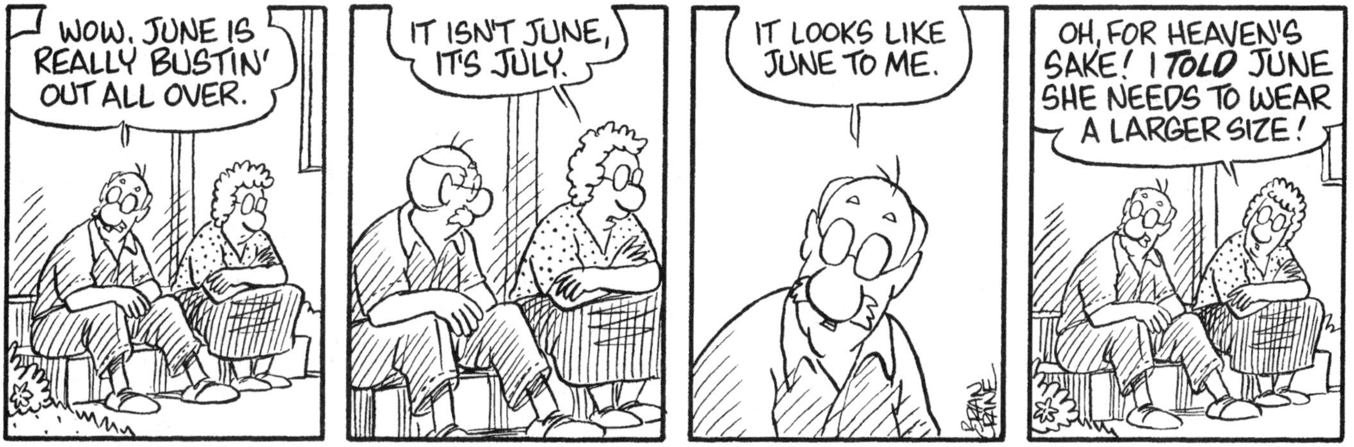
WOW. JUNE IS REALLY BUSTIN' OUT ALL OVER.
IT ISN'T JUNE, IT'S JULY.
IT LOOKS LIKE JUNE TO ME.
OH, FOR HEAVEN'S SAKE! I TOLD JUNE SHE NEEDS TO WEAR A LARGER SIZE!

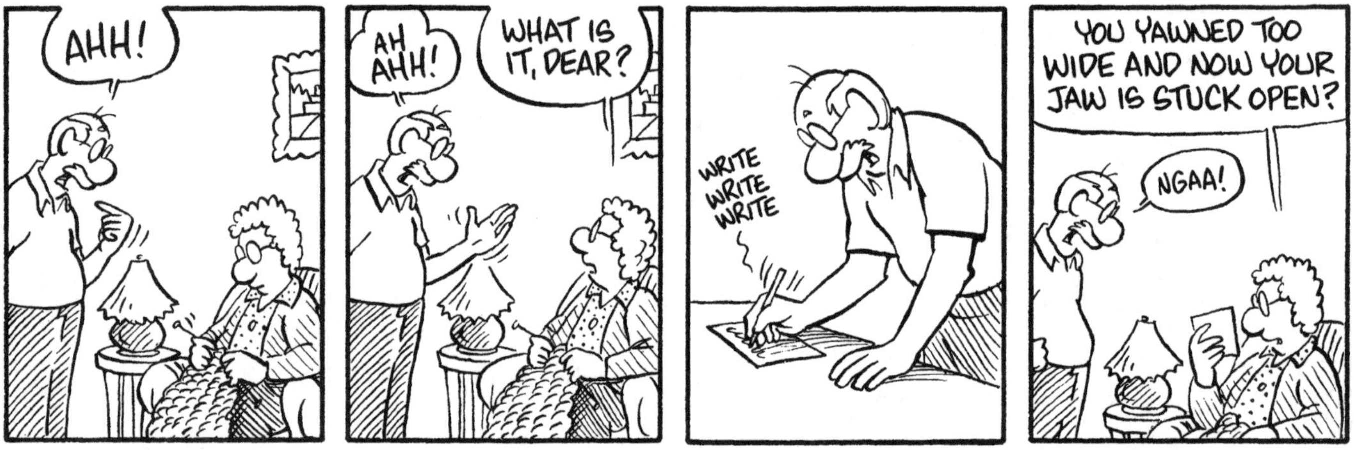
AHH!
AH AHH!
WHAT IS IT, DEAR?
WRITE WRITE WRITE
YOU YAWNED TOO WIDE AND NOW YOUR JAW IS STUCK OPEN?
NGAA!

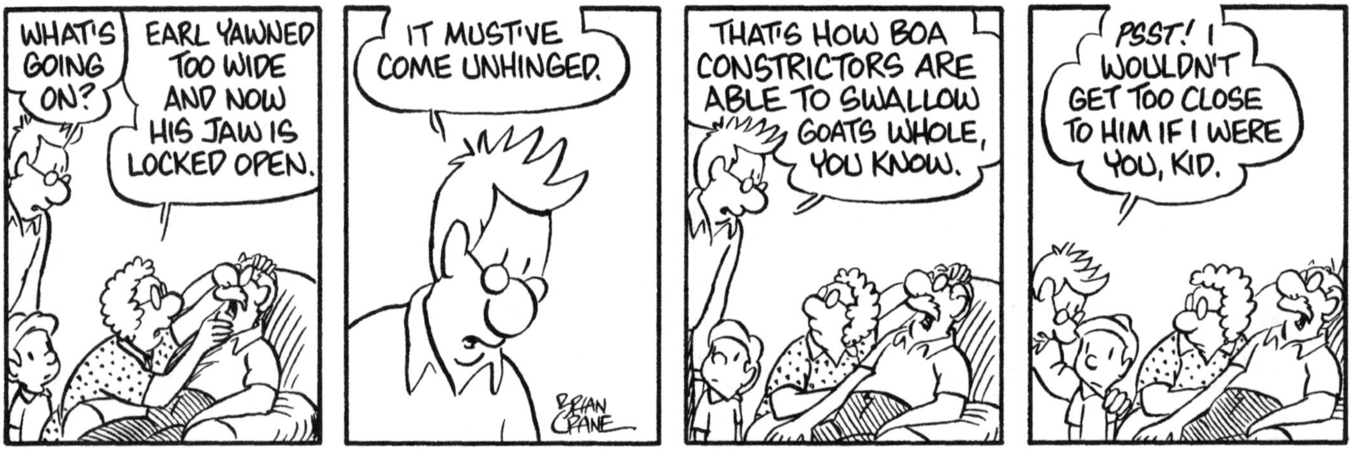
WHAT'S GOING ON?
EARL YAWNED TOO WIDE AND NOW HIS JAW IS LOCKED OPEN.
IT MUST'VE COME UNHINGED.
BRIAN CRANE
THAT'S HOW BOA CONSTRICTORS ARE ABLE TO SWALLOW GOATS WHOLE, YOU KNOW.
PSST! I WOULDN'T GET TOO CLOSE TO HIM IF I WERE YOU, KID.

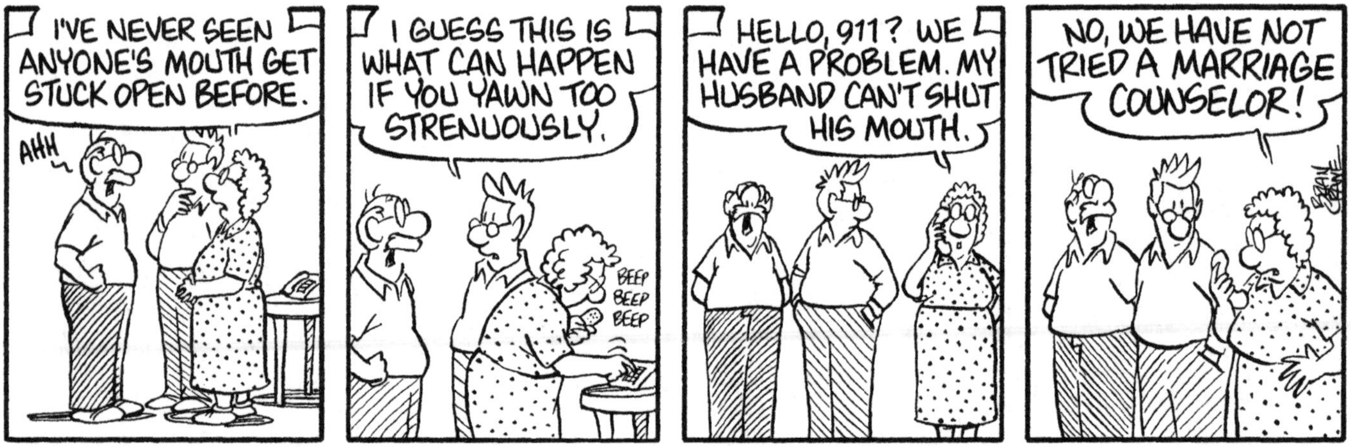
I'VE NEVER SEEN ANYONE'S MOUTH GET STUCK OPEN BEFORE.
AHH
I GUESS THIS IS WHAT CAN HAPPEN IF YOU YAWN TOO STRENUOUSLY.
BEEP BEEP BEEP
HELLO, 911? WE HAVE A PROBLEM. MY HUSBAND CAN'T SHUT HIS MOUTH.
NO, WE HAVE NOT TRIED A MARRIAGE COUNSELOR!

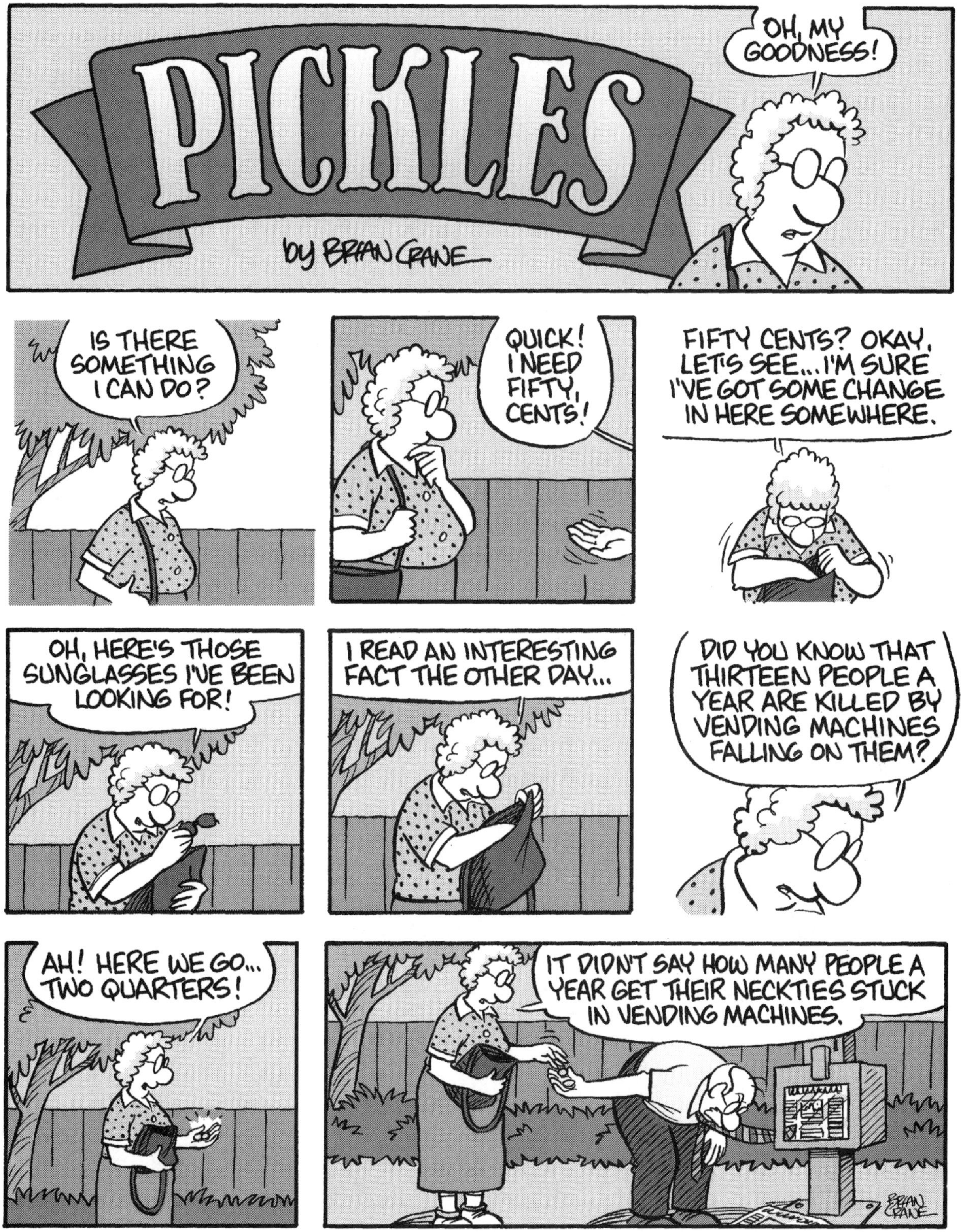
PICKLES
by BRIAN CRANE
OH, MY GOODNESS!
IS THERE SOMETHING I CAN DO?
QUICK! I NEED FIFTY CENTS!
FIFTY CENTS? OKAY, LET'S SEE... I'M SURE I'VE GOT SOME CHANGE IN HERE SOMEWHERE.
OH, HERE'S THOSE SUNGLASSES I'VE BEEN LOOKING FOR!
I READ AN INTERESTING FACT THE OTHER DAY...
DID YOU KNOW THAT THIRTEEN PEOPLE A YEAR ARE KILLED BY VENDING MACHINES FALLING ON THEM?
AH! HERE WE GO... TWO QUARTERS!
IT DIDN'T SAY HOW MANY PEOPLE A YEAR GET THEIR NECKTIES STUCK IN VENDING MACHINES.
BRIAN CRANE

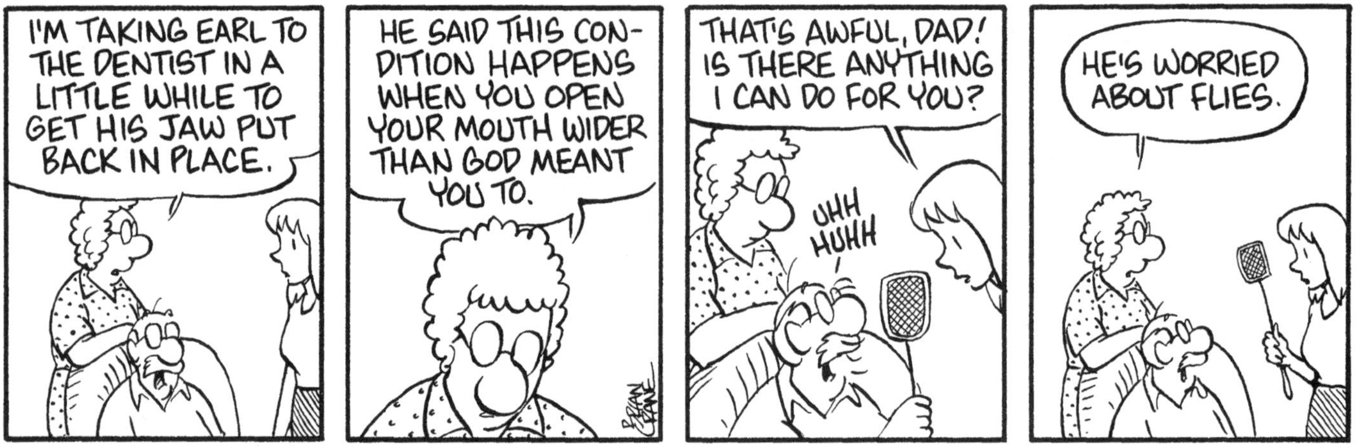
I'M TAKING EARL TO THE DENTIST IN A LITTLE WHILE TO GET HIS JAW PUT BACK IN PLACE.
HE SAID THIS CONDITION HAPPENS WHEN YOU OPEN YOUR MOUTH WIDER THAN GOD MEANT YOU TO.
THAT'S AWFUL, DAD! IS THERE ANYTHING I CAN DO FOR YOU?
UHH HUHH
HE'S WORRIED ABOUT FLIES.

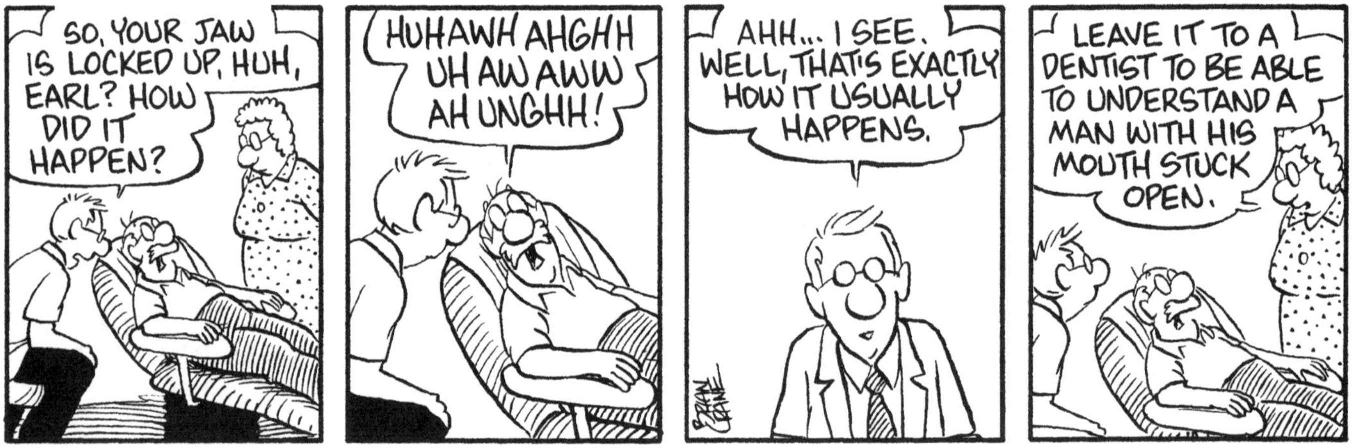
SO, YOUR JAW IS LOCKED UP, HUH, EARL? HOW DID IT HAPPEN?
HUHAWH AHGHH UH AW AWW AH UNGHH!
AHH... I SEE. WELL, THAT'S EXACTLY HOW IT USUALLY HAPPENS.
LEAVE IT TO A DENTIST TO BE ABLE TO UNDERSTAND A MAN WITH HIS MOUTH STUCK OPEN.

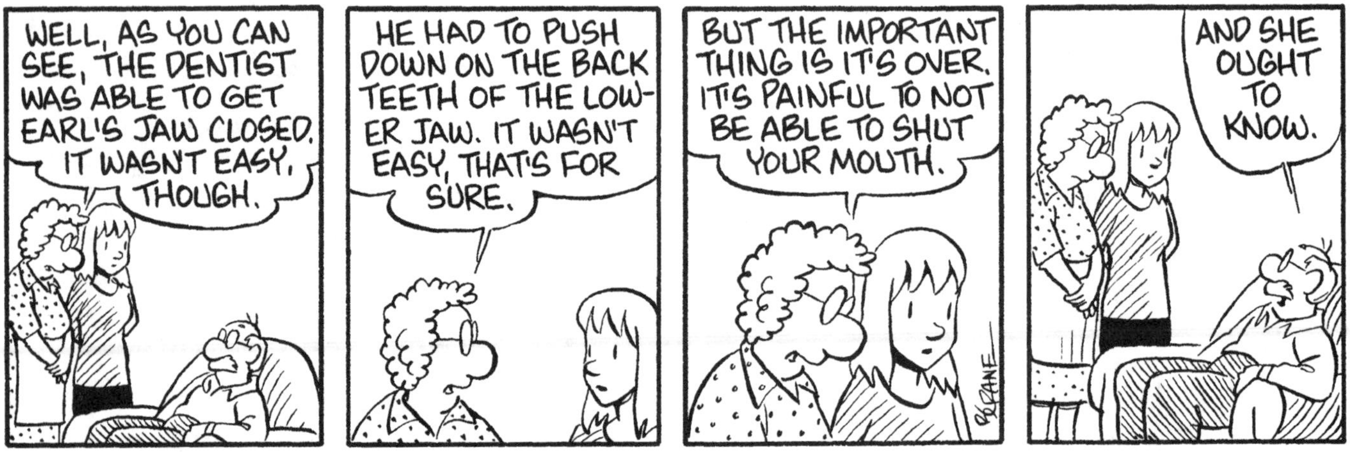
WELL, AS YOU CAN SEE, THE DENTIST WAS ABLE TO GET EARL'S JAW CLOSED. IT WASN'T EASY, THOUGH.
HE HAD TO PUSH DOWN ON THE BACK TEETH OF THE LOWER JAW. IT WASN'T EASY, THAT'S FOR SURE.
BUT THE IMPORTANT THING IS IT'S OVER. IT'S PAINFUL TO NOT BE ABLE TO SHUT YOUR MOUTH.
AND SHE OUGHT TO KNOW.

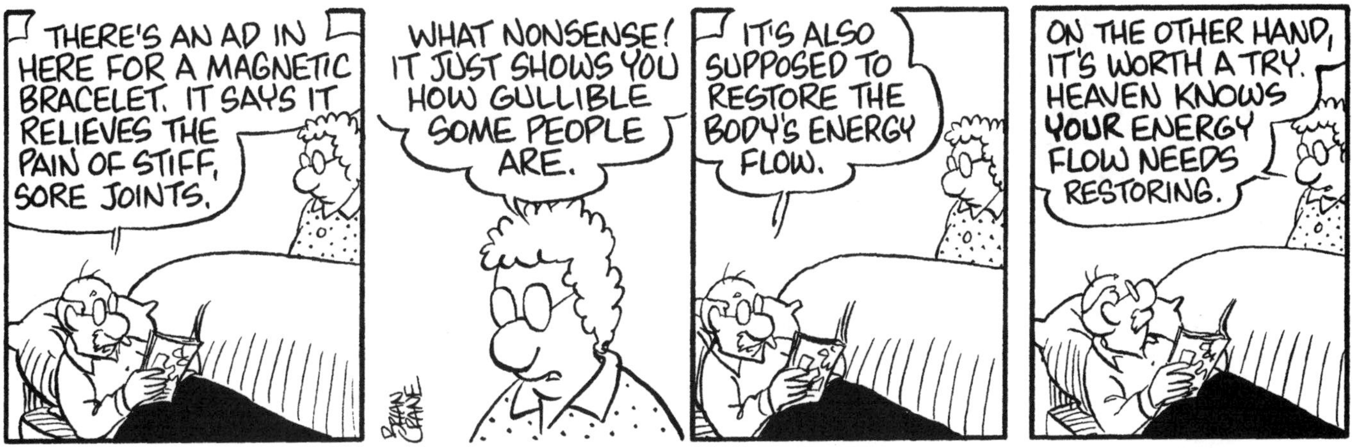
THERE'S AN AD IN HERE FOR A MAGNETIC BRACELET. IT SAYS IT RELIEVES THE PAIN OF STIFF, SORE JOINTS.
WHAT NONSENSE! IT JUST SHOWS YOU HOW GULLIBLE SOME PEOPLE ARE.
IT'S ALSO SUPPOSED TO RESTORE THE BODY'S ENERGY FLOW.
ON THE OTHER HAND, IT'S WORTH A TRY. HEAVEN KNOWS **YOUR** ENERGY FLOW NEEDS RESTORING.

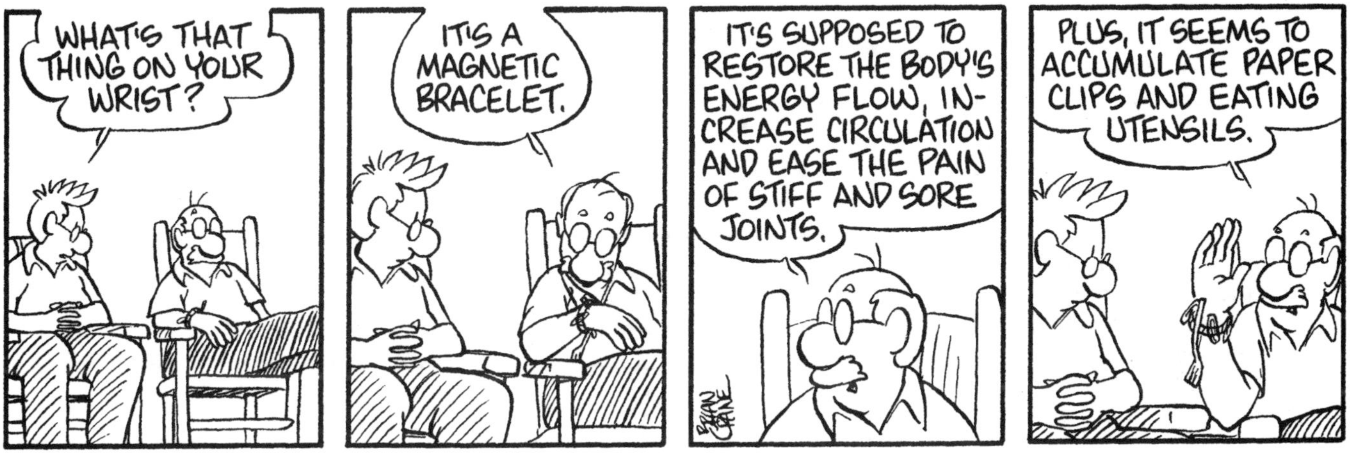
WHAT'S THAT THING ON YOUR WRIST?
IT'S A MAGNETIC BRACELET.
IT'S SUPPOSED TO RESTORE THE BODY'S ENERGY FLOW, INCREASE CIRCULATION AND EASE THE PAIN OF STIFF AND SORE JOINTS.
PLUS, IT SEEMS TO ACCUMULATE PAPER CLIPS AND EATING UTENSILS.

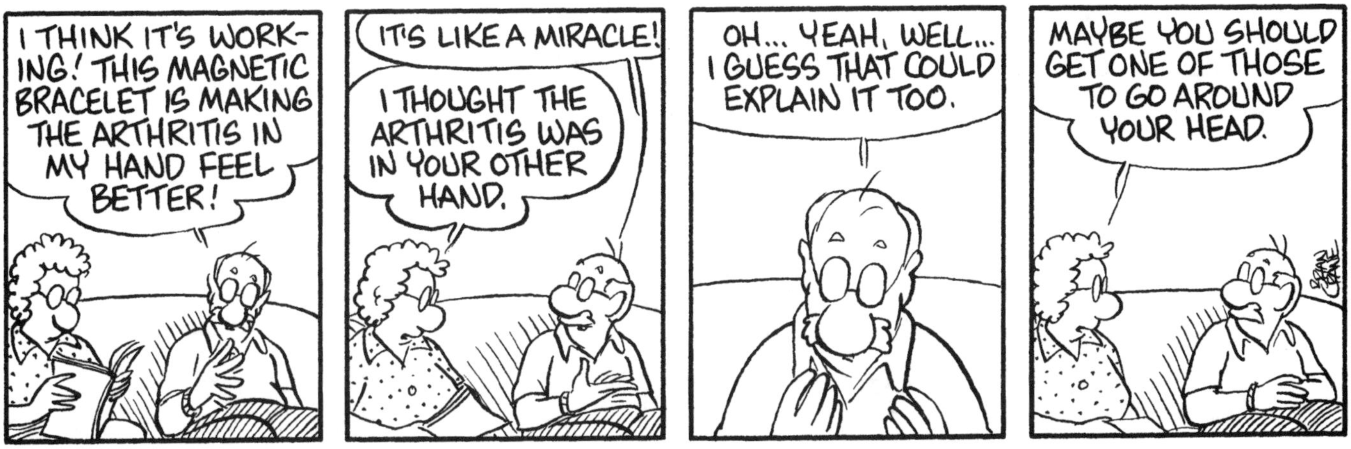
I THINK IT'S WORKING! THIS MAGNETIC BRACELET IS MAKING THE ARTHRITIS IN MY HAND FEEL BETTER!
IT'S LIKE A MIRACLE!
I THOUGHT THE ARTHRITIS WAS IN YOUR OTHER HAND.
OH... YEAH, WELL... I GUESS THAT COULD EXPLAIN IT TOO.
MAYBE YOU SHOULD GET ONE OF THOSE TO GO AROUND YOUR HEAD.

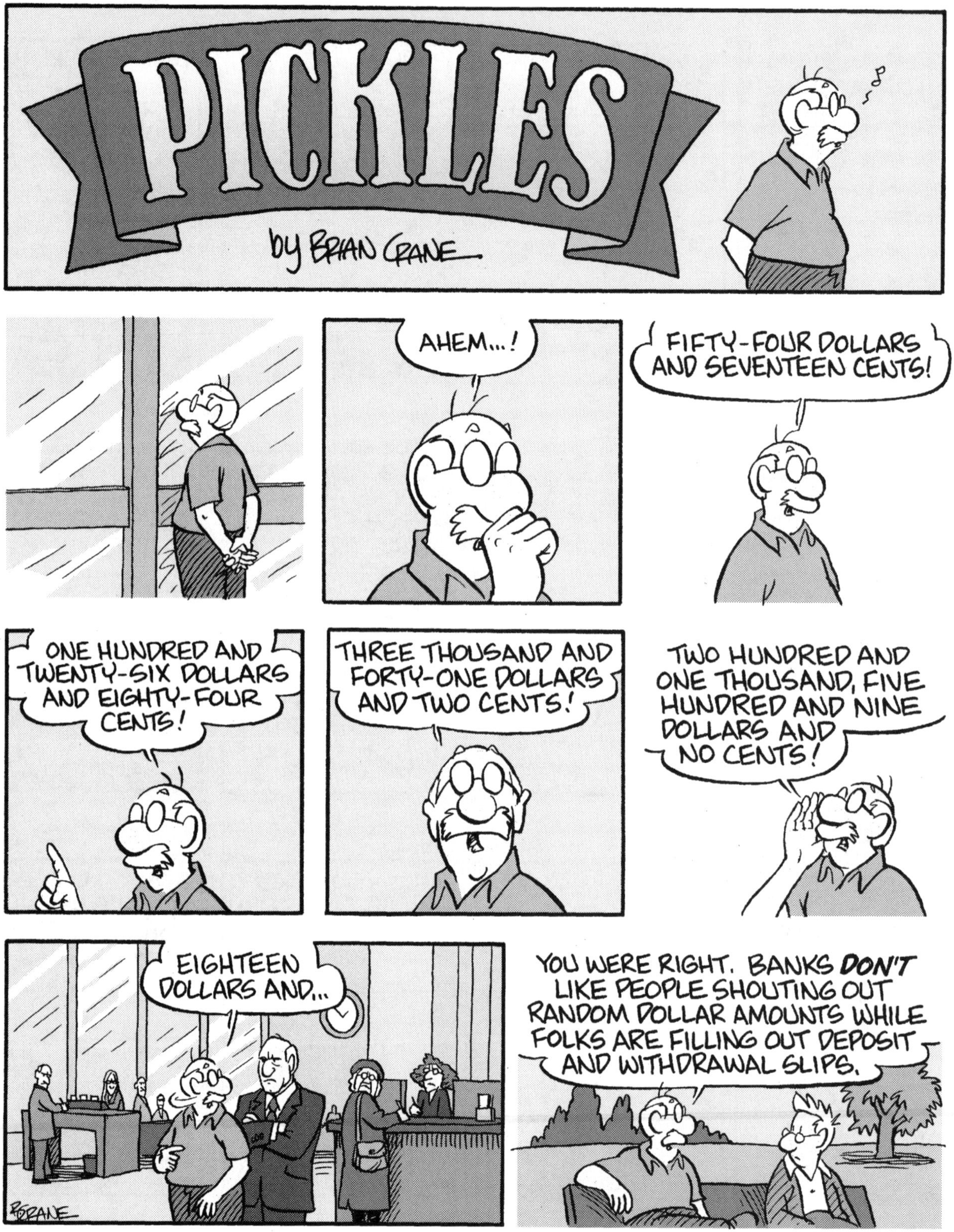
PICKLES
by BRIAN CRANE
AHEM...!
FIFTY-FOUR DOLLARS AND SEVENTEEN CENTS!
ONE HUNDRED AND TWENTY-SIX DOLLARS AND EIGHTY-FOUR CENTS!
THREE THOUSAND AND FORTY-ONE DOLLARS AND TWO CENTS!
TWO HUNDRED AND ONE THOUSAND, FIVE HUNDRED AND NINE DOLLARS AND NO CENTS!
EIGHTEEN DOLLARS AND...
B CRANE
YOU WERE RIGHT. BANKS **DON'T** LIKE PEOPLE SHOUTING OUT RANDOM DOLLAR AMOUNTS WHILE FOLKS ARE FILLING OUT DEPOSIT AND WITHDRAWAL SLIPS.

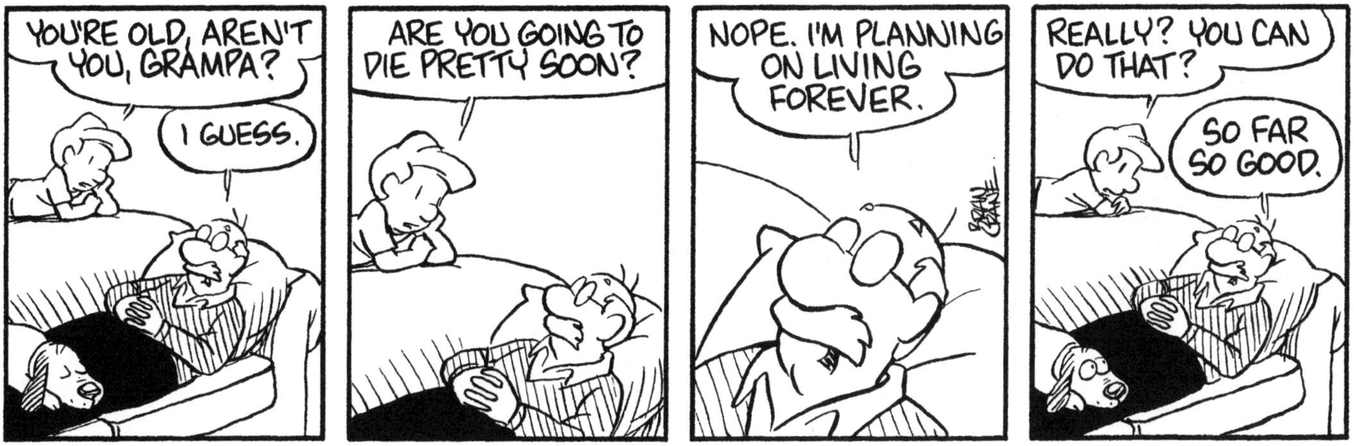
YOU'RE OLD, AREN'T YOU, GRAMPA?
I GUESS.
ARE YOU GOING TO DIE PRETTY SOON?
NOPE. I'M PLANNING ON LIVING FOREVER.
REALLY? YOU CAN DO THAT?
SO FAR SO GOOD.

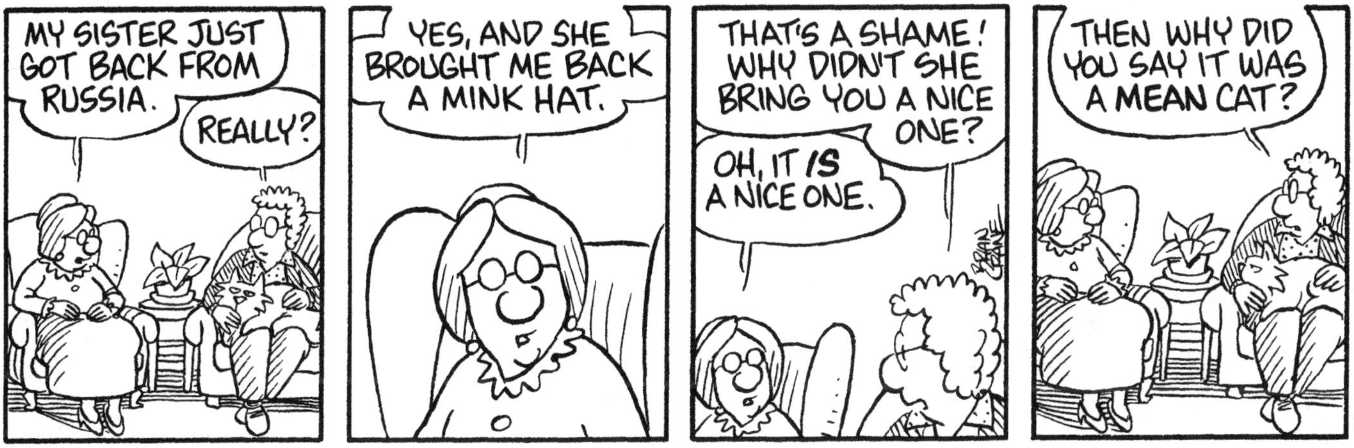
MY SISTER JUST GOT BACK FROM RUSSIA.
REALLY?
YES, AND SHE BROUGHT ME BACK A MINK HAT.
THAT'S A SHAME! WHY DIDN'T SHE BRING YOU A NICE ONE?
OH, IT **IS** A NICE ONE.
THEN WHY DID YOU SAY IT WAS A **MEAN** CAT?

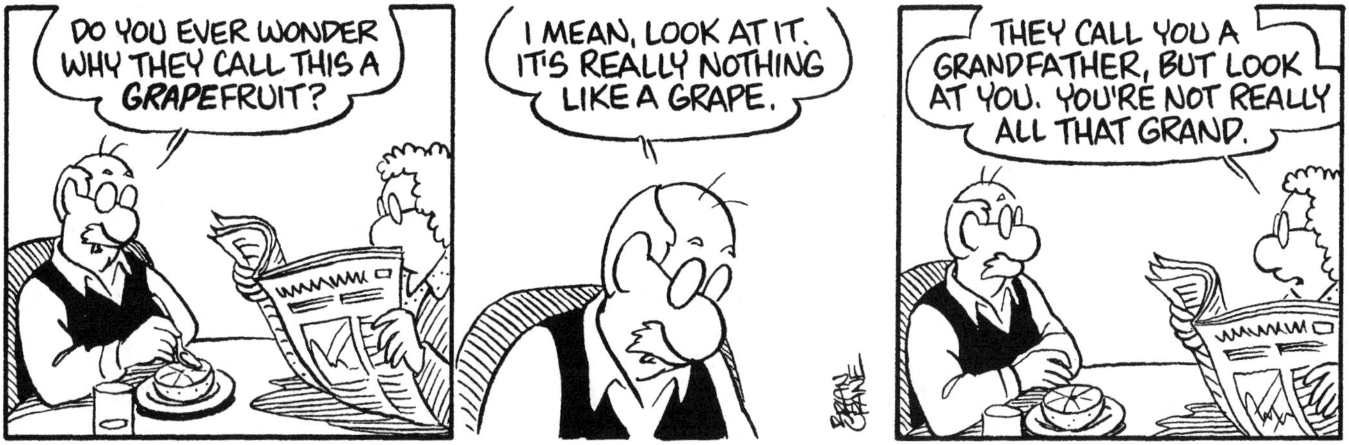
DO YOU EVER WONDER WHY THEY CALL THIS A **GRAPE**FRUIT?
I MEAN, LOOK AT IT. IT'S REALLY NOTHING LIKE A GRAPE.
THEY CALL YOU A GRANDFATHER, BUT LOOK AT YOU. YOU'RE NOT REALLY ALL THAT GRAND.

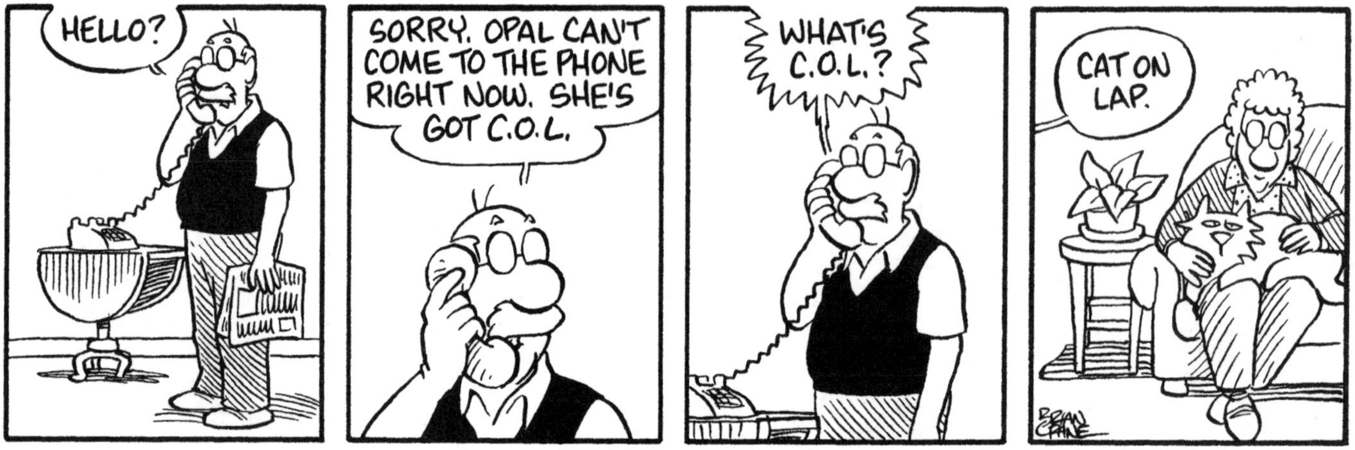
HELLO?
SORRY. OPAL CAN'T COME TO THE PHONE RIGHT NOW. SHE'S GOT C.O.L.
WHAT'S C.O.L.?
CAT ON LAP.
BRIAN CRANE

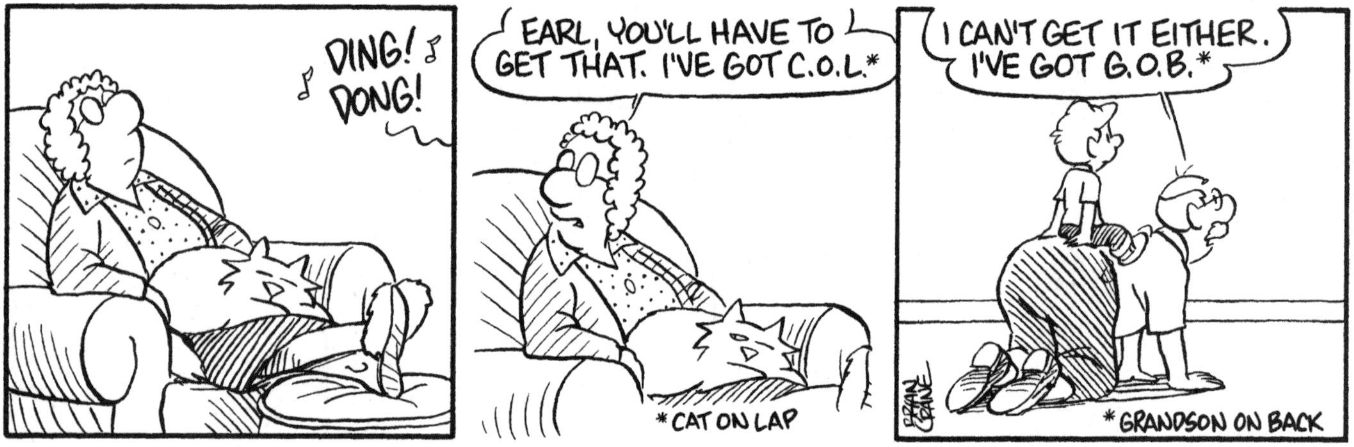
DING! DONG!
EARL, YOU'LL HAVE TO GET THAT. I'VE GOT C.O.L.*
*CAT ON LAP
I CAN'T GET IT EITHER. I'VE GOT G.O.B.*
*GRANDSON ON BACK
BRIAN CRANE

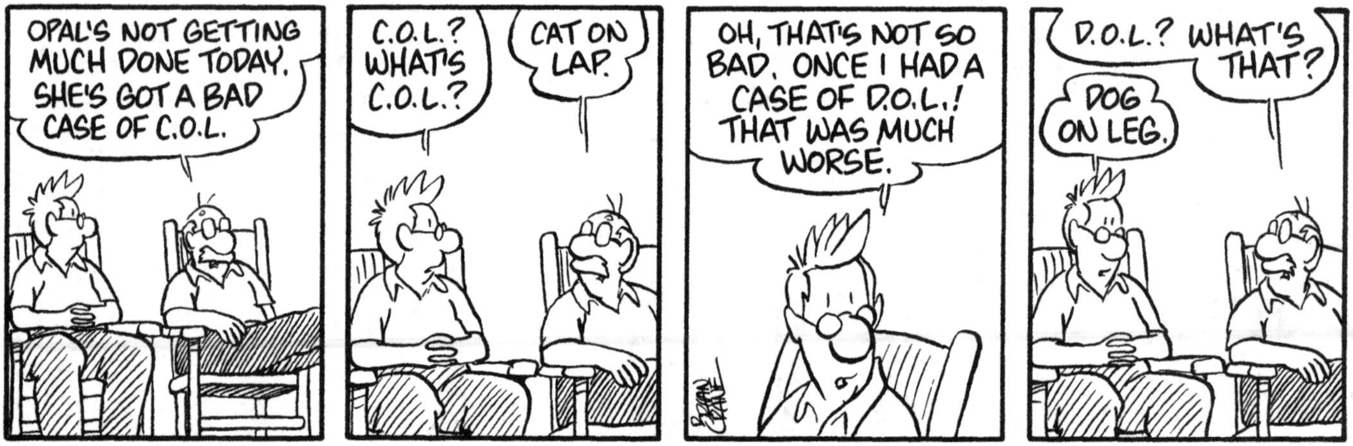
OPAL'S NOT GETTING MUCH DONE TODAY. SHE'S GOT A BAD CASE OF C.O.L.
C.O.L.? WHAT'S C.O.L.?
CAT ON LAP.
OH, THAT'S NOT SO BAD. ONCE I HAD A CASE OF D.O.L.! THAT WAS MUCH WORSE.
BRIAN CRANE
D.O.L.? WHAT'S THAT?
DOG ON LEG.

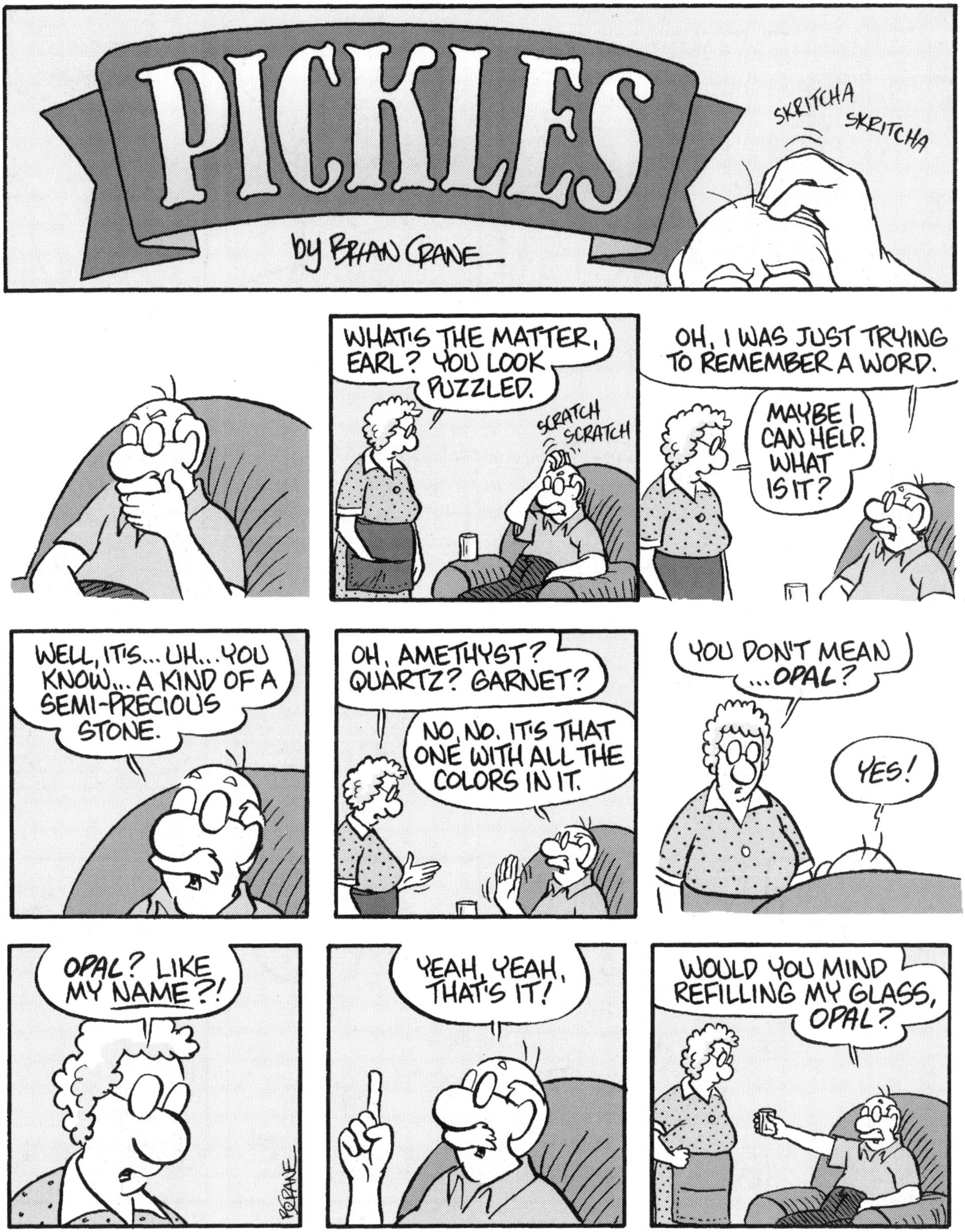
PICKLES
by BRIAN CRANE
SKRITCHA SKRITCHA
WHAT'S THE MATTER, EARL? YOU LOOK PUZZLED.
SCRATCH SCRATCH
OH, I WAS JUST TRYING TO REMEMBER A WORD.
MAYBE I CAN HELP. WHAT IS IT?
WELL, IT'S... UH... YOU KNOW... A KIND OF A SEMI-PRECIOUS STONE.
OH, AMETHYST? QUARTZ? GARNET?
NO, NO. IT'S THAT ONE WITH ALL THE COLORS IN IT.
YOU DON'T MEAN ...OPAL?
YES!
OPAL? LIKE MY NAME?!
YEAH, YEAH, THAT'S IT!
WOULD YOU MIND REFILLING MY GLASS, OPAL?

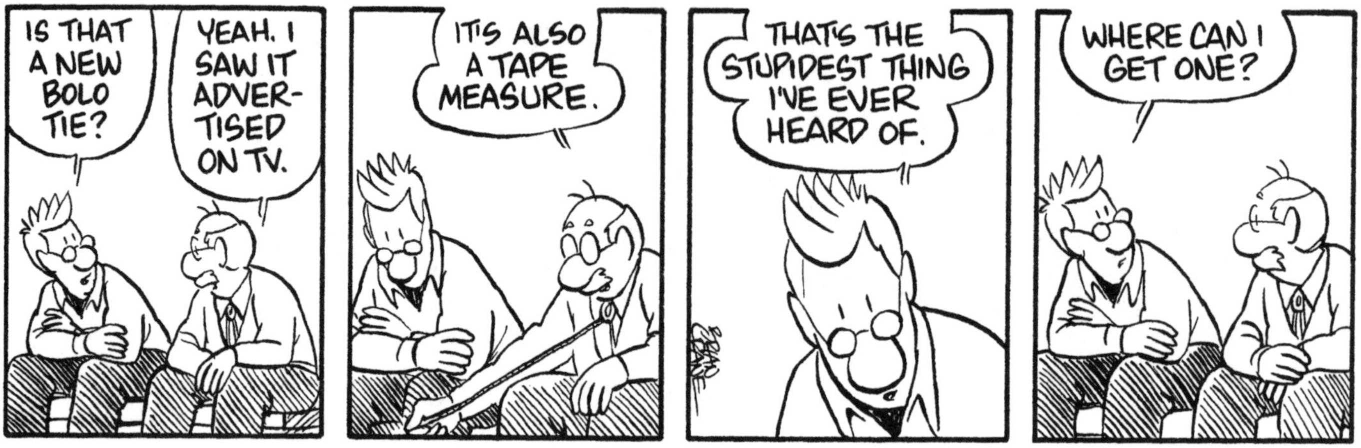
IS THAT A NEW BOLO TIE?
YEAH. I SAW IT ADVERTISED ON TV.
IT'S ALSO A TAPE MEASURE.
THAT'S THE STUPIDEST THING I'VE EVER HEARD OF.
WHERE CAN I GET ONE?

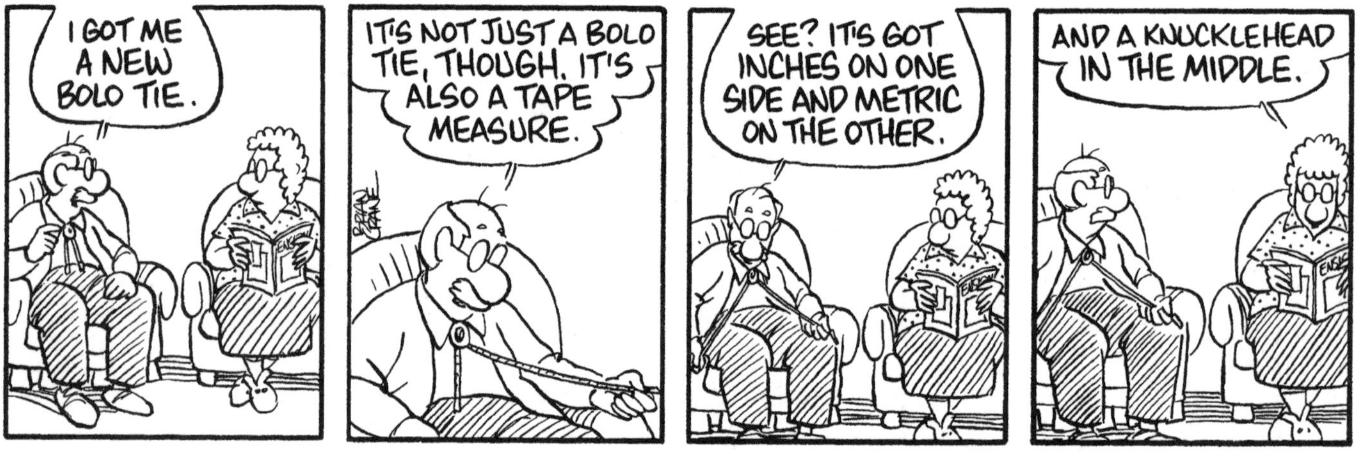
I GOT ME A NEW BOLO TIE.
IT'S NOT JUST A BOLO TIE, THOUGH. IT'S ALSO A TAPE MEASURE.
SEE? IT'S GOT INCHES ON ONE SIDE AND METRIC ON THE OTHER.
AND A KNUCKLEHEAD IN THE MIDDLE.

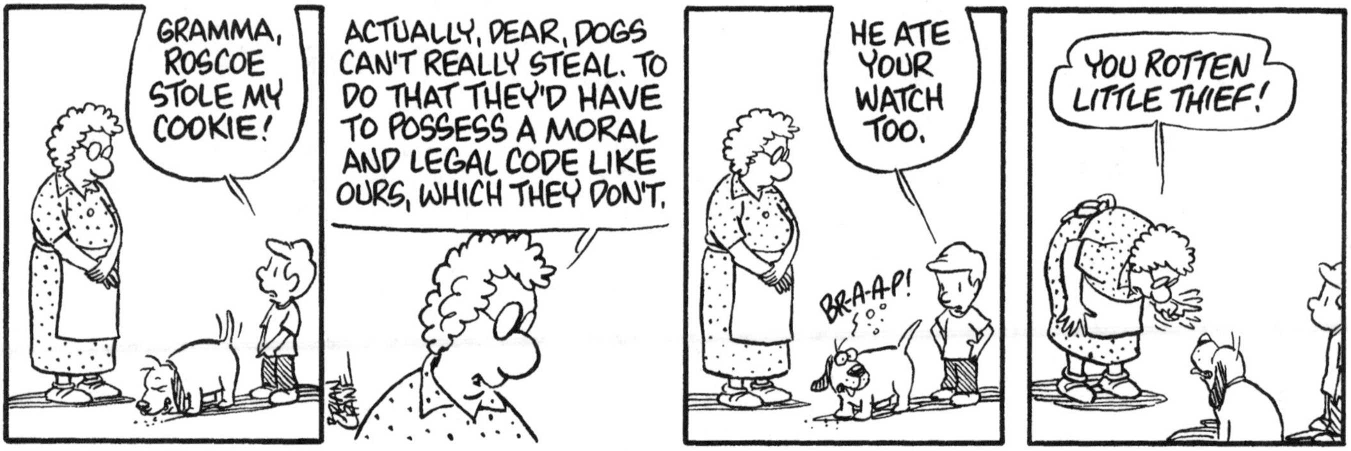
GRAMMA, ROSCOE STOLE MY COOKIE!
ACTUALLY, DEAR, DOGS CAN'T REALLY STEAL. TO DO THAT THEY'D HAVE TO POSSESS A MORAL AND LEGAL CODE LIKE OURS, WHICH THEY DON'T.
HE ATE YOUR WATCH TOO.
BR-A-A-P!
YOU ROTTEN LITTLE THIEF!

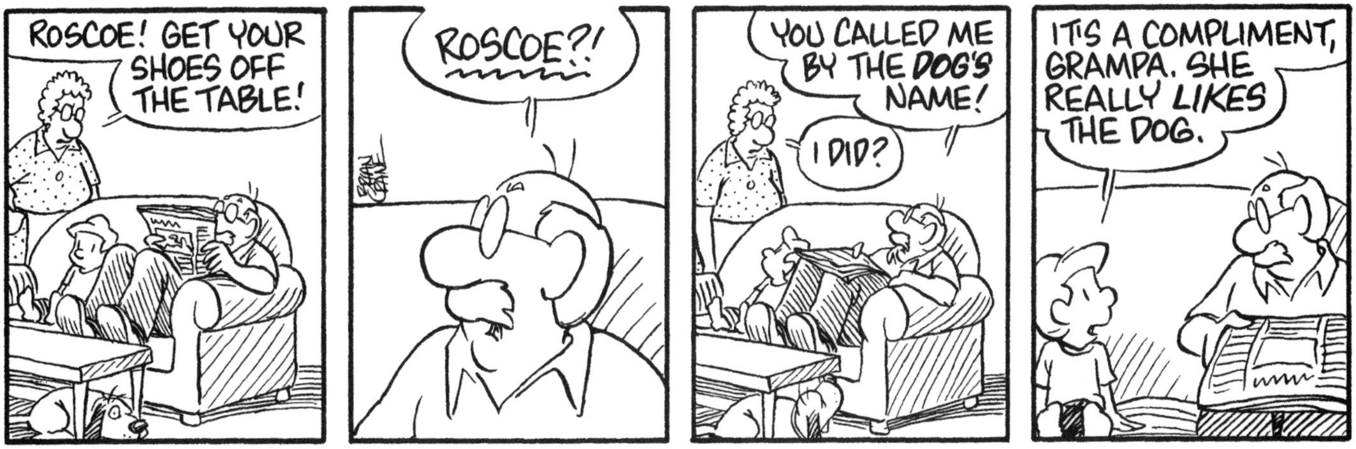
ROSCOE! GET YOUR SHOES OFF THE TABLE!
ROSCOE?!
YOU CALLED ME BY THE DOG'S NAME!
I DID?
IT'S A COMPLIMENT, GRAMPA. SHE REALLY LIKES THE DOG.

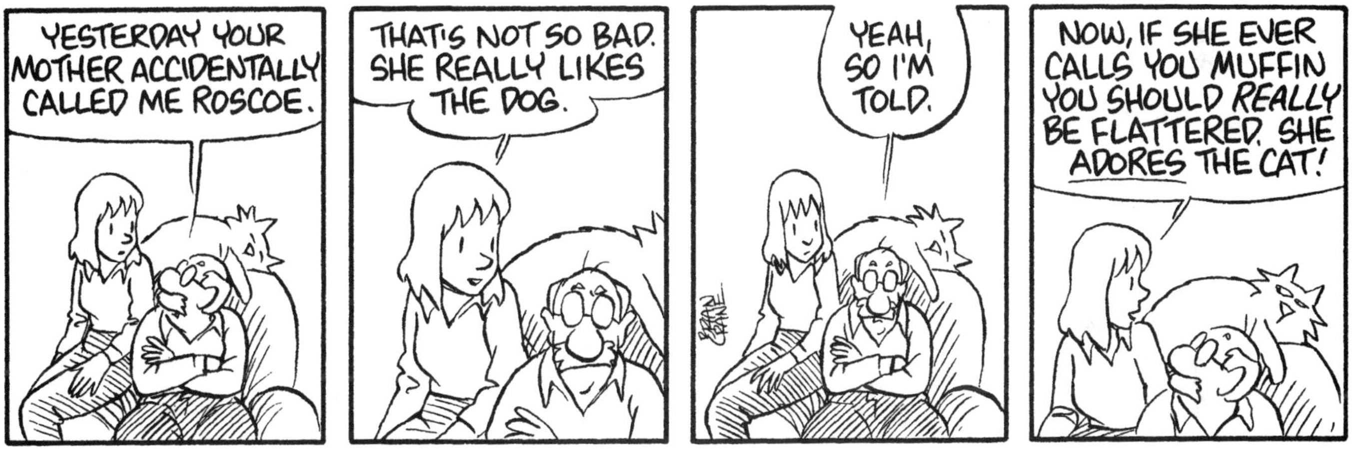
YESTERDAY YOUR MOTHER ACCIDENTALLY CALLED ME ROSCOE.
THAT'S NOT SO BAD. SHE REALLY LIKES THE DOG.
YEAH, SO I'M TOLD.
NOW, IF SHE EVER CALLS YOU MUFFIN YOU SHOULD REALLY BE FLATTERED. SHE ADORES THE CAT!

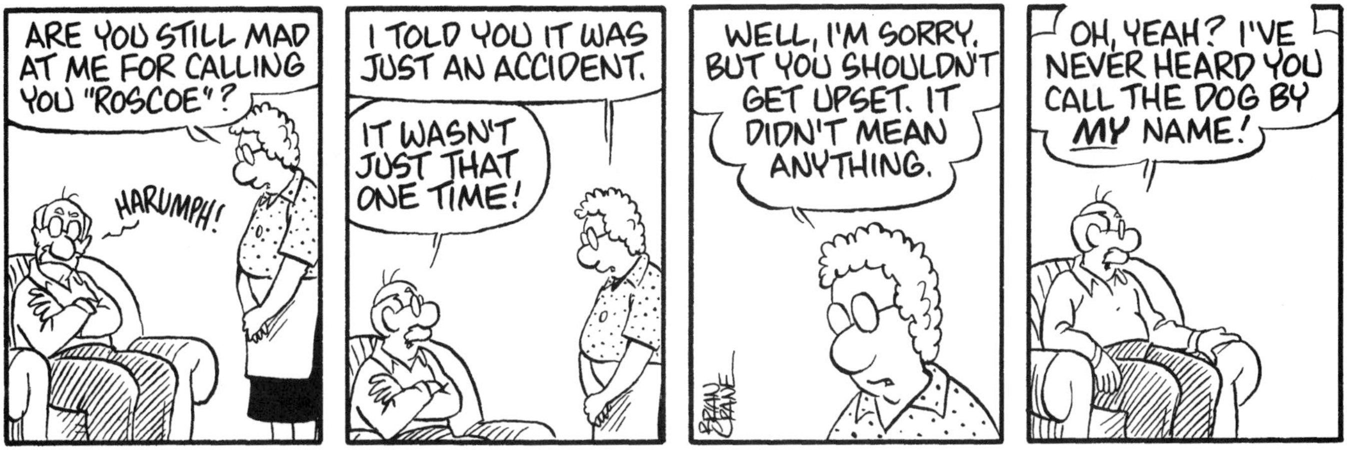
ARE YOU STILL MAD AT ME FOR CALLING YOU "ROSCOE"?
HARUMPH!
I TOLD YOU IT WAS JUST AN ACCIDENT.
IT WASN'T JUST THAT ONE TIME!
WELL, I'M SORRY. BUT YOU SHOULDN'T GET UPSET. IT DIDN'T MEAN ANYTHING.
OH, YEAH? I'VE NEVER HEARD YOU CALL THE DOG BY MY NAME!

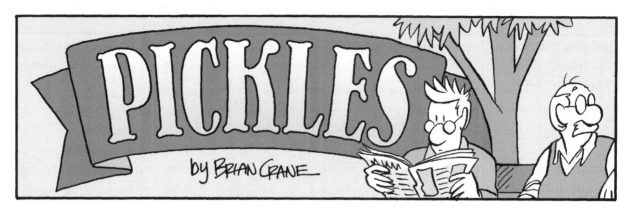

# PICKLES

## by Brian Crane

NEVER BUY A PIG IN A POKE.

ROTATE THE SHOES YOU WEAR. THEY'LL LAST LONGER THAT WAY.

DON'T SIT ON THE COLD GROUND. YOU'LL GET GALLOPING CONSUMPTION.

SOAP IS JUST AS GOOD AS SHAMPOO.

NEVER EAT AT A PLACE WITH A VIEW. THEY'RE SELLING THE VIEW, NOT THE FOOD.

AS SOON AS YOU CAN COUNT TWELVE BUBBLES, IT'S TIME FLIP THE PANCAKES.

AT MY AGE I KNOW ALL THE ANSWERS, BUT NOBODY ASKS ME THE QUESTIONS.

YOUR SHOES SHOULD MATCH YOUR BELT.

THAT DOESN'T STOP ME, MIND YOU.

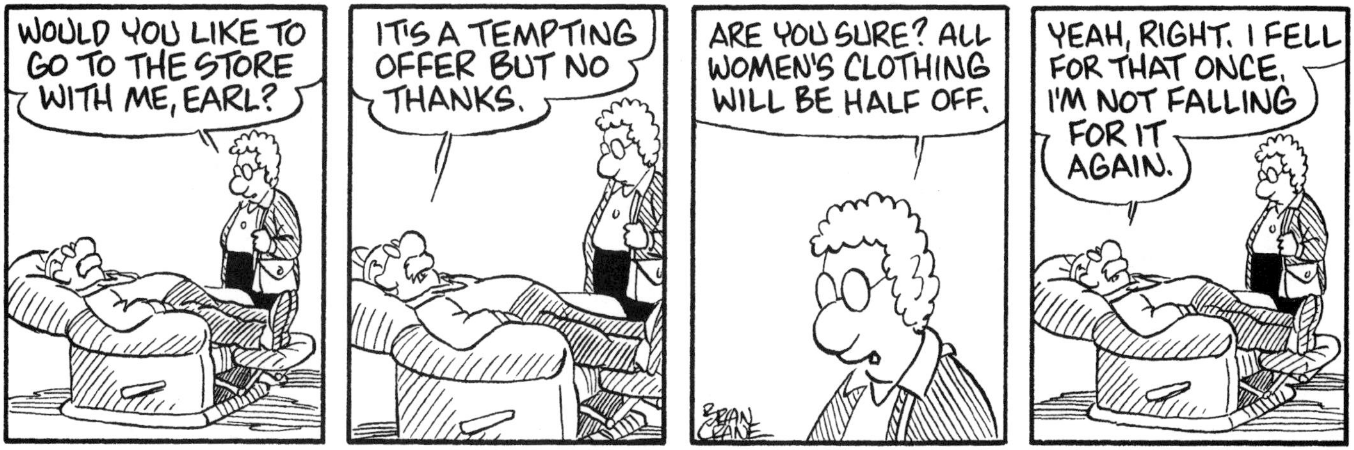
WOULD YOU LIKE TO GO TO THE STORE WITH ME, EARL?
IT'S A TEMPTING OFFER BUT NO THANKS.
ARE YOU SURE? ALL WOMEN'S CLOTHING WILL BE HALF OFF.
YEAH, RIGHT. I FELL FOR THAT ONCE. I'M NOT FALLING FOR IT AGAIN.

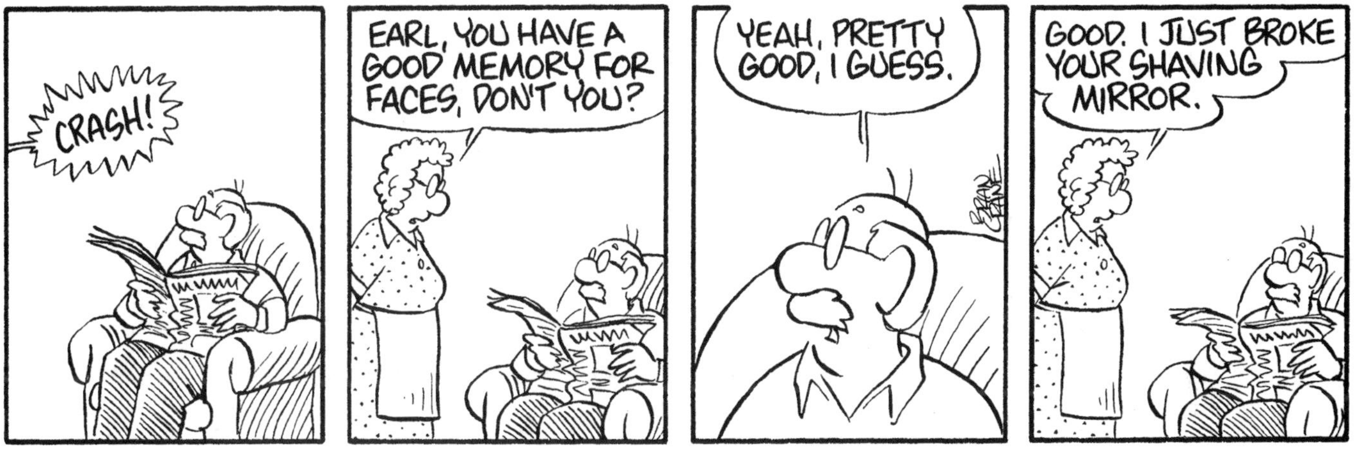
CRASH!
EARL, YOU HAVE A GOOD MEMORY FOR FACES, DON'T YOU?
YEAH, PRETTY GOOD, I GUESS.
GOOD. I JUST BROKE YOUR SHAVING MIRROR.

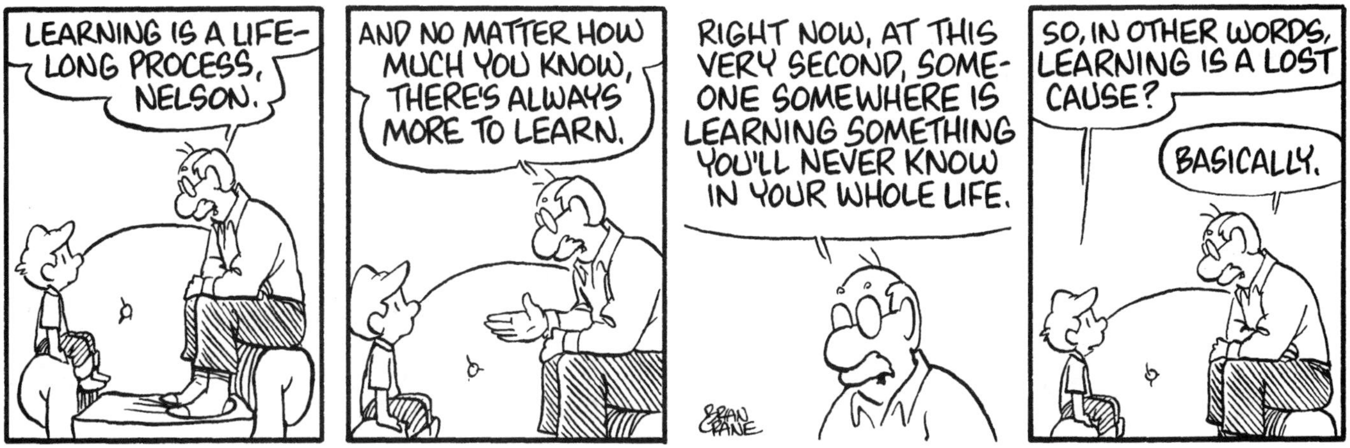
LEARNING IS A LIFE-LONG PROCESS, NELSON.
AND NO MATTER HOW MUCH YOU KNOW, THERE'S ALWAYS MORE TO LEARN.
RIGHT NOW, AT THIS VERY SECOND, SOME-ONE SOMEWHERE IS LEARNING SOMETHING YOU'LL NEVER KNOW IN YOUR WHOLE LIFE.
SO, IN OTHER WORDS, LEARNING IS A LOST CAUSE?
BASICALLY.

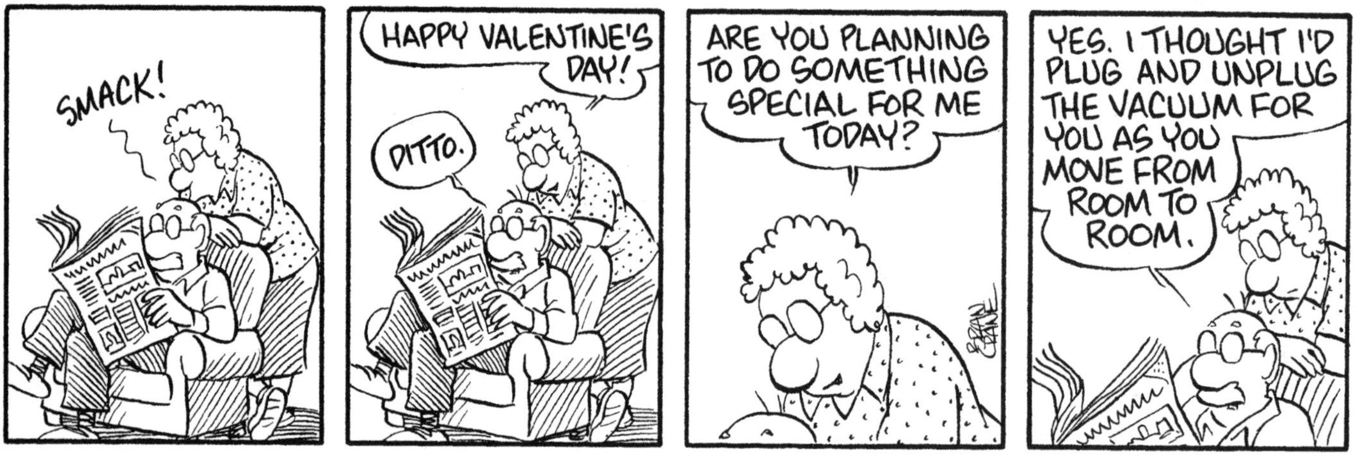
SMACK!
HAPPY VALENTINE'S DAY!
DITTO.
ARE YOU PLANNING TO DO SOMETHING SPECIAL FOR ME TODAY?
YES. I THOUGHT I'D PLUG AND UNPLUG THE VACUUM FOR YOU AS YOU MOVE FROM ROOM TO ROOM.

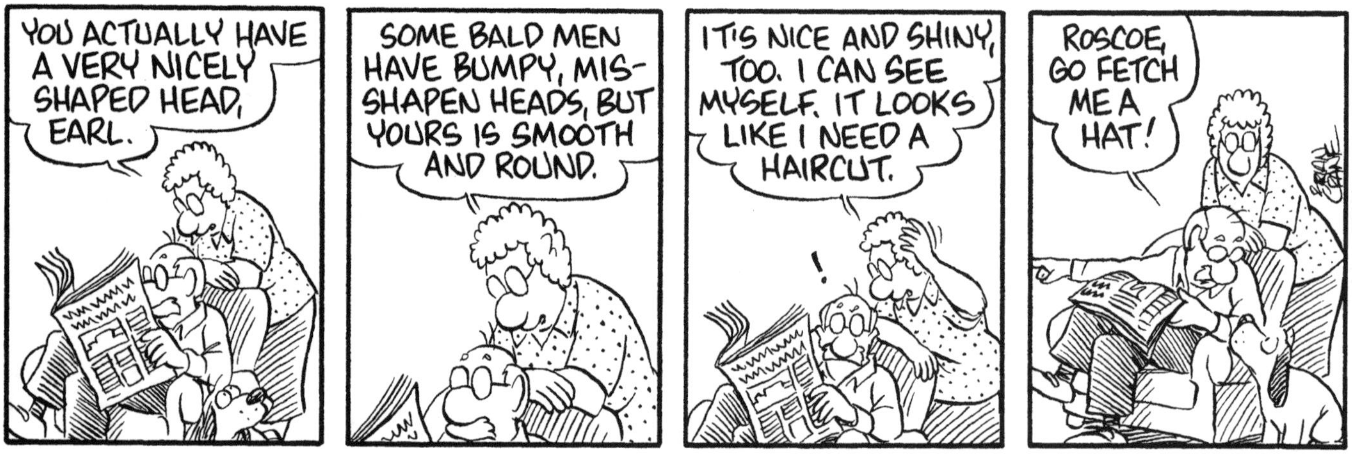
YOU ACTUALLY HAVE A VERY NICELY SHAPED HEAD, EARL.
SOME BALD MEN HAVE BUMPY, MIS-SHAPEN HEADS, BUT YOURS IS SMOOTH AND ROUND.
IT'S NICE AND SHINY, TOO. I CAN SEE MYSELF. IT LOOKS LIKE I NEED A HAIRCUT.
!
ROSCOE, GO FETCH ME A HAT!

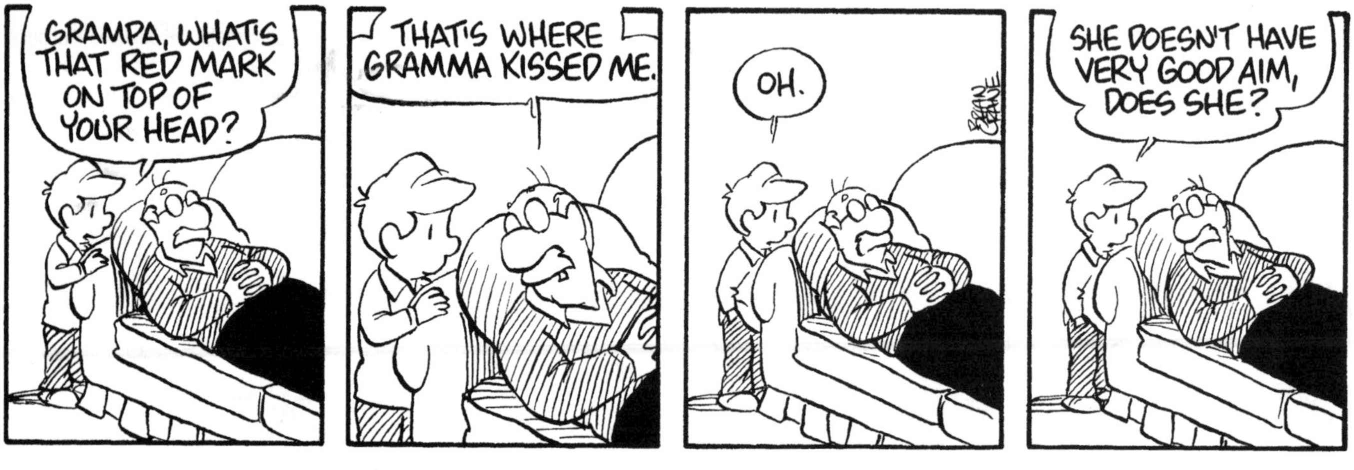
GRAMPA, WHAT'S THAT RED MARK ON TOP OF YOUR HEAD?
THAT'S WHERE GRAMMA KISSED ME.
OH.
SHE DOESN'T HAVE VERY GOOD AIM, DOES SHE?

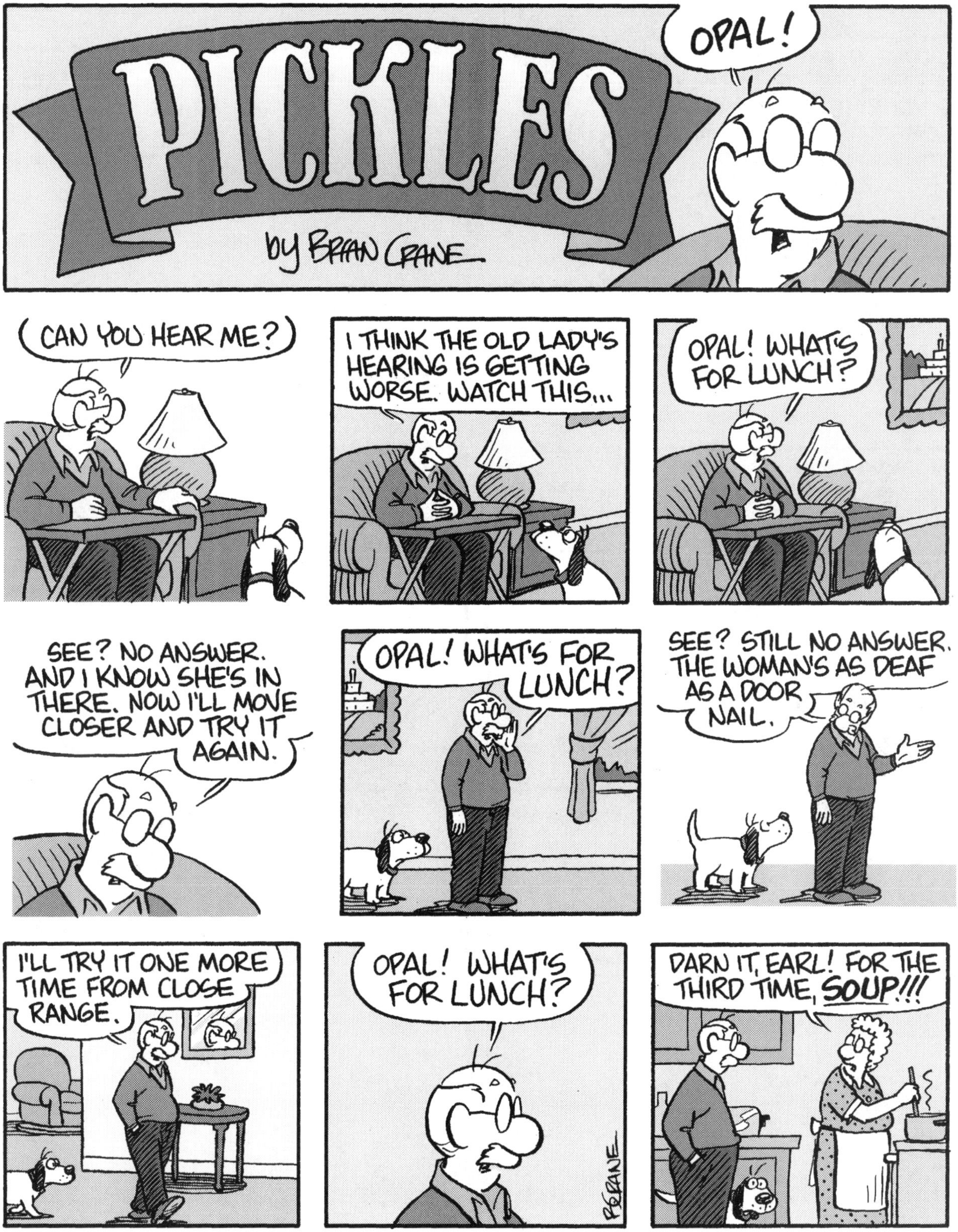
OPAL!
PICKLES
by BRIAN CRANE
CAN YOU HEAR ME?
I THINK THE OLD LADY'S HEARING IS GETTING WORSE. WATCH THIS...
OPAL! WHAT'S FOR LUNCH?
SEE? NO ANSWER. AND I KNOW SHE'S IN THERE. NOW I'LL MOVE CLOSER AND TRY IT AGAIN.
OPAL! WHAT'S FOR LUNCH?
SEE? STILL NO ANSWER. THE WOMAN'S AS DEAF AS A DOOR NAIL.
I'LL TRY IT ONE MORE TIME FROM CLOSE RANGE.
OPAL! WHAT'S FOR LUNCH?
DARN IT, EARL! FOR THE THIRD TIME, SOUP!!!

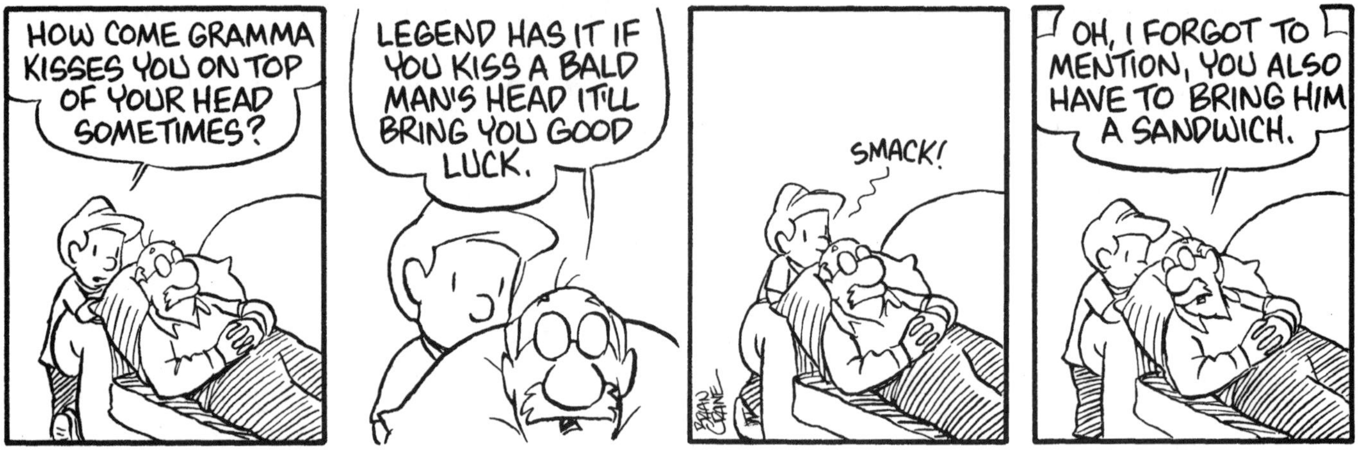
HOW COME GRAMMA KISSES YOU ON TOP OF YOUR HEAD SOMETIMES?
LEGEND HAS IT IF YOU KISS A BALD MAN'S HEAD IT'LL BRING YOU GOOD LUCK.
SMACK!
OH, I FORGOT TO MENTION, YOU ALSO HAVE TO BRING HIM A SANDWICH.

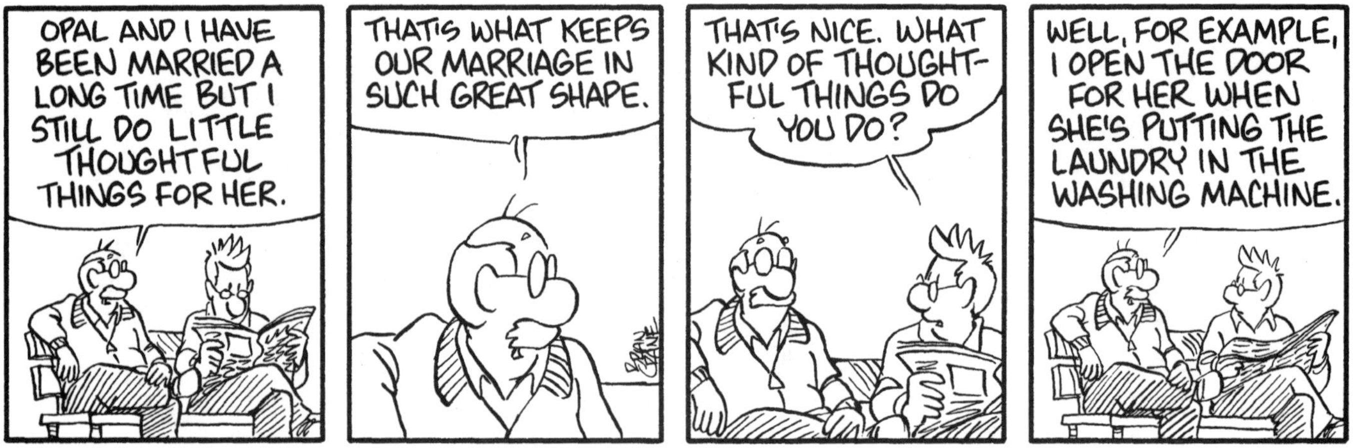
OPAL AND I HAVE BEEN MARRIED A LONG TIME BUT I STILL DO LITTLE THOUGHTFUL THINGS FOR HER.
THAT'S WHAT KEEPS OUR MARRIAGE IN SUCH GREAT SHAPE.
THAT'S NICE. WHAT KIND OF THOUGHTFUL THINGS DO YOU DO?
WELL, FOR EXAMPLE, I OPEN THE DOOR FOR HER WHEN SHE'S PUTTING THE LAUNDRY IN THE WASHING MACHINE.

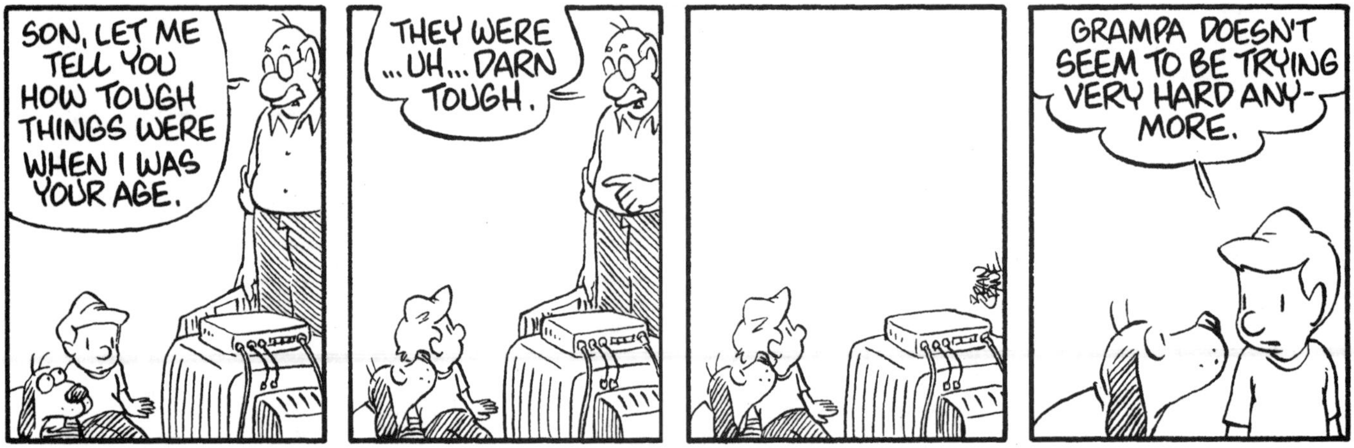
SON, LET ME TELL YOU HOW TOUGH THINGS WERE WHEN I WAS YOUR AGE.
THEY WERE ...UH... DARN TOUGH.
GRAMPA DOESN'T SEEM TO BE TRYING VERY HARD ANYMORE.

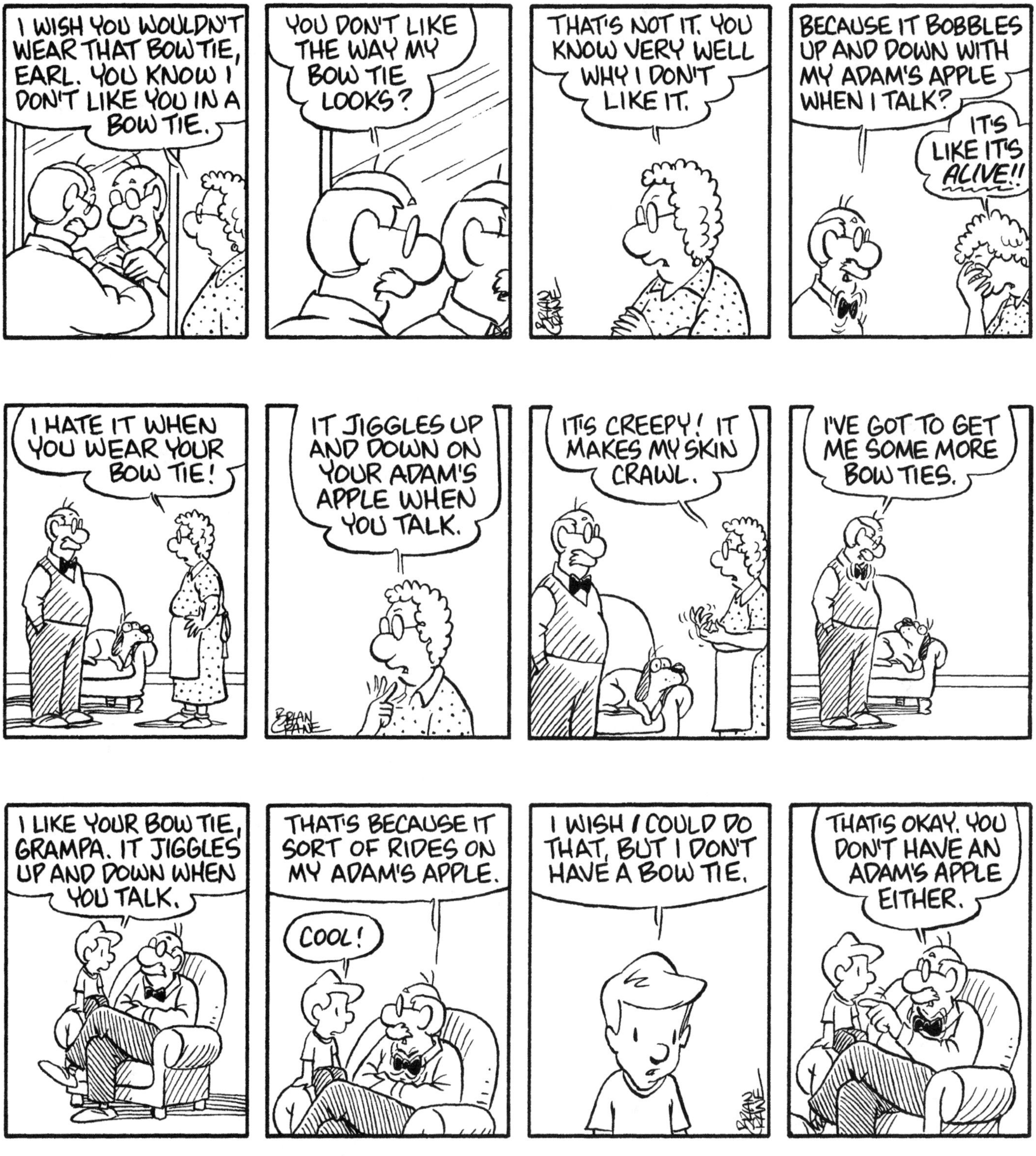
I WISH YOU WOULDN'T WEAR THAT BOW TIE, EARL. YOU KNOW I DON'T LIKE YOU IN A BOW TIE.
YOU DON'T LIKE THE WAY MY BOW TIE LOOKS?
THAT'S NOT IT. YOU KNOW VERY WELL WHY I DON'T LIKE IT.
BECAUSE IT BOBBLES UP AND DOWN WITH MY ADAM'S APPLE WHEN I TALK?
IT'S LIKE IT'S ALIVE!!
I HATE IT WHEN YOU WEAR YOUR BOW TIE!
IT JIGGLES UP AND DOWN ON YOUR ADAM'S APPLE WHEN YOU TALK.
IT'S CREEPY! IT MAKES MY SKIN CRAWL.
I'VE GOT TO GET ME SOME MORE BOW TIES.
I LIKE YOUR BOW TIE, GRAMPA. IT JIGGLES UP AND DOWN WHEN YOU TALK.
THAT'S BECAUSE IT SORT OF RIDES ON MY ADAM'S APPLE.
COOL!
I WISH I COULD DO THAT, BUT I DON'T HAVE A BOW TIE.
THAT'S OKAY. YOU DON'T HAVE AN ADAM'S APPLE EITHER.

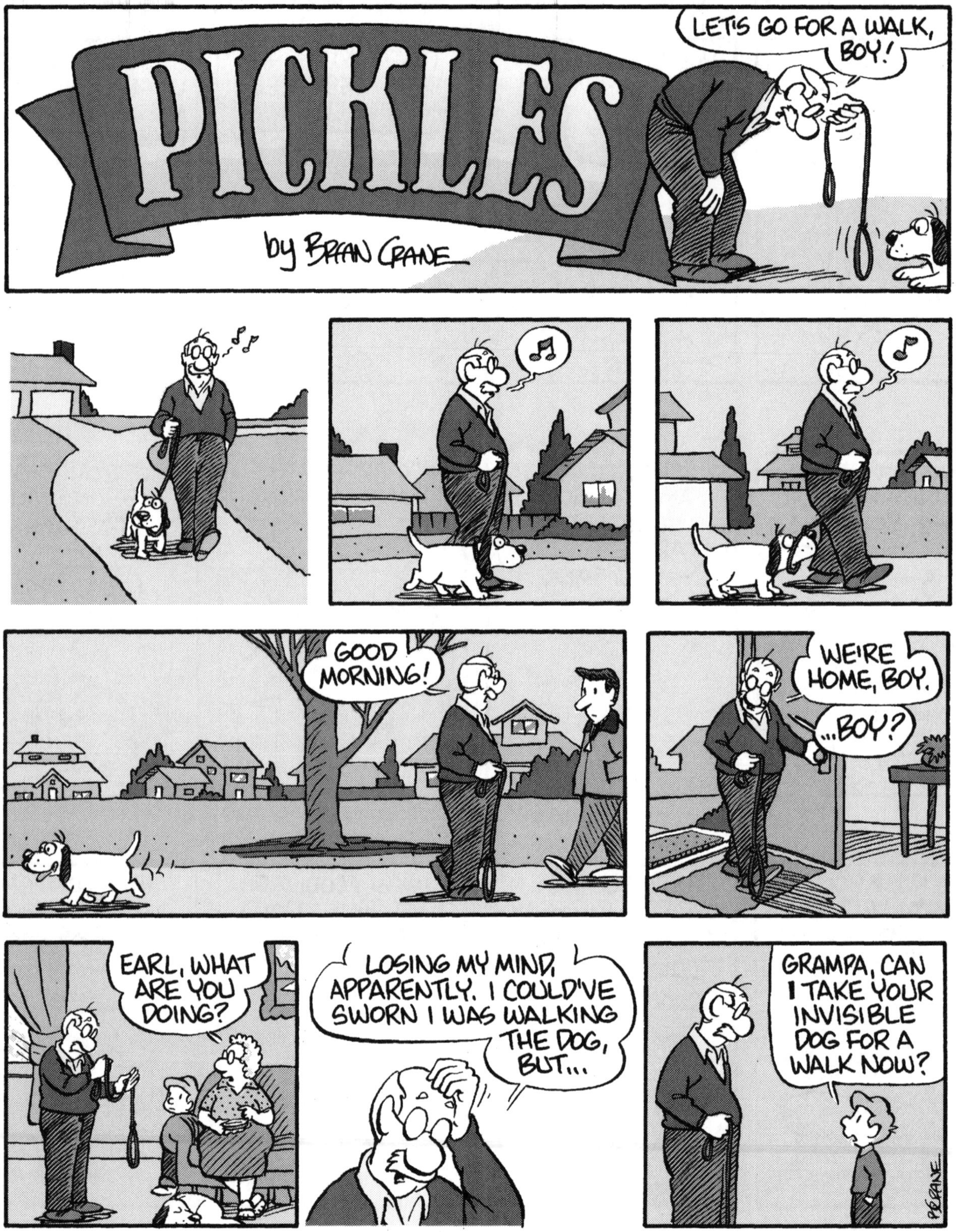
PICKLES
by BRIAN CRANE
LET'S GO FOR A WALK, BOY!
GOOD MORNING!
WE'RE HOME, BOY.
...BOY?
EARL, WHAT ARE YOU DOING?
LOSING MY MIND, APPARENTLY. I COULD'VE SWORN I WAS WALKING THE DOG, BUT...
GRAMPA, CAN I TAKE YOUR INVISIBLE DOG FOR A WALK NOW?

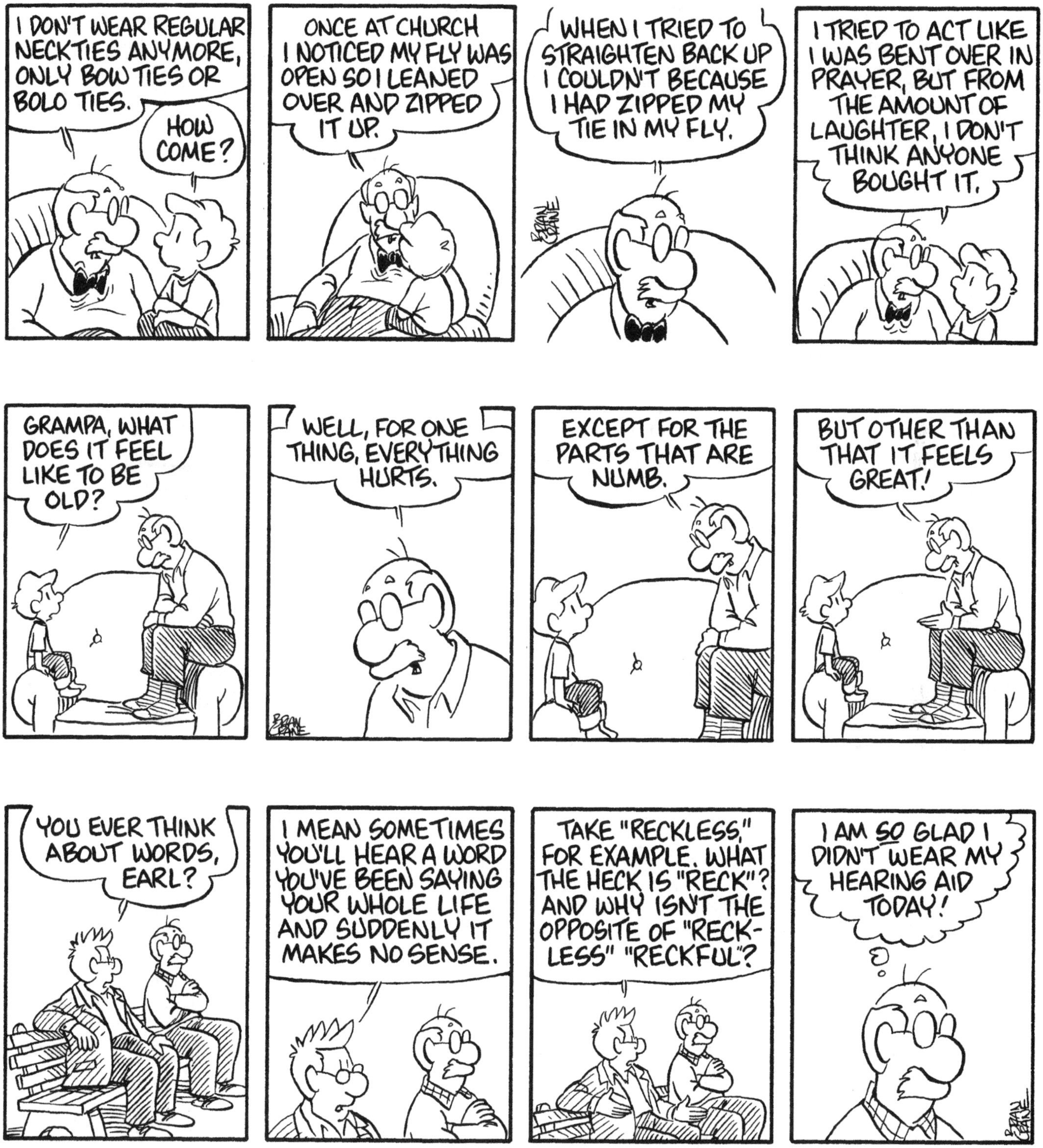
I DON'T WEAR REGULAR NECKTIES ANYMORE, ONLY BOW TIES OR BOLO TIES.
HOW COME?
ONCE AT CHURCH I NOTICED MY FLY WAS OPEN SO I LEANED OVER AND ZIPPED IT UP.
WHEN I TRIED TO STRAIGHTEN BACK UP I COULDN'T BECAUSE I HAD ZIPPED MY TIE IN MY FLY.
I TRIED TO ACT LIKE I WAS BENT OVER IN PRAYER, BUT FROM THE AMOUNT OF LAUGHTER, I DON'T THINK ANYONE BOUGHT IT.
GRAMPA, WHAT DOES IT FEEL LIKE TO BE OLD?
WELL, FOR ONE THING, EVERYTHING HURTS.
EXCEPT FOR THE PARTS THAT ARE NUMB.
BUT OTHER THAN THAT IT FEELS GREAT!
YOU EVER THINK ABOUT WORDS, EARL?
I MEAN SOMETIMES YOU'LL HEAR A WORD YOU'VE BEEN SAYING YOUR WHOLE LIFE AND SUDDENLY IT MAKES NO SENSE.
TAKE "RECKLESS," FOR EXAMPLE. WHAT THE HECK IS "RECK"? AND WHY ISN'T THE OPPOSITE OF "RECK-LESS" "RECKFUL"?
I AM SO GLAD I DIDN'T WEAR MY HEARING AID TODAY!

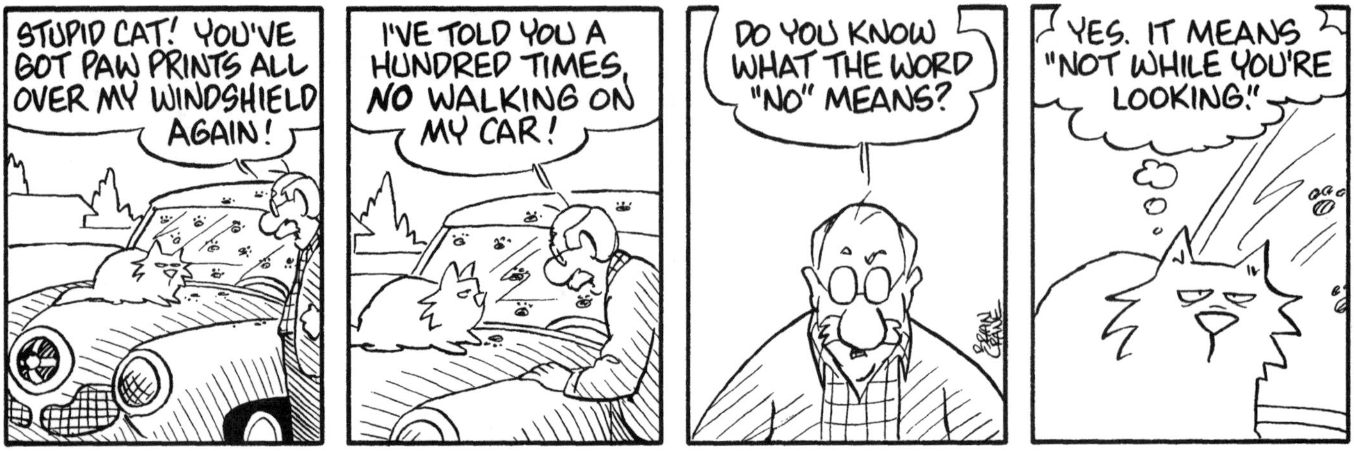
STUPID CAT! YOU'VE GOT PAW PRINTS ALL OVER MY WINDSHIELD AGAIN!
I'VE TOLD YOU A HUNDRED TIMES, NO WALKING ON MY CAR!
DO YOU KNOW WHAT THE WORD "NO" MEANS?
YES. IT MEANS "NOT WHILE YOU'RE LOOKING."

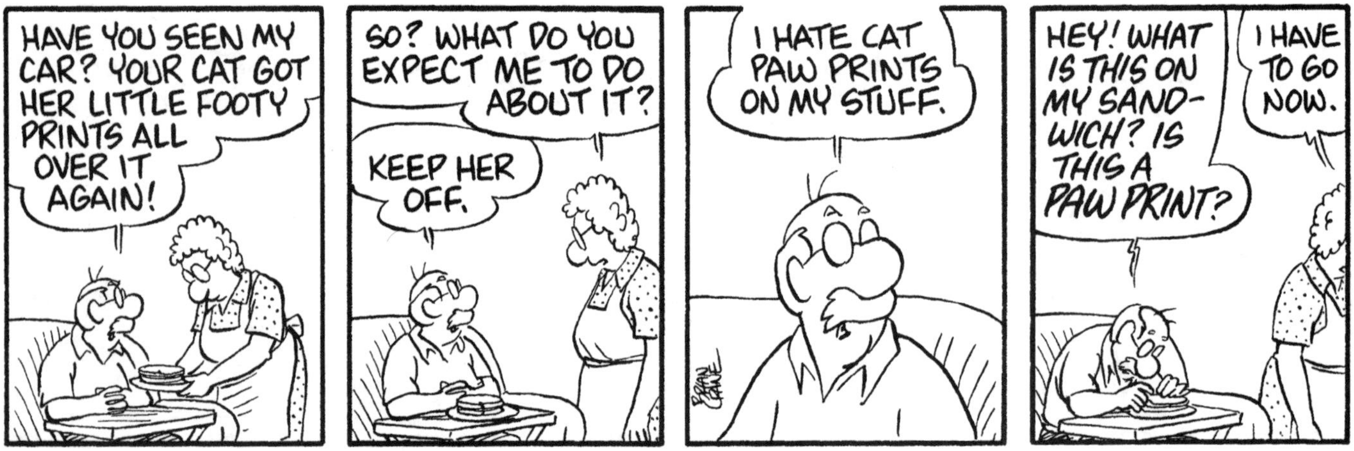
HAVE YOU SEEN MY CAR? YOUR CAT GOT HER LITTLE FOOTY PRINTS ALL OVER IT AGAIN!
SO? WHAT DO YOU EXPECT ME TO DO ABOUT IT?
KEEP HER OFF.
I HATE CAT PAW PRINTS ON MY STUFF.
HEY! WHAT IS THIS ON MY SANDWICH? IS THIS A PAW PRINT?
I HAVE TO GO NOW.

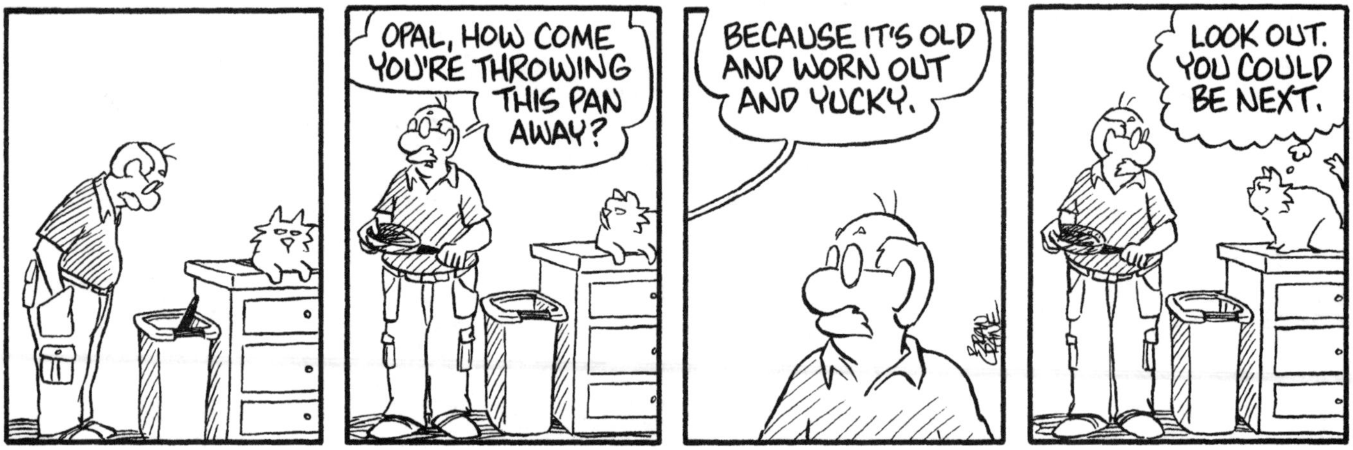
OPAL, HOW COME YOU'RE THROWING THIS PAN AWAY?
BECAUSE IT'S OLD AND WORN OUT AND YUCKY.
LOOK OUT. YOU COULD BE NEXT.

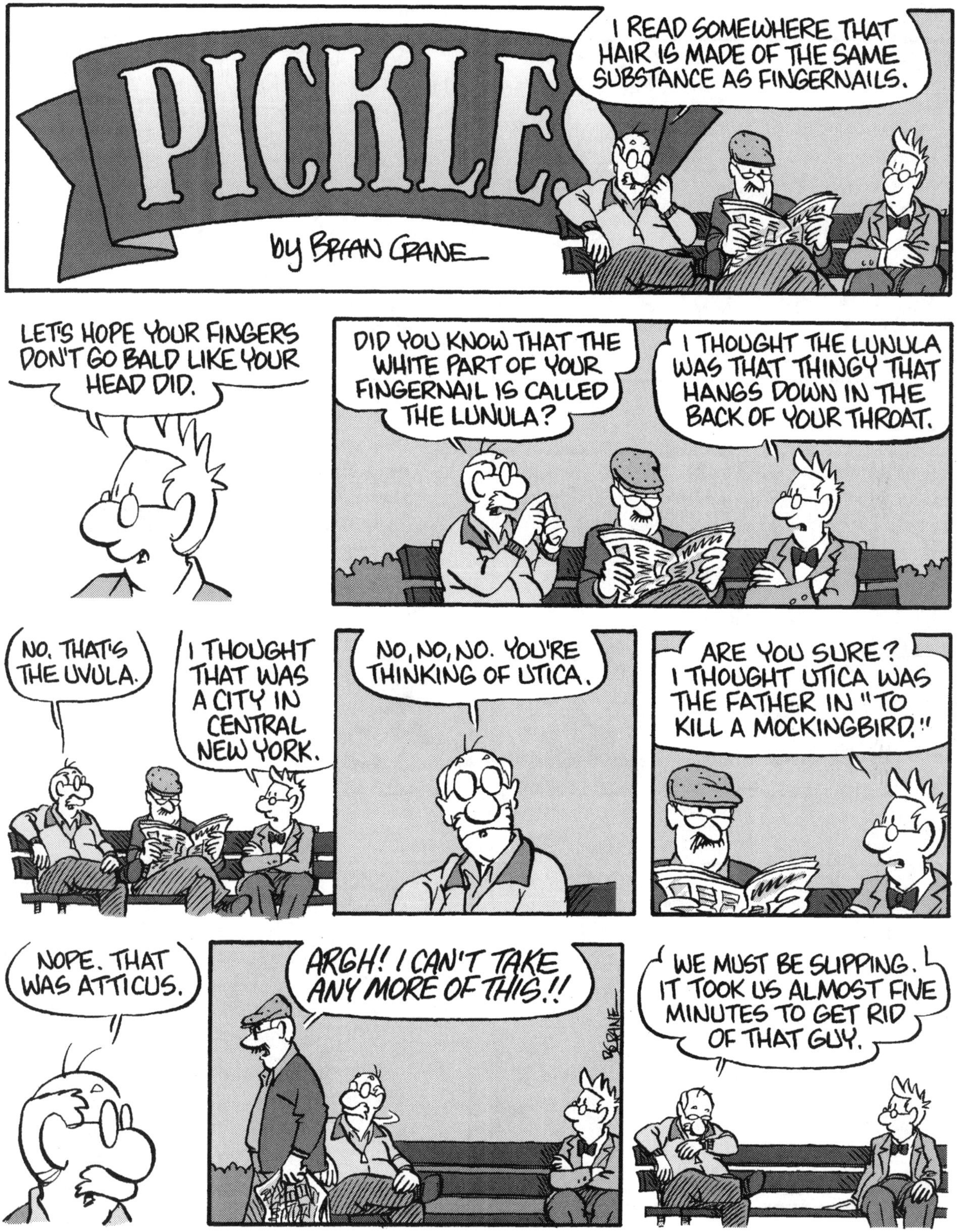
PICKLES
by BRIAN CRANE
I READ SOMEWHERE THAT HAIR IS MADE OF THE SAME SUBSTANCE AS FINGERNAILS.
LET'S HOPE YOUR FINGERS DON'T GO BALD LIKE YOUR HEAD DID.
DID YOU KNOW THAT THE WHITE PART OF YOUR FINGERNAIL IS CALLED THE LUNULA?
I THOUGHT THE LUNULA WAS THAT THINGY THAT HANGS DOWN IN THE BACK OF YOUR THROAT.
NO. THAT'S THE UVULA.
I THOUGHT THAT WAS A CITY IN CENTRAL NEW YORK.
NO, NO, NO. YOU'RE THINKING OF UTICA.
ARE YOU SURE? I THOUGHT UTICA WAS THE FATHER IN "TO KILL A MOCKINGBIRD."
NOPE. THAT WAS ATTICUS.
ARGH! I CAN'T TAKE ANY MORE OF THIS!!
WE MUST BE SLIPPING. IT TOOK US ALMOST FIVE MINUTES TO GET RID OF THAT GUY.

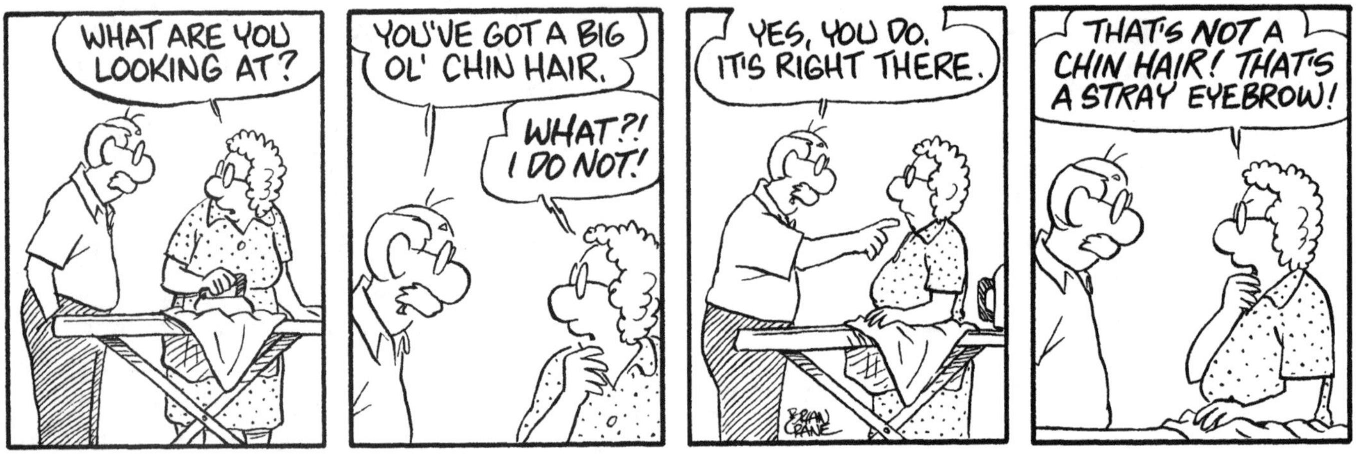
WHAT ARE YOU LOOKING AT?
YOU'VE GOT A BIG OL' CHIN HAIR.
WHAT?! I DO NOT!
YES, YOU DO. IT'S RIGHT THERE.
THAT'S NOT A CHIN HAIR! THAT'S A STRAY EYEBROW!

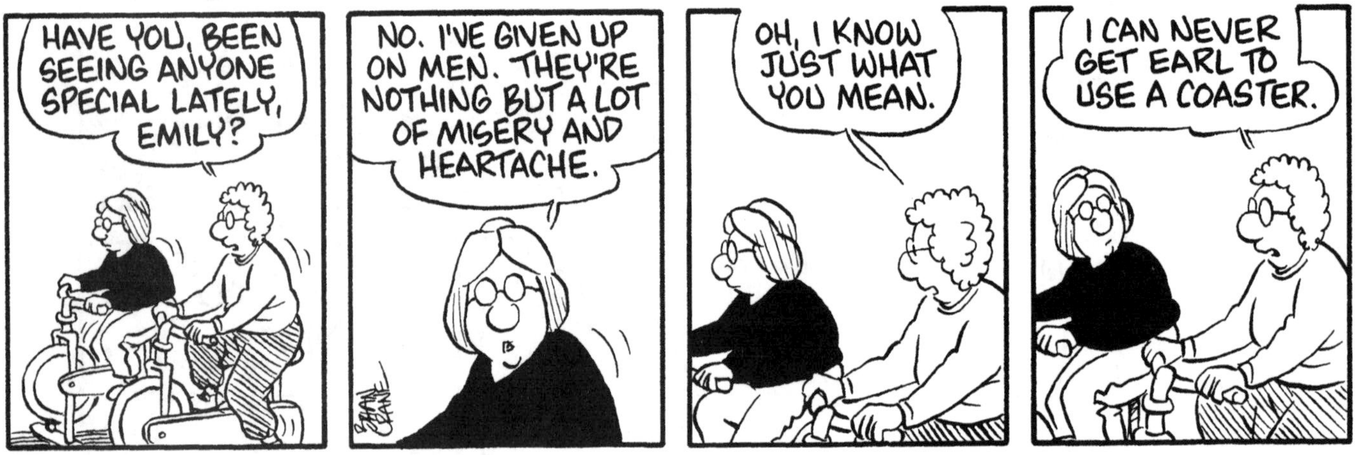
HAVE YOU, BEEN SEEING ANYONE SPECIAL LATELY, EMILY?
NO. I'VE GIVEN UP ON MEN. THEY'RE NOTHING BUT A LOT OF MISERY AND HEARTACHE.
OH, I KNOW JUST WHAT YOU MEAN.
I CAN NEVER GET EARL TO USE A COASTER.

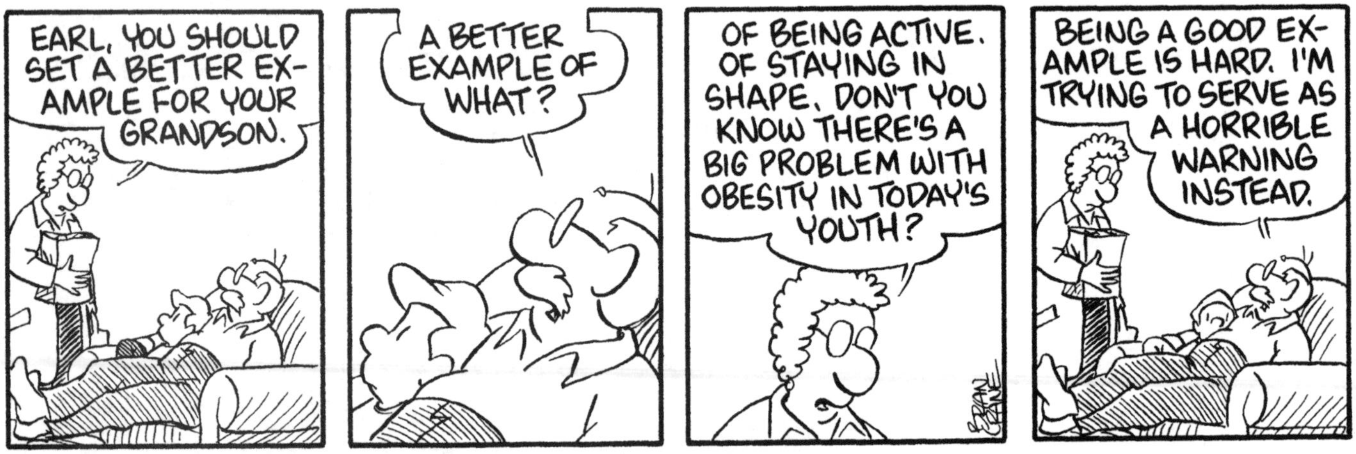
EARL, YOU SHOULD SET A BETTER EX-AMPLE FOR YOUR GRANDSON.
A BETTER EXAMPLE OF WHAT?
OF BEING ACTIVE. OF STAYING IN SHAPE. DON'T YOU KNOW THERE'S A BIG PROBLEM WITH OBESITY IN TODAY'S YOUTH?
BEING A GOOD EX-AMPLE IS HARD. I'M TRYING TO SERVE AS A HORRIBLE WARNING INSTEAD.

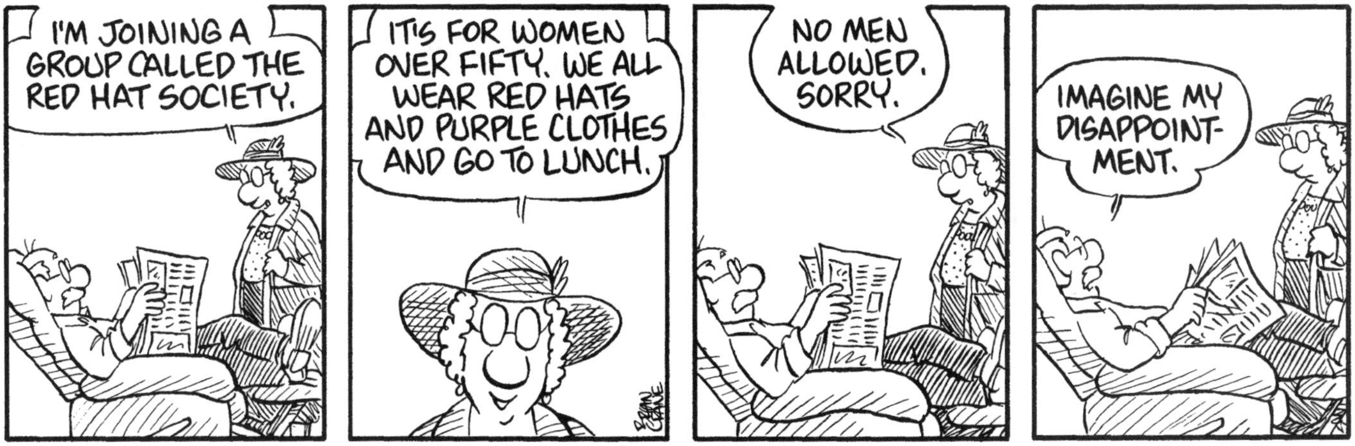
I'M JOINING A GROUP CALLED THE RED HAT SOCIETY.
IT'S FOR WOMEN OVER FIFTY. WE ALL WEAR RED HATS AND PURPLE CLOTHES AND GO TO LUNCH.
NO MEN ALLOWED. SORRY.
IMAGINE MY DISAPPOINTMENT.

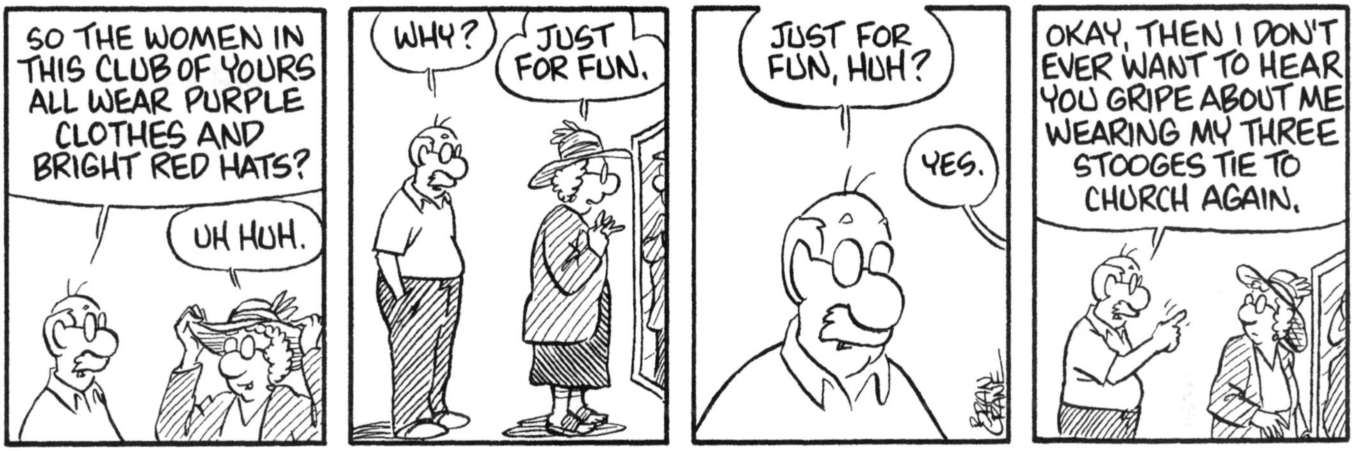
SO THE WOMEN IN THIS CLUB OF YOURS ALL WEAR PURPLE CLOTHES AND BRIGHT RED HATS?
UH HUH.
WHY?
JUST FOR FUN.
JUST FOR FUN, HUH?
YES.
OKAY, THEN I DON'T EVER WANT TO HEAR YOU GRIPE ABOUT ME WEARING MY THREE STOOGES TIE TO CHURCH AGAIN.

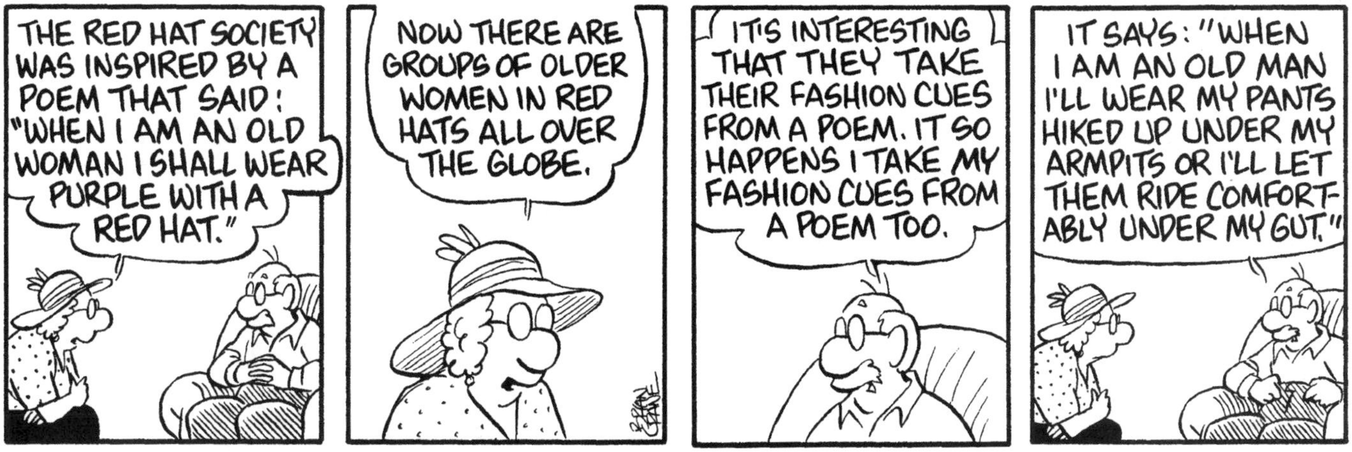
THE RED HAT SOCIETY WAS INSPIRED BY A POEM THAT SAID: "WHEN I AM AN OLD WOMAN I SHALL WEAR PURPLE WITH A RED HAT."
NOW THERE ARE GROUPS OF OLDER WOMEN IN RED HATS ALL OVER THE GLOBE.
IT'S INTERESTING THAT THEY TAKE THEIR FASHION CUES FROM A POEM. IT SO HAPPENS I TAKE MY FASHION CUES FROM A POEM TOO.
IT SAYS: "WHEN I AM AN OLD MAN I'LL WEAR MY PANTS HIKED UP UNDER MY ARMPITS OR I'LL LET THEM RIDE COMFORTABLY UNDER MY GUT."

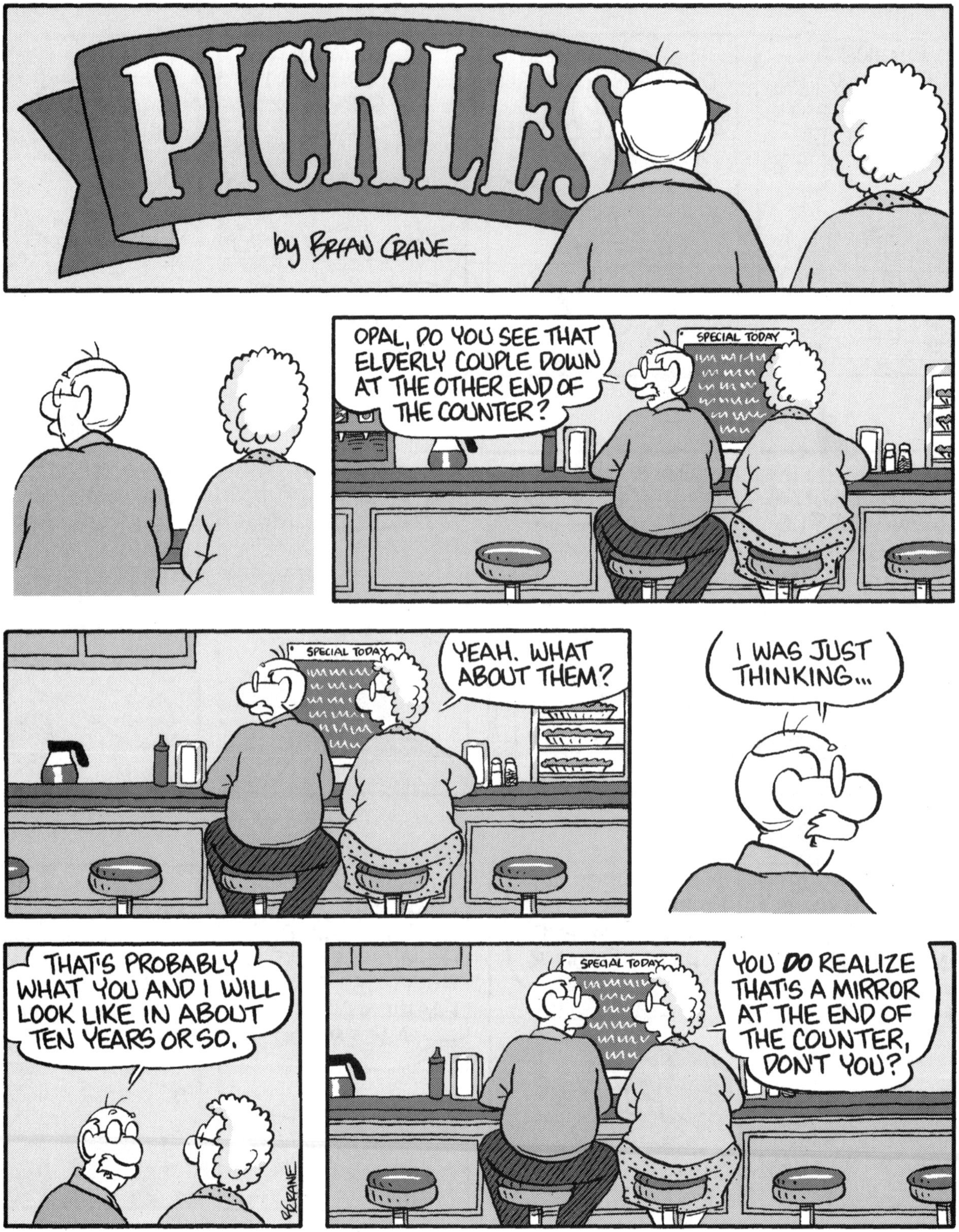
PICKLES
by BRIAN CRANE
OPAL, DO YOU SEE THAT ELDERLY COUPLE DOWN AT THE OTHER END OF THE COUNTER?
SPECIAL TODAY
YEAH. WHAT ABOUT THEM?
I WAS JUST THINKING...
THAT'S PROBABLY WHAT YOU AND I WILL LOOK LIKE IN ABOUT TEN YEARS OR SO.
YOU **DO** REALIZE THAT'S A MIRROR AT THE END OF THE COUNTER, DON'T YOU?
B.CRANE

Panel 1: I JUST DON'T SEE WHY YOU WANT TO JOIN THAT RED HAT LADIES CLUB.

Panel 2: SOMETIMES I FEEL A LITTLE LONELY AND SOCIALLY ISOLATED.

Panel 3: WHY? YOU'VE GOT ME.

Panel 4: THAT'S TRUE, BUT... SHH! MY SHOW'S BACK ON.

Panel 5: MY WIFE JOINED SOME KIND OF WOMEN'S CLUB.

Panel 6: APPARENTLY THEY DRESS UP IN BRIGHT RED HATS AND PURPLE CLOTHES. WHY?

Panel 7: GOOD QUESTION. SHE SAYS IT'S FUN TO GO OUT TO LUNCH WEARING GAUDY OUTFITS.

Panel 8: AND YET IF I WEAR PLAIDS AND STRIPES SHE HAS A COW.

Panel 9: YOU'RE BACK. HOW WAS YOUR LUNCH WITH THE RED HAT LADIES? GOOD.

Panel 10: WHAT KINDS OF THINGS DO THEY DO? DO THEY SUPPORT CIVIC CAUSES, HELP WITH DISASTER RELIEF, THAT KIND OF STUFF?

Panel 11: NO, MOSTLY WE JUST EAT AND TALK AND LAUGH.

Panel 12: AND NO MEN ARE ALLOWED? WHO DO YOU THINK WE LAUGH AT?

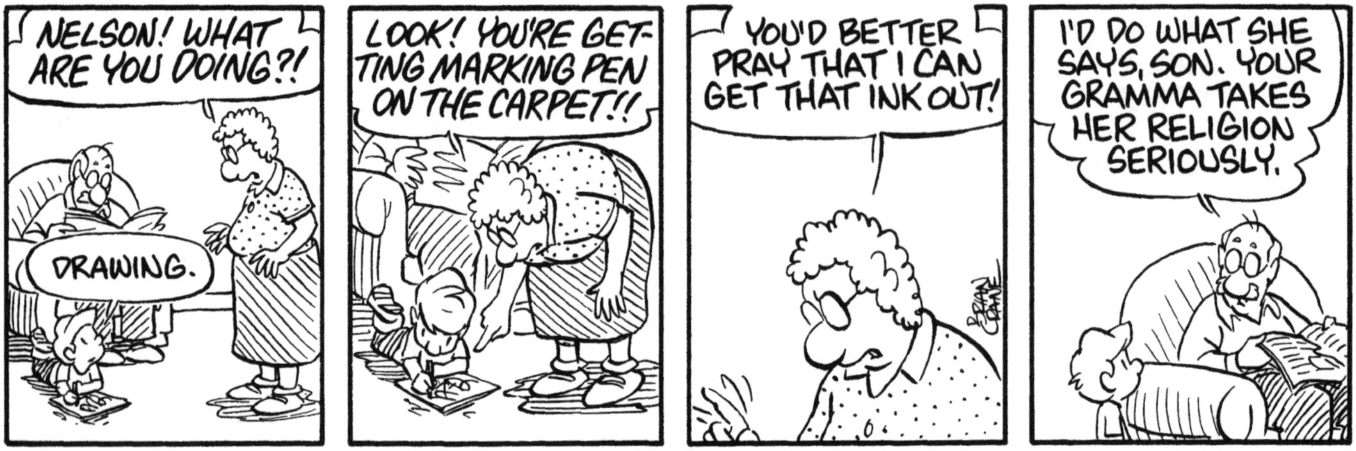
NELSON! WHAT ARE YOU DOING?!
DRAWING.
LOOK! YOU'RE GETTING MARKING PEN ON THE CARPET!!
YOU'D BETTER PRAY THAT I CAN GET THAT INK OUT!
I'D DO WHAT SHE SAYS, SON. YOUR GRAMMA TAKES HER RELIGION SERIOUSLY.

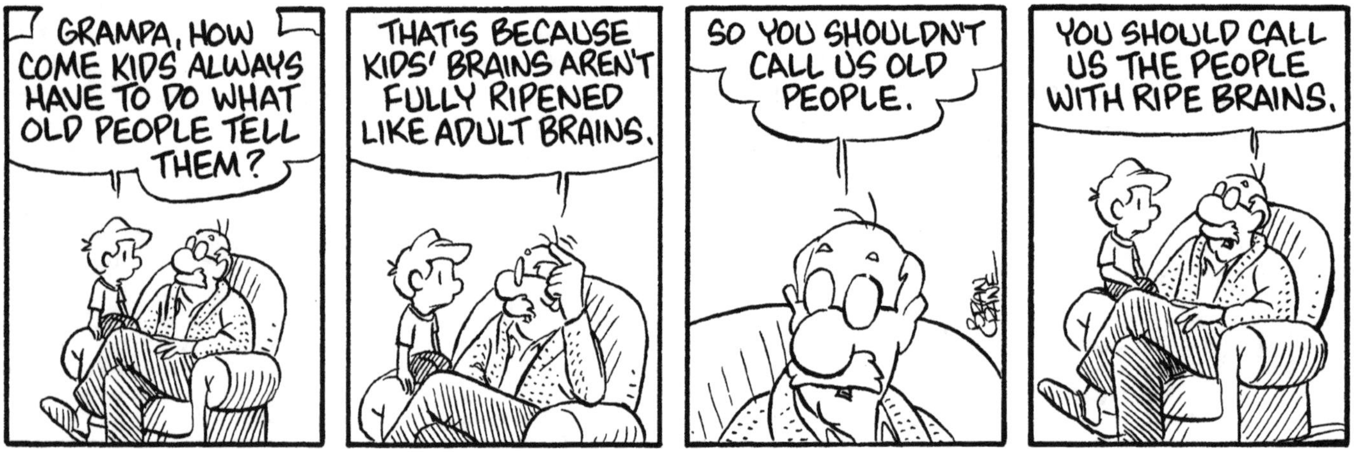
GRAMPA, HOW COME KIDS ALWAYS HAVE TO DO WHAT OLD PEOPLE TELL THEM?
THAT'S BECAUSE KIDS' BRAINS AREN'T FULLY RIPENED LIKE ADULT BRAINS.
SO YOU SHOULDN'T CALL US OLD PEOPLE.
YOU SHOULD CALL US THE PEOPLE WITH RIPE BRAINS.

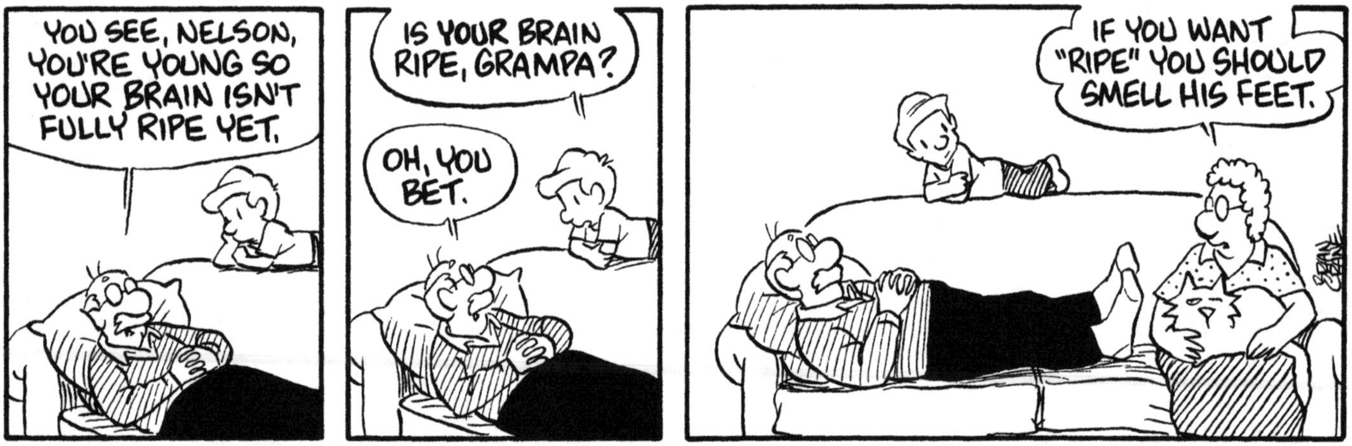
YOU SEE, NELSON, YOU'RE YOUNG SO YOUR BRAIN ISN'T FULLY RIPE YET.
IS YOUR BRAIN RIPE, GRAMPA?
OH, YOU BET.
IF YOU WANT "RIPE" YOU SHOULD SMELL HIS FEET.

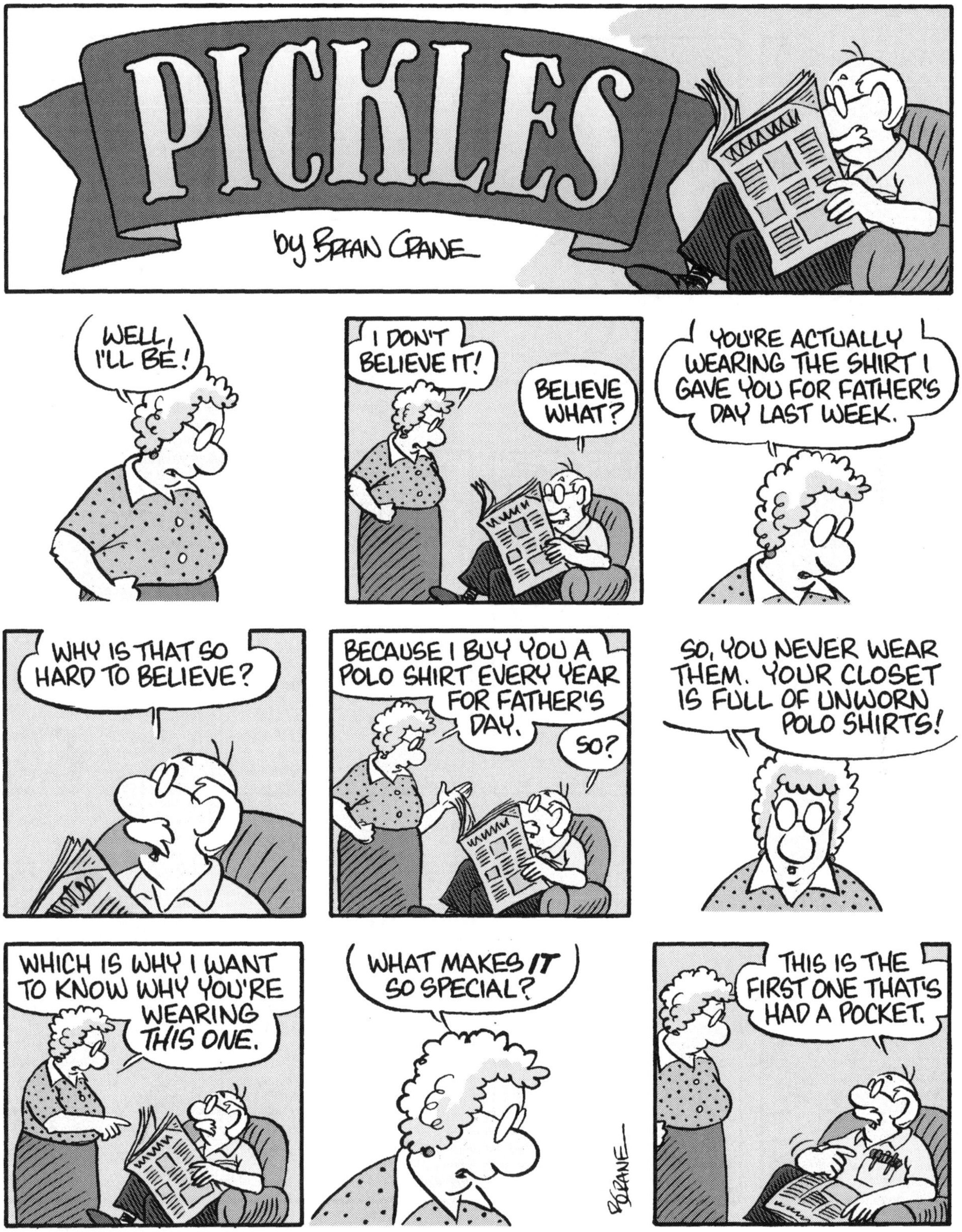
PICKLES
by BRIAN CRANE
WELL, I'LL BE!
I DON'T BELIEVE IT!
BELIEVE WHAT?
YOU'RE ACTUALLY WEARING THE SHIRT I GAVE YOU FOR FATHER'S DAY LAST WEEK.
WHY IS THAT SO HARD TO BELIEVE?
BECAUSE I BUY YOU A POLO SHIRT EVERY YEAR FOR FATHER'S DAY.
SO?
SO, YOU NEVER WEAR THEM. YOUR CLOSET IS FULL OF UNWORN POLO SHIRTS!
WHICH IS WHY I WANT TO KNOW WHY YOU'RE WEARING THIS ONE.
WHAT MAKES IT SO SPECIAL?
THIS IS THE FIRST ONE THAT'S HAD A POCKET.
B CRANE

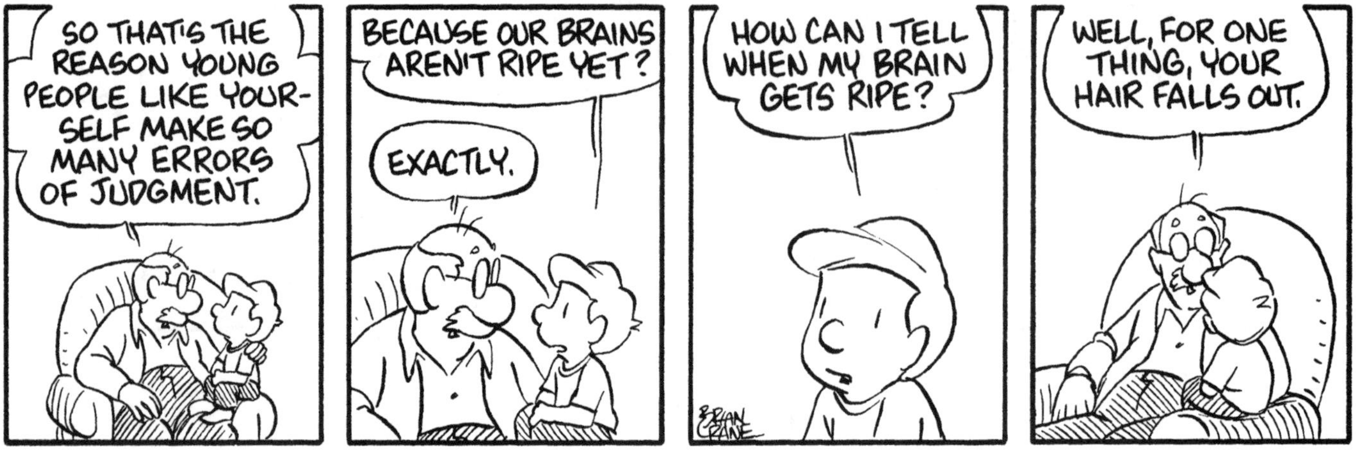
SO THAT'S THE REASON YOUNG PEOPLE LIKE YOUR-SELF MAKE SO MANY ERRORS OF JUDGMENT.
BECAUSE OUR BRAINS AREN'T RIPE YET?
EXACTLY.
HOW CAN I TELL WHEN MY BRAIN GETS RIPE?
WELL, FOR ONE THING, YOUR HAIR FALLS OUT.

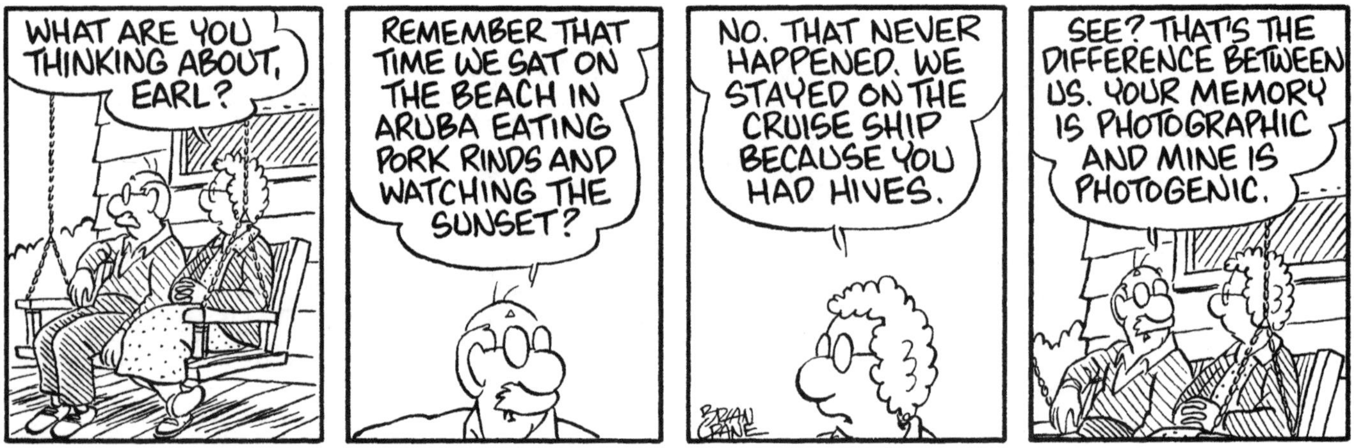
WHAT ARE YOU THINKING ABOUT, EARL?
REMEMBER THAT TIME WE SAT ON THE BEACH IN ARUBA EATING PORK RINDS AND WATCHING THE SUNSET?
NO. THAT NEVER HAPPENED. WE STAYED ON THE CRUISE SHIP BECAUSE YOU HAD HIVES.
SEE? THAT'S THE DIFFERENCE BETWEEN US. YOUR MEMORY IS PHOTOGRAPHIC AND MINE IS PHOTOGENIC.

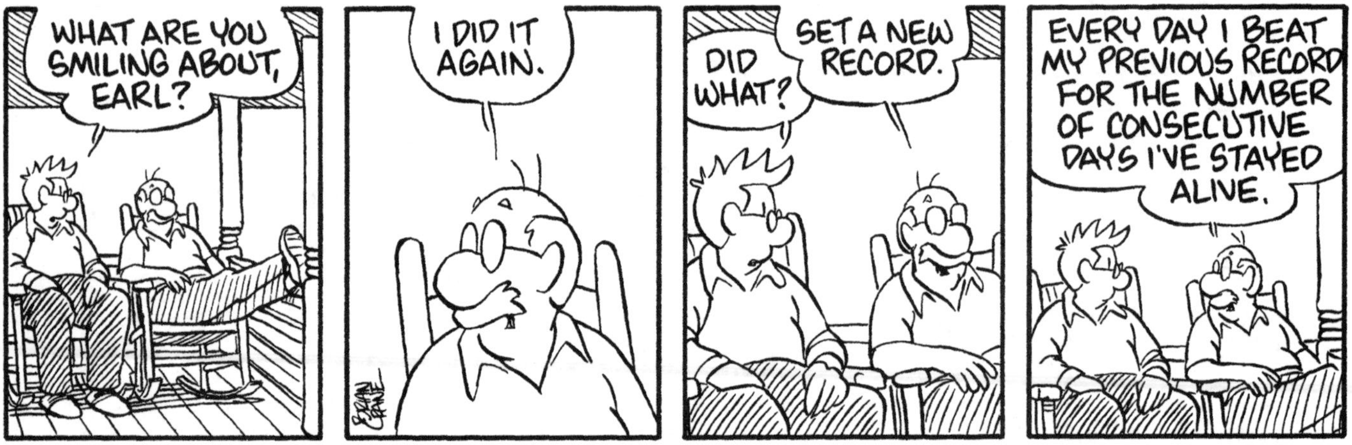
WHAT ARE YOU SMILING ABOUT, EARL?
I DID IT AGAIN.
DID WHAT?
SET A NEW RECORD.
EVERY DAY I BEAT MY PREVIOUS RECORD FOR THE NUMBER OF CONSECUTIVE DAYS I'VE STAYED ALIVE.

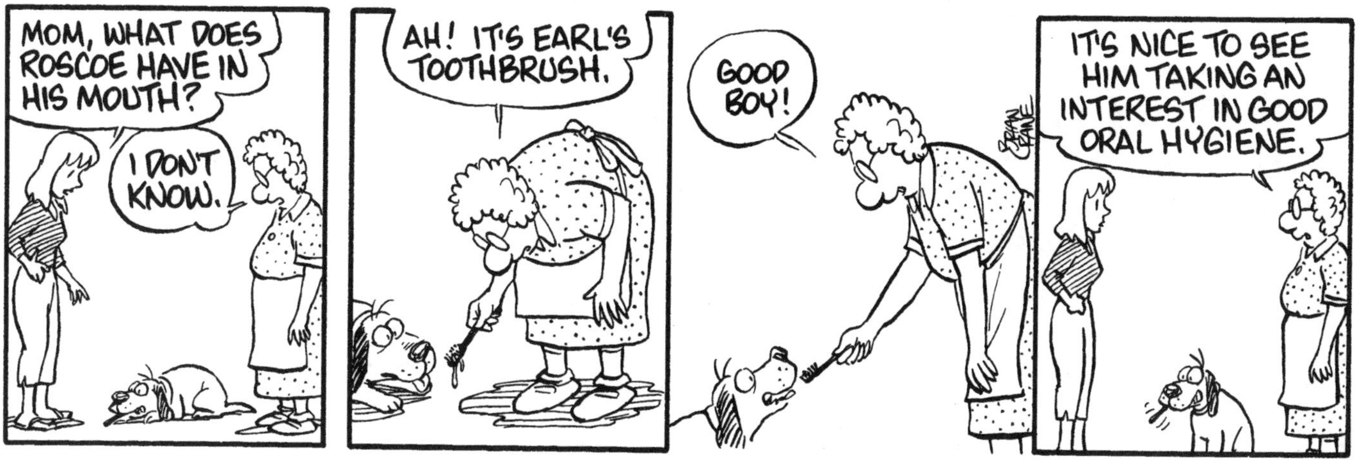
MOM, WHAT DOES ROSCOE HAVE IN HIS MOUTH?
I DON'T KNOW.
AH! IT'S EARL'S TOOTHBRUSH.
GOOD BOY!
IT'S NICE TO SEE HIM TAKING AN INTEREST IN GOOD ORAL HYGIENE.

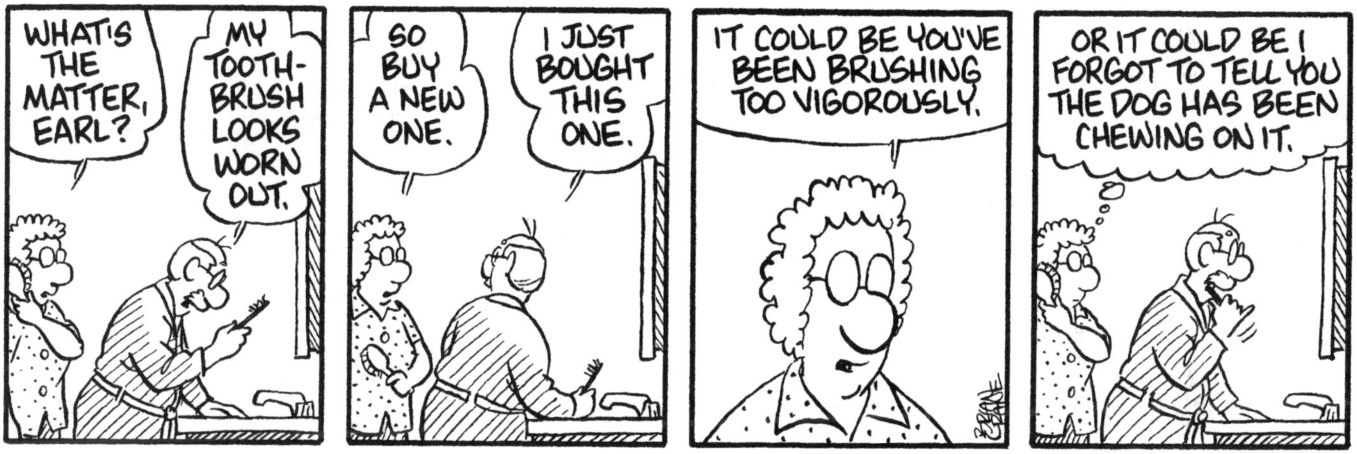
WHAT'S THE MATTER, EARL?
MY TOOTH-BRUSH LOOKS WORN OUT.
SO BUY A NEW ONE.
I JUST BOUGHT THIS ONE.
IT COULD BE YOU'VE BEEN BRUSHING TOO VIGOROUSLY.
OR IT COULD BE I FORGOT TO TELL YOU THE DOG HAS BEEN CHEWING ON IT.

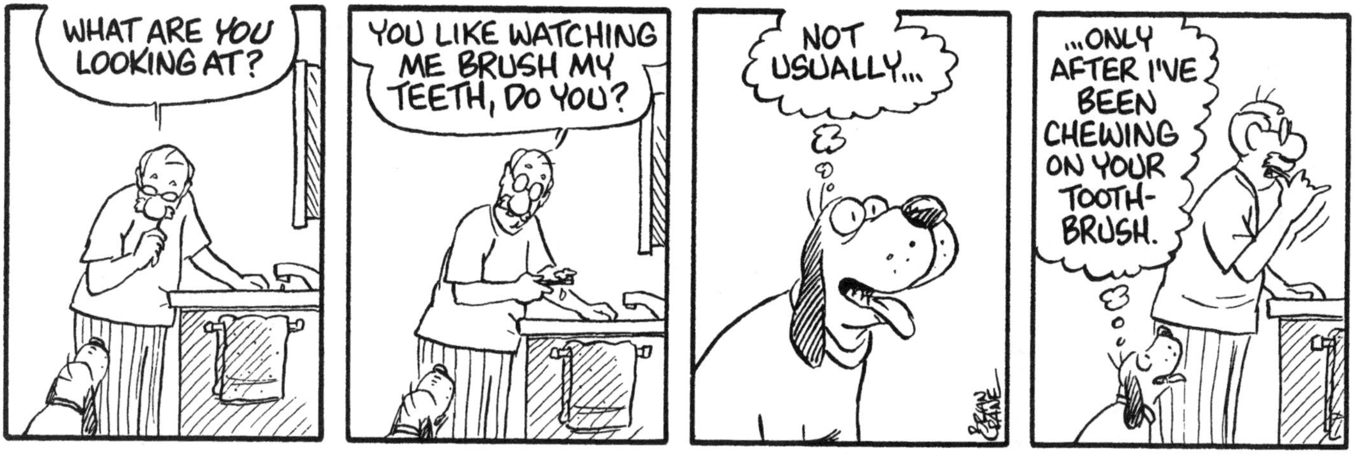
WHAT ARE YOU LOOKING AT?
YOU LIKE WATCHING ME BRUSH MY TEETH, DO YOU?
NOT USUALLY...
...ONLY AFTER I'VE BEEN CHEWING ON YOUR TOOTH-BRUSH.

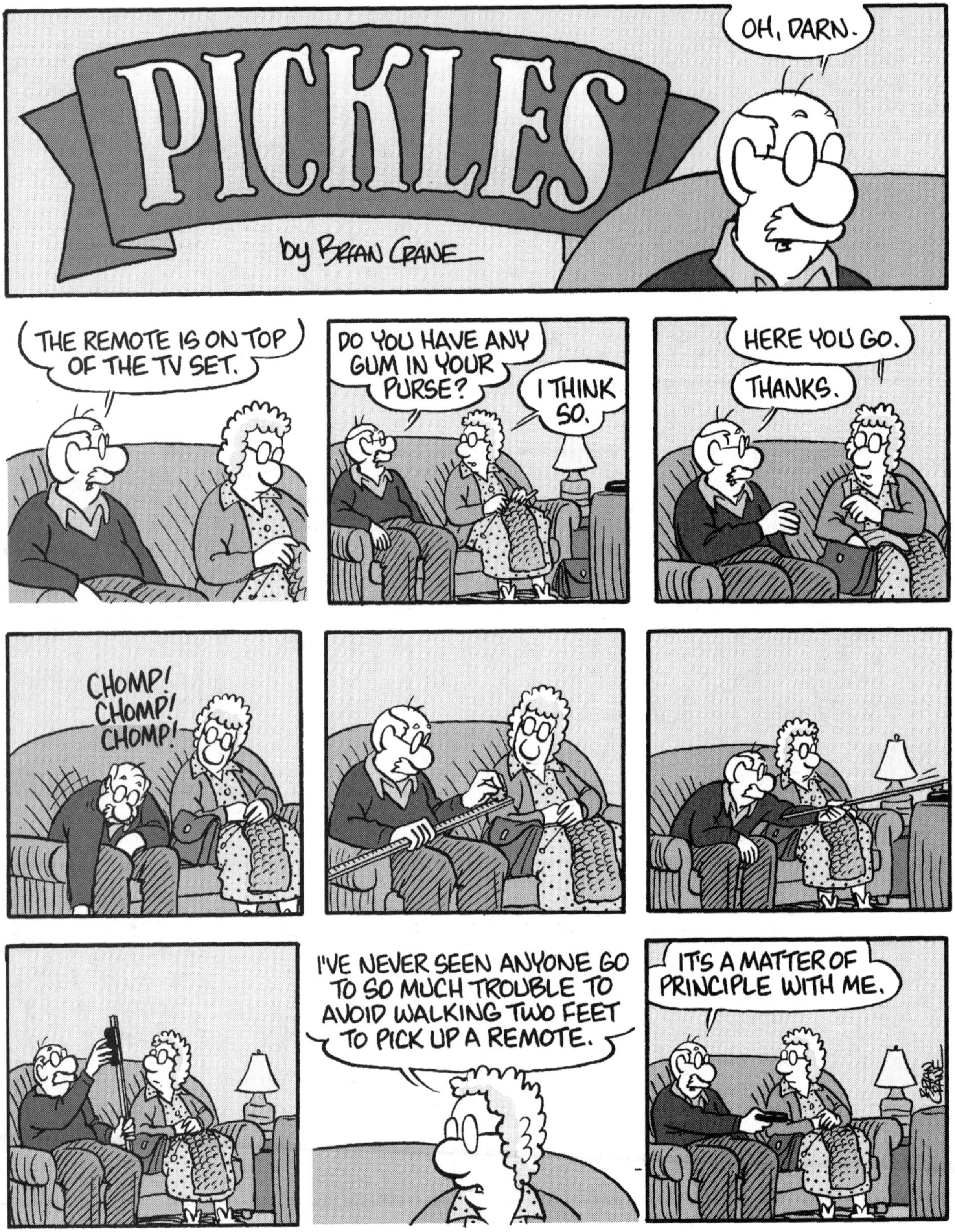
OH, DARN.
PICKLES
by BRIAN CRANE
THE REMOTE IS ON TOP OF THE TV SET.
DO YOU HAVE ANY GUM IN YOUR PURSE?
I THINK SO.
HERE YOU GO.
THANKS.
CHOMP! CHOMP! CHOMP!
I'VE NEVER SEEN ANYONE GO TO SO MUCH TROUBLE TO AVOID WALKING TWO FEET TO PICK UP A REMOTE.
IT'S A MATTER OF PRINCIPLE WITH ME.

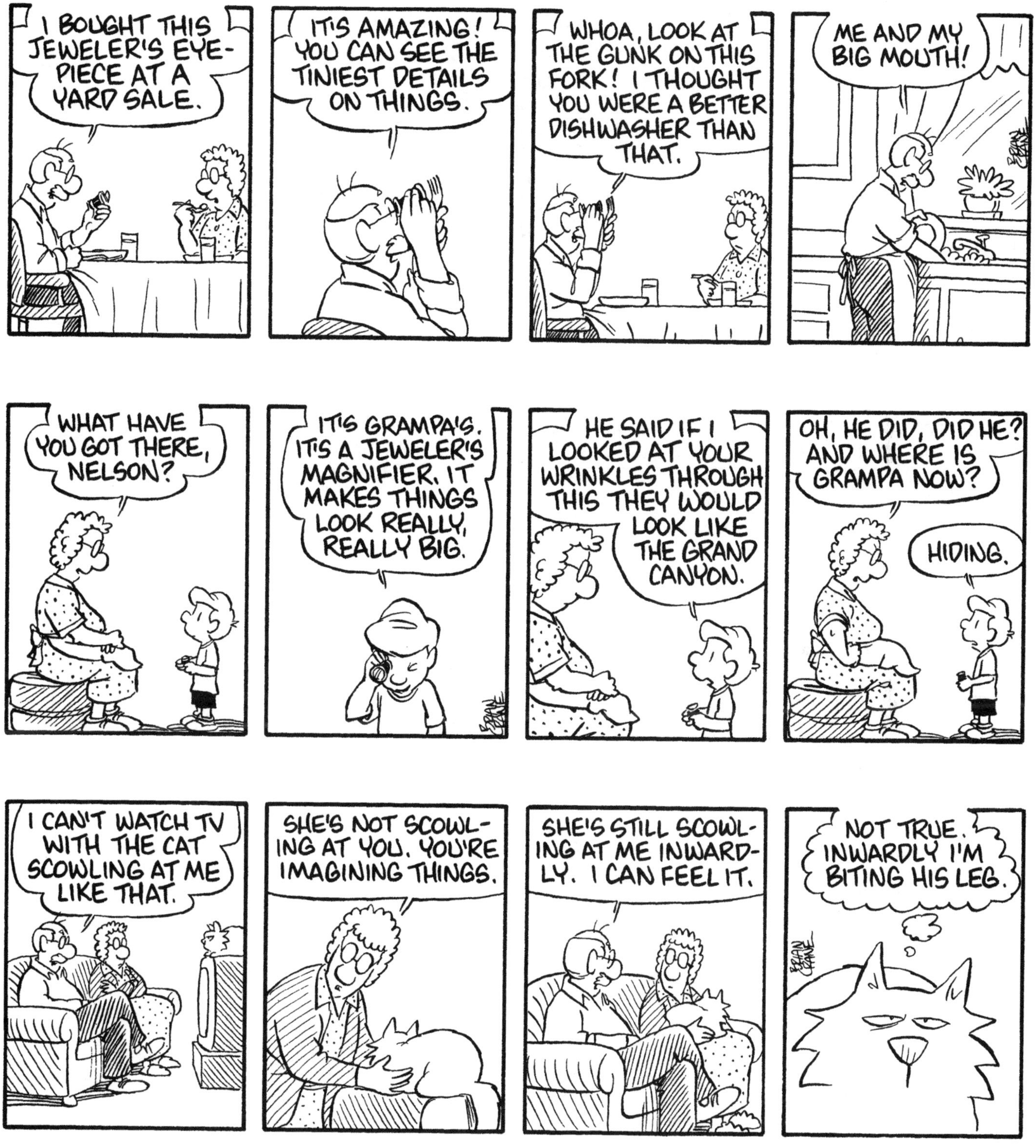
I BOUGHT THIS JEWELER'S EYE-PIECE AT A YARD SALE.
IT'S AMAZING! YOU CAN SEE THE TINIEST DETAILS ON THINGS.
WHOA, LOOK AT THE GUNK ON THIS FORK! I THOUGHT YOU WERE A BETTER DISHWASHER THAN THAT.
ME AND MY BIG MOUTH!
WHAT HAVE YOU GOT THERE, NELSON?
IT'S GRAMPA'S. IT'S A JEWELER'S MAGNIFIER. IT MAKES THINGS LOOK REALLY, REALLY BIG.
HE SAID IF I LOOKED AT YOUR WRINKLES THROUGH THIS THEY WOULD LOOK LIKE THE GRAND CANYON.
OH, HE DID, DID HE? AND WHERE IS GRAMPA NOW?
HIDING.
I CAN'T WATCH TV WITH THE CAT SCOWLING AT ME LIKE THAT.
SHE'S NOT SCOWLING AT YOU. YOU'RE IMAGINING THINGS.
SHE'S STILL SCOWLING AT ME INWARDLY. I CAN FEEL IT.
NOT TRUE. INWARDLY I'M BITING HIS LEG.

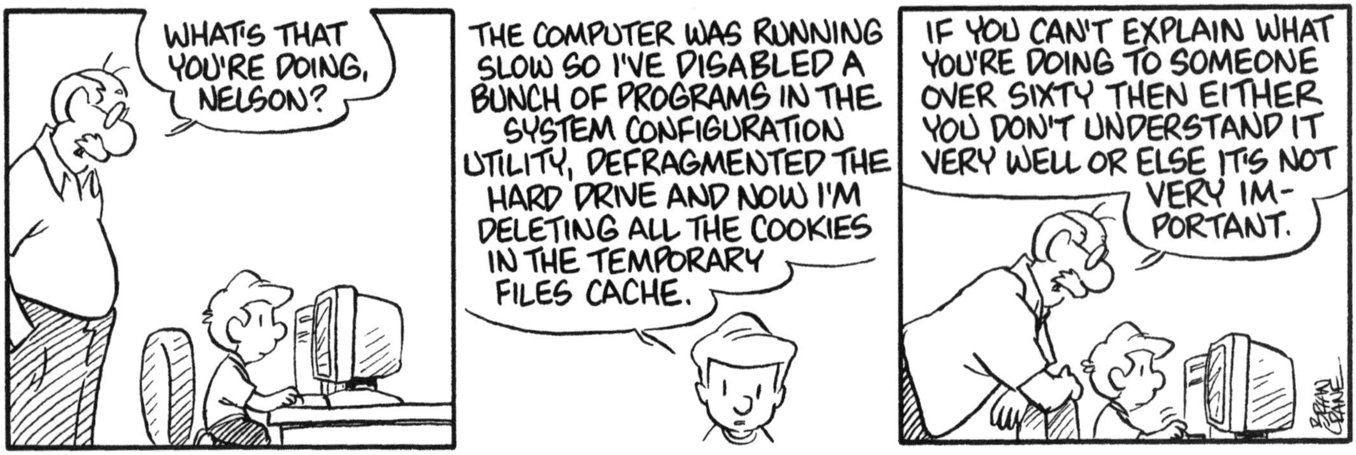
WHAT'S THAT YOU'RE DOING, NELSON?
THE COMPUTER WAS RUNNING SLOW SO I'VE DISABLED A BUNCH OF PROGRAMS IN THE SYSTEM CONFIGURATION UTILITY, DEFRAGMENTED THE HARD DRIVE AND NOW I'M DELETING ALL THE COOKIES IN THE TEMPORARY FILES CACHE.
IF YOU CAN'T EXPLAIN WHAT YOU'RE DOING TO SOMEONE OVER SIXTY THEN EITHER YOU DON'T UNDERSTAND IT VERY WELL OR ELSE IT'S NOT VERY IM-PORTANT.

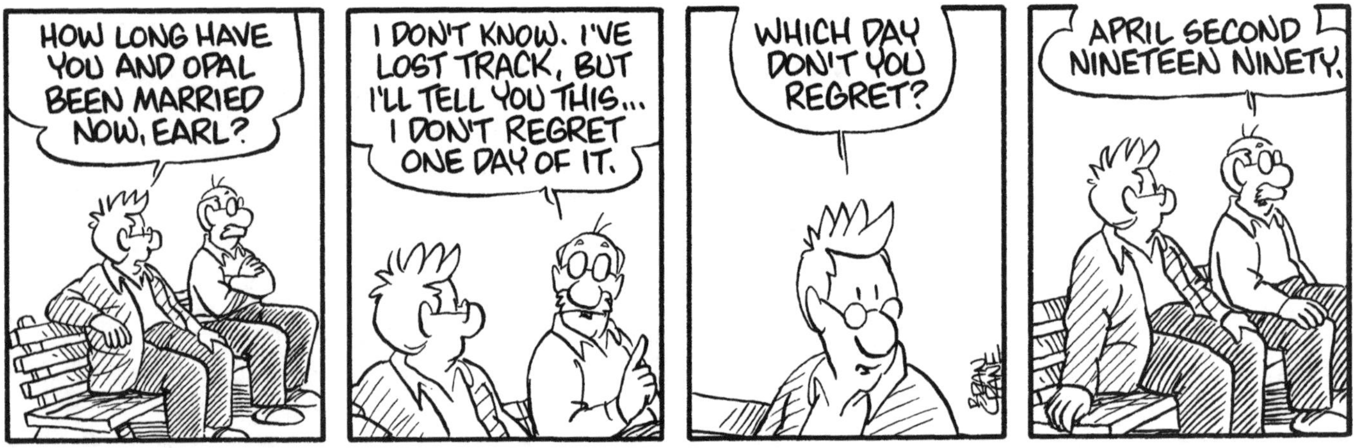
HOW LONG HAVE YOU AND OPAL BEEN MARRIED NOW, EARL?
I DON'T KNOW. I'VE LOST TRACK, BUT I'LL TELL YOU THIS... I DON'T REGRET ONE DAY OF IT.
WHICH DAY DON'T YOU REGRET?
APRIL SECOND NINETEEN NINETY.

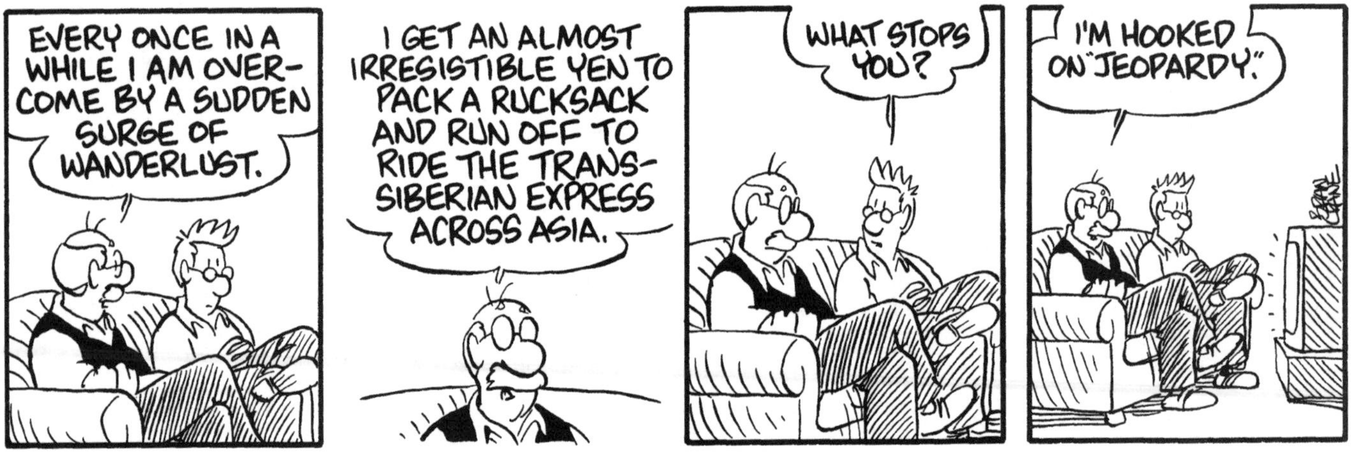
EVERY ONCE IN A WHILE I AM OVER-COME BY A SUDDEN SURGE OF WANDERLUST.
I GET AN ALMOST IRRESISTIBLE YEN TO PACK A RUCKSACK AND RUN OFF TO RIDE THE TRANS-SIBERIAN EXPRESS ACROSS ASIA.
WHAT STOPS YOU?
I'M HOOKED ON "JEOPARDY."

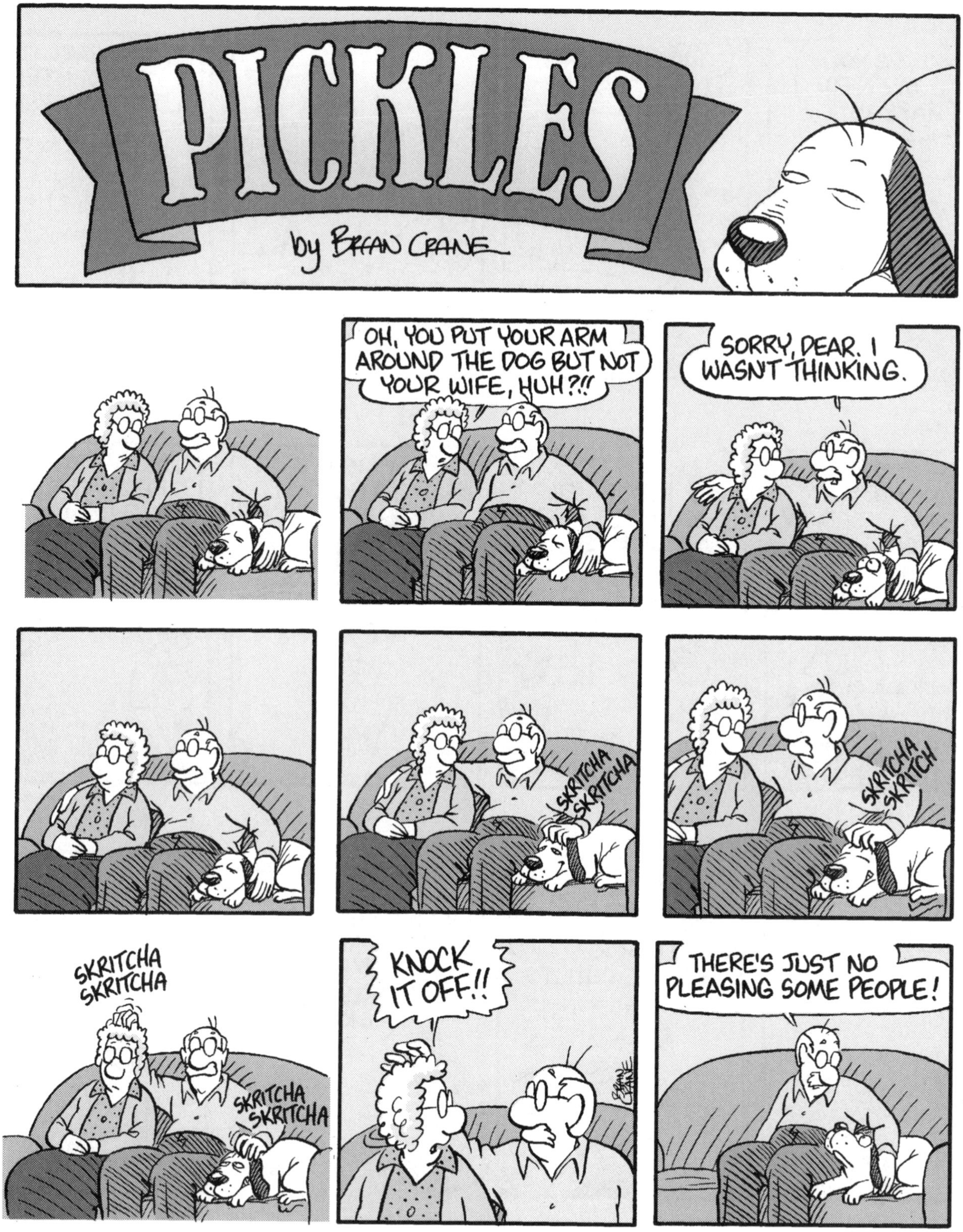
PICKLES
by Brian Crane
OH, YOU PUT YOUR ARM AROUND THE DOG BUT NOT YOUR WIFE, HUH?!!
SORRY, DEAR. I WASN'T THINKING.
SKRITCHA SKRITCHA
SKRITCHA SKRITCH
SKRITCHA SKRITCHA
SKRITCHA SKRITCHA
KNOCK IT OFF!!
THERE'S JUST NO PLEASING SOME PEOPLE!

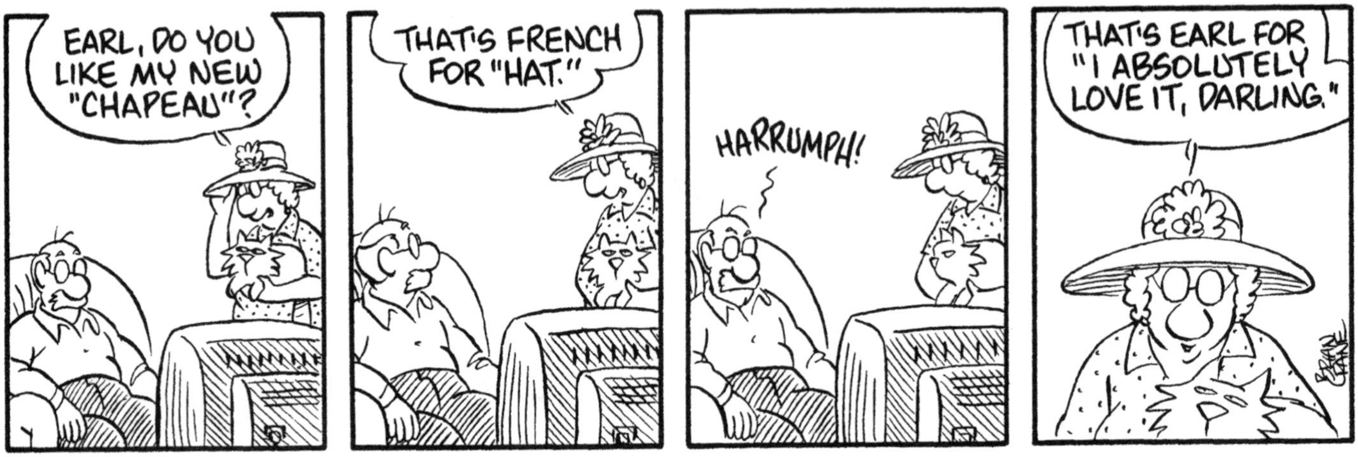
EARL, DO YOU LIKE MY NEW "CHAPEAU"?
THAT'S FRENCH FOR "HAT."
HARRUMPH!
THAT'S EARL FOR "I ABSOLUTELY LOVE IT, DARLING."

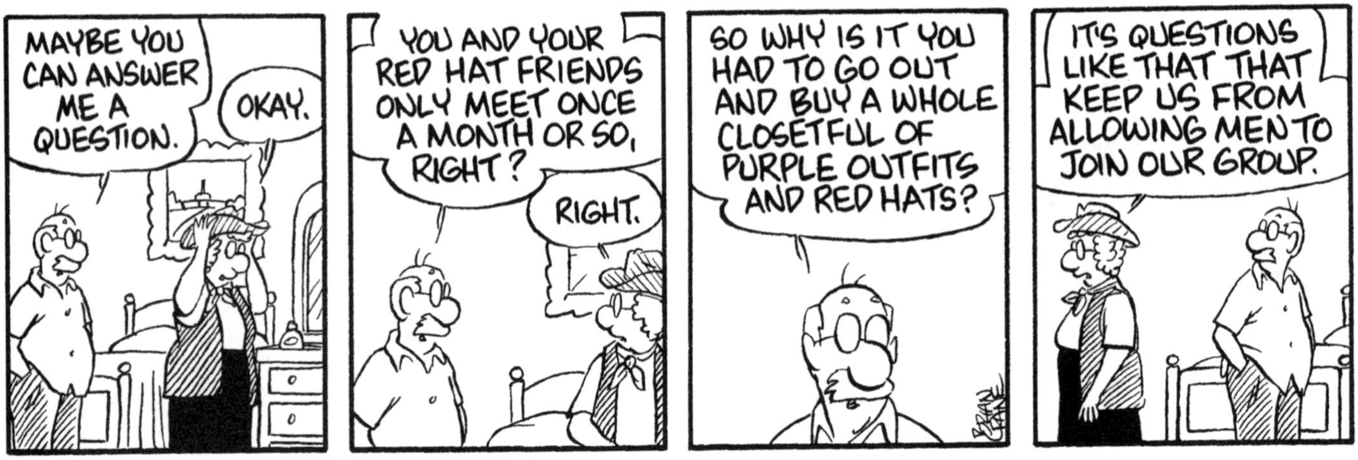
MAYBE YOU CAN ANSWER ME A QUESTION.
OKAY.
YOU AND YOUR RED HAT FRIENDS ONLY MEET ONCE A MONTH OR SO, RIGHT?
RIGHT.
SO WHY IS IT YOU HAD TO GO OUT AND BUY A WHOLE CLOSETFUL OF PURPLE OUTFITS AND RED HATS?
IT'S QUESTIONS LIKE THAT THAT KEEP US FROM ALLOWING MEN TO JOIN OUR GROUP.

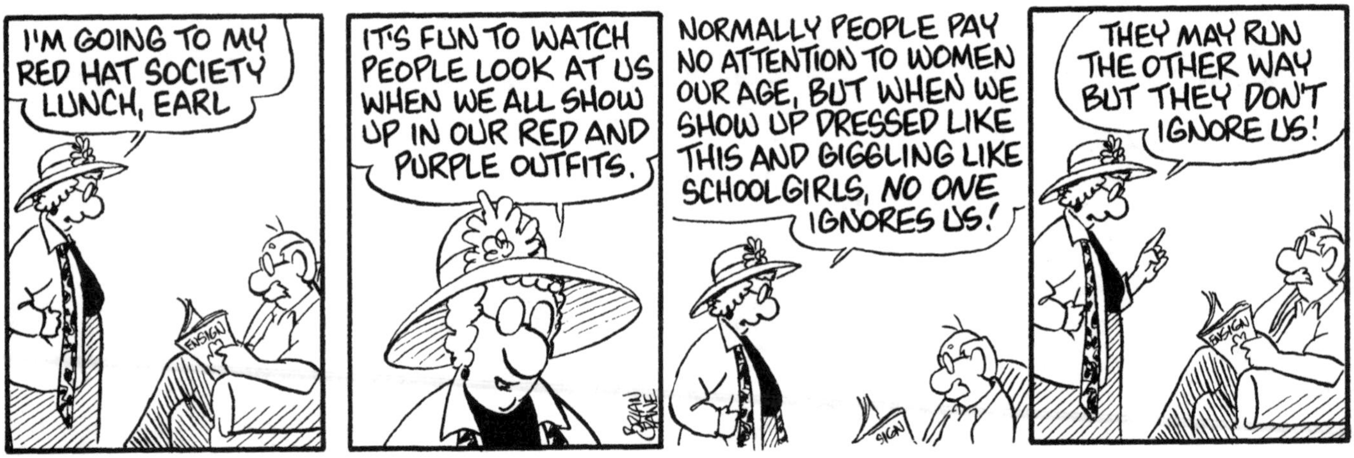
I'M GOING TO MY RED HAT SOCIETY LUNCH, EARL
IT'S FUN TO WATCH PEOPLE LOOK AT US WHEN WE ALL SHOW UP IN OUR RED AND PURPLE OUTFITS.
NORMALLY PEOPLE PAY NO ATTENTION TO WOMEN OUR AGE, BUT WHEN WE SHOW UP DRESSED LIKE THIS AND GIGGLING LIKE SCHOOLGIRLS, NO ONE IGNORES US!
THEY MAY RUN THE OTHER WAY BUT THEY DON'T IGNORE US!

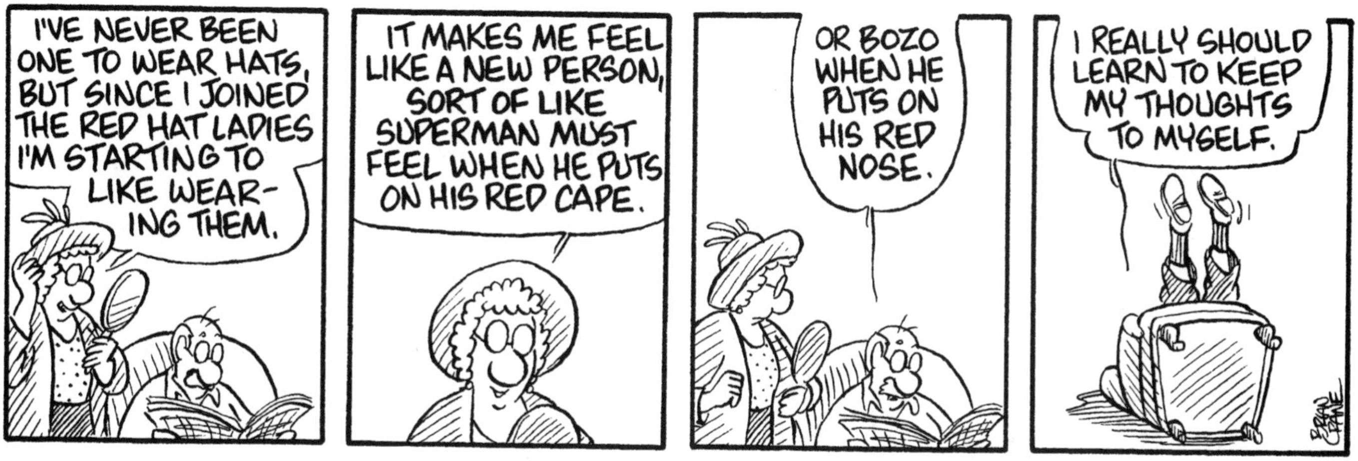
I'VE NEVER BEEN ONE TO WEAR HATS, BUT SINCE I JOINED THE RED HAT LADIES I'M STARTING TO LIKE WEARING THEM.
IT MAKES ME FEEL LIKE A NEW PERSON, SORT OF LIKE SUPERMAN MUST FEEL WHEN HE PUTS ON HIS RED CAPE.
OR BOZO WHEN HE PUTS ON HIS RED NOSE.
I REALLY SHOULD LEARN TO KEEP MY THOUGHTS TO MYSELF.

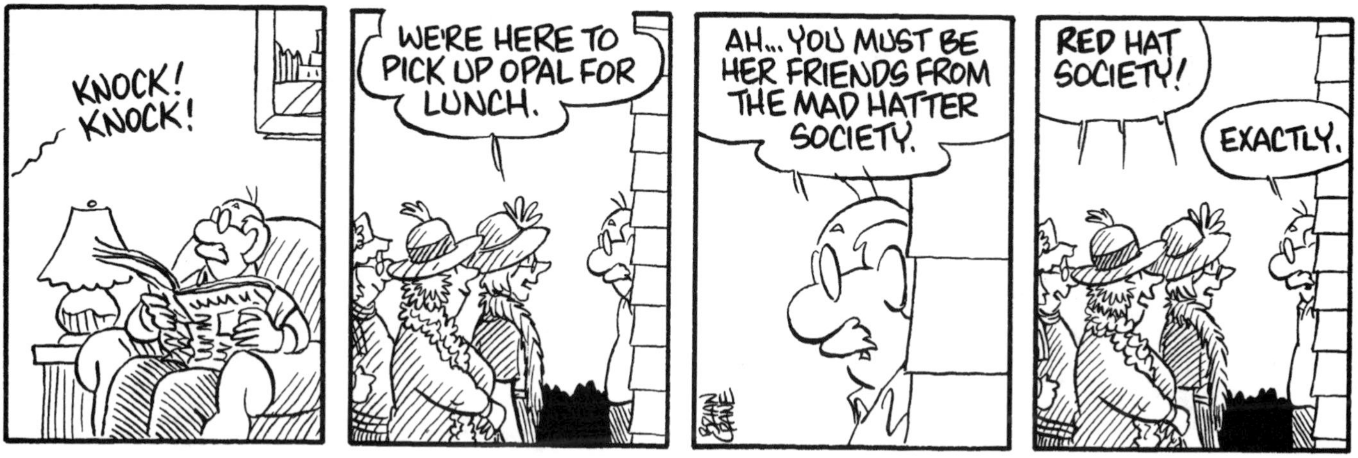
KNOCK! KNOCK!
WE'RE HERE TO PICK UP OPAL FOR LUNCH.
AH... YOU MUST BE HER FRIENDS FROM THE MAD HATTER SOCIETY.
RED HAT SOCIETY!
EXACTLY.

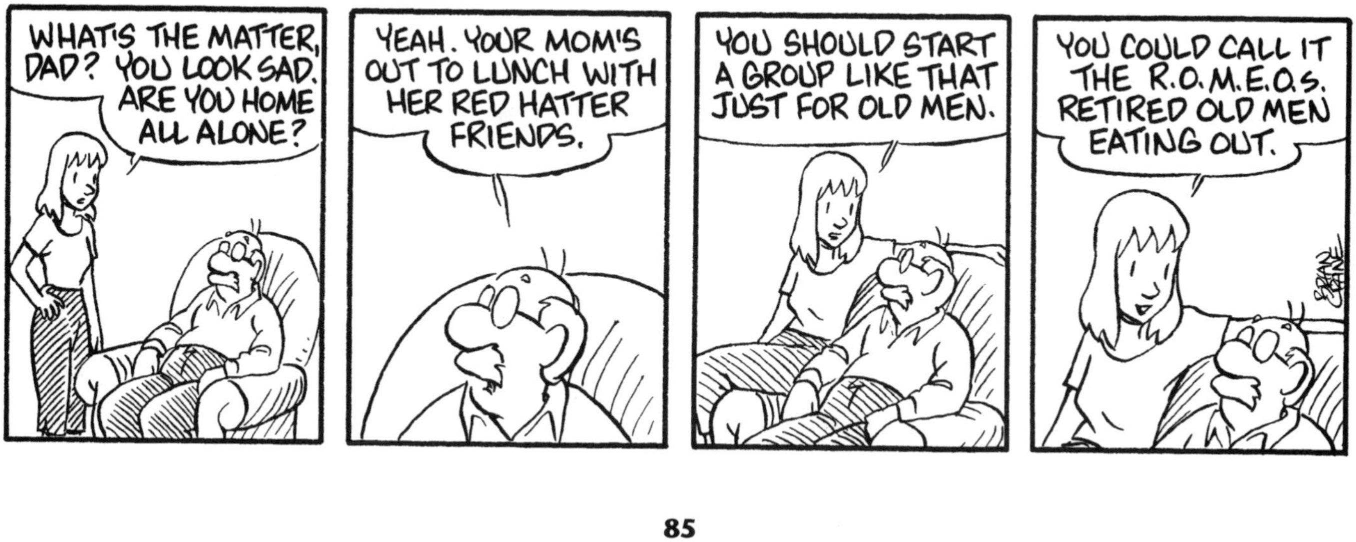
WHAT'S THE MATTER, DAD? YOU LOOK SAD. ARE YOU HOME ALL ALONE?
YEAH. YOUR MOM'S OUT TO LUNCH WITH HER RED HATTER FRIENDS.
YOU SHOULD START A GROUP LIKE THAT JUST FOR OLD MEN.
YOU COULD CALL IT THE R.O.M.E.O.S. RETIRED OLD MEN EATING OUT.

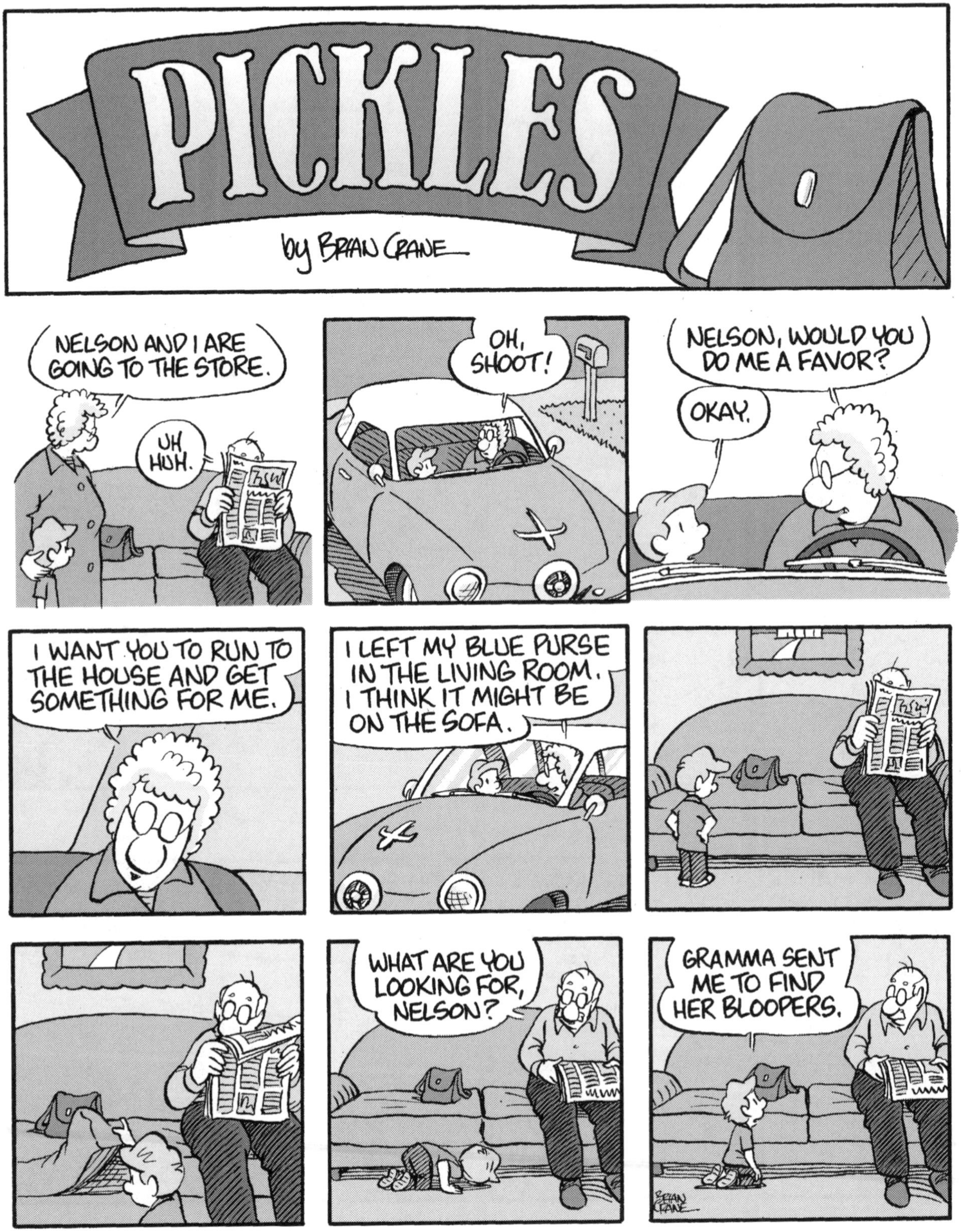
PICKLES
by BRIAN CRANE
NELSON AND I ARE GOING TO THE STORE.
UH HUH.
OH, SHOOT!
NELSON, WOULD YOU DO ME A FAVOR?
OKAY.
I WANT YOU TO RUN TO THE HOUSE AND GET SOMETHING FOR ME.
I LEFT MY BLUE PURSE IN THE LIVING ROOM. I THINK IT MIGHT BE ON THE SOFA.
WHAT ARE YOU LOOKING FOR, NELSON?
GRAMMA SENT ME TO FIND HER BLOOPERS.
BRIAN CRANE

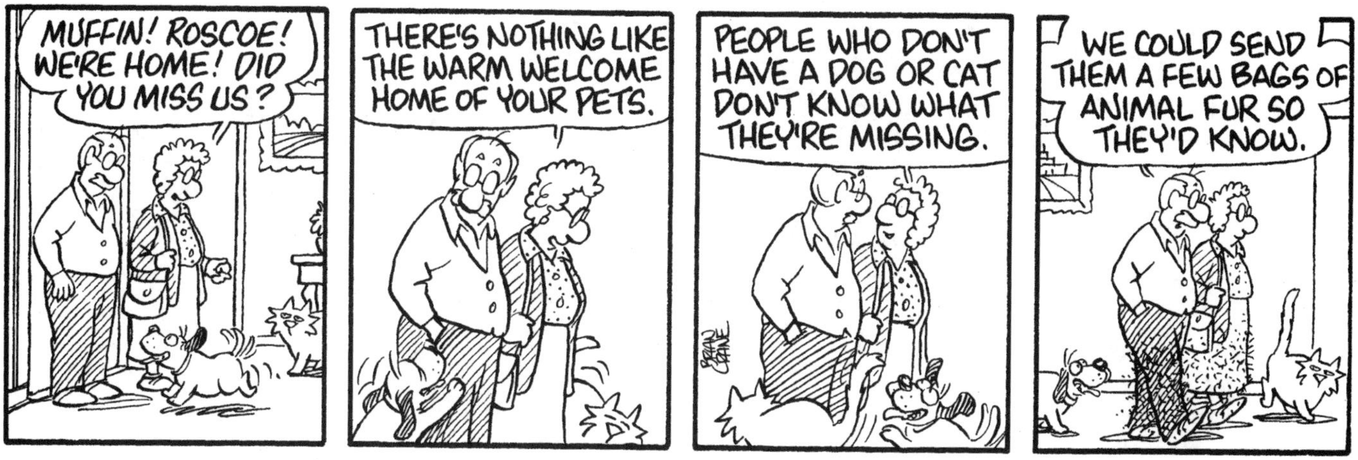
MUFFIN! ROSCOE! WE'RE HOME! DID YOU MISS US?
THERE'S NOTHING LIKE THE WARM WELCOME HOME OF YOUR PETS.
PEOPLE WHO DON'T HAVE A DOG OR CAT DON'T KNOW WHAT THEY'RE MISSING.
WE COULD SEND THEM A FEW BAGS OF ANIMAL FUR SO THEY'D KNOW.

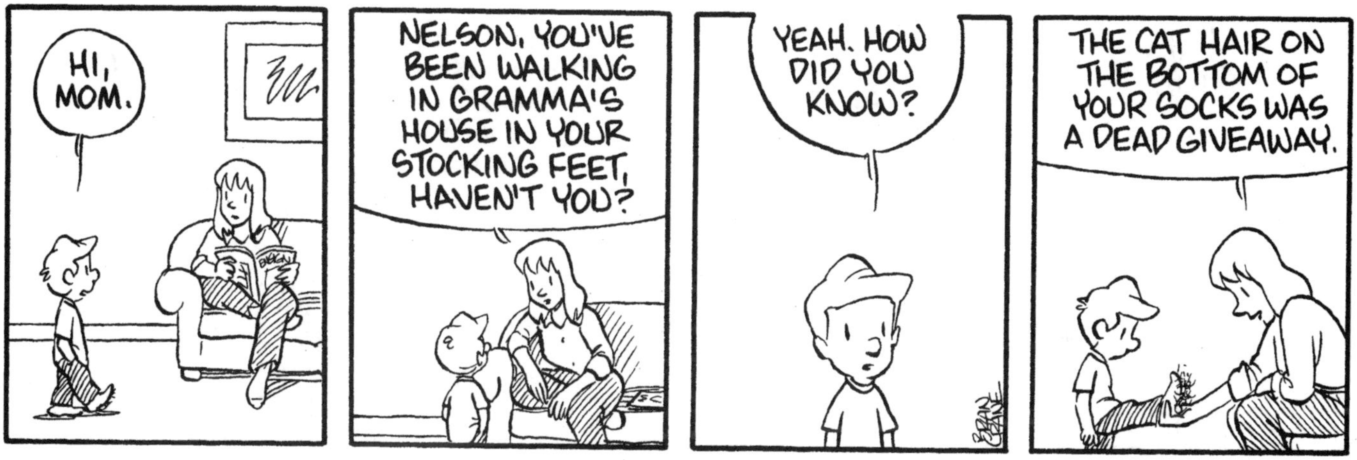
HI, MOM.
NELSON, YOU'VE BEEN WALKING IN GRAMMA'S HOUSE IN YOUR STOCKING FEET, HAVEN'T YOU?
YEAH. HOW DID YOU KNOW?
THE CAT HAIR ON THE BOTTOM OF YOUR SOCKS WAS A DEAD GIVEAWAY.

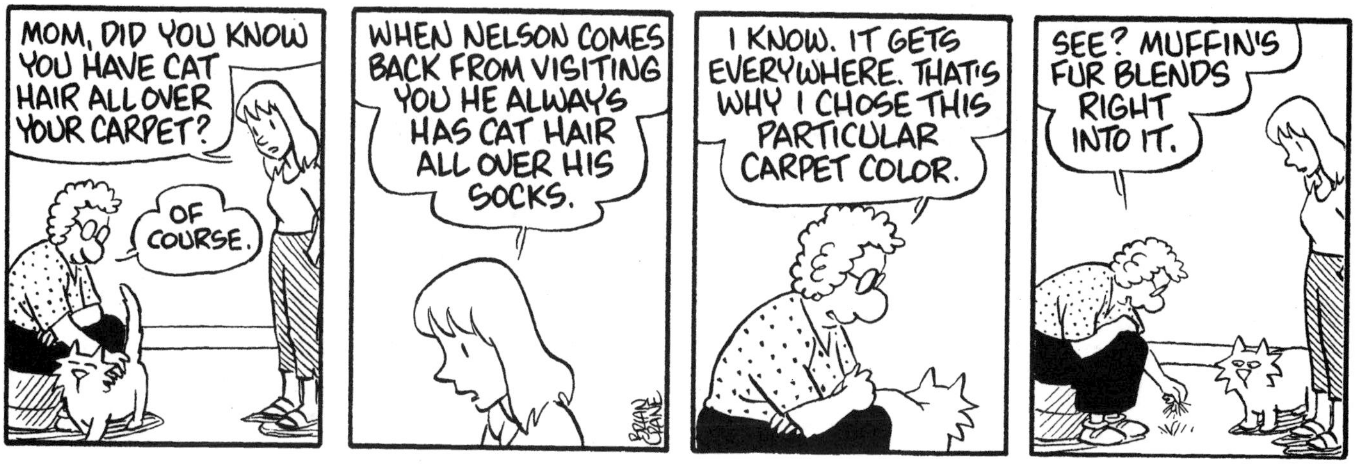
MOM, DID YOU KNOW YOU HAVE CAT HAIR ALL OVER YOUR CARPET?
OF COURSE.
WHEN NELSON COMES BACK FROM VISITING YOU HE ALWAYS HAS CAT HAIR ALL OVER HIS SOCKS.
I KNOW. IT GETS EVERYWHERE. THAT'S WHY I CHOSE THIS PARTICULAR CARPET COLOR.
SEE? MUFFIN'S FUR BLENDS RIGHT INTO IT.

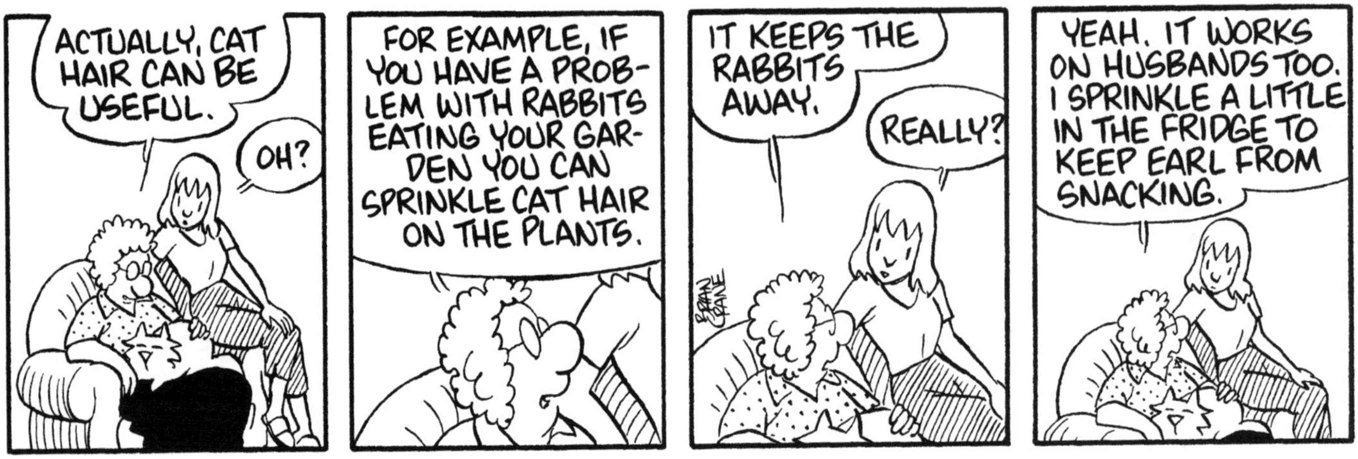
ACTUALLY, CAT HAIR CAN BE USEFUL.
OH?
FOR EXAMPLE, IF YOU HAVE A PROBLEM WITH RABBITS EATING YOUR GARDEN YOU CAN SPRINKLE CAT HAIR ON THE PLANTS.
IT KEEPS THE RABBITS AWAY.
REALLY?
YEAH. IT WORKS ON HUSBANDS TOO. I SPRINKLE A LITTLE IN THE FRIDGE TO KEEP EARL FROM SNACKING.

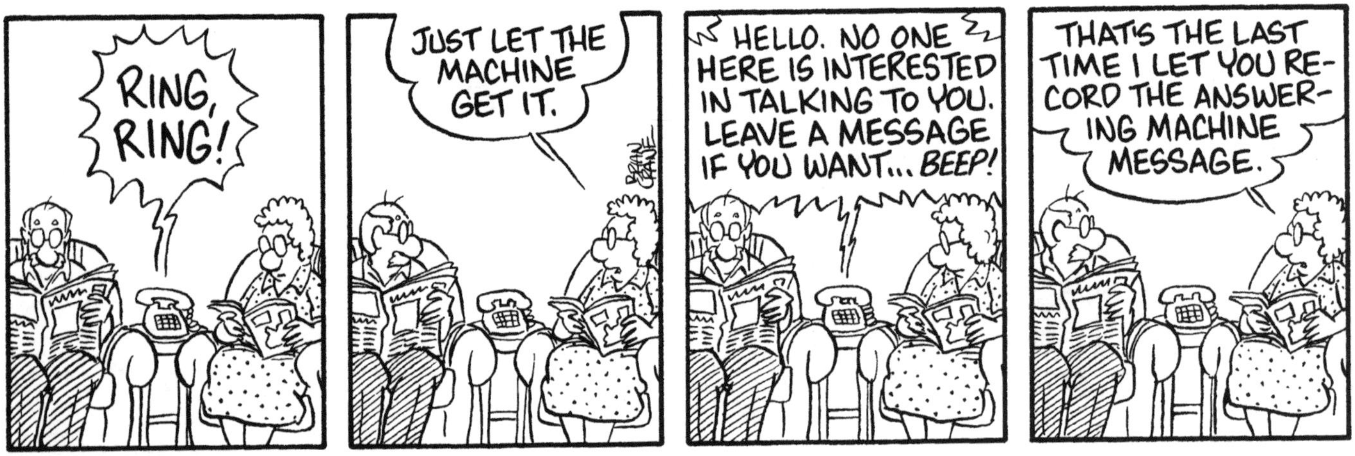
RING, RING!
JUST LET THE MACHINE GET IT.
HELLO. NO ONE HERE IS INTERESTED IN TALKING TO YOU. LEAVE A MESSAGE IF YOU WANT... *BEEP!*
THAT'S THE LAST TIME I LET YOU RECORD THE ANSWERING MACHINE MESSAGE.

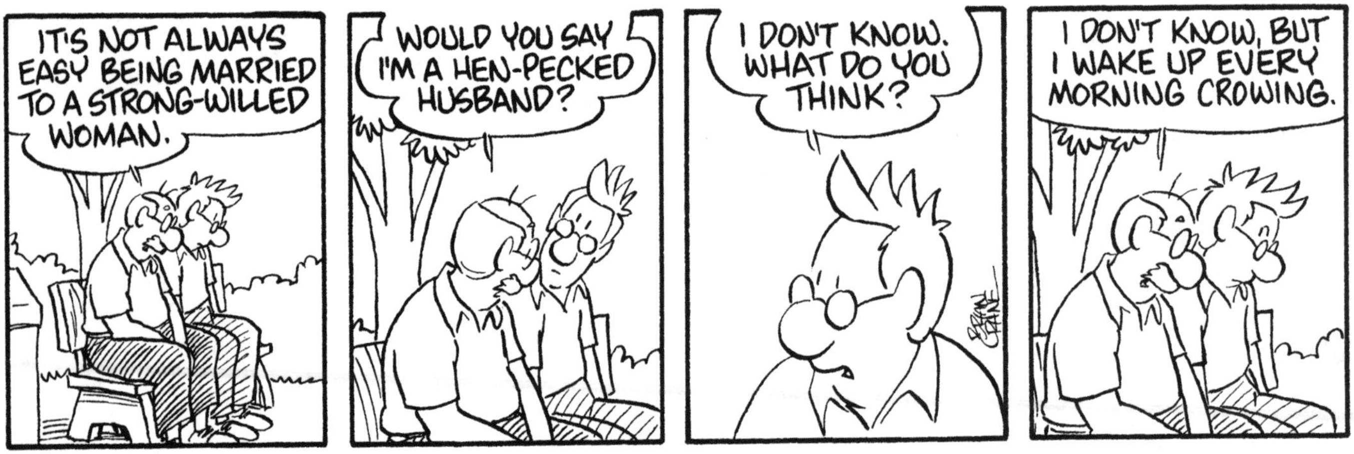
IT'S NOT ALWAYS EASY BEING MARRIED TO A STRONG-WILLED WOMAN.
WOULD YOU SAY I'M A HEN-PECKED HUSBAND?
I DON'T KNOW. WHAT DO YOU THINK?
I DON'T KNOW, BUT I WAKE UP EVERY MORNING CROWING.

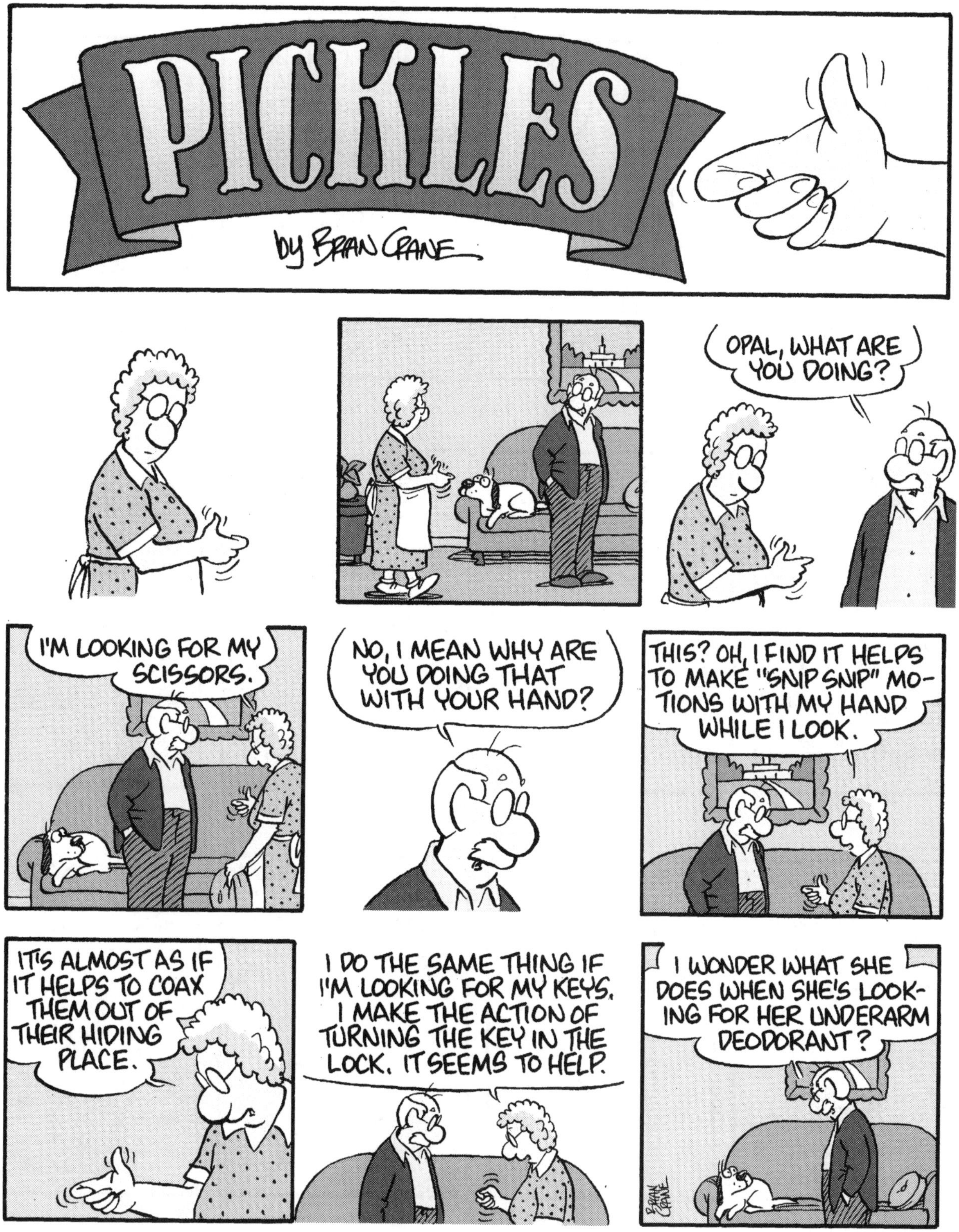

PICKLES
by BRIAN CRANE
OPAL, WHAT ARE YOU DOING?
I'M LOOKING FOR MY SCISSORS.
NO, I MEAN WHY ARE YOU DOING THAT WITH YOUR HAND?
THIS? OH, I FIND IT HELPS TO MAKE "SNIP SNIP" MOTIONS WITH MY HAND WHILE I LOOK.
IT'S ALMOST AS IF IT HELPS TO COAX THEM OUT OF THEIR HIDING PLACE.
I DO THE SAME THING IF I'M LOOKING FOR MY KEYS. I MAKE THE ACTION OF TURNING THE KEY IN THE LOCK. IT SEEMS TO HELP.
I WONDER WHAT SHE DOES WHEN SHE'S LOOKING FOR HER UNDERARM DEODORANT?
BRIAN CRANE

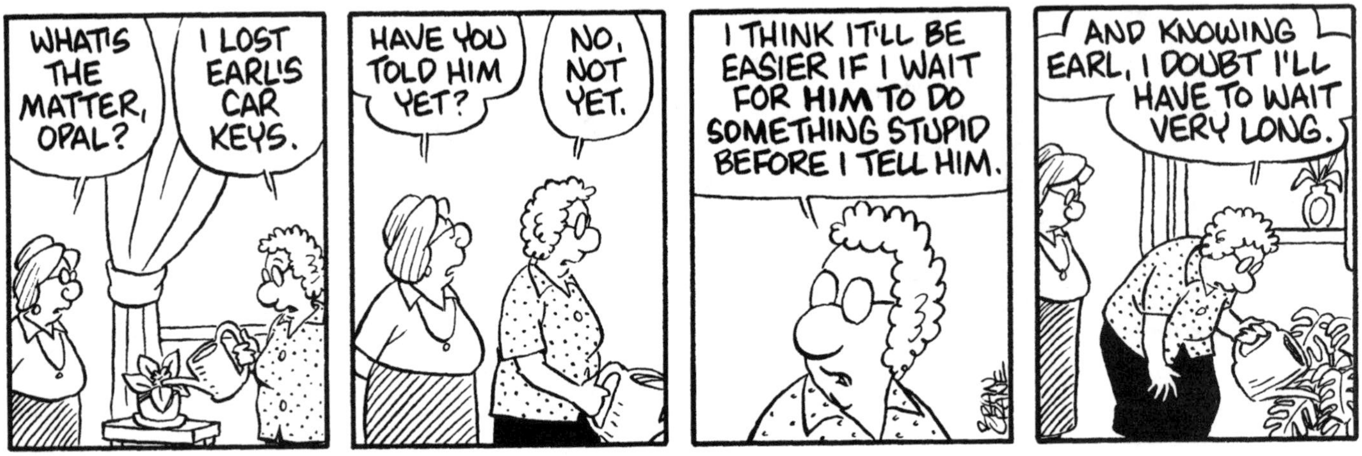
WHAT'S THE MATTER, OPAL?
I LOST EARL'S CAR KEYS.
HAVE YOU TOLD HIM YET?
NO, NOT YET.
I THINK IT'LL BE EASIER IF I WAIT FOR **HIM** TO DO SOMETHING STUPID BEFORE I TELL HIM.
AND KNOWING EARL, I DOUBT I'LL HAVE TO WAIT VERY LONG.

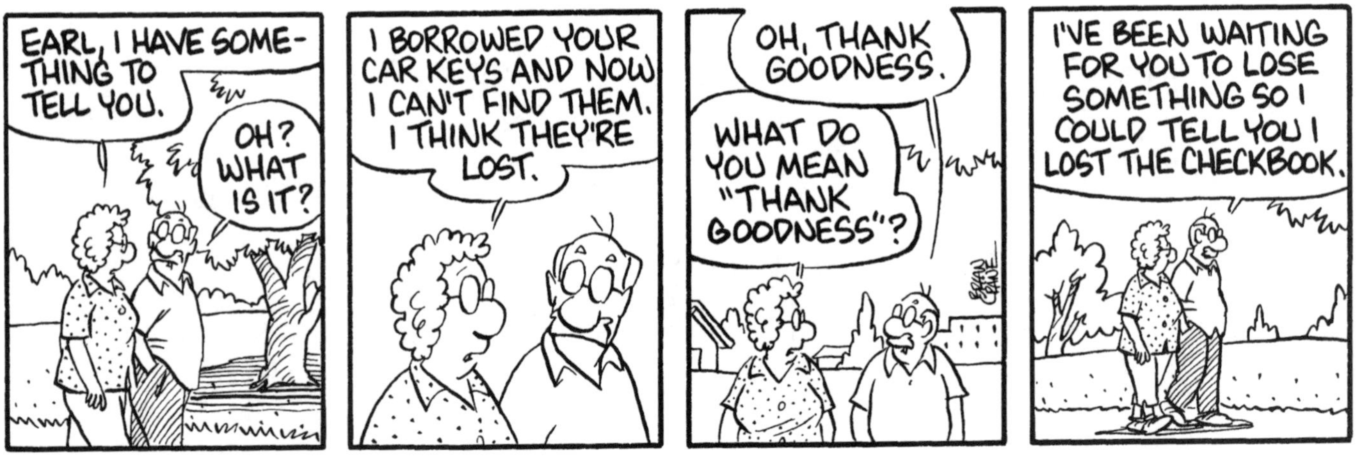
EARL, I HAVE SOMETHING TO TELL YOU.
OH? WHAT IS IT?
I BORROWED YOUR CAR KEYS AND NOW I CAN'T FIND THEM. I THINK THEY'RE LOST.
OH, THANK GOODNESS.
WHAT DO YOU MEAN "THANK GOODNESS"?
I'VE BEEN WAITING FOR YOU TO LOSE SOMETHING SO I COULD TELL YOU I LOST THE CHECKBOOK.

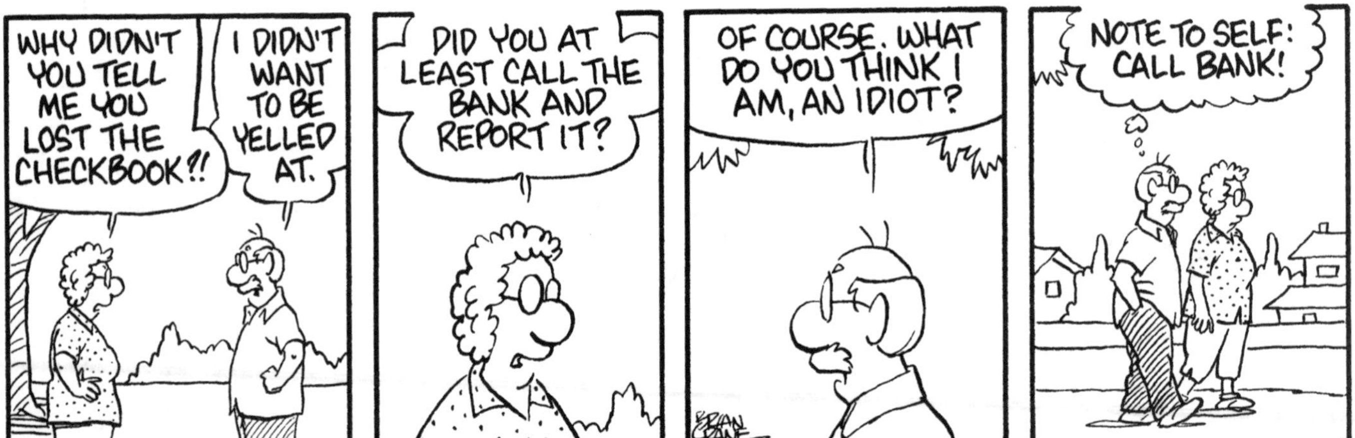
WHY DIDN'T YOU TELL ME YOU LOST THE CHECKBOOK?!
I DIDN'T WANT TO BE YELLED AT.
DID YOU AT LEAST CALL THE BANK AND REPORT IT?
OF COURSE. WHAT DO YOU THINK I AM, AN IDIOT?
NOTE TO SELF: CALL BANK!

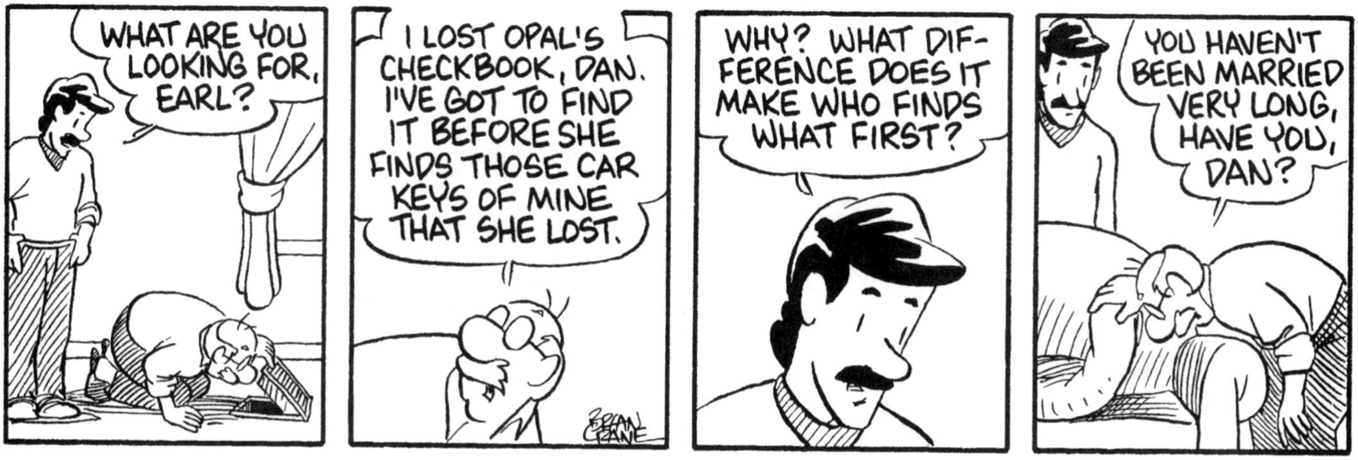
WHAT ARE YOU LOOKING FOR, EARL?
I LOST OPAL'S CHECKBOOK, DAN. I'VE GOT TO FIND IT BEFORE SHE FINDS THOSE CAR KEYS OF MINE THAT SHE LOST.
WHY? WHAT DIFFERENCE DOES IT MAKE WHO FINDS WHAT FIRST?
YOU HAVEN'T BEEN MARRIED VERY LONG, HAVE YOU, DAN?

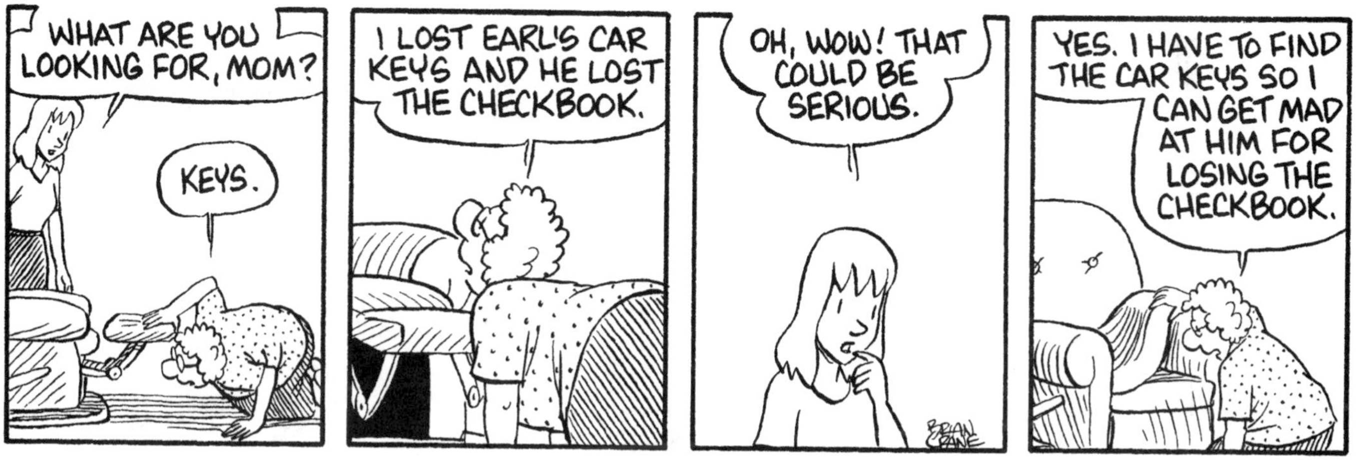
WHAT ARE YOU LOOKING FOR, MOM?
KEYS.
I LOST EARL'S CAR KEYS AND HE LOST THE CHECKBOOK.
OH, WOW! THAT COULD BE SERIOUS.
YES. I HAVE TO FIND THE CAR KEYS SO I CAN GET MAD AT HIM FOR LOSING THE CHECKBOOK.

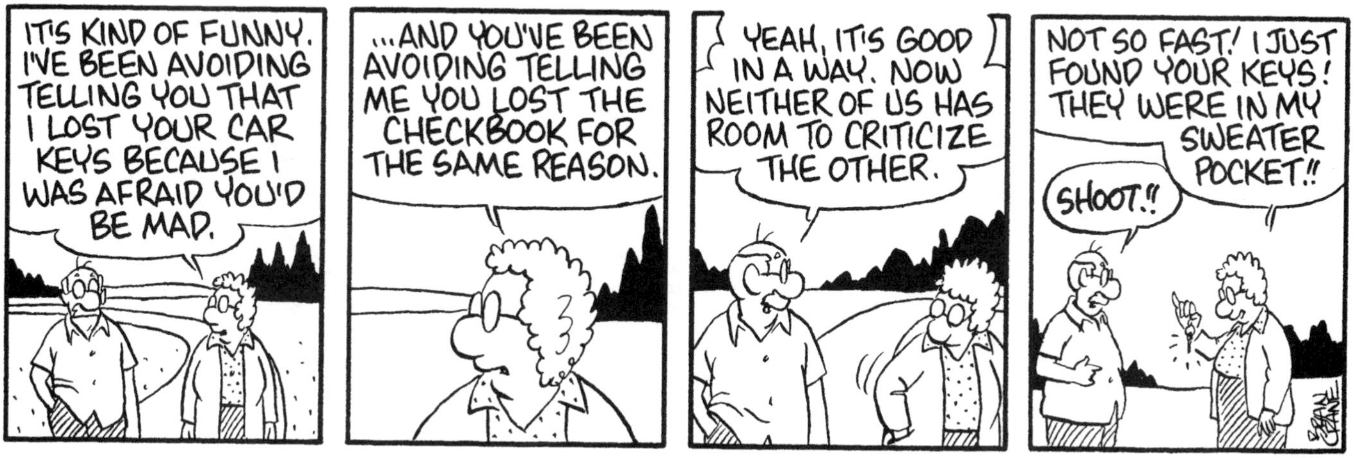
IT'S KIND OF FUNNY. I'VE BEEN AVOIDING TELLING YOU THAT I LOST YOUR CAR KEYS BECAUSE I WAS AFRAID YOU'D BE MAD.
...AND YOU'VE BEEN AVOIDING TELLING ME YOU LOST THE CHECKBOOK FOR THE SAME REASON.
YEAH, IT'S GOOD IN A WAY. NOW NEITHER OF US HAS ROOM TO CRITICIZE THE OTHER.
NOT SO FAST! I JUST FOUND YOUR KEYS! THEY WERE IN MY SWEATER POCKET!!
SHOOT!!

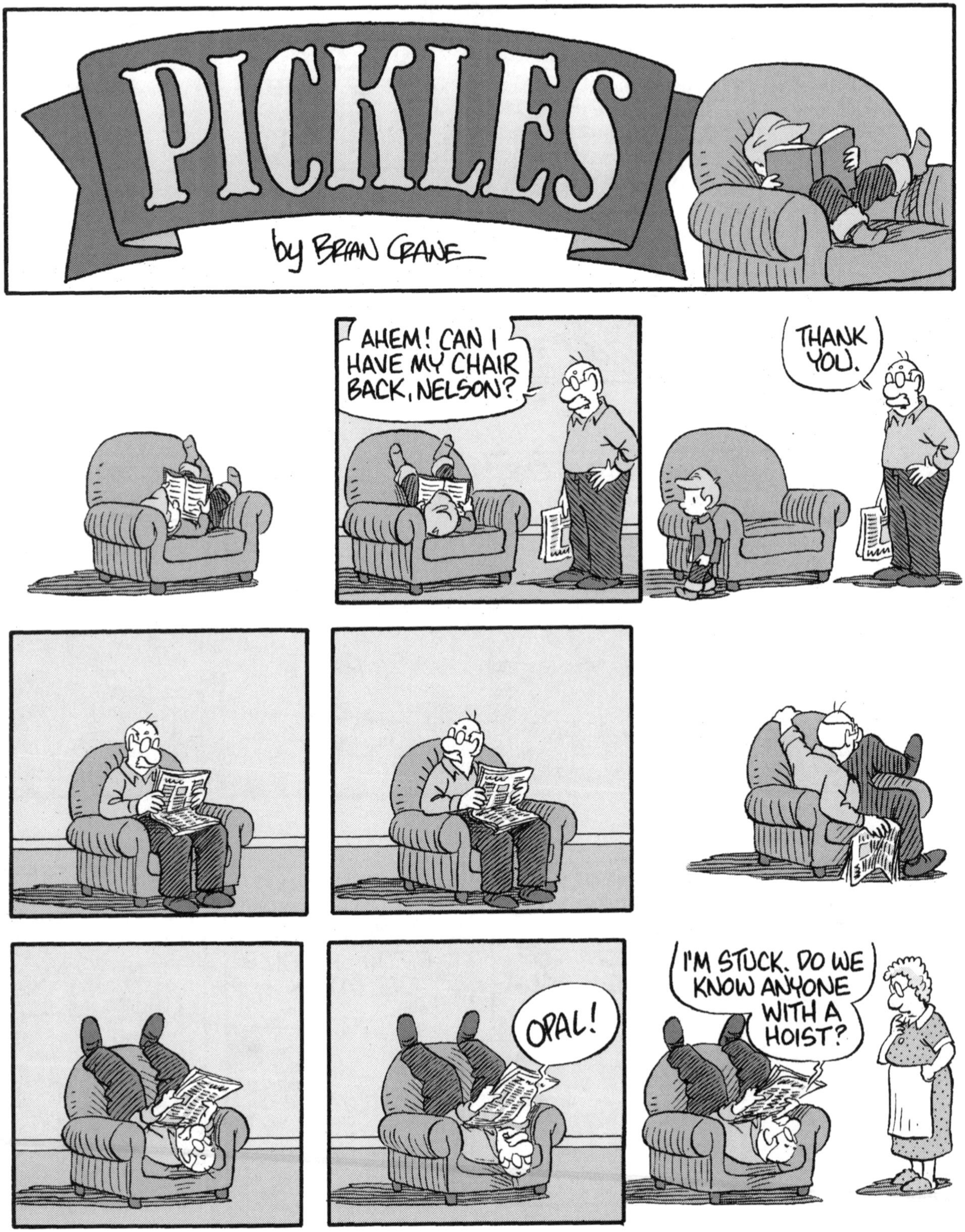
PICKLES
by BRIAN CRANE
AHEM! CAN I HAVE MY CHAIR BACK, NELSON?
THANK YOU.
OPAL!
I'M STUCK. DO WE KNOW ANYONE WITH A HOIST?

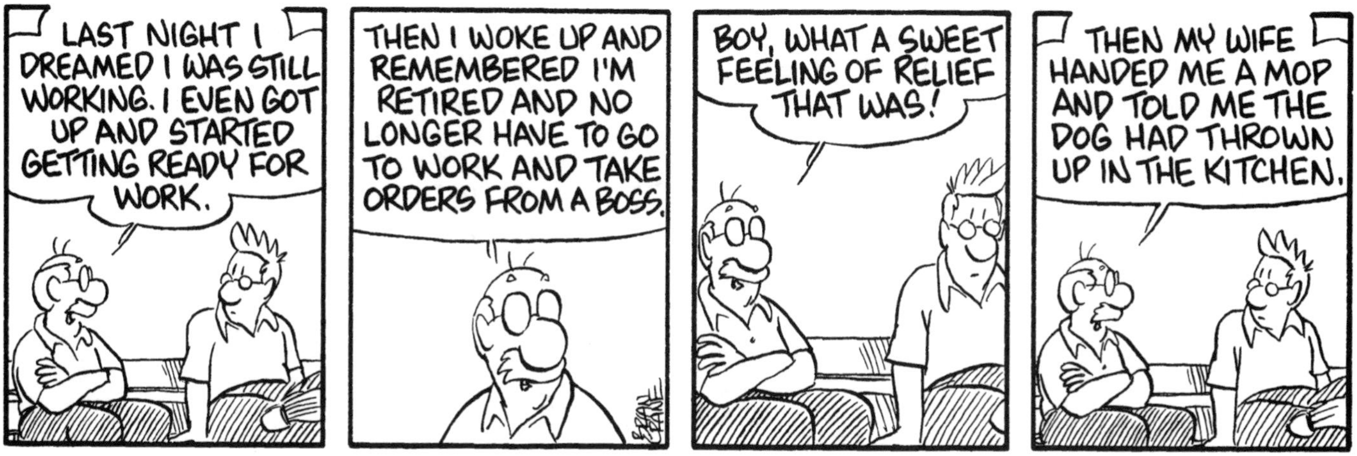
LAST NIGHT I DREAMED I WAS STILL WORKING. I EVEN GOT UP AND STARTED GETTING READY FOR WORK.
THEN I WOKE UP AND REMEMBERED I'M RETIRED AND NO LONGER HAVE TO GO TO WORK AND TAKE ORDERS FROM A BOSS.
BOY, WHAT A SWEET FEELING OF RELIEF THAT WAS!
THEN MY WIFE HANDED ME A MOP AND TOLD ME THE DOG HAD THROWN UP IN THE KITCHEN.

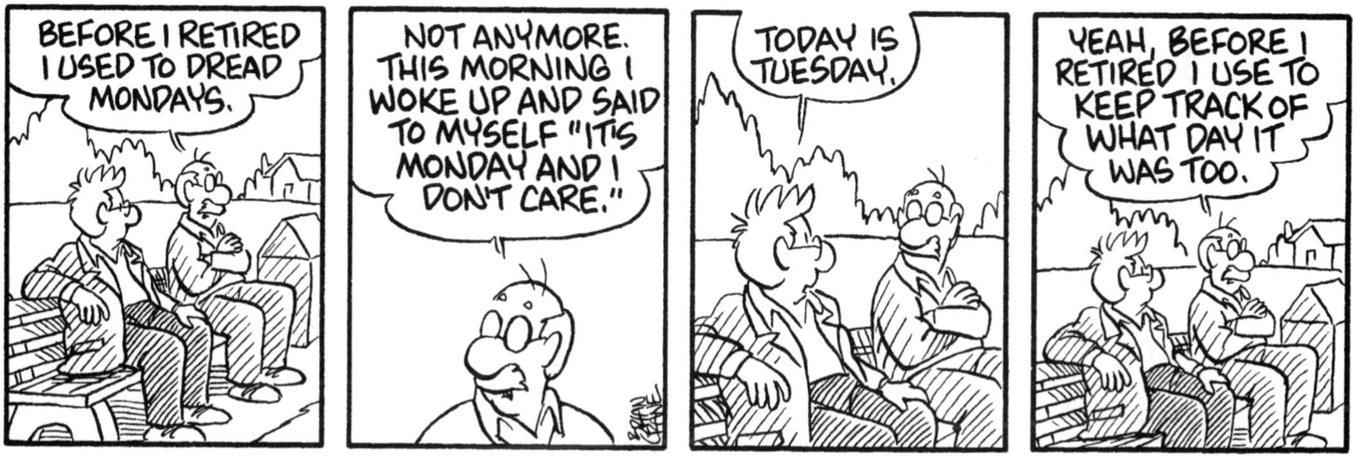
BEFORE I RETIRED I USED TO DREAD MONDAYS.
NOT ANYMORE. THIS MORNING I WOKE UP AND SAID TO MYSELF "IT'S MONDAY AND I DON'T CARE."
TODAY IS TUESDAY.
YEAH, BEFORE I RETIRED I USE TO KEEP TRACK OF WHAT DAY IT WAS TOO.

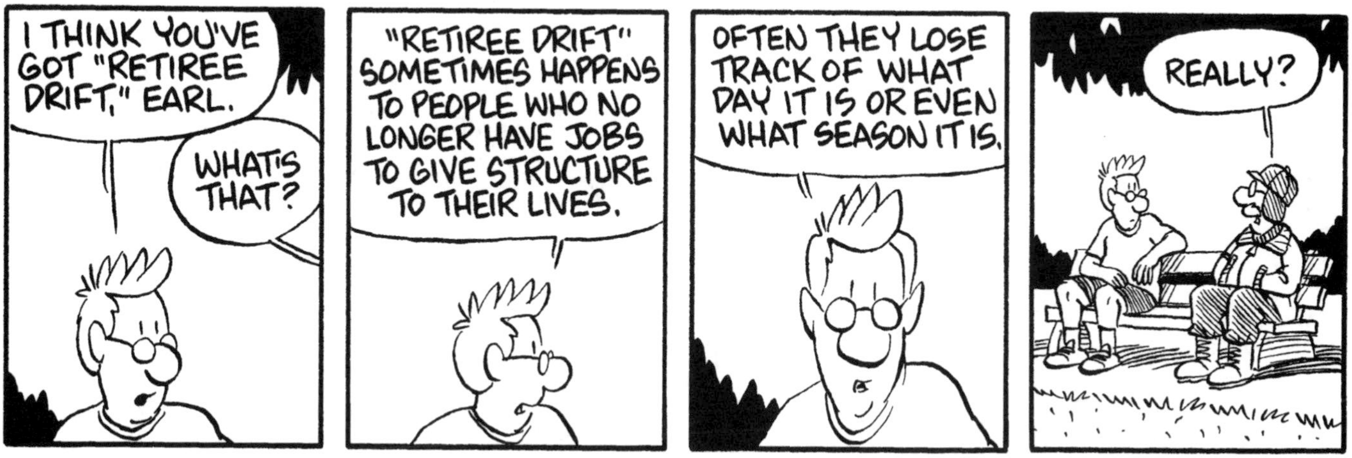
I THINK YOU'VE GOT "RETIREE DRIFT," EARL.
WHAT'S THAT?
"RETIREE DRIFT" SOMETIMES HAPPENS TO PEOPLE WHO NO LONGER HAVE JOBS TO GIVE STRUCTURE TO THEIR LIVES.
OFTEN THEY LOSE TRACK OF WHAT DAY IT IS OR EVEN WHAT SEASON IT IS.
REALLY?

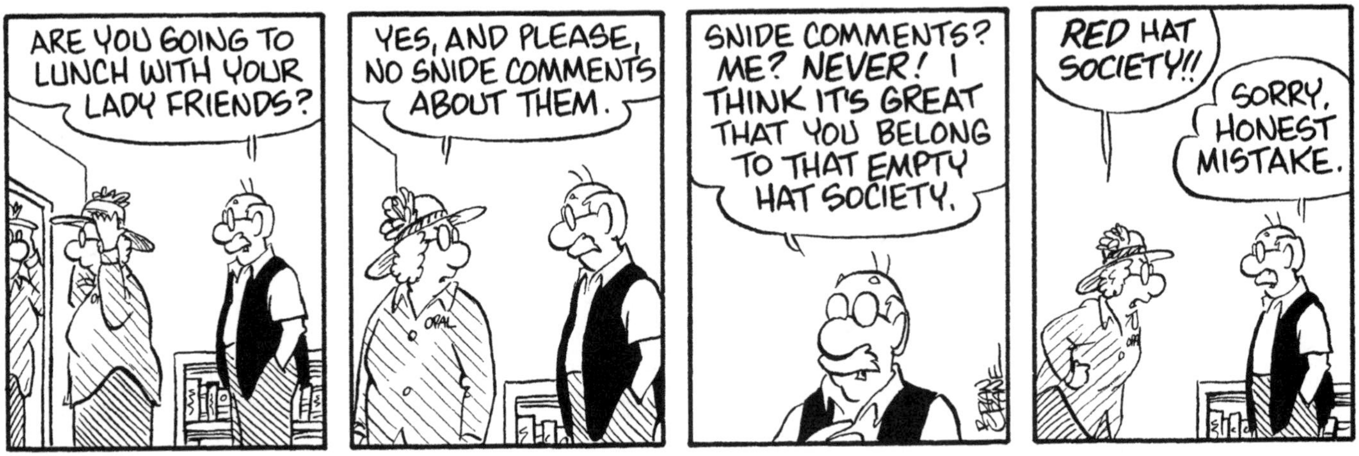
ARE YOU GOING TO LUNCH WITH YOUR LADY FRIENDS?
YES, AND PLEASE, NO SNIDE COMMENTS ABOUT THEM.
OPAL
SNIDE COMMENTS? ME? NEVER! I THINK IT'S GREAT THAT YOU BELONG TO THAT EMPTY HAT SOCIETY.
RED HAT SOCIETY!!
SORRY, HONEST MISTAKE.

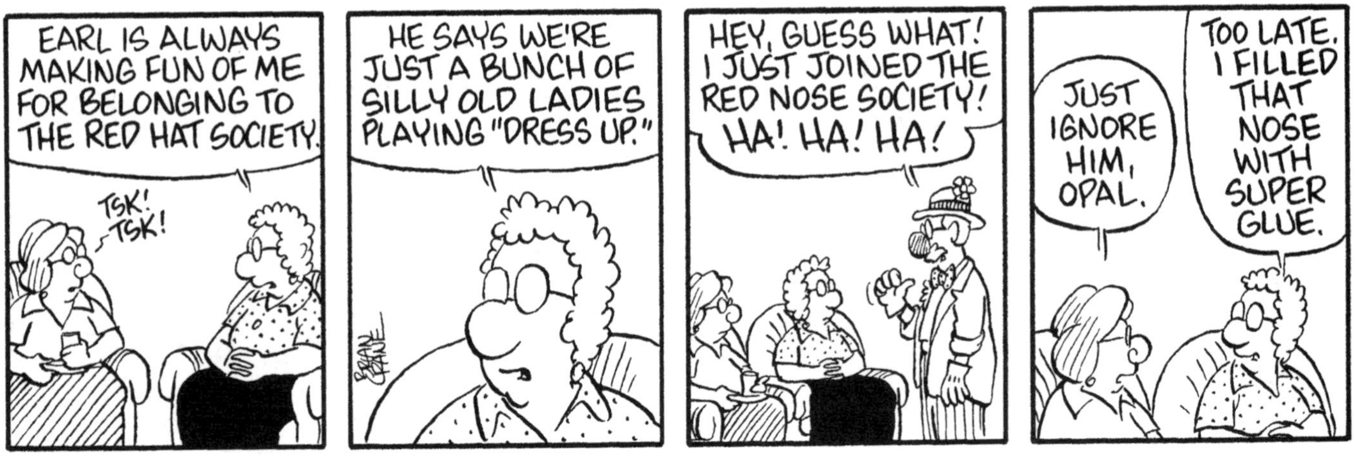
EARL IS ALWAYS MAKING FUN OF ME FOR BELONGING TO THE RED HAT SOCIETY.
TSK! TSK!
HE SAYS WE'RE JUST A BUNCH OF SILLY OLD LADIES PLAYING "DRESS UP."
HEY, GUESS WHAT! I JUST JOINED THE RED NOSE SOCIETY! HA! HA! HA!
JUST IGNORE HIM, OPAL.
TOO LATE. I FILLED THAT NOSE WITH SUPER GLUE.

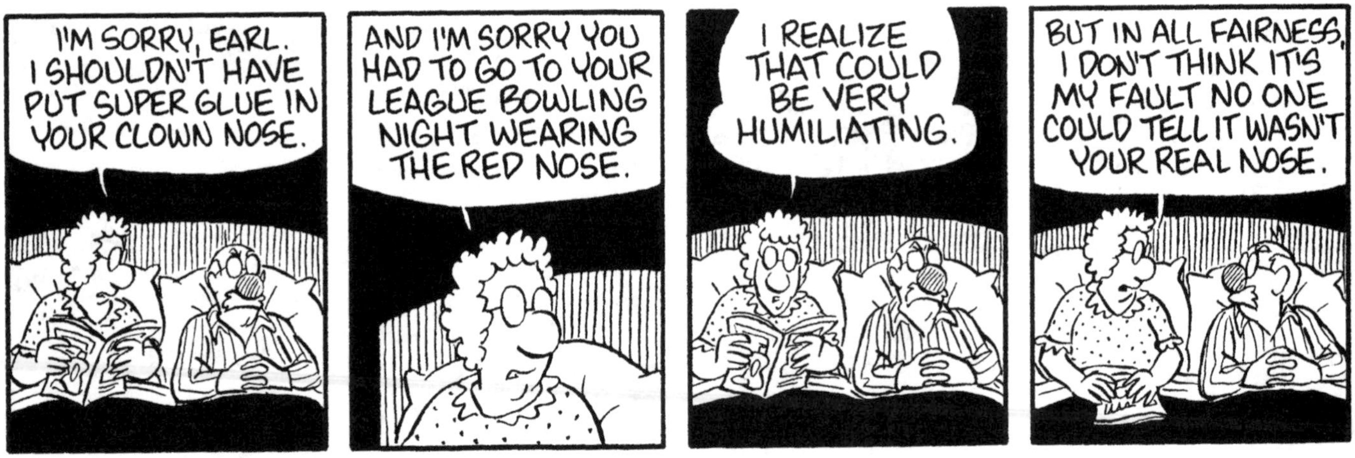
I'M SORRY, EARL. I SHOULDN'T HAVE PUT SUPER GLUE IN YOUR CLOWN NOSE.
AND I'M SORRY YOU HAD TO GO TO YOUR LEAGUE BOWLING NIGHT WEARING THE RED NOSE.
I REALIZE THAT COULD BE VERY HUMILIATING.
BUT IN ALL FAIRNESS, I DON'T THINK IT'S MY FAULT NO ONE COULD TELL IT WASN'T YOUR REAL NOSE.

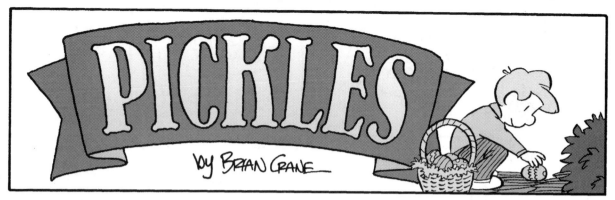

# PICKLES
### by Brian Crane

WHAT HAVE YOU GOT THERE, SON?

MY EASTER BASKET.

OH, HAVE YOU BEEN ON AN EASTER EGG HUNT?

YEAH!

AHH... SO THE EASTER BUNNY CAME AND LAID EGGS ALL OVER THE YARD. WHAT'RE YOU GOING TO DO WITH THEM?

EAT THEM!

WOW, REALLY? YOU'D EAT SOMETHING THAT CAME OUT OF A RABBIT? I HOPE YOU'RE AT LEAST GOING TO WASH THEM.

LOOK AT THE SIZE OF THESE EGGS! HARD TO BELIEVE THEY CAME OUT OF A LITTLE BUNNY, HUH? BOY, THAT MUST'VE HURT!

COME TO THINK OF IT, I THOUGHT I HEARD SOMETHING SCREAMING IN PAIN IN THE GARDEN THIS MORNING.

EARL, WHY DO YOU HAVE NELSON'S EASTER BASKET?

HE SAID HE DIDN'T WANT IT.

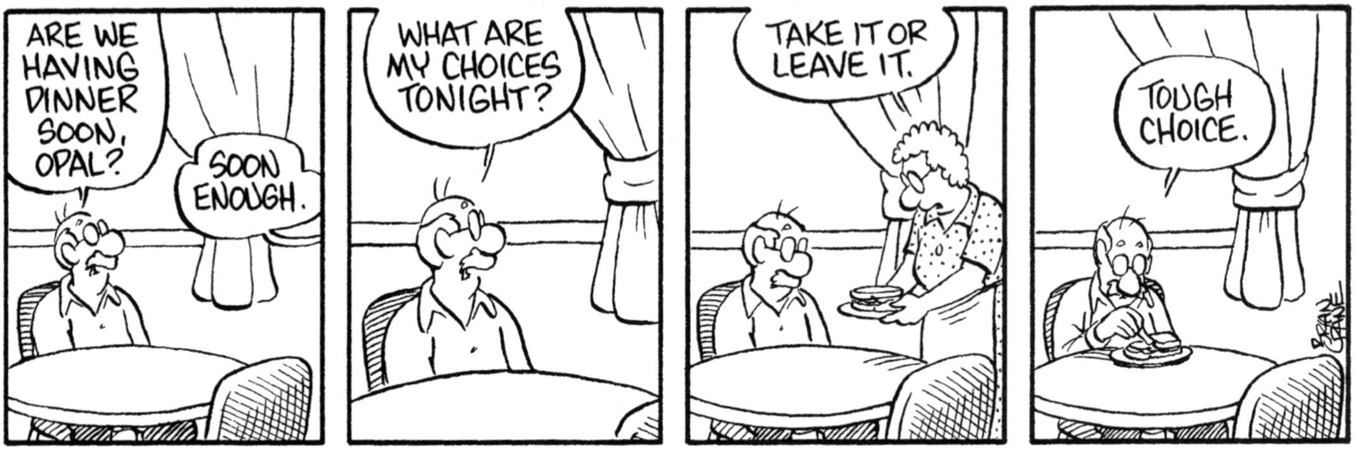
ARE WE HAVING DINNER SOON, OPAL?
SOON ENOUGH.
WHAT ARE MY CHOICES TONIGHT?
TAKE IT OR LEAVE IT.
TOUGH CHOICE.

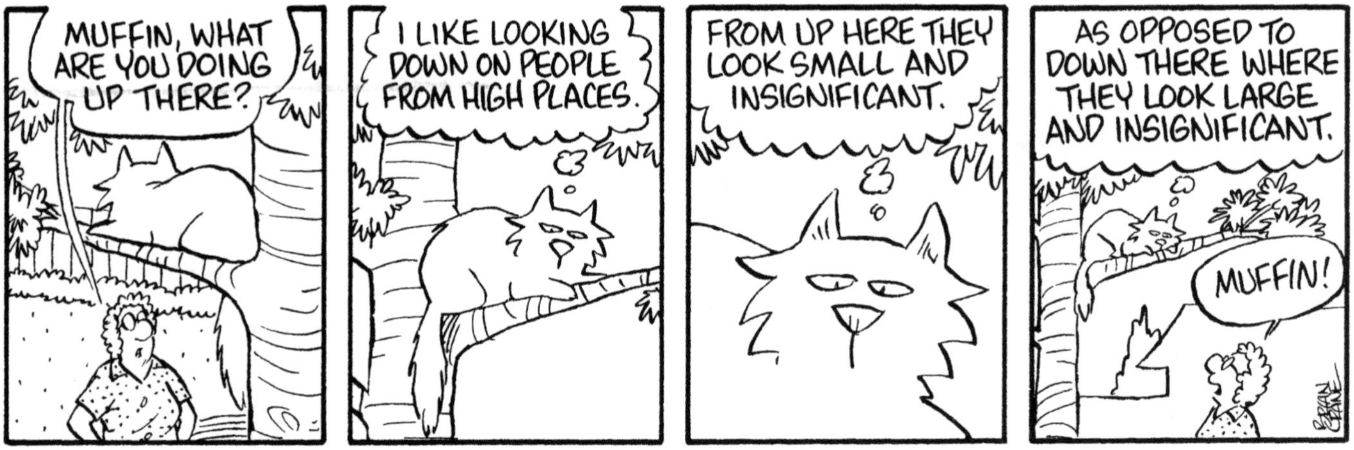
MUFFIN, WHAT ARE YOU DOING UP THERE?
I LIKE LOOKING DOWN ON PEOPLE FROM HIGH PLACES.
FROM UP HERE THEY LOOK SMALL AND INSIGNIFICANT.
AS OPPOSED TO DOWN THERE WHERE THEY LOOK LARGE AND INSIGNIFICANT.
MUFFIN!

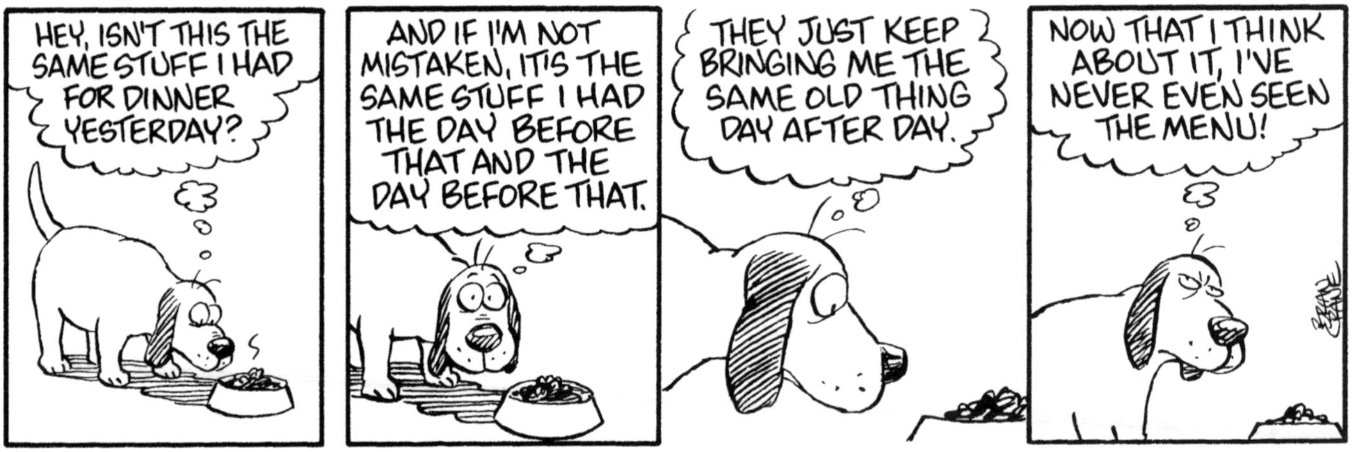
HEY, ISN'T THIS THE SAME STUFF I HAD FOR DINNER YESTERDAY?
AND IF I'M NOT MISTAKEN, IT'S THE SAME STUFF I HAD THE DAY BEFORE THAT AND THE DAY BEFORE THAT.
THEY JUST KEEP BRINGING ME THE SAME OLD THING DAY AFTER DAY.
NOW THAT I THINK ABOUT IT, I'VE NEVER EVEN SEEN THE MENU!

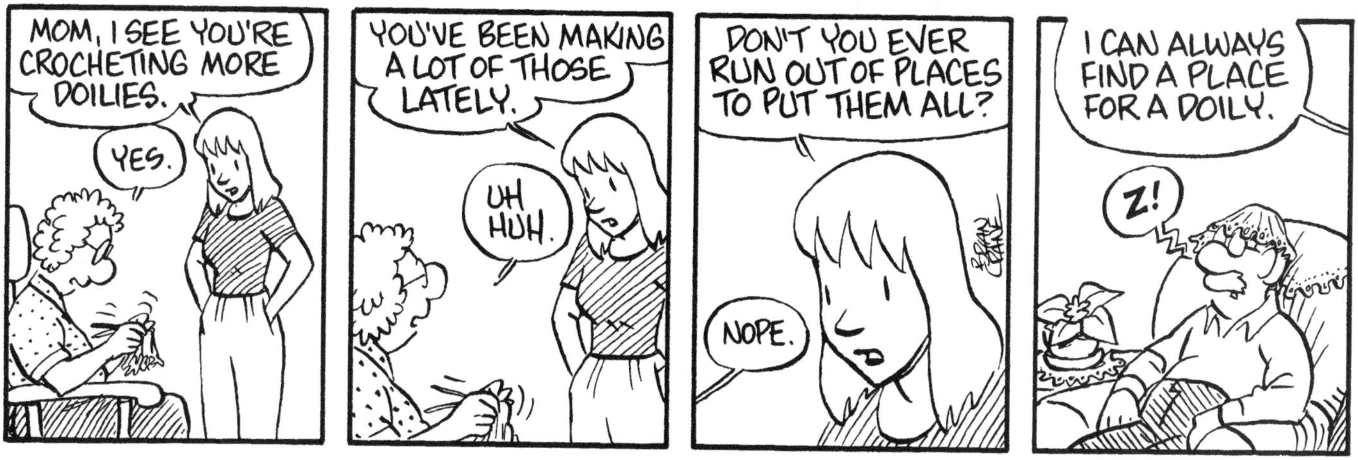
MOM, I SEE YOU'RE CROCHETING MORE DOILIES.
YES.
YOU'VE BEEN MAKING A LOT OF THOSE LATELY.
UH HUH.
DON'T YOU EVER RUN OUT OF PLACES TO PUT THEM ALL?
NOPE.
I CAN ALWAYS FIND A PLACE FOR A DOILY.
Z!

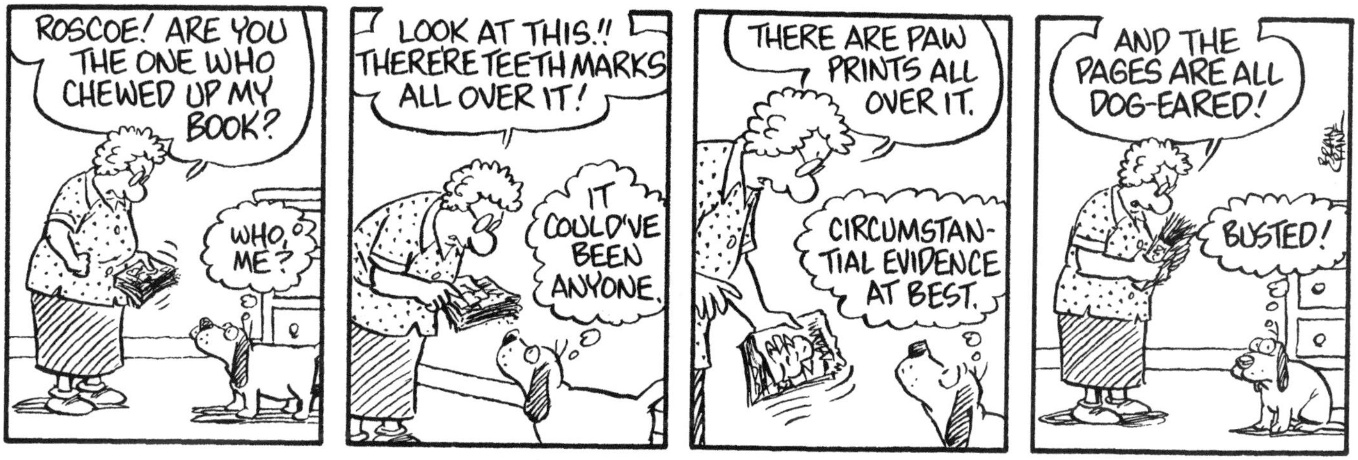
ROSCOE! ARE YOU THE ONE WHO CHEWED UP MY BOOK?
WHO, ME?
LOOK AT THIS!! THERE'RE TEETH MARKS ALL OVER IT!
IT COULD'VE BEEN ANYONE.
THERE ARE PAW PRINTS ALL OVER IT.
CIRCUMSTAN-TIAL EVIDENCE AT BEST.
AND THE PAGES ARE ALL DOG-EARED!
BUSTED!

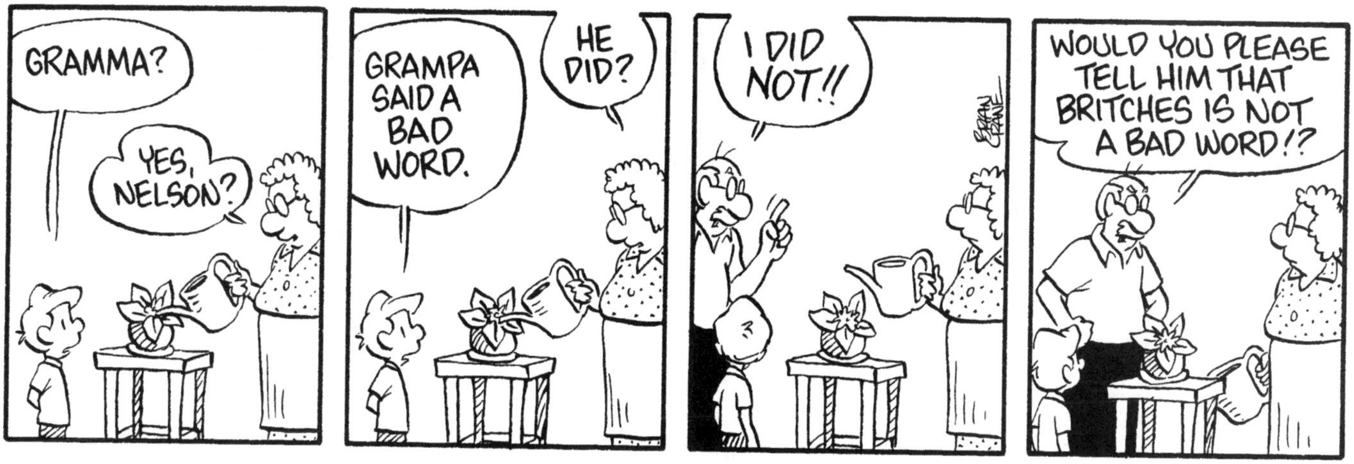
GRAMMA?
YES, NELSON?
GRAMPA SAID A BAD WORD.
HE DID?
I DID NOT!!
WOULD YOU PLEASE TELL HIM THAT BRITCHES IS NOT A BAD WORD!?

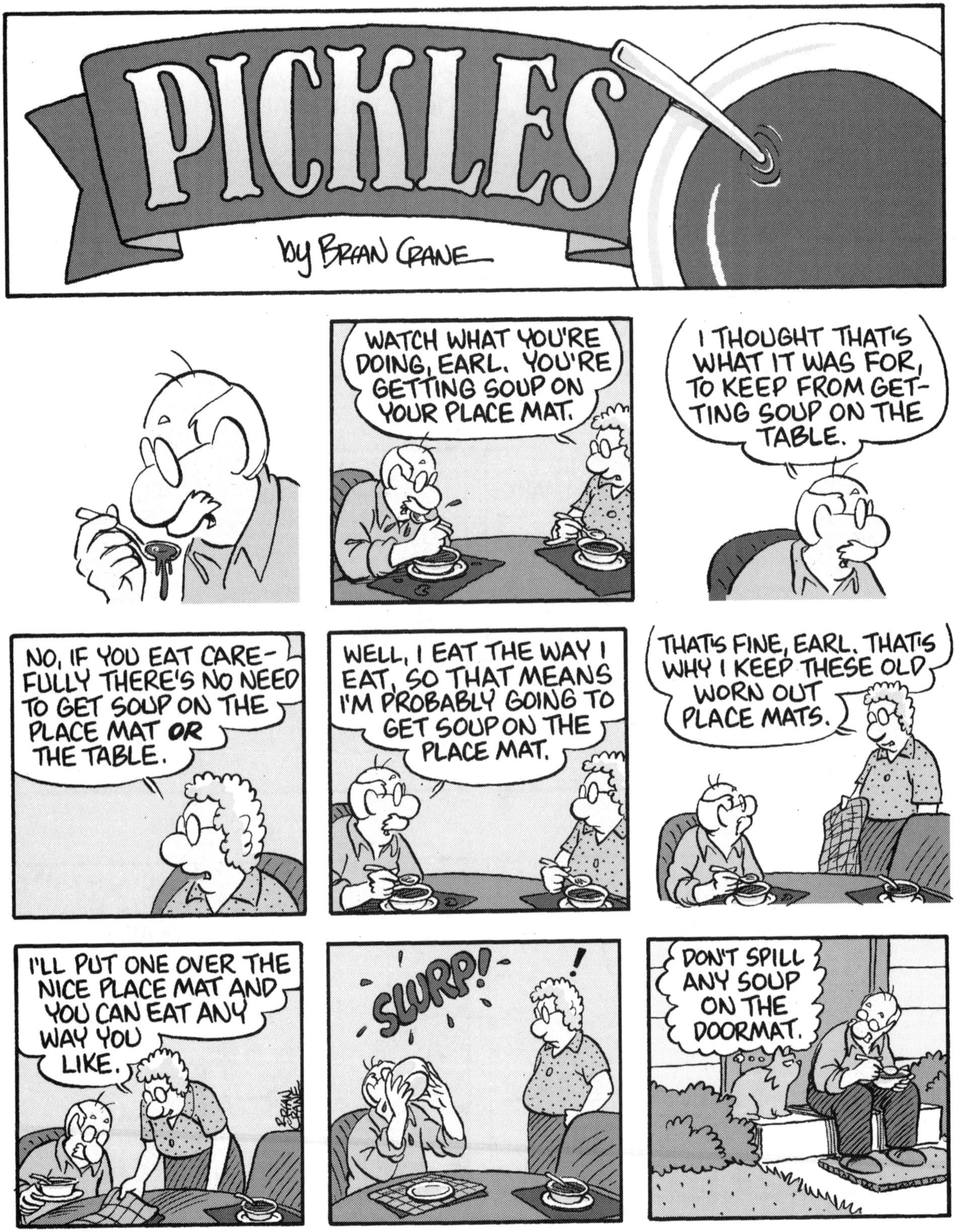
PICKLES
by BRIAN CRANE
WATCH WHAT YOU'RE DOING, EARL. YOU'RE GETTING SOUP ON YOUR PLACE MAT.
I THOUGHT THAT'S WHAT IT WAS FOR, TO KEEP FROM GETTING SOUP ON THE TABLE.
NO, IF YOU EAT CAREFULLY THERE'S NO NEED TO GET SOUP ON THE PLACE MAT OR THE TABLE.
WELL, I EAT THE WAY I EAT, SO THAT MEANS I'M PROBABLY GOING TO GET SOUP ON THE PLACE MAT.
THAT'S FINE, EARL. THAT'S WHY I KEEP THESE OLD WORN OUT PLACE MATS.
I'LL PUT ONE OVER THE NICE PLACE MAT AND YOU CAN EAT ANY WAY YOU LIKE.
SLURP!
!
DON'T SPILL ANY SOUP ON THE DOORMAT.

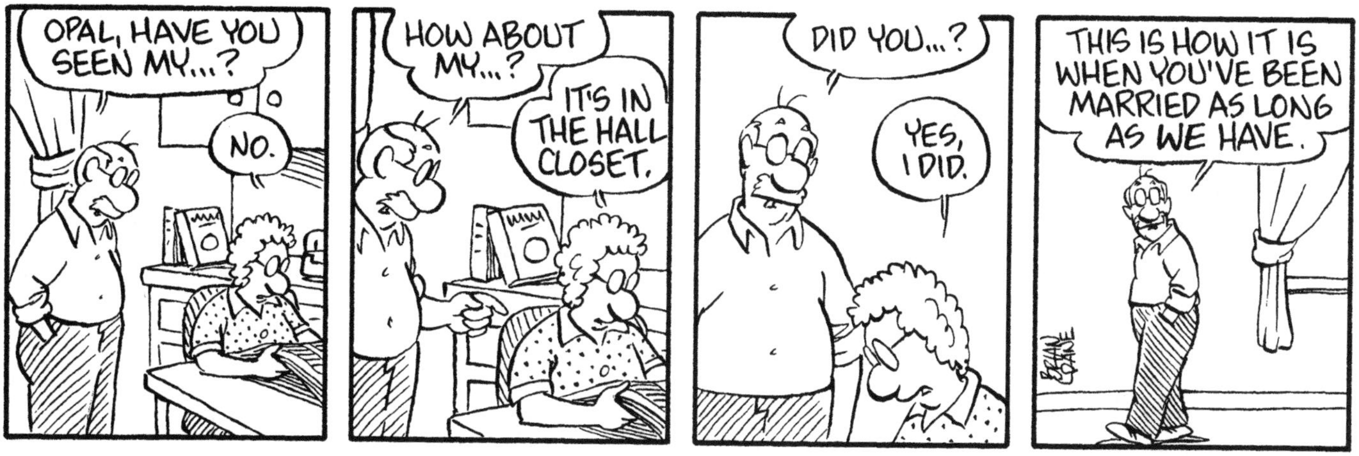
OPAL, HAVE YOU SEEN MY...?
NO.
HOW ABOUT MY...?
IT'S IN THE HALL CLOSET.
DID YOU...?
YES, I DID.
THIS IS HOW IT IS WHEN YOU'VE BEEN MARRIED AS LONG AS WE HAVE.

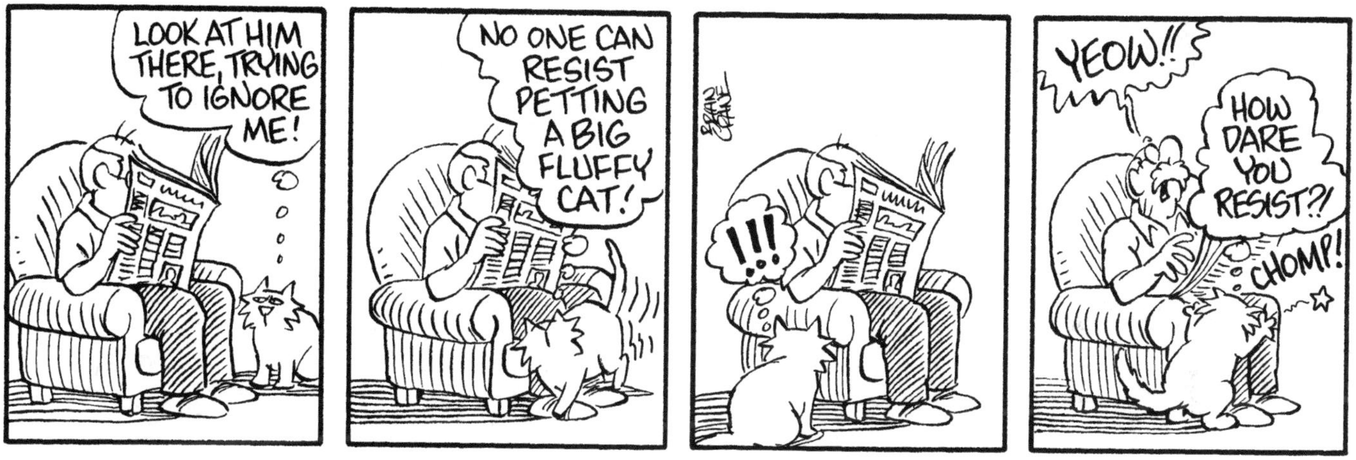
LOOK AT HIM THERE, TRYING TO IGNORE ME!
NO ONE CAN RESIST PETTING A BIG FLUFFY CAT!
!!!
YEOW!!
HOW DARE YOU RESIST?!
CHOMP!

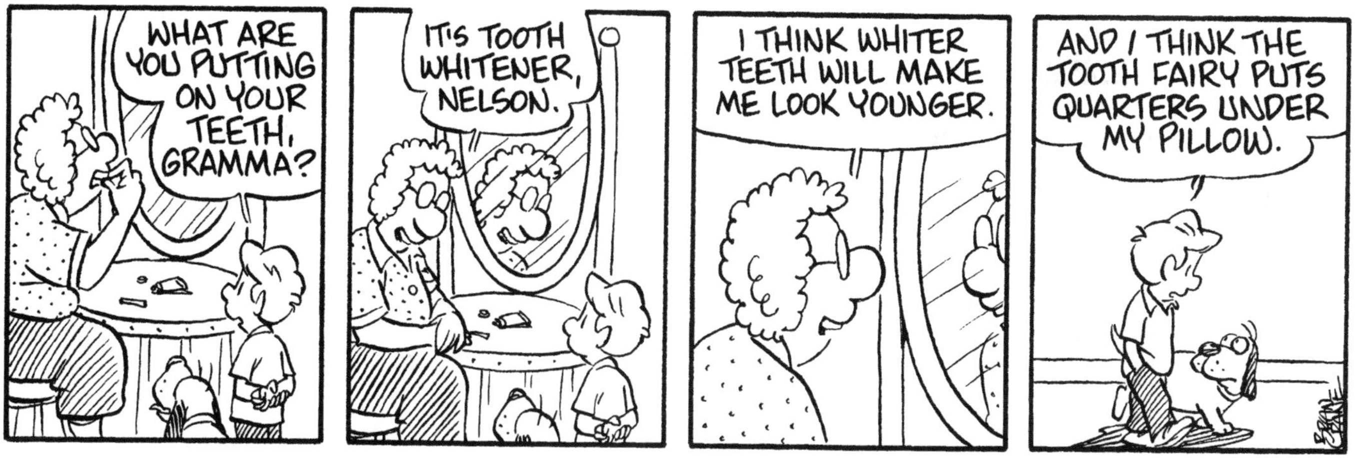
WHAT ARE YOU PUTTING ON YOUR TEETH, GRAMMA?
IT'S TOOTH WHITENER, NELSON.
I THINK WHITER TEETH WILL MAKE ME LOOK YOUNGER.
AND I THINK THE TOOTH FAIRY PUTS QUARTERS UNDER MY PILLOW.

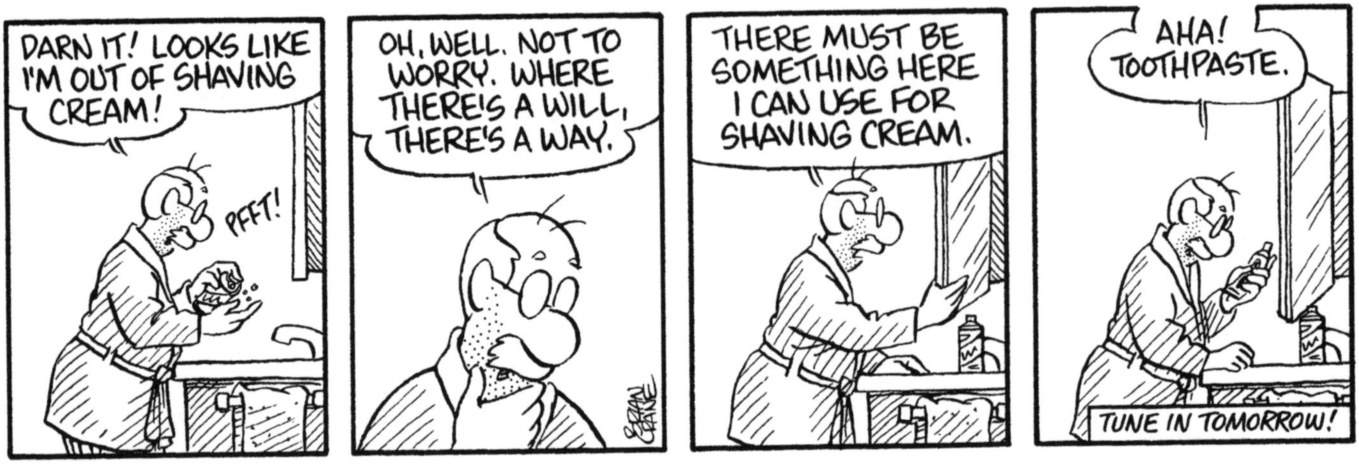
DARN IT! LOOKS LIKE I'M OUT OF SHAVING CREAM!
PFFT!
OH, WELL. NOT TO WORRY. WHERE THERE'S A WILL, THERE'S A WAY.
THERE MUST BE SOMETHING HERE I CAN USE FOR SHAVING CREAM.
AHA! TOOTHPASTE.
TUNE IN TOMORROW!

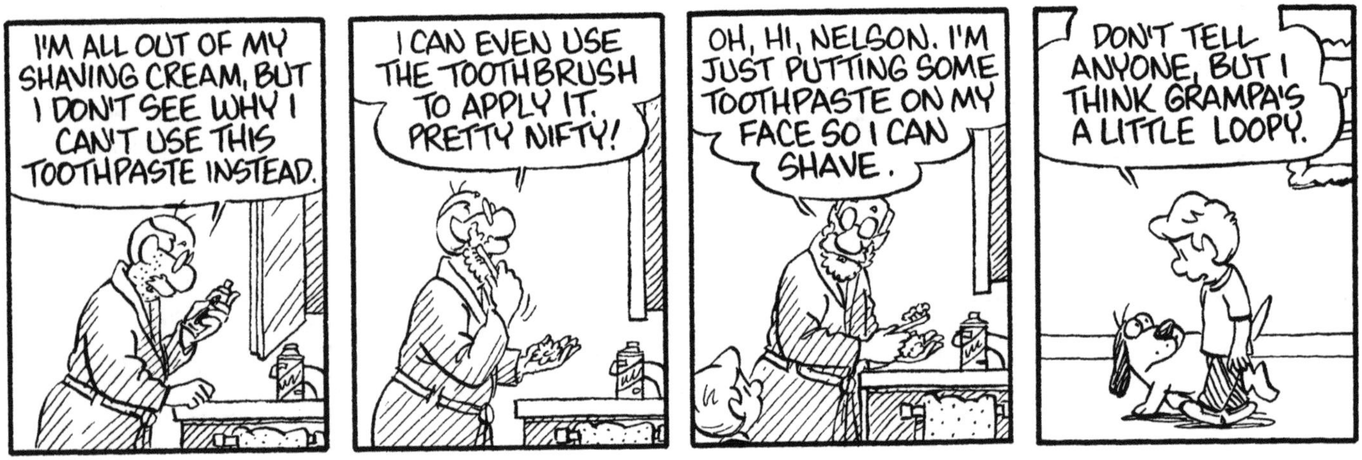
I'M ALL OUT OF MY SHAVING CREAM, BUT I DON'T SEE WHY I CAN'T USE THIS TOOTHPASTE INSTEAD.
I CAN EVEN USE THE TOOTHBRUSH TO APPLY IT. PRETTY NIFTY!
OH, HI, NELSON. I'M JUST PUTTING SOME TOOTHPASTE ON MY FACE SO I CAN SHAVE.
DON'T TELL ANYONE, BUT I THINK GRAMPA'S A LITTLE LOOPY.

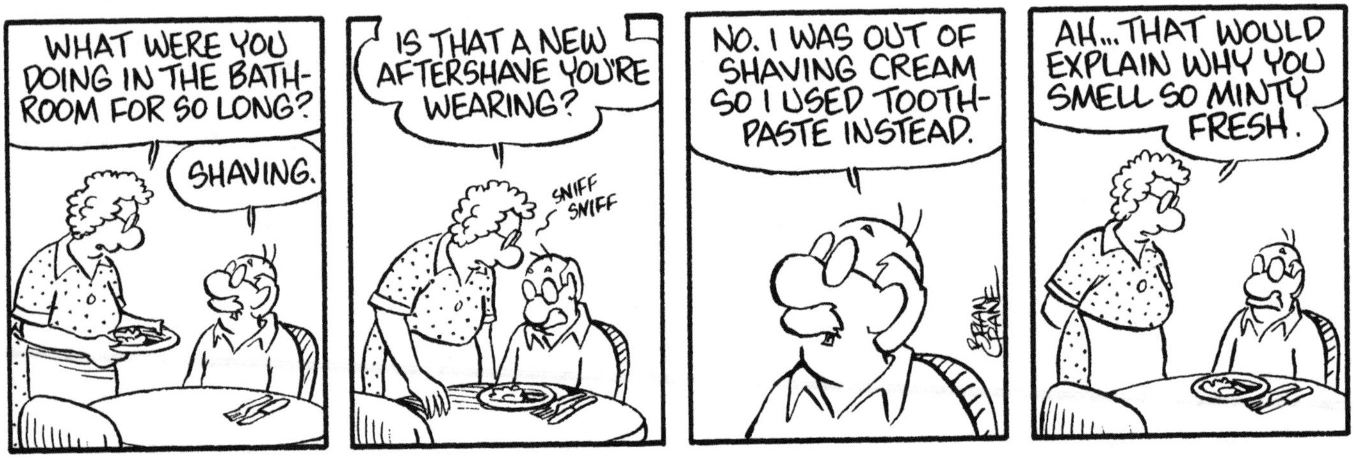
WHAT WERE YOU DOING IN THE BATHROOM FOR SO LONG?
SHAVING.
IS THAT A NEW AFTERSHAVE YOU'RE WEARING?
SNIFF SNIFF
NO. I WAS OUT OF SHAVING CREAM SO I USED TOOTHPASTE INSTEAD.
AH...THAT WOULD EXPLAIN WHY YOU SMELL SO MINTY FRESH.

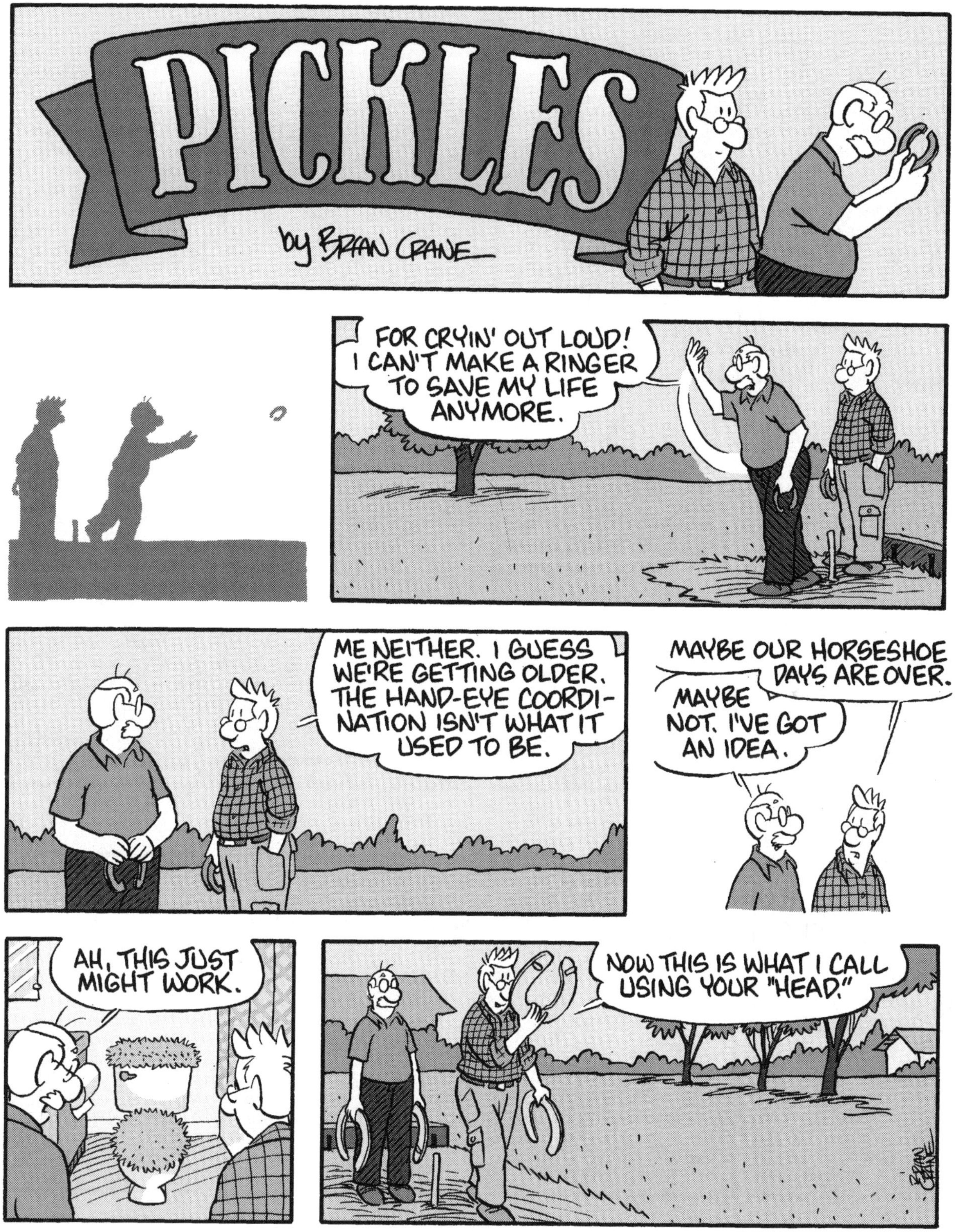
PICKLES
by BRIAN CRANE
FOR CRYIN' OUT LOUD! I CAN'T MAKE A RINGER TO SAVE MY LIFE ANYMORE.
ME NEITHER. I GUESS WE'RE GETTING OLDER. THE HAND-EYE COORDINATION ISN'T WHAT IT USED TO BE.
MAYBE OUR HORSESHOE DAYS ARE OVER.
MAYBE NOT. I'VE GOT AN IDEA.
AH, THIS JUST MIGHT WORK.
NOW THIS IS WHAT I CALL USING YOUR "HEAD."

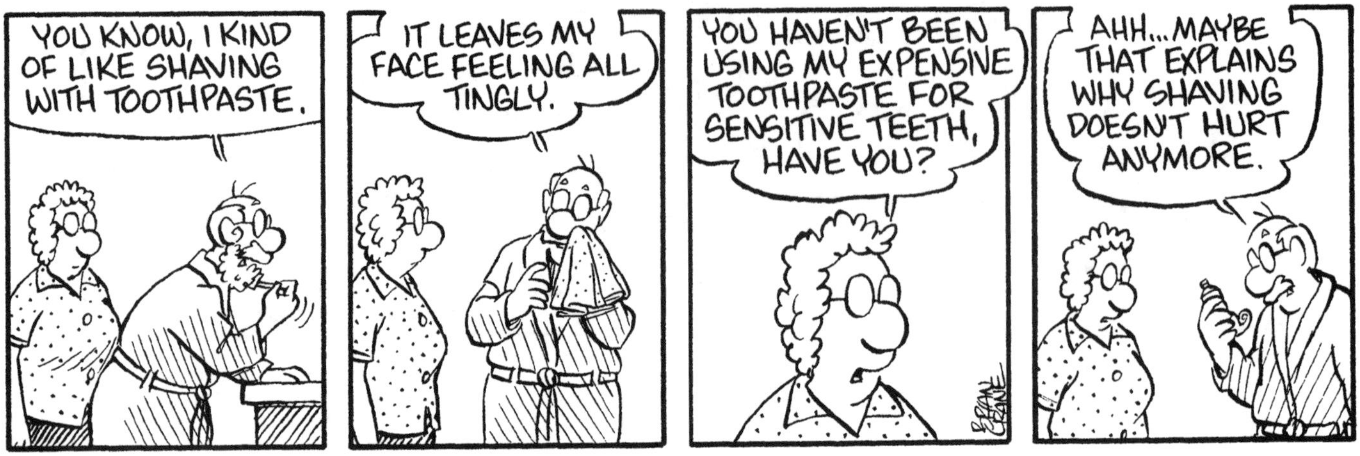
YOU KNOW, I KIND OF LIKE SHAVING WITH TOOTHPASTE.
IT LEAVES MY FACE FEELING ALL TINGLY.
YOU HAVEN'T BEEN USING MY EXPENSIVE TOOTHPASTE FOR SENSITIVE TEETH, HAVE YOU?
AHH... MAYBE THAT EXPLAINS WHY SHAVING DOESN'T HURT ANYMORE.

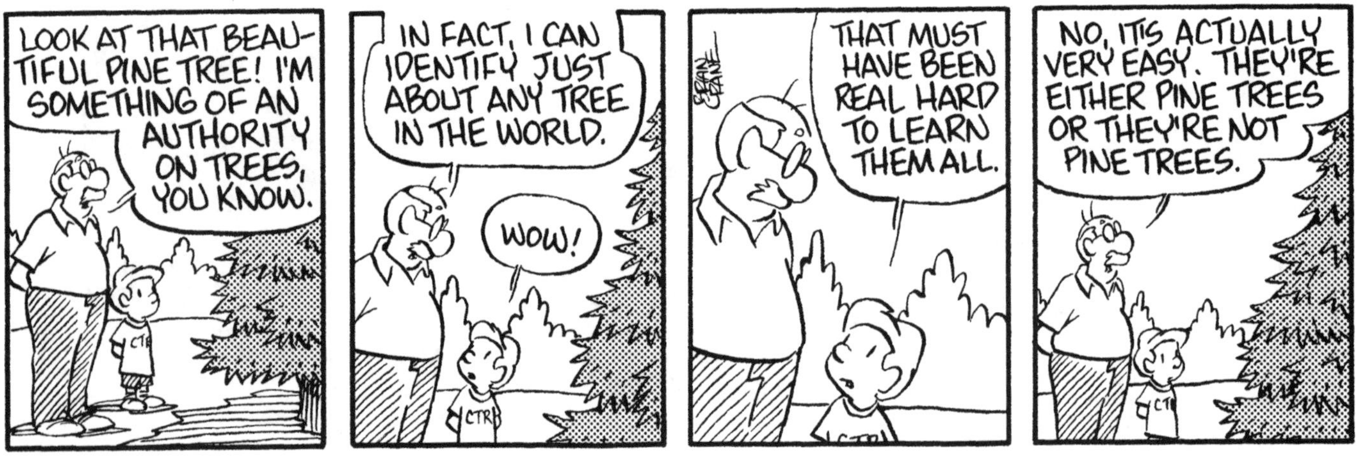
LOOK AT THAT BEAUTIFUL PINE TREE! I'M SOMETHING OF AN AUTHORITY ON TREES, YOU KNOW.
CTR
IN FACT, I CAN IDENTIFY JUST ABOUT ANY TREE IN THE WORLD.
WOW!
CTR
THAT MUST HAVE BEEN REAL HARD TO LEARN THEM ALL.
NO, IT'S ACTUALLY VERY EASY. THEY'RE EITHER PINE TREES OR THEY'RE NOT PINE TREES.

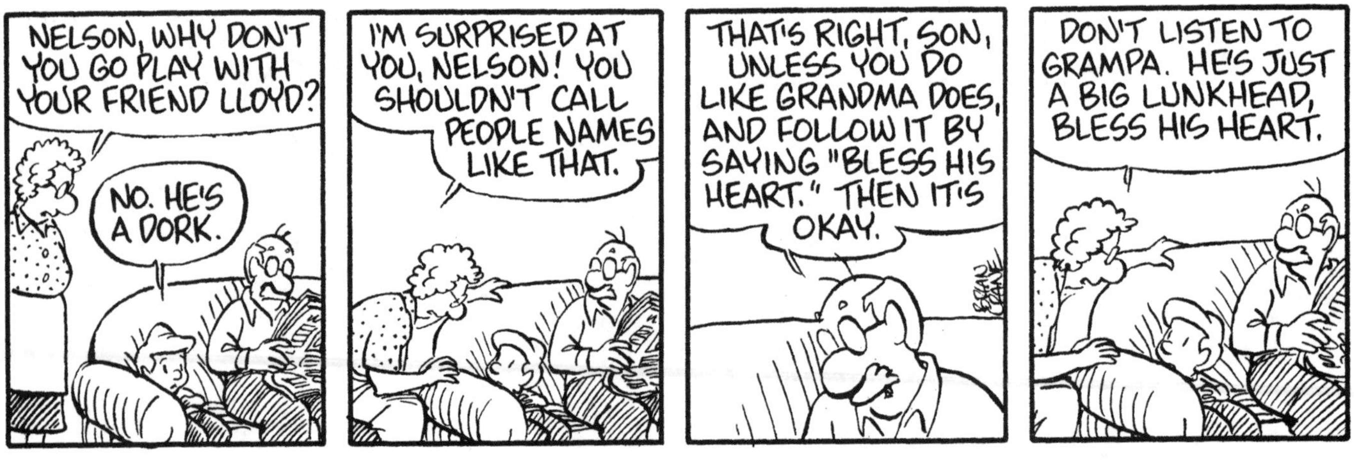
NELSON, WHY DON'T YOU GO PLAY WITH YOUR FRIEND LLOYD?
NO. HE'S A DORK.
I'M SURPRISED AT YOU, NELSON! YOU SHOULDN'T CALL PEOPLE NAMES LIKE THAT.
THAT'S RIGHT, SON, UNLESS YOU DO LIKE GRANDMA DOES, AND FOLLOW IT BY SAYING "BLESS HIS HEART." THEN IT'S OKAY.
DON'T LISTEN TO GRAMPA. HE'S JUST A BIG LUNKHEAD, BLESS HIS HEART.

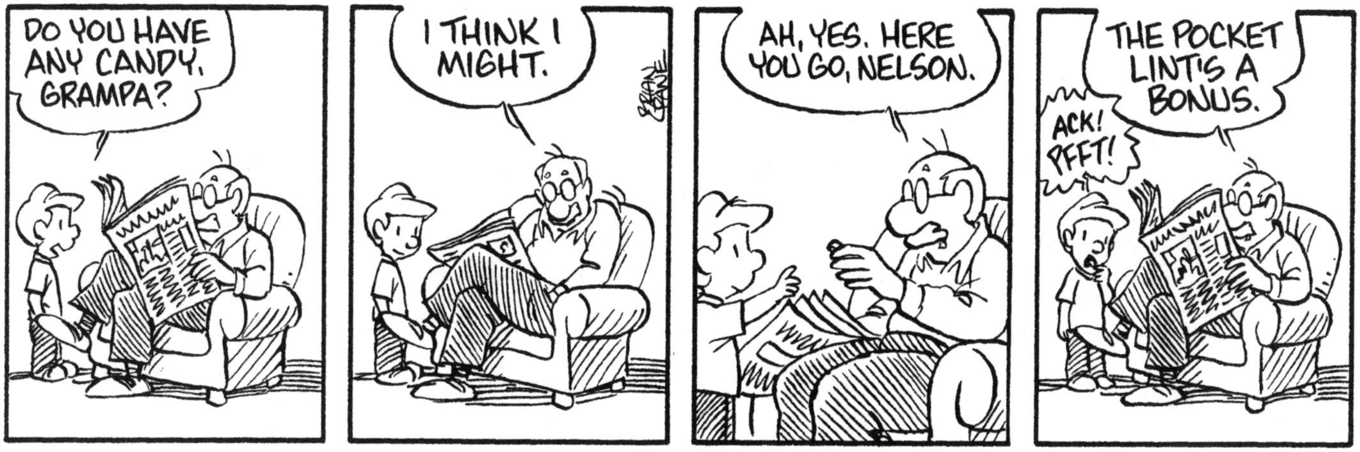
DO YOU HAVE ANY CANDY, GRAMPA?
I THINK I MIGHT.
AH, YES. HERE YOU GO, NELSON.
THE POCKET LINT'S A BONUS.
ACK! PFFT!

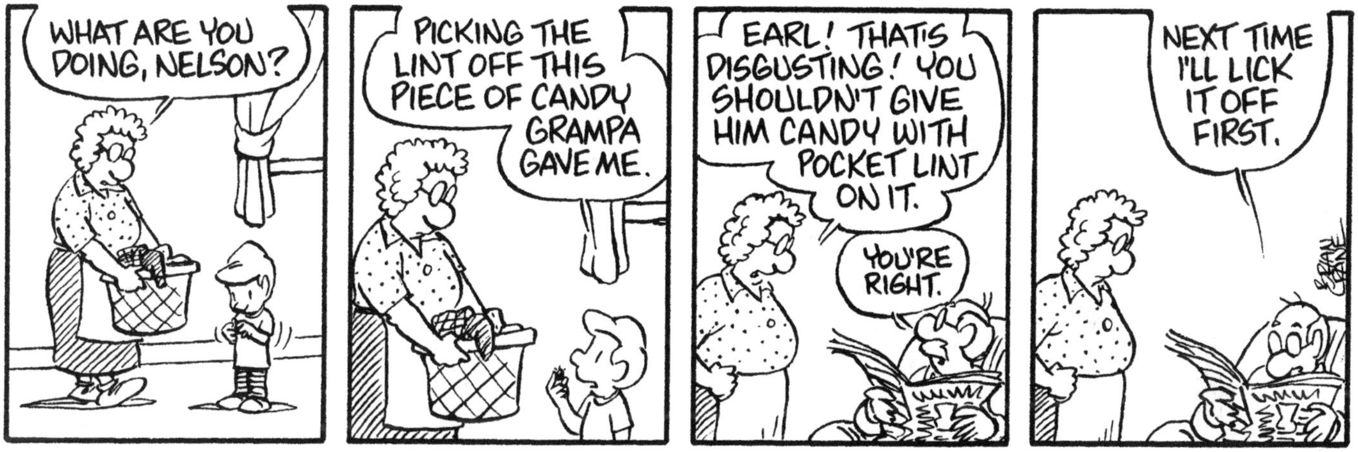
WHAT ARE YOU DOING, NELSON?
PICKING THE LINT OFF THIS PIECE OF CANDY GRAMPA GAVE ME.
EARL! THAT'S DISGUSTING! YOU SHOULDN'T GIVE HIM CANDY WITH POCKET LINT ON IT.
YOU'RE RIGHT.
NEXT TIME I'LL LICK IT OFF FIRST.

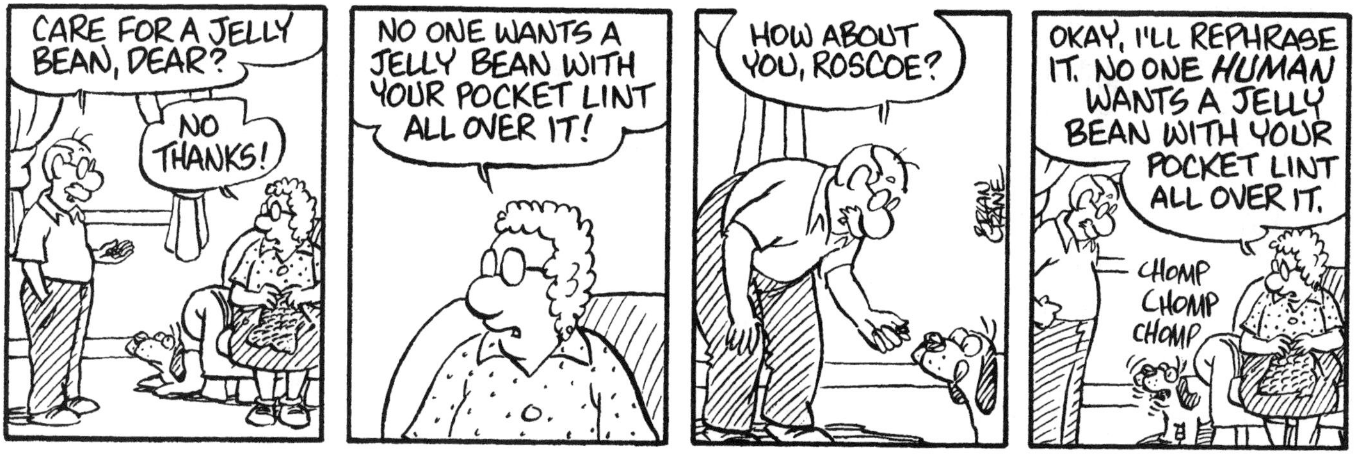
CARE FOR A JELLY BEAN, DEAR?
NO THANKS!
NO ONE WANTS A JELLY BEAN WITH YOUR POCKET LINT ALL OVER IT!
HOW ABOUT YOU, ROSCOE?
OKAY, I'LL REPHRASE IT. NO ONE *HUMAN* WANTS A JELLY BEAN WITH YOUR POCKET LINT ALL OVER IT.
CHOMP
CHOMP
CHOMP

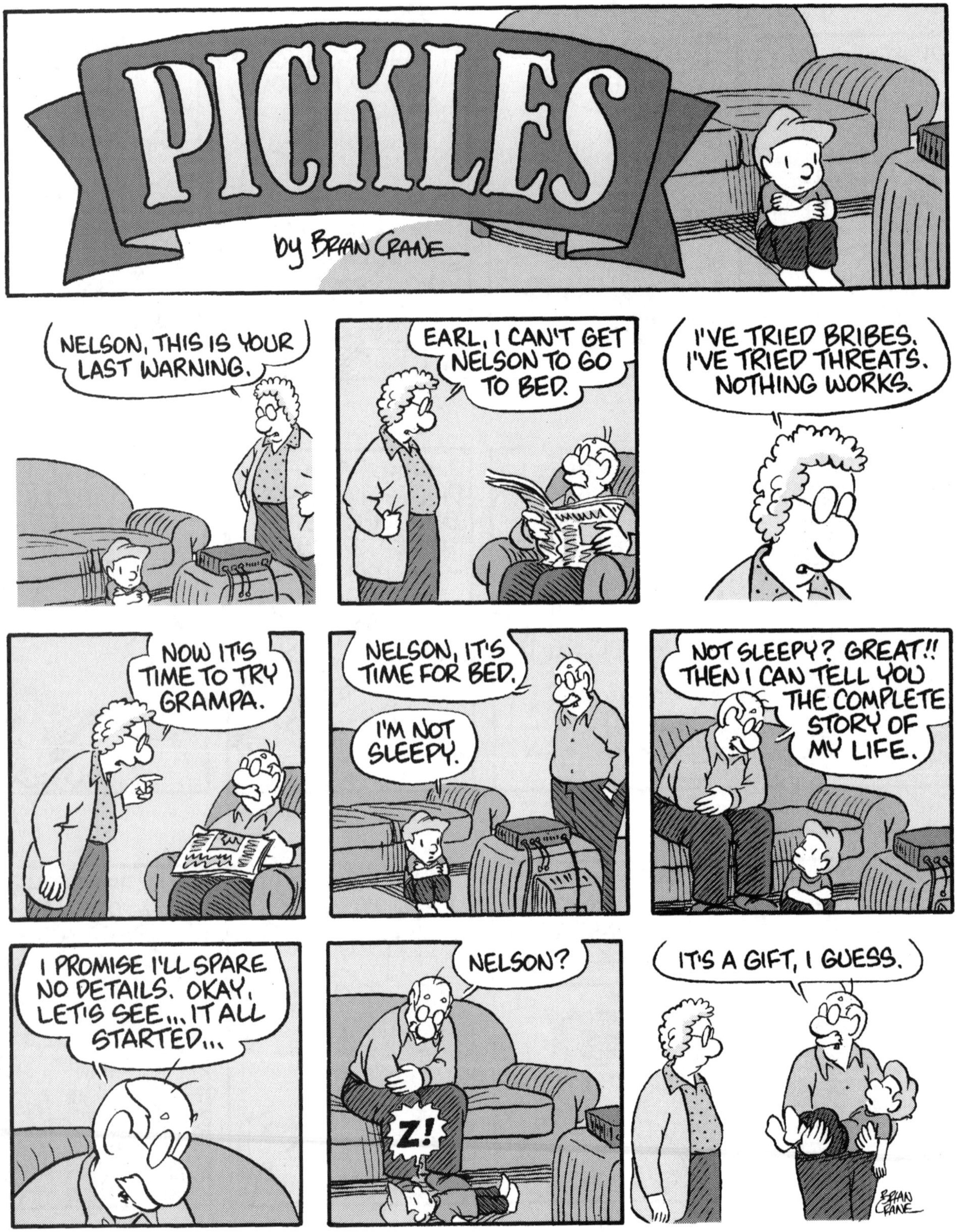
PICKLES
by BRIAN CRANE
NELSON, THIS IS YOUR LAST WARNING.
EARL, I CAN'T GET NELSON TO GO TO BED.
I'VE TRIED BRIBES. I'VE TRIED THREATS. NOTHING WORKS.
NOW IT'S TIME TO TRY GRAMPA.
NELSON, IT'S TIME FOR BED.
I'M NOT SLEEPY.
NOT SLEEPY? GREAT!! THEN I CAN TELL YOU THE COMPLETE STORY OF MY LIFE.
I PROMISE I'LL SPARE NO DETAILS. OKAY, LET'S SEE... IT ALL STARTED...
NELSON?
Z!
IT'S A GIFT, I GUESS.
BRIAN CRANE

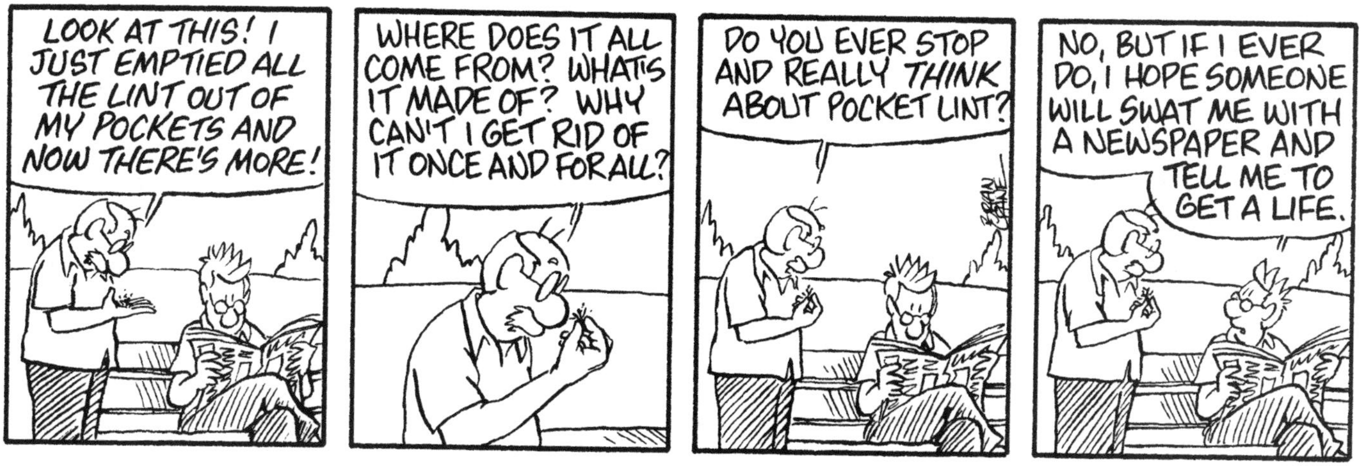
LOOK AT THIS! I JUST EMPTIED ALL THE LINT OUT OF MY POCKETS AND NOW THERE'S MORE!
WHERE DOES IT ALL COME FROM? WHAT'S IT MADE OF? WHY CAN'T I GET RID OF IT ONCE AND FOR ALL?
DO YOU EVER STOP AND REALLY *THINK* ABOUT POCKET LINT?
NO, BUT IF I EVER DO, I HOPE SOMEONE WILL SWAT ME WITH A NEWSPAPER AND TELL ME TO GET A LIFE.

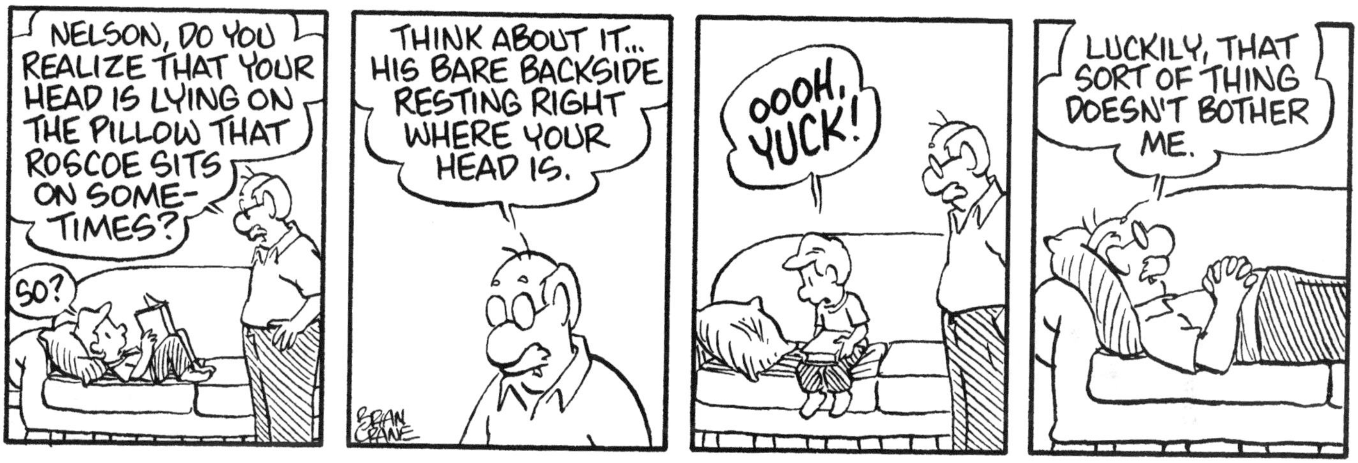
NELSON, DO YOU REALIZE THAT YOUR HEAD IS LYING ON THE PILLOW THAT ROSCOE SITS ON SOMETIMES?
SO?
THINK ABOUT IT... HIS BARE BACKSIDE RESTING RIGHT WHERE YOUR HEAD IS.
OOOH, YUCK!
LUCKILY, THAT SORT OF THING DOESN'T BOTHER ME.

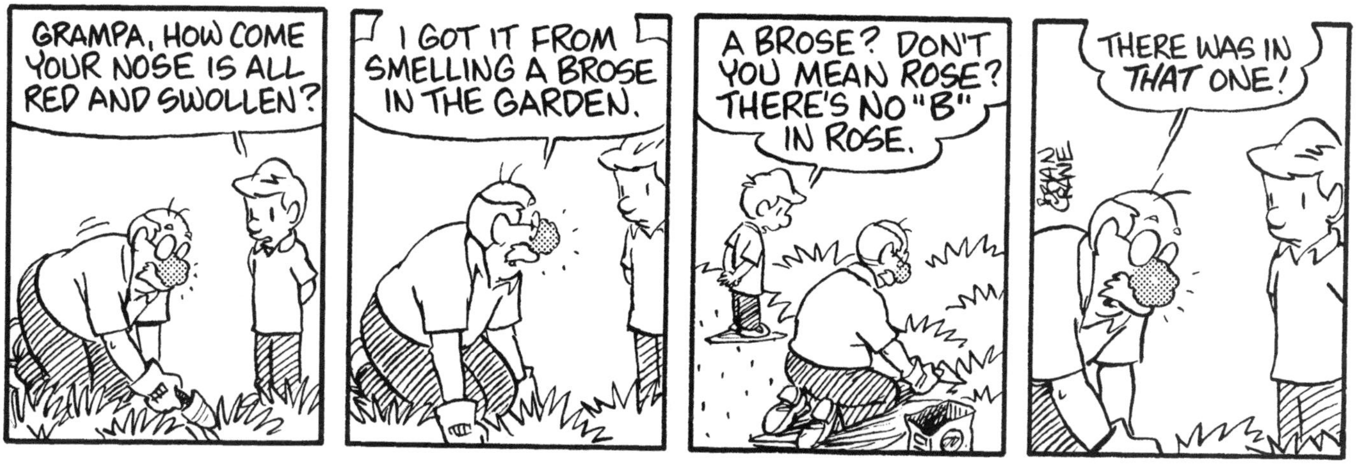
GRAMPA, HOW COME YOUR NOSE IS ALL RED AND SWOLLEN?
I GOT IT FROM SMELLING A BROSE IN THE GARDEN.
A BROSE? DON'T YOU MEAN ROSE? THERE'S NO "B" IN ROSE.
THERE WAS IN *THAT* ONE!

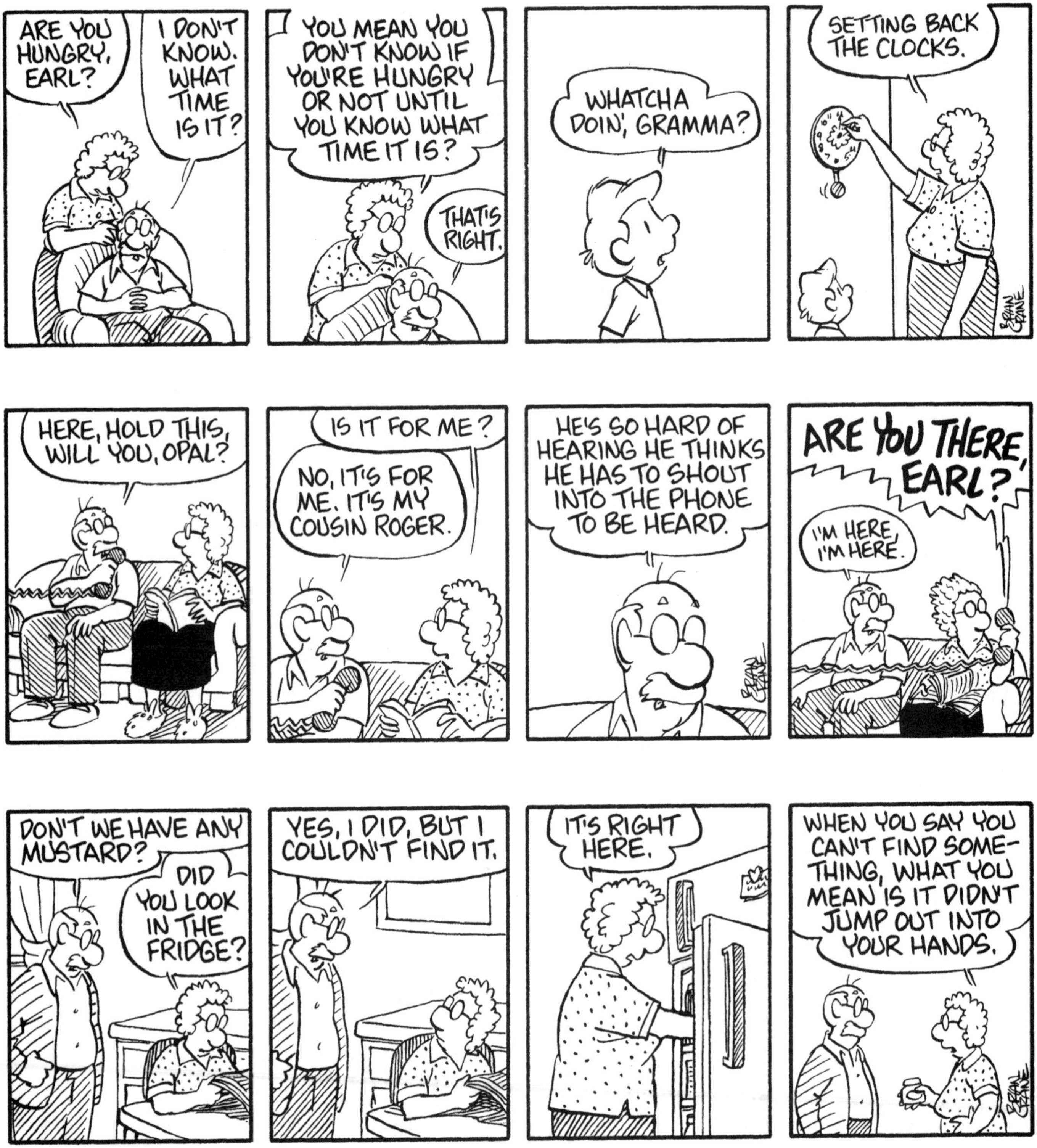
ARE YOU HUNGRY, EARL?
I DON'T KNOW. WHAT TIME IS IT?
YOU MEAN YOU DON'T KNOW IF YOU'RE HUNGRY OR NOT UNTIL YOU KNOW WHAT TIME IT IS?
THAT'S RIGHT.
WHATCHA DOIN', GRAMMA?
SETTING BACK THE CLOCKS.
BRIAN CRANE
HERE, HOLD THIS, WILL YOU, OPAL?
IS IT FOR ME?
NO, IT'S FOR ME. IT'S MY COUSIN ROGER.
HE'S SO HARD OF HEARING HE THINKS HE HAS TO SHOUT INTO THE PHONE TO BE HEARD.
ARE YOU THERE, EARL?
I'M HERE, I'M HERE.
DON'T WE HAVE ANY MUSTARD?
DID YOU LOOK IN THE FRIDGE?
YES, I DID, BUT I COULDN'T FIND IT.
IT'S RIGHT HERE.
WHEN YOU SAY YOU CAN'T FIND SOMETHING, WHAT YOU MEAN IS IT DIDN'T JUMP OUT INTO YOUR HANDS.
BRIAN CRANE

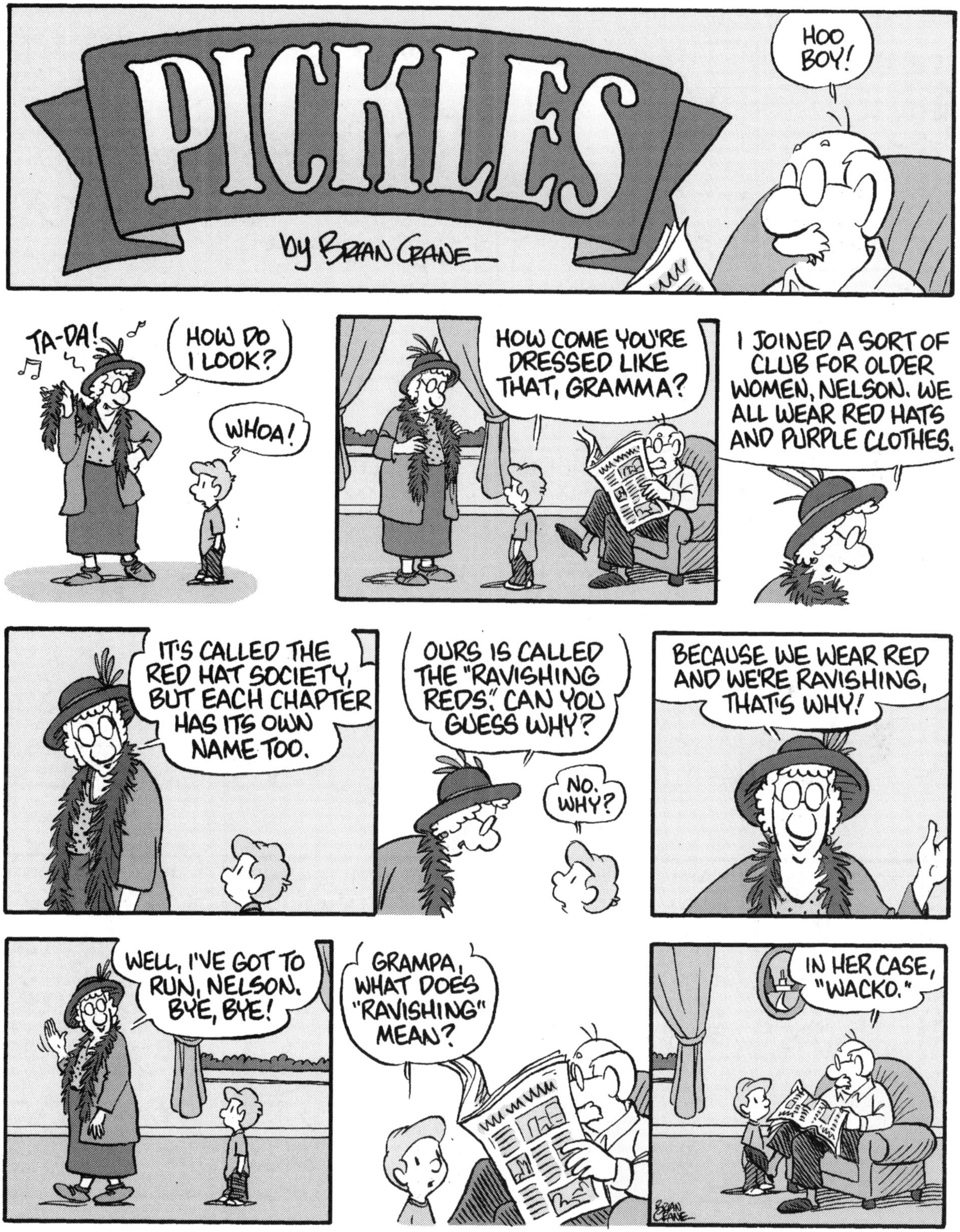
PICKLES
by BRIAN CRANE
HOO BOY!
TA-DA!
HOW DO I LOOK?
WHOA!
HOW COME YOU'RE DRESSED LIKE THAT, GRAMMA?
I JOINED A SORT OF CLUB FOR OLDER WOMEN, NELSON. WE ALL WEAR RED HATS AND PURPLE CLOTHES.
IT'S CALLED THE RED HAT SOCIETY, BUT EACH CHAPTER HAS ITS OWN NAME TOO.
OURS IS CALLED THE "RAVISHING REDS". CAN YOU GUESS WHY?
NO. WHY?
BECAUSE WE WEAR RED AND WE'RE RAVISHING, THAT'S WHY!
WELL, I'VE GOT TO RUN, NELSON. BYE, BYE!
GRAMPA, WHAT DOES "RAVISHING" MEAN?
IN HER CASE, "WACKO."
BRIAN CRANE

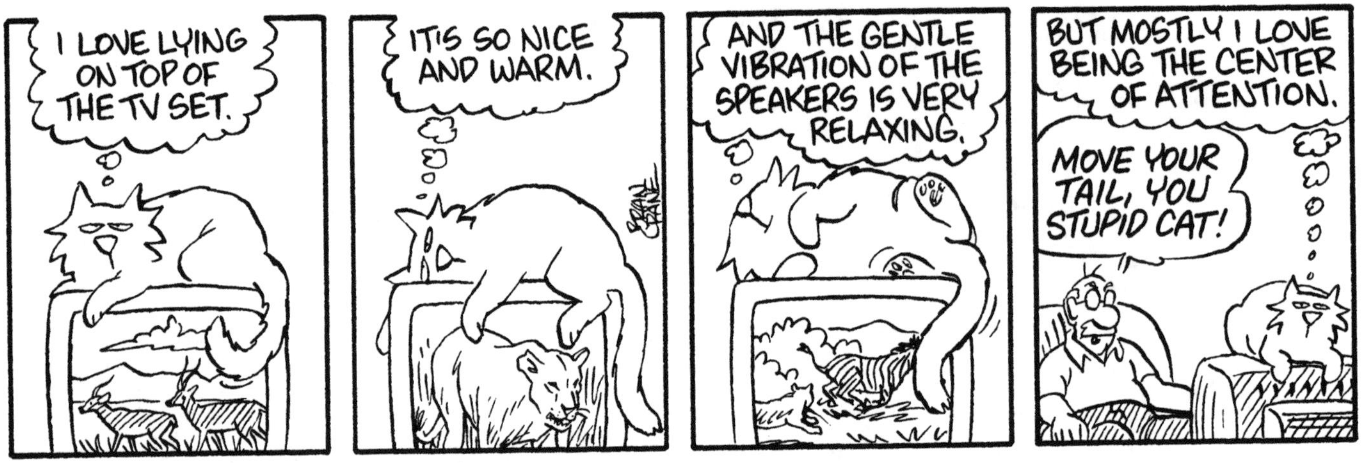
I LOVE LYING ON TOP OF THE TV SET.
IT'S SO NICE AND WARM.
AND THE GENTLE VIBRATION OF THE SPEAKERS IS VERY RELAXING.
BUT MOSTLY I LOVE BEING THE CENTER OF ATTENTION.
MOVE YOUR TAIL, YOU STUPID CAT!

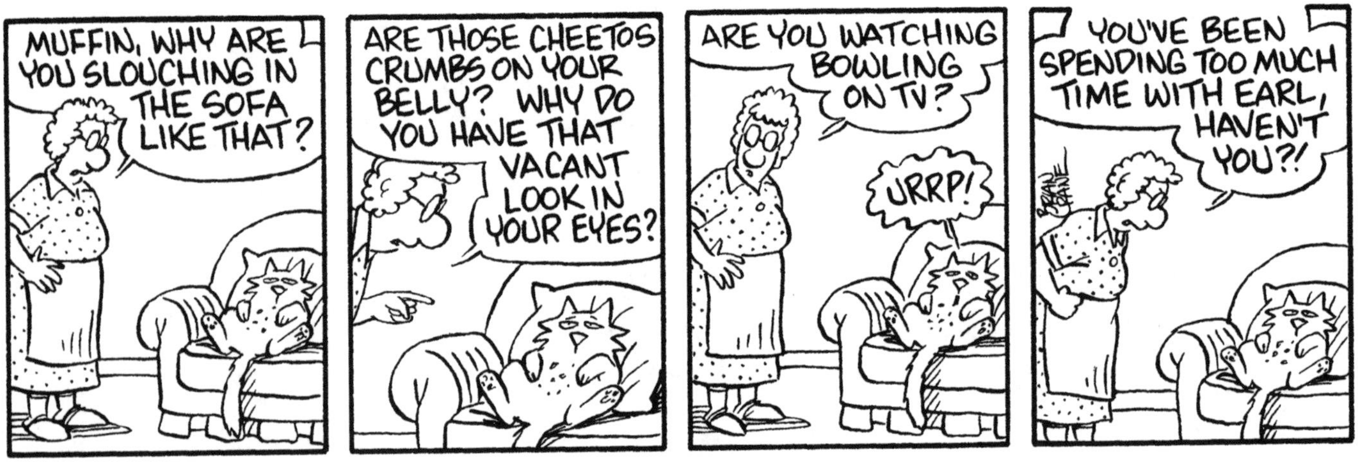
MUFFIN, WHY ARE YOU SLOUCHING IN THE SOFA LIKE THAT?
ARE THOSE CHEETOS CRUMBS ON YOUR BELLY? WHY DO YOU HAVE THAT VACANT LOOK IN YOUR EYES?
ARE YOU WATCHING BOWLING ON TV?
URRP!
YOU'VE BEEN SPENDING TOO MUCH TIME WITH EARL, HAVEN'T YOU?!

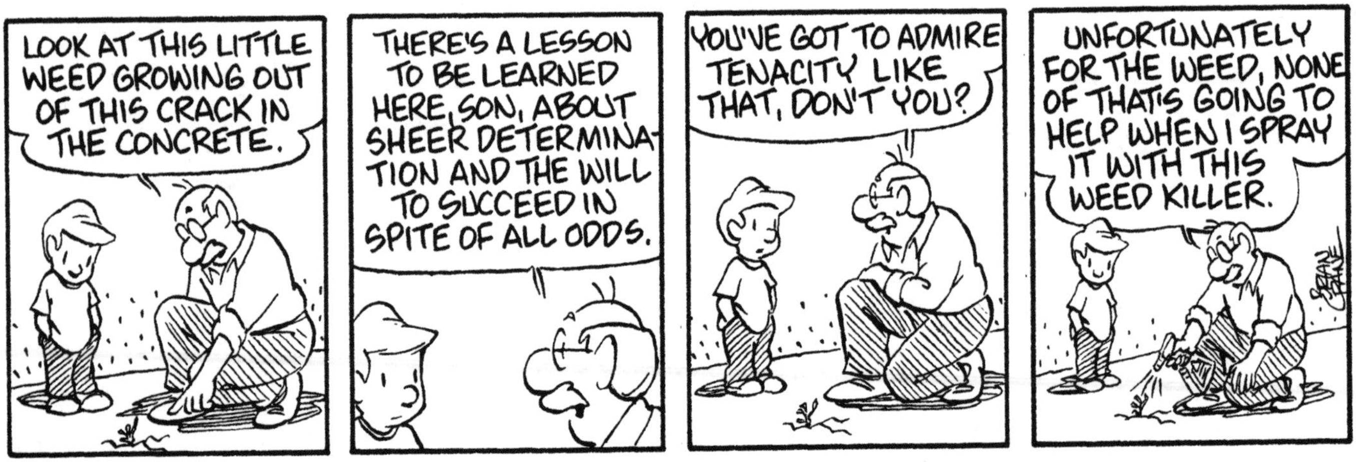
LOOK AT THIS LITTLE WEED GROWING OUT OF THIS CRACK IN THE CONCRETE.
THERE'S A LESSON TO BE LEARNED HERE, SON, ABOUT SHEER DETERMINATION AND THE WILL TO SUCCEED IN SPITE OF ALL ODDS.
YOU'VE GOT TO ADMIRE TENACITY LIKE THAT, DON'T YOU?
UNFORTUNATELY FOR THE WEED, NONE OF THAT'S GOING TO HELP WHEN I SPRAY IT WITH THIS WEED KILLER.

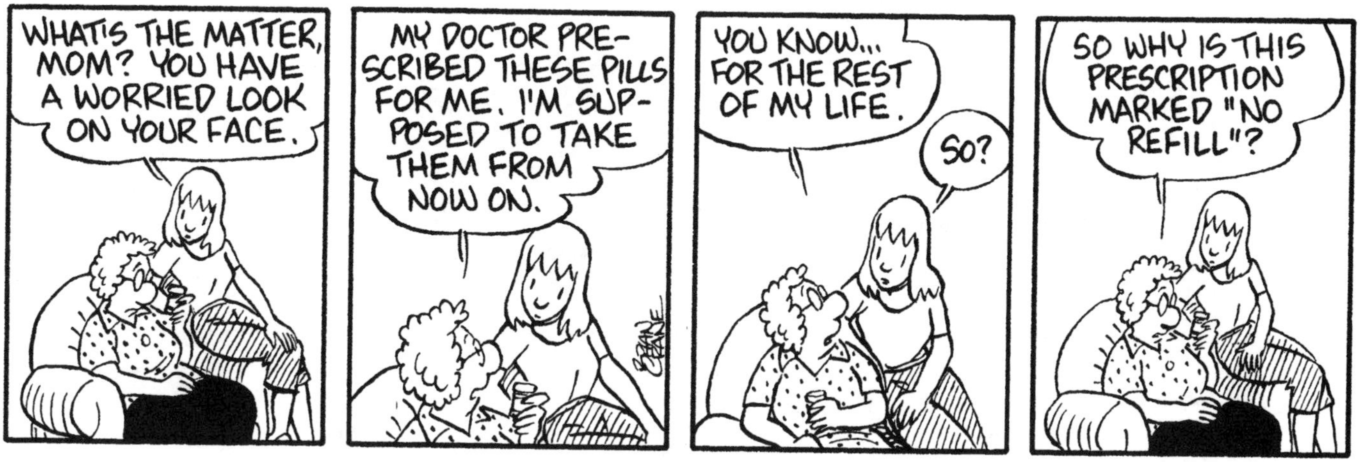
WHAT'S THE MATTER, MOM? YOU HAVE A WORRIED LOOK ON YOUR FACE.
MY DOCTOR PRESCRIBED THESE PILLS FOR ME. I'M SUPPOSED TO TAKE THEM FROM NOW ON.
YOU KNOW... FOR THE REST OF MY LIFE.
SO?
SO WHY IS THIS PRESCRIPTION MARKED "NO REFILL"?

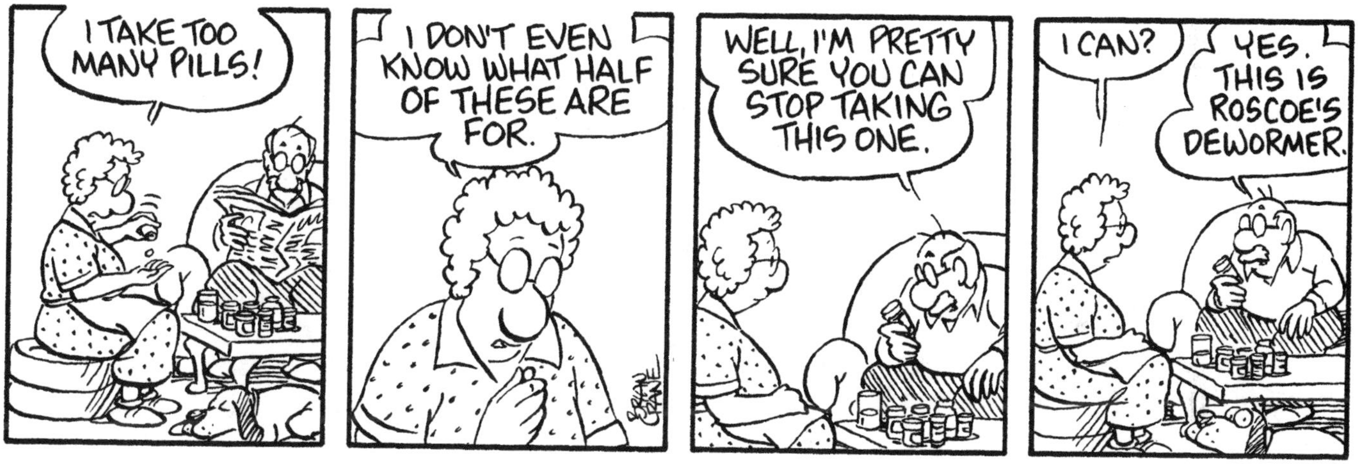
I TAKE TOO MANY PILLS!
I DON'T EVEN KNOW WHAT HALF OF THESE ARE FOR.
WELL, I'M PRETTY SURE YOU CAN STOP TAKING THIS ONE.
I CAN?
YES. THIS IS ROSCOE'S DEWORMER.

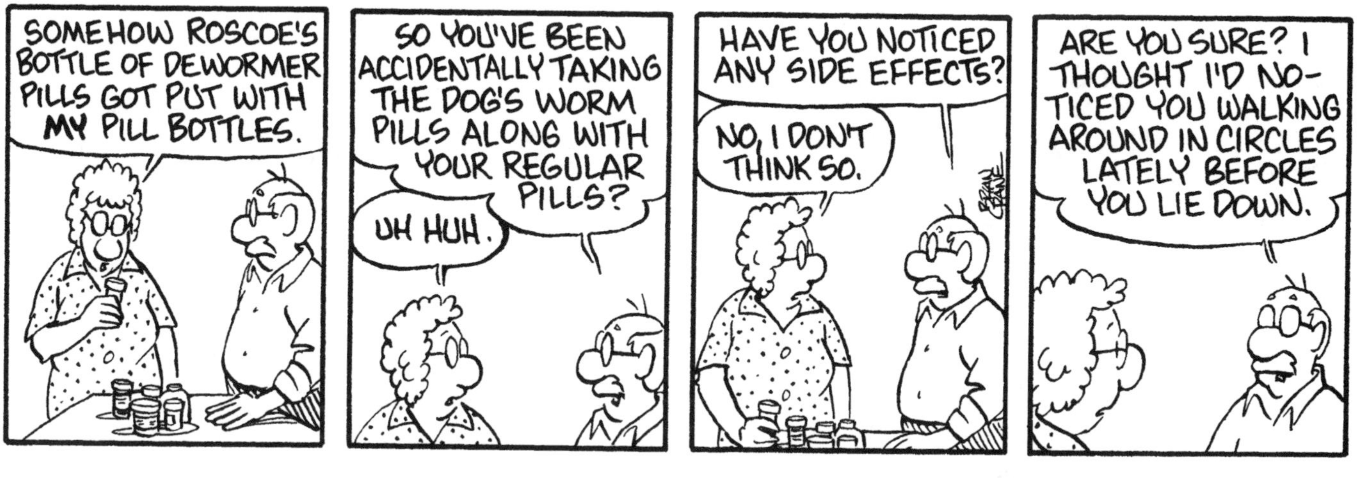
SOMEHOW ROSCOE'S BOTTLE OF DEWORMER PILLS GOT PUT WITH MY PILL BOTTLES.
SO YOU'VE BEEN ACCIDENTALLY TAKING THE DOG'S WORM PILLS ALONG WITH YOUR REGULAR PILLS?
UH HUH.
HAVE YOU NOTICED ANY SIDE EFFECTS?
NO, I DON'T THINK SO.
ARE YOU SURE? I THOUGHT I'D NOTICED YOU WALKING AROUND IN CIRCLES LATELY BEFORE YOU LIE DOWN.

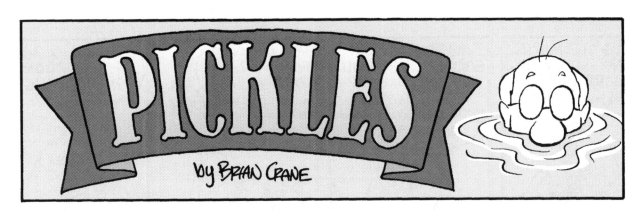

**PICKLES**

by Brian Crane

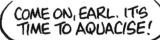
COME ON, EARL. IT'S TIME TO AQUACISE!

GLRB

I'M GLAD YOU DECIDED TO JOIN MY AQUACISE CLASS, EARL. IT'S A GREAT WORKOUT AND IT'S FUN.

TOO BAD IT'S SO CROWDED.

YEAH, BUT WHAT CAN YOU DO?

OOPS! I THINK I LOST MY TRUNKS!!

NOPE. THEY'RE STILL THERE. HEY, WHERE'D EVERYONE GO?

EARL!

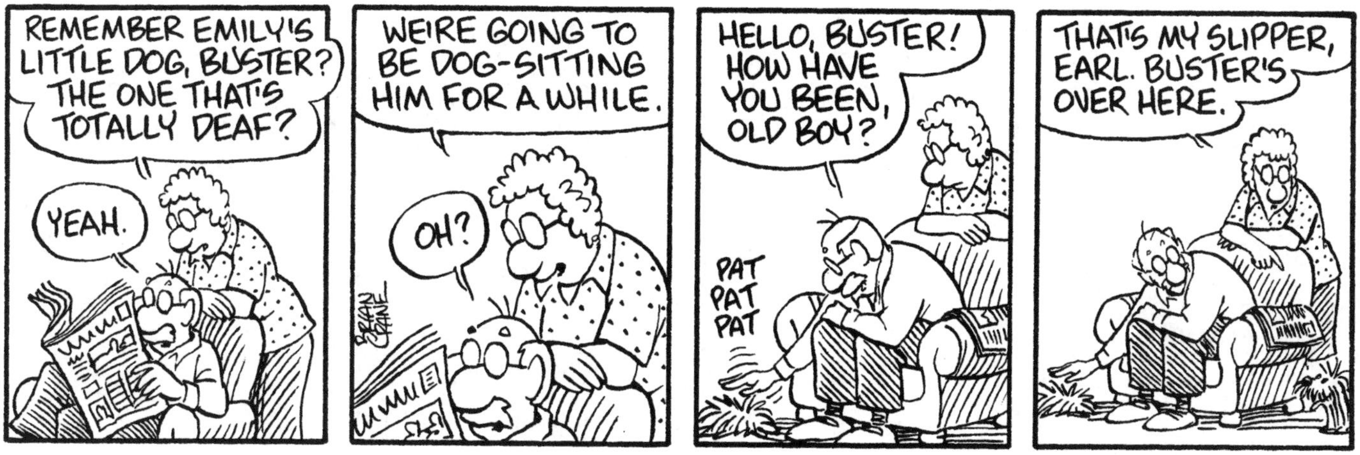
REMEMBER EMILY'S LITTLE DOG, BUSTER? THE ONE THAT'S TOTALLY DEAF?
YEAH.
WE'RE GOING TO BE DOG-SITTING HIM FOR A WHILE.
OH?
HELLO, BUSTER! HOW HAVE YOU BEEN, OLD BOY?
PAT PAT PAT
THAT'S MY SLIPPER, EARL. BUSTER'S OVER HERE.

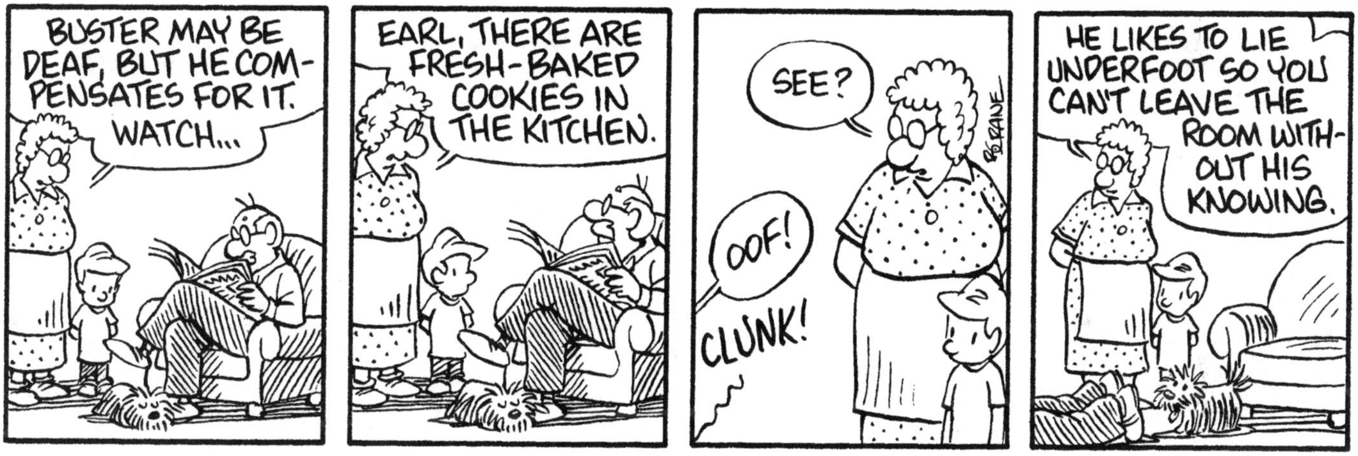
BUSTER MAY BE DEAF, BUT HE COMPENSATES FOR IT. WATCH...
EARL, THERE ARE FRESH-BAKED COOKIES IN THE KITCHEN.
SEE?
OOF!
CLUNK!
HE LIKES TO LIE UNDERFOOT SO YOU CAN'T LEAVE THE ROOM WITHOUT HIS KNOWING.

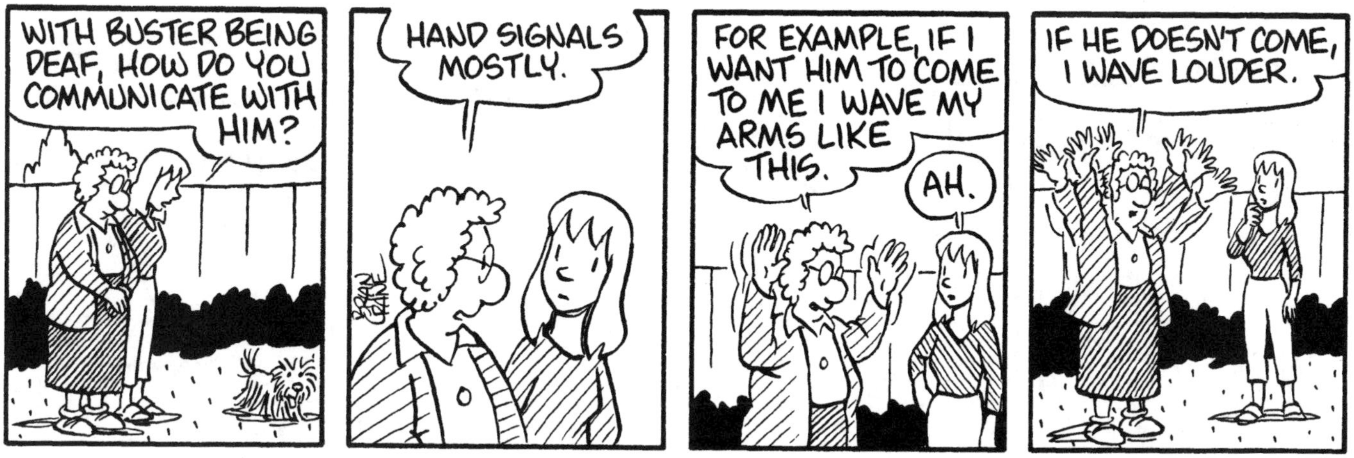
WITH BUSTER BEING DEAF, HOW DO YOU COMMUNICATE WITH HIM?
HAND SIGNALS MOSTLY.
FOR EXAMPLE, IF I WANT HIM TO COME TO ME I WAVE MY ARMS LIKE THIS.
AH.
IF HE DOESN'T COME, I WAVE LOUDER.

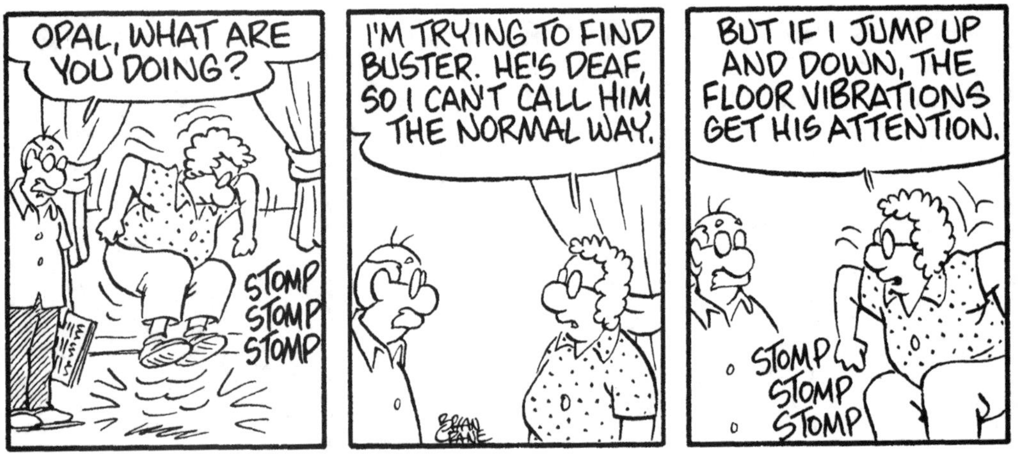
OPAL, WHAT ARE YOU DOING?
STOMP STOMP STOMP
I'M TRYING TO FIND BUSTER. HE'S DEAF, SO I CAN'T CALL HIM THE NORMAL WAY.
BUT IF I JUMP UP AND DOWN, THE FLOOR VIBRATIONS GET HIS ATTENTION.
STOMP STOMP STOMP
NOT TO MENTION THE PEOPLE AT THE SEISMOGRAPHIC STATION.

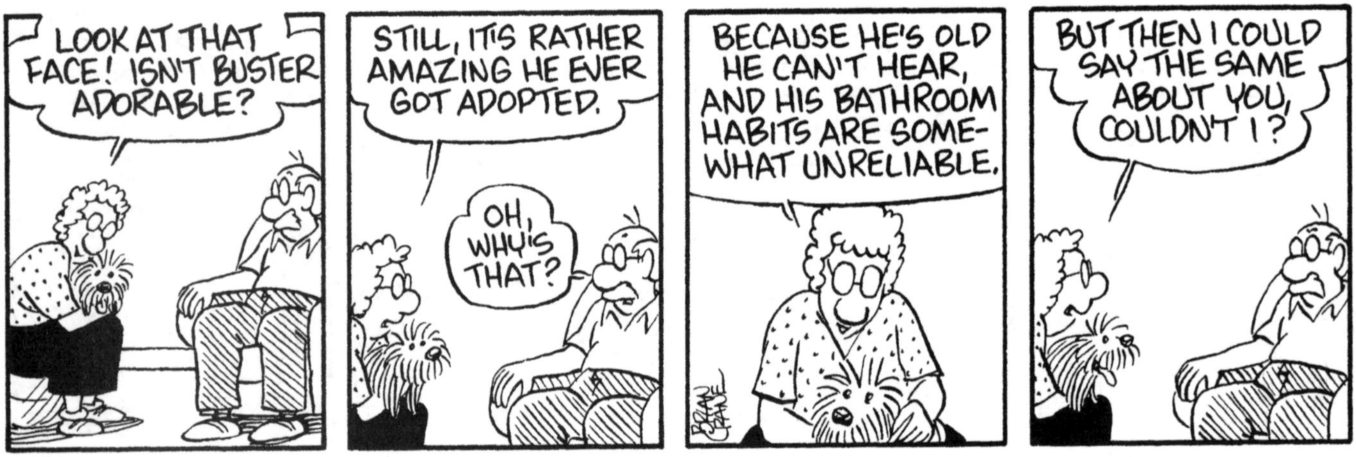
LOOK AT THAT FACE! ISN'T BUSTER ADORABLE?
STILL, IT'S RATHER AMAZING HE EVER GOT ADOPTED.
OH, WHY'S THAT?
BECAUSE HE'S OLD HE CAN'T HEAR, AND HIS BATHROOM HABITS ARE SOMEWHAT UNRELIABLE.
BUT THEN I COULD SAY THE SAME ABOUT YOU, COULDN'T I?

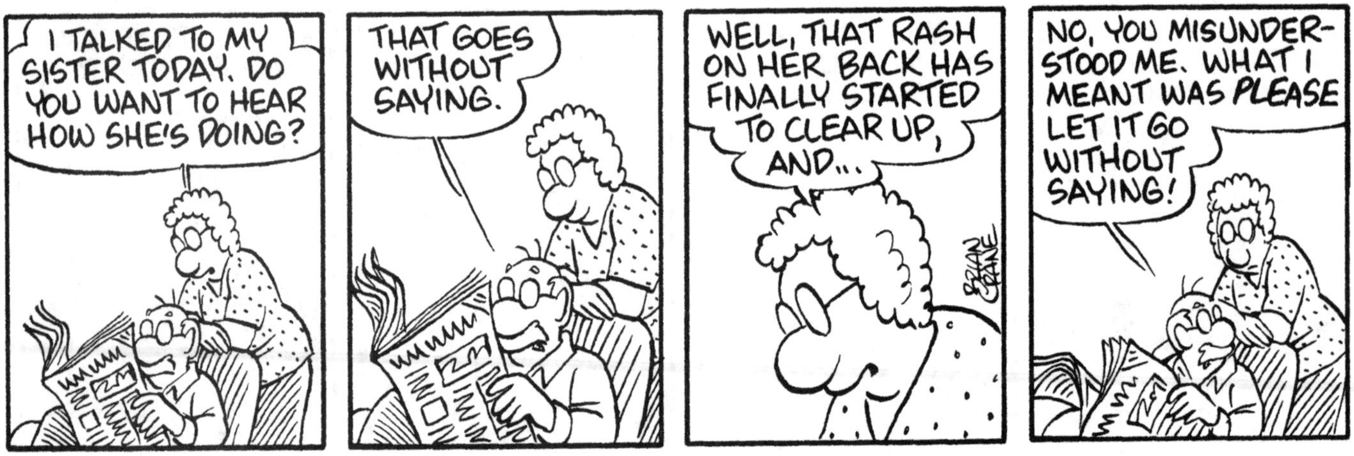
I TALKED TO MY SISTER TODAY. DO YOU WANT TO HEAR HOW SHE'S DOING?
THAT GOES WITHOUT SAYING.
WELL, THAT RASH ON HER BACK HAS FINALLY STARTED TO CLEAR UP, AND...
NO, YOU MISUNDERSTOOD ME. WHAT I MEANT WAS PLEASE LET IT GO WITHOUT SAYING!

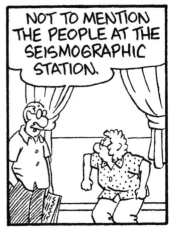

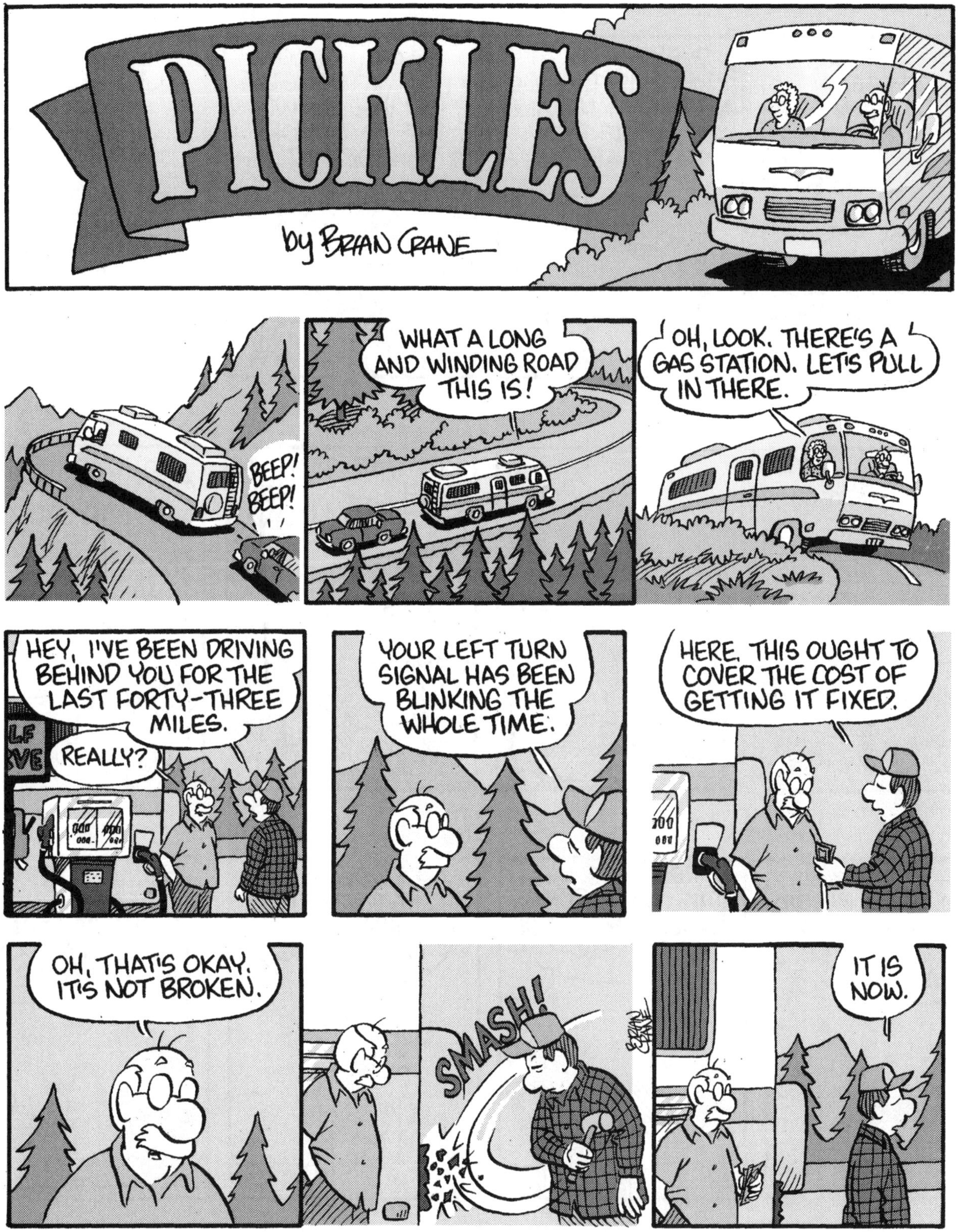
PICKLES
by BRIAN CRANE
BEEP! BEEP!
WHAT A LONG AND WINDING ROAD THIS IS!
OH, LOOK. THERE'S A GAS STATION. LET'S PULL IN THERE.
HEY, I'VE BEEN DRIVING BEHIND YOU FOR THE LAST FORTY-THREE MILES.
REALLY?
YOUR LEFT TURN SIGNAL HAS BEEN BLINKING THE WHOLE TIME.
HERE. THIS OUGHT TO COVER THE COST OF GETTING IT FIXED.
OH, THAT'S OKAY. IT'S NOT BROKEN.
SMASH!
IT IS NOW.

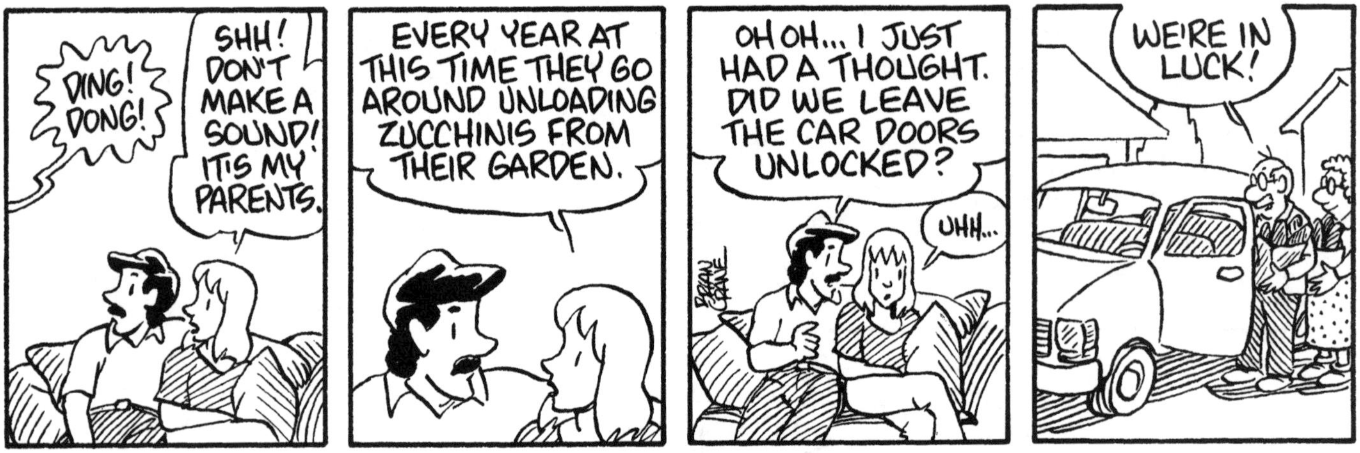
DING! DONG!
SHH! DON'T MAKE A SOUND! IT'S MY PARENTS.
EVERY YEAR AT THIS TIME THEY GO AROUND UNLOADING ZUCCHINIS FROM THEIR GARDEN.
OH OH... I JUST HAD A THOUGHT. DID WE LEAVE THE CAR DOORS UNLOCKED?
UHH...
WE'RE IN LUCK!

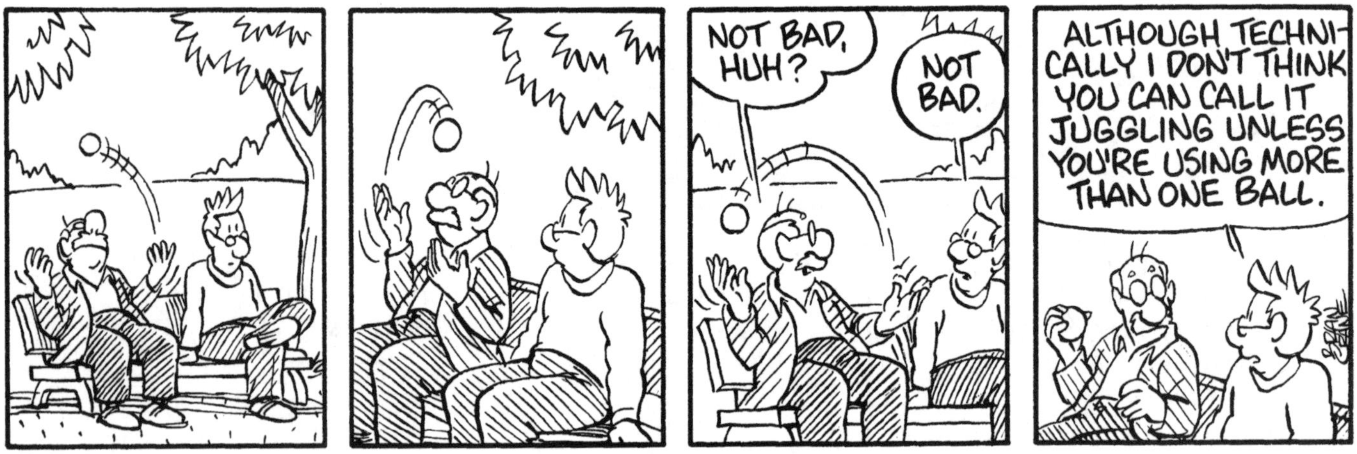
NOT BAD, HUH?
NOT BAD.
ALTHOUGH TECHNICALLY I DON'T THINK YOU CAN CALL IT JUGGLING UNLESS YOU'RE USING MORE THAN ONE BALL.

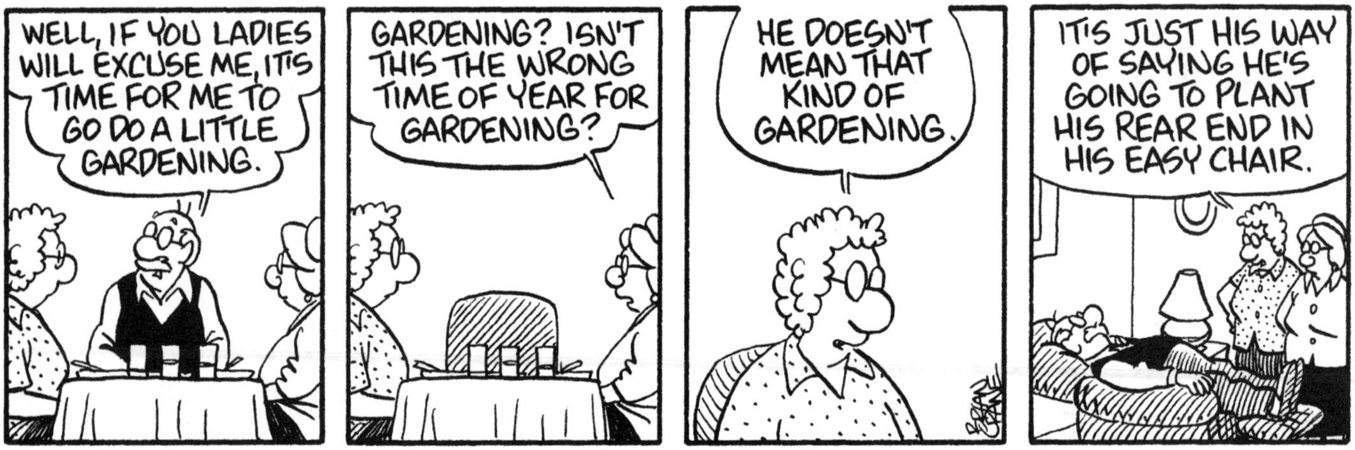
WELL, IF YOU LADIES WILL EXCUSE ME, IT'S TIME FOR ME TO GO DO A LITTLE GARDENING.
GARDENING? ISN'T THIS THE WRONG TIME OF YEAR FOR GARDENING?
HE DOESN'T MEAN THAT KIND OF GARDENING.
IT'S JUST HIS WAY OF SAYING HE'S GOING TO PLANT HIS REAR END IN HIS EASY CHAIR.

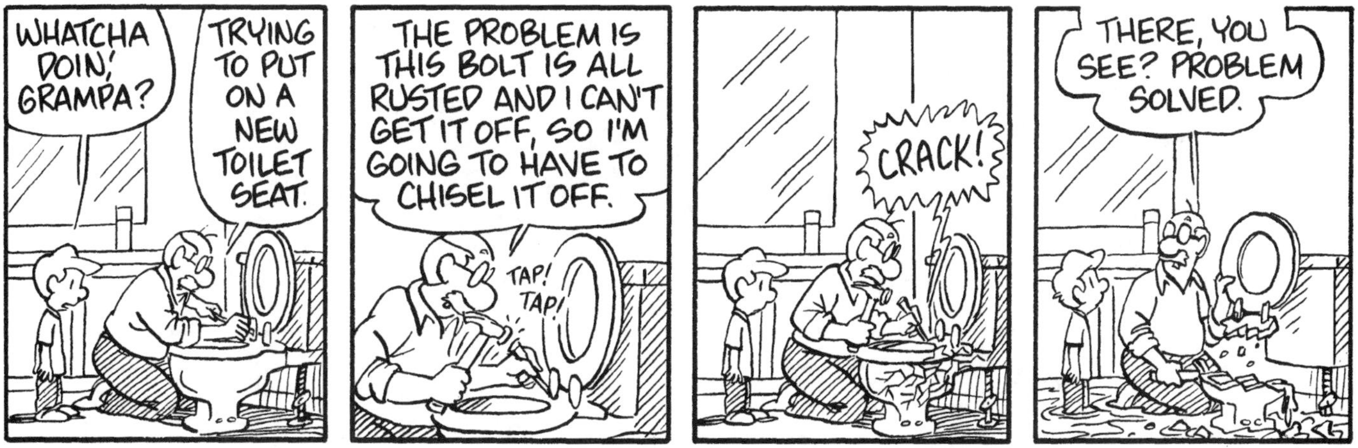
WHATCHA DOIN', GRAMPA?
TRYING TO PUT ON A NEW TOILET SEAT.
THE PROBLEM IS THIS BOLT IS ALL RUSTED AND I CAN'T GET IT OFF, SO I'M GOING TO HAVE TO CHISEL IT OFF.
TAP! TAP!
CRACK!
THERE, YOU SEE? PROBLEM SOLVED.

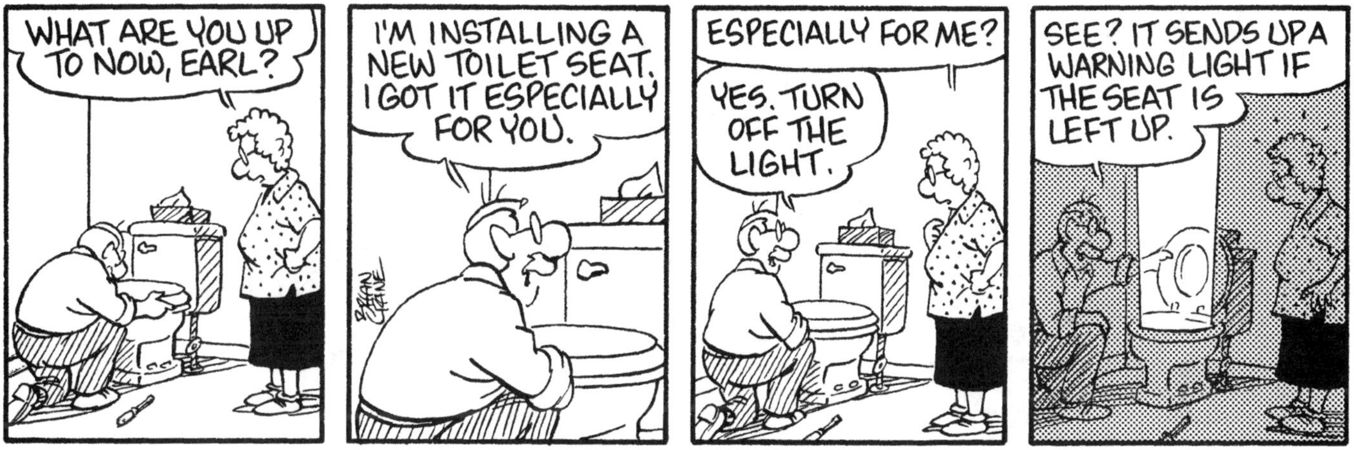
WHAT ARE YOU UP TO NOW, EARL?
I'M INSTALLING A NEW TOILET SEAT. I GOT IT ESPECIALLY FOR YOU.
ESPECIALLY FOR ME?
YES. TURN OFF THE LIGHT.
SEE? IT SENDS UP A WARNING LIGHT IF THE SEAT IS LEFT UP.

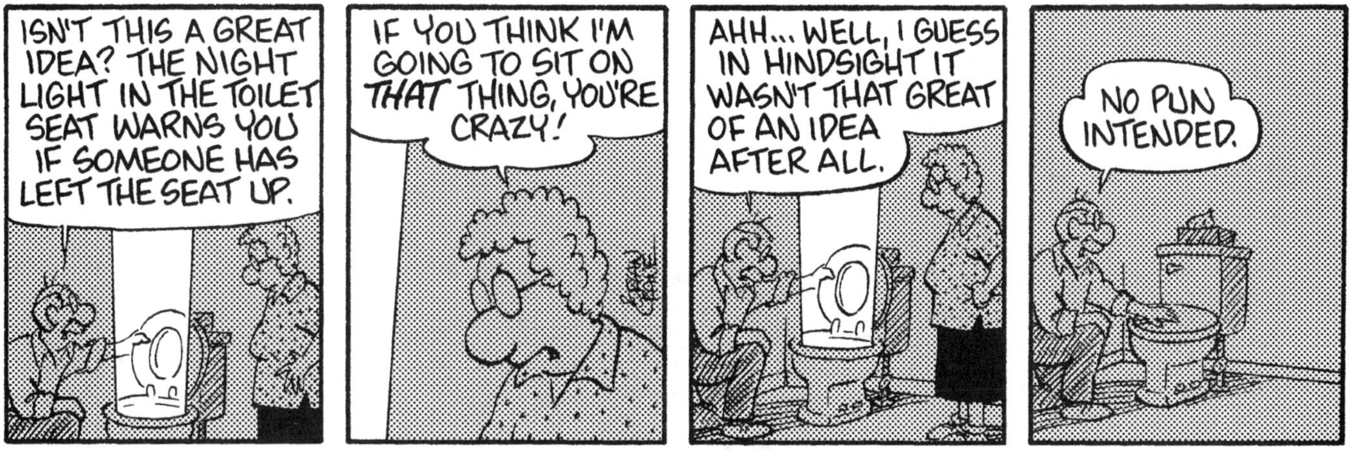
ISN'T THIS A GREAT IDEA? THE NIGHT LIGHT IN THE TOILET SEAT WARNS YOU IF SOMEONE HAS LEFT THE SEAT UP.
IF YOU THINK I'M GOING TO SIT ON THAT THING, YOU'RE CRAZY!
AHH... WELL, I GUESS IN HINDSIGHT IT WASN'T THAT GREAT OF AN IDEA AFTER ALL.
NO PUN INTENDED.

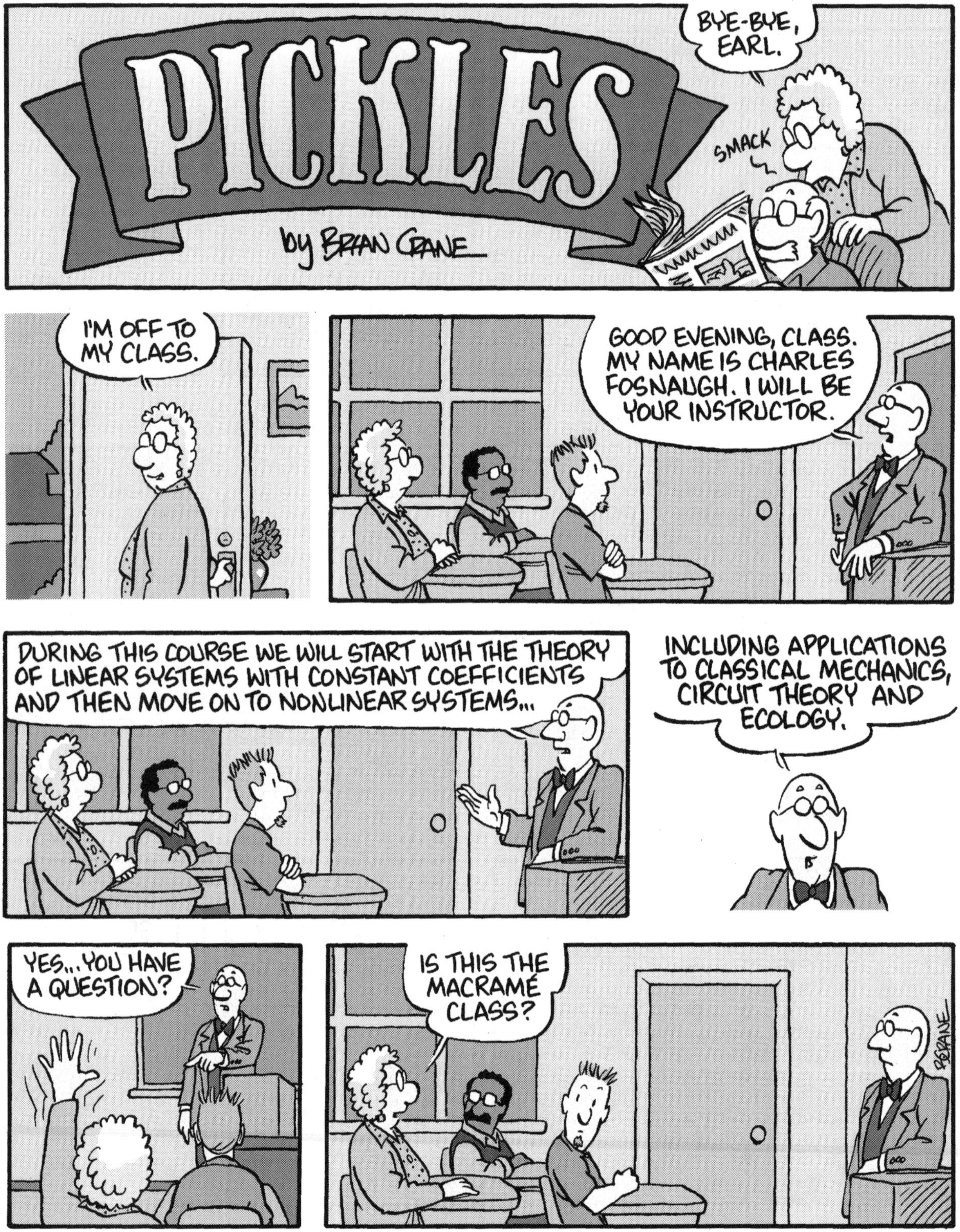
PICKLES
by BRIAN CRANE
BYE-BYE, EARL.
SMACK
I'M OFF TO MY CLASS.
GOOD EVENING, CLASS. MY NAME IS CHARLES FOSNAUGH. I WILL BE YOUR INSTRUCTOR.
DURING THIS COURSE WE WILL START WITH THE THEORY OF LINEAR SYSTEMS WITH CONSTANT COEFFICIENTS AND THEN MOVE ON TO NONLINEAR SYSTEMS...
INCLUDING APPLICATIONS TO CLASSICAL MECHANICS, CIRCUIT THEORY AND ECOLOGY.
YES... YOU HAVE A QUESTION?
IS THIS THE MACRAMÉ CLASS?
B CRANE

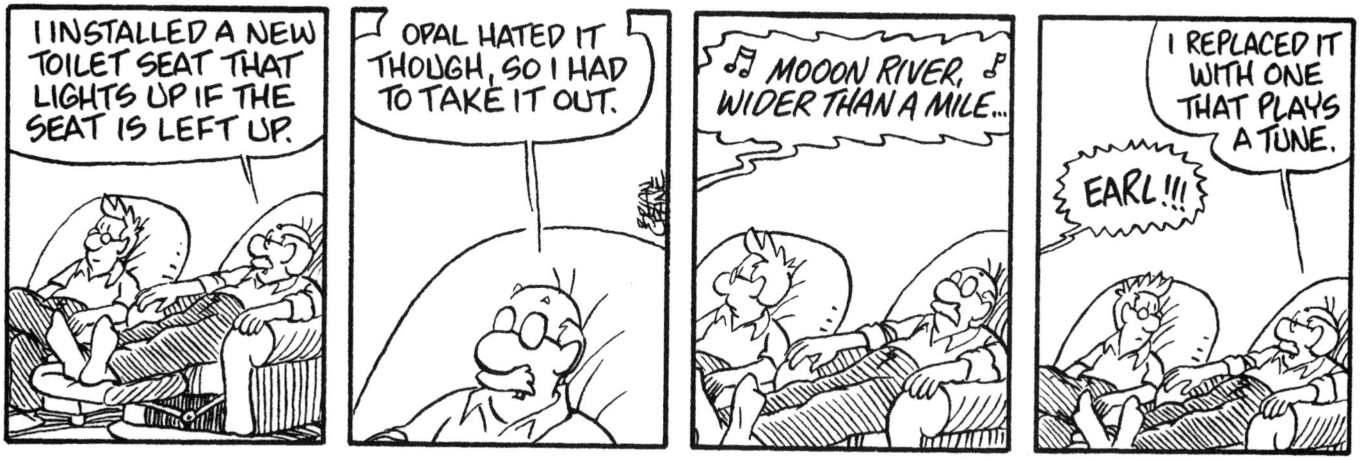
I INSTALLED A NEW TOILET SEAT THAT LIGHTS UP IF THE SEAT IS LEFT UP.
OPAL HATED IT THOUGH, SO I HAD TO TAKE IT OUT.
♪ MOOON RIVER, WIDER THAN A MILE... ♪
I REPLACED IT WITH ONE THAT PLAYS A TUNE.
EARL!!!

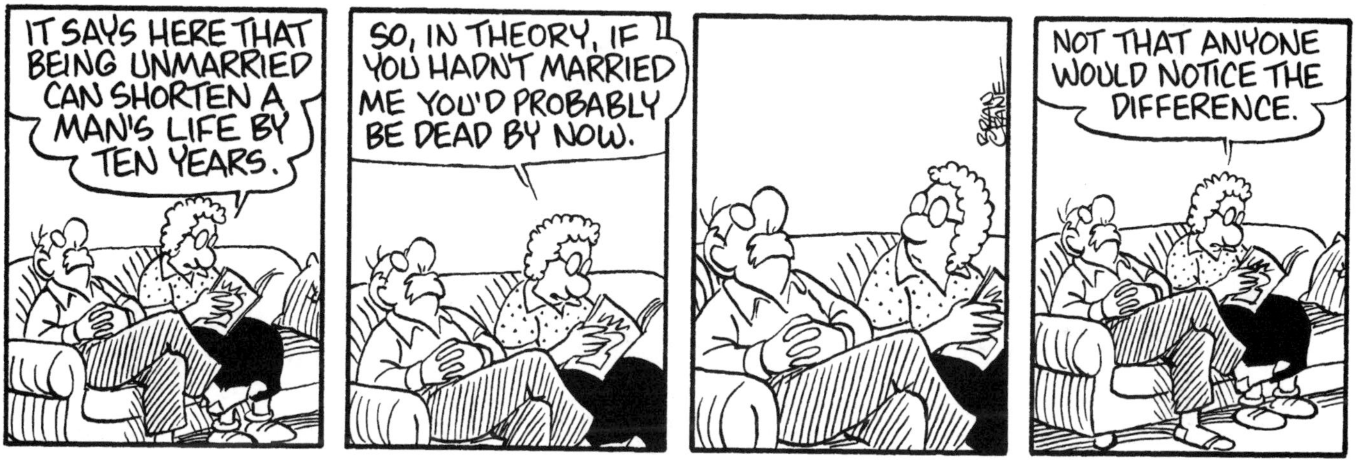
IT SAYS HERE THAT BEING UNMARRIED CAN SHORTEN A MAN'S LIFE BY TEN YEARS.
SO, IN THEORY, IF YOU HADN'T MARRIED ME YOU'D PROBABLY BE DEAD BY NOW.
NOT THAT ANYONE WOULD NOTICE THE DIFFERENCE.

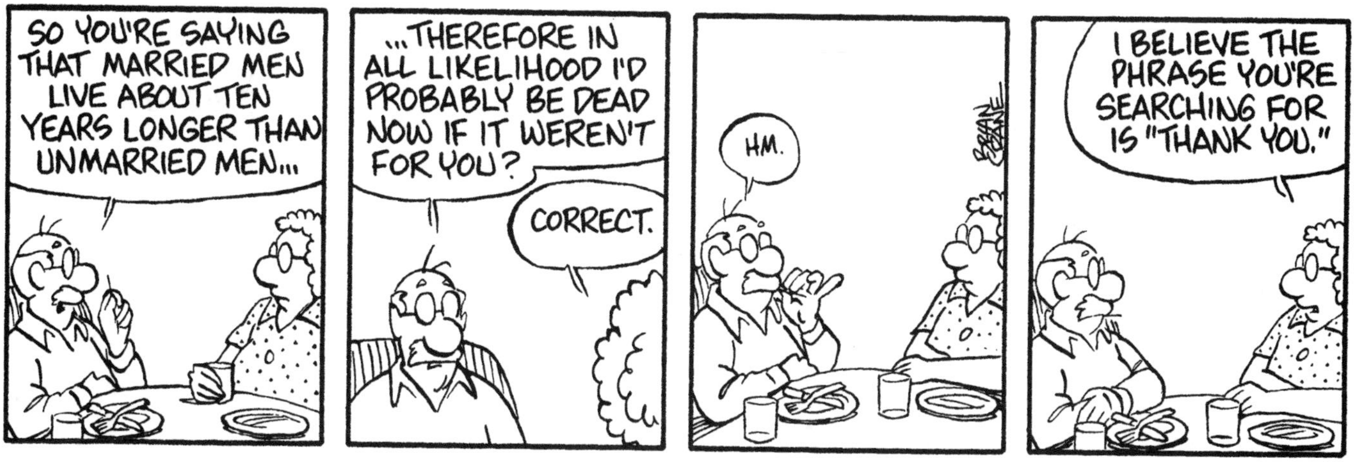
SO YOU'RE SAYING THAT MARRIED MEN LIVE ABOUT TEN YEARS LONGER THAN UNMARRIED MEN...
...THEREFORE IN ALL LIKELIHOOD I'D PROBABLY BE DEAD NOW IF IT WEREN'T FOR YOU?
CORRECT.
HM.
I BELIEVE THE PHRASE YOU'RE SEARCHING FOR IS "THANK YOU."

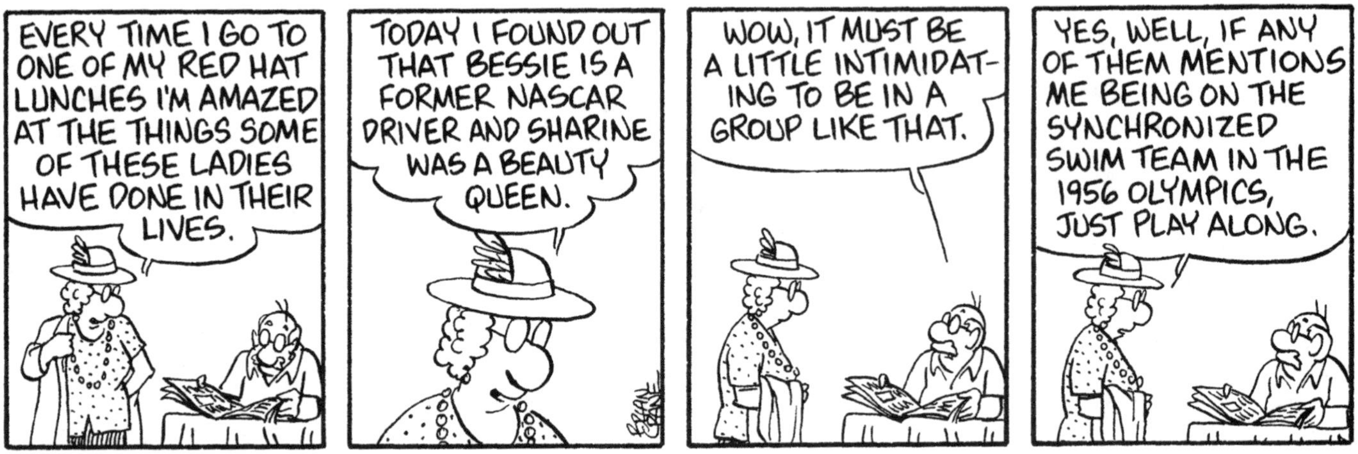
EVERY TIME I GO TO ONE OF MY RED HAT LUNCHES I'M AMAZED AT THE THINGS SOME OF THESE LADIES HAVE DONE IN THEIR LIVES.
TODAY I FOUND OUT THAT BESSIE IS A FORMER NASCAR DRIVER AND SHARINE WAS A BEAUTY QUEEN.
WOW, IT MUST BE A LITTLE INTIMIDATING TO BE IN A GROUP LIKE THAT.
YES, WELL, IF ANY OF THEM MENTIONS ME BEING ON THE SYNCHRONIZED SWIM TEAM IN THE 1956 OLYMPICS, JUST PLAY ALONG.

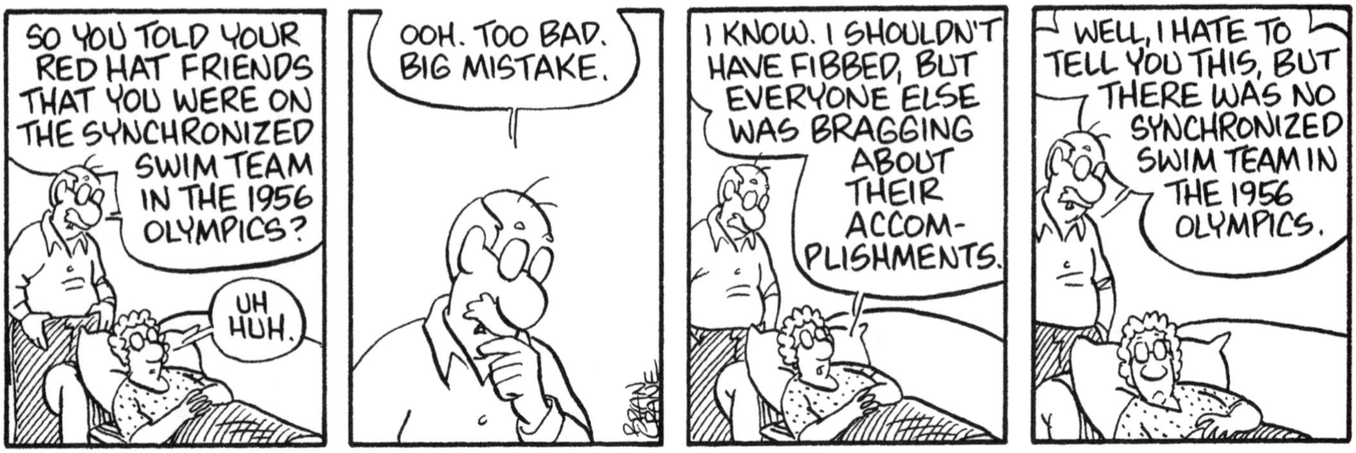
SO YOU TOLD YOUR RED HAT FRIENDS THAT YOU WERE ON THE SYNCHRONIZED SWIM TEAM IN THE 1956 OLYMPICS?
UH HUH.
OOH. TOO BAD. BIG MISTAKE.
I KNOW. I SHOULDN'T HAVE FIBBED, BUT EVERYONE ELSE WAS BRAGGING ABOUT THEIR ACCOMPLISHMENTS.
WELL, I HATE TO TELL YOU THIS, BUT THERE WAS NO SYNCHRONIZED SWIM TEAM IN THE 1956 OLYMPICS.

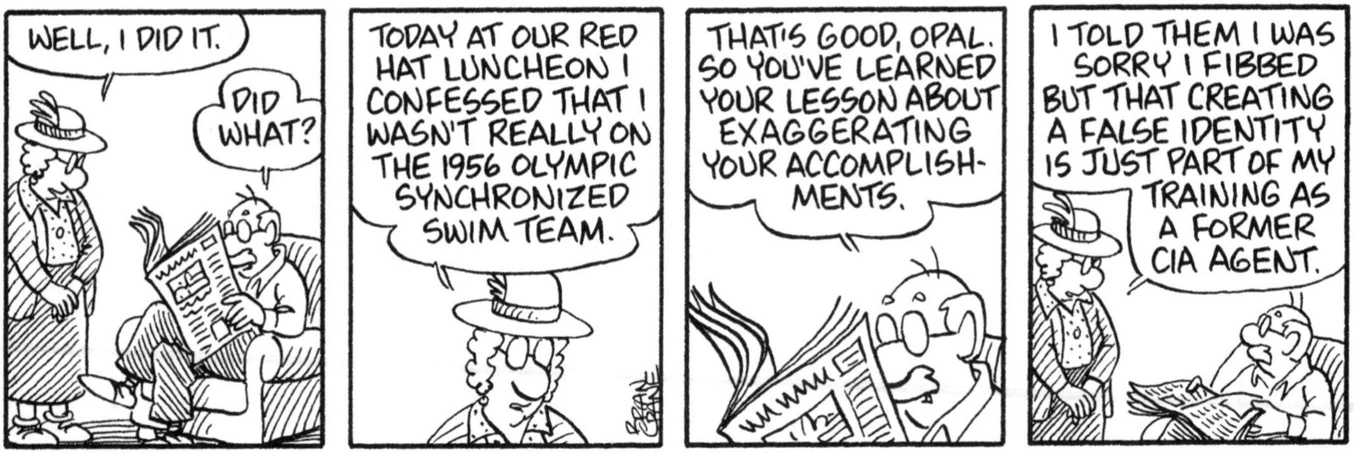
WELL, I DID IT.
DID WHAT?
TODAY AT OUR RED HAT LUNCHEON I CONFESSED THAT I WASN'T REALLY ON THE 1956 OLYMPIC SYNCHRONIZED SWIM TEAM.
THAT'S GOOD, OPAL. SO YOU'VE LEARNED YOUR LESSON ABOUT EXAGGERATING YOUR ACCOMPLISHMENTS.
I TOLD THEM I WAS SORRY I FIBBED BUT THAT CREATING A FALSE IDENTITY IS JUST PART OF MY TRAINING AS A FORMER CIA AGENT.

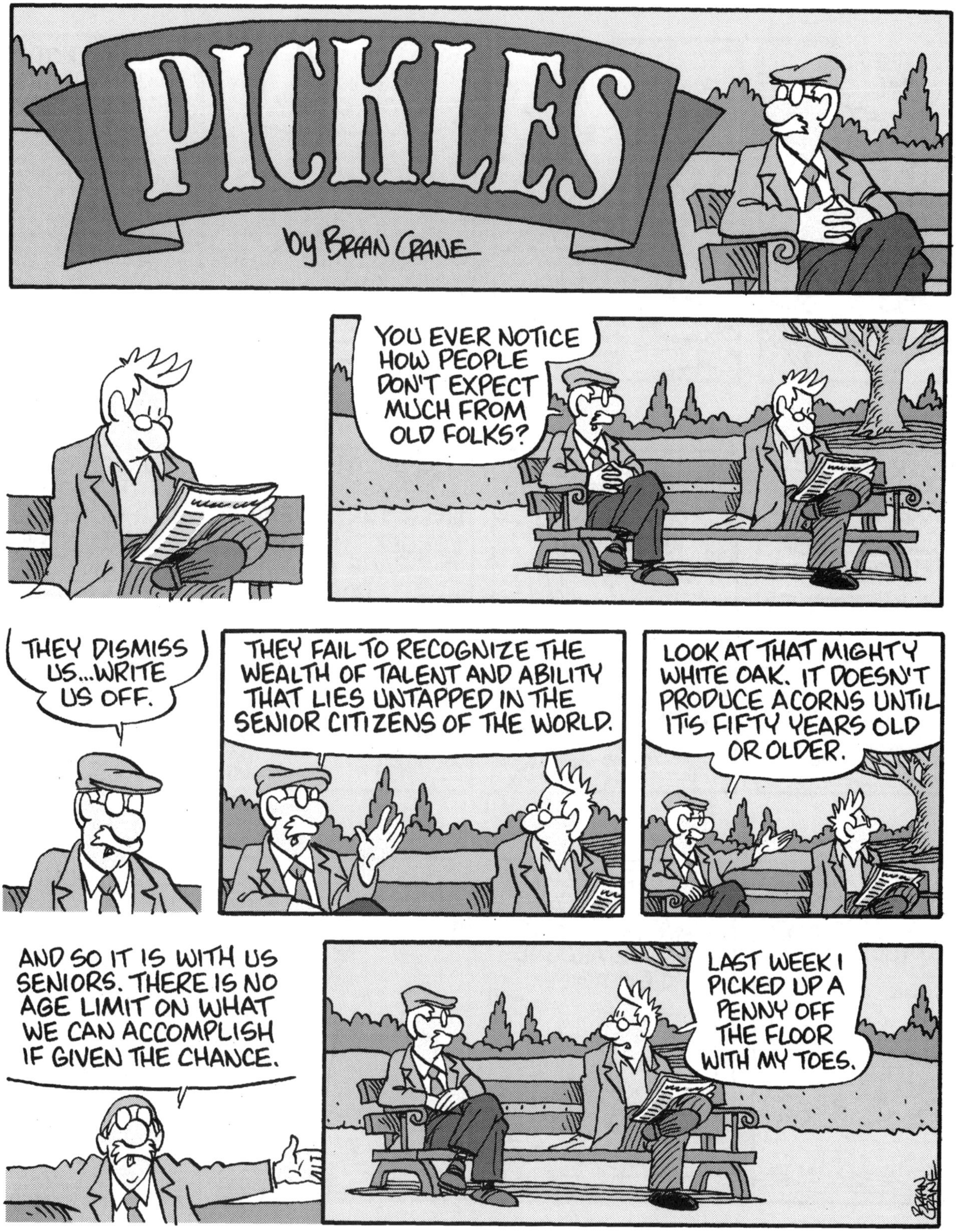
PICKLES
by Brian Crane
YOU EVER NOTICE HOW PEOPLE DON'T EXPECT MUCH FROM OLD FOLKS?
THEY DISMISS US...WRITE US OFF.
THEY FAIL TO RECOGNIZE THE WEALTH OF TALENT AND ABILITY THAT LIES UNTAPPED IN THE SENIOR CITIZENS OF THE WORLD.
LOOK AT THAT MIGHTY WHITE OAK. IT DOESN'T PRODUCE ACORNS UNTIL IT'S FIFTY YEARS OLD OR OLDER.
AND SO IT IS WITH US SENIORS. THERE IS NO AGE LIMIT ON WHAT WE CAN ACCOMPLISH IF GIVEN THE CHANCE.
LAST WEEK I PICKED UP A PENNY OFF THE FLOOR WITH MY TOES.

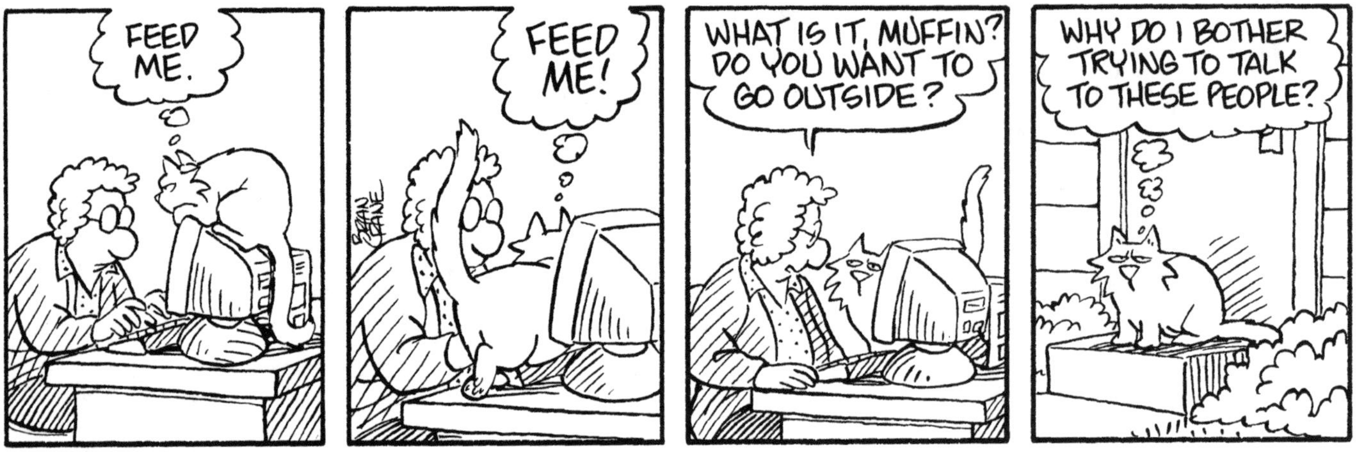
FEED ME.
FEED ME!
WHAT IS IT, MUFFIN? DO YOU WANT TO GO OUTSIDE?
WHY DO I BOTHER TRYING TO TALK TO THESE PEOPLE?

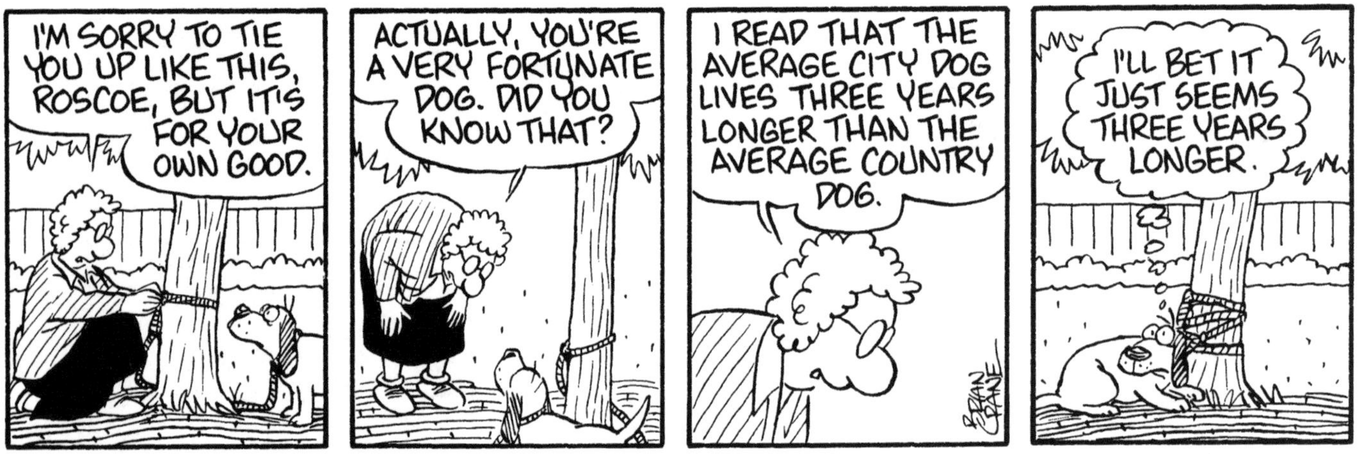
I'M SORRY TO TIE YOU UP LIKE THIS, ROSCOE, BUT IT'S FOR YOUR OWN GOOD.
ACTUALLY, YOU'RE A VERY FORTUNATE DOG. DID YOU KNOW THAT?
I READ THAT THE AVERAGE CITY DOG LIVES THREE YEARS LONGER THAN THE AVERAGE COUNTRY DOG.
I'LL BET IT JUST SEEMS THREE YEARS LONGER.

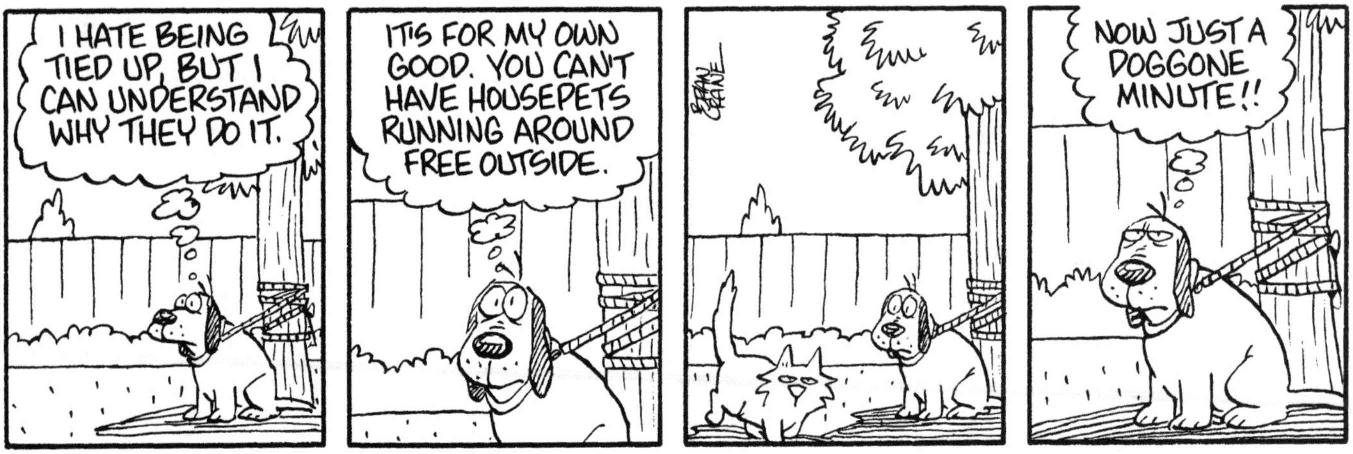
I HATE BEING TIED UP, BUT I CAN UNDERSTAND WHY THEY DO IT.
IT'S FOR MY OWN GOOD. YOU CAN'T HAVE HOUSEPETS RUNNING AROUND FREE OUTSIDE.
NOW JUST A DOGGONE MINUTE!!

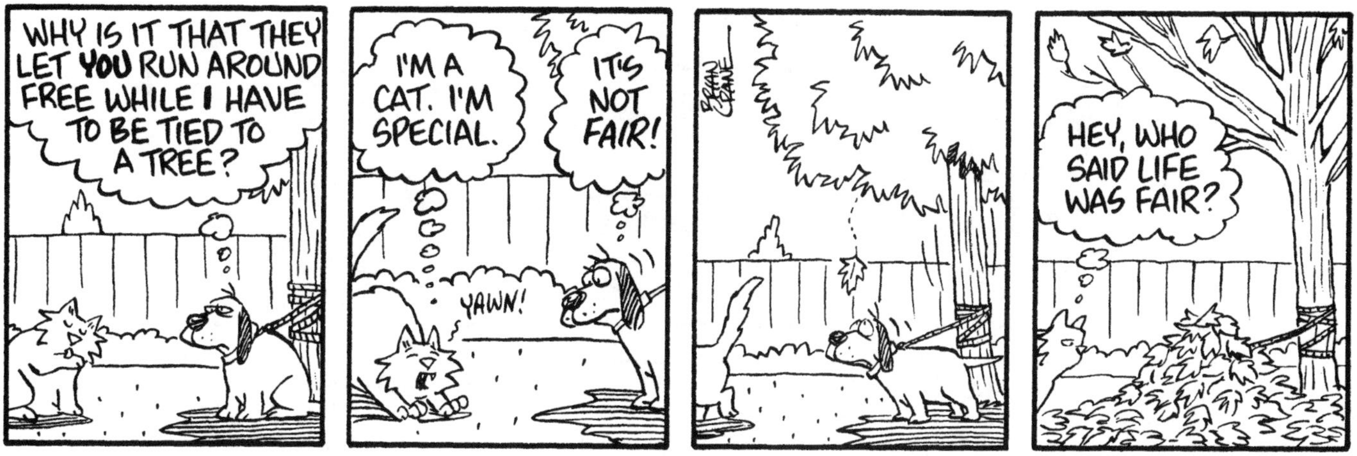
WHY IS IT THAT THEY LET **YOU** RUN AROUND FREE WHILE **I** HAVE TO BE TIED TO A TREE?
I'M A CAT. I'M SPECIAL.
YAWN!
IT'S NOT **FAIR!**
HEY, WHO SAID LIFE WAS FAIR?

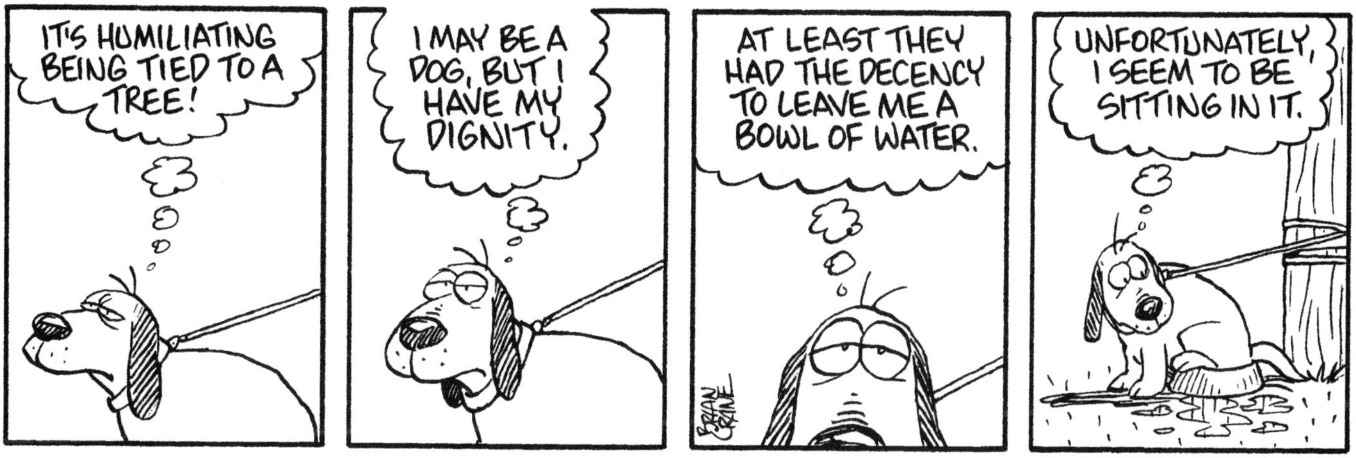
IT'S HUMILIATING BEING TIED TO A TREE!
I MAY BE A DOG, BUT I HAVE MY DIGNITY.
AT LEAST THEY HAD THE DECENCY TO LEAVE ME A BOWL OF WATER.
UNFORTUNATELY, I SEEM TO BE SITTING IN IT.

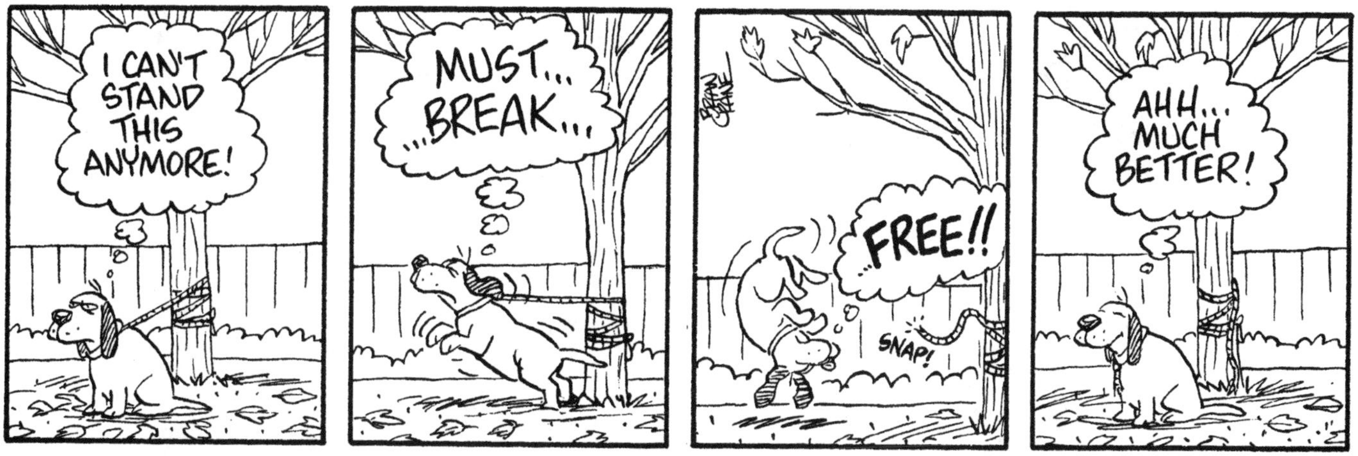
I CAN'T STAND THIS ANYMORE!
MUST... ...BREAK...
FREE!!
SNAP!
AHH... MUCH BETTER!

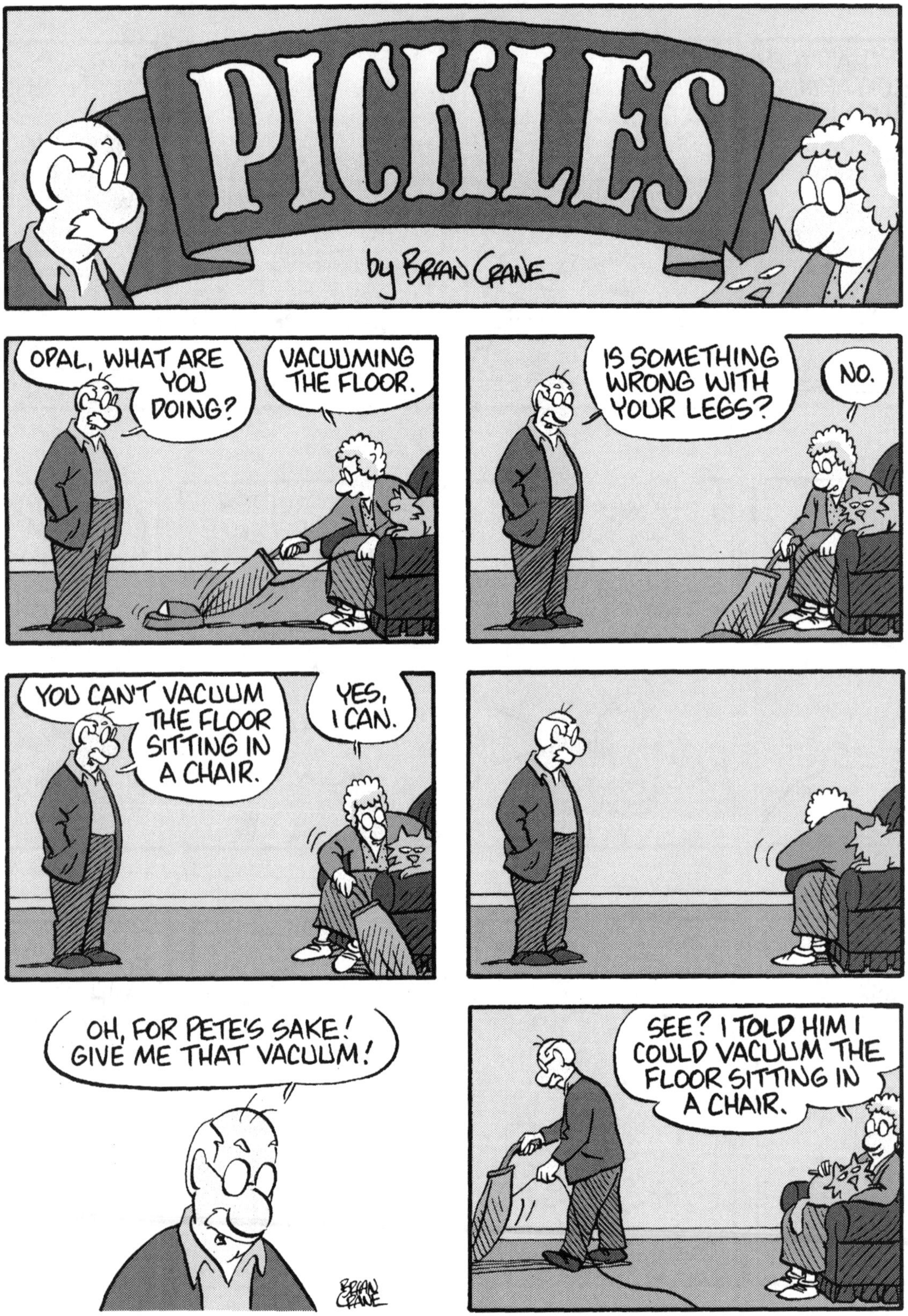
PICKLES
by BRIAN CRANE
OPAL, WHAT ARE YOU DOING?
VACUUMING THE FLOOR.
IS SOMETHING WRONG WITH YOUR LEGS?
NO.
YOU CAN'T VACUUM THE FLOOR SITTING IN A CHAIR.
YES, I CAN.
OH, FOR PETE'S SAKE! GIVE ME THAT VACUUM!
BRIAN CRANE
SEE? I TOLD HIM I COULD VACUUM THE FLOOR SITTING IN A CHAIR.

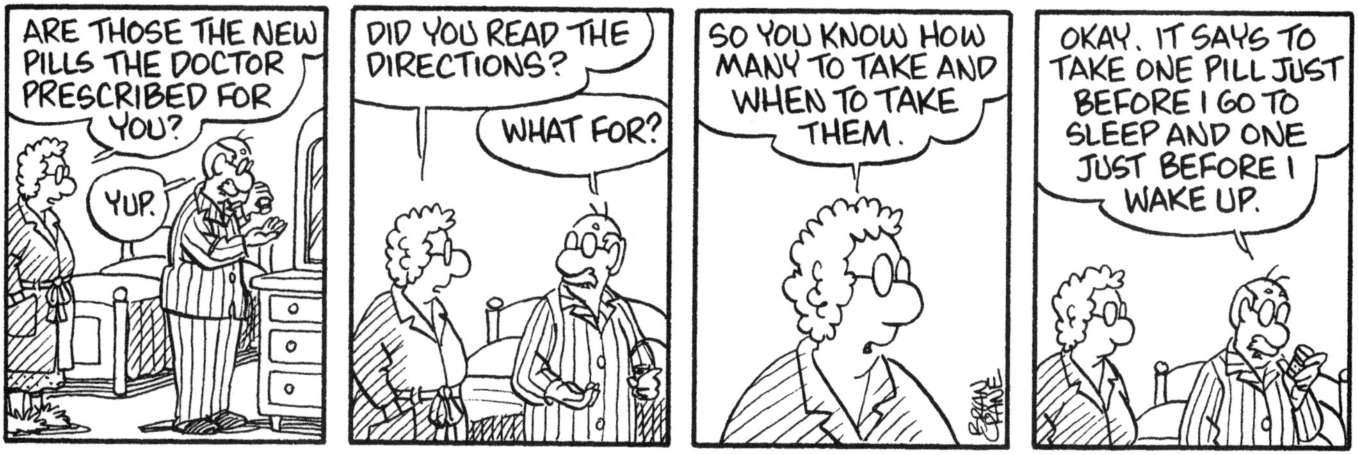
ARE THOSE THE NEW PILLS THE DOCTOR PRESCRIBED FOR YOU?
YUP.
DID YOU READ THE DIRECTIONS?
WHAT FOR?
SO YOU KNOW HOW MANY TO TAKE AND WHEN TO TAKE THEM.
OKAY. IT SAYS TO TAKE ONE PILL JUST BEFORE I GO TO SLEEP AND ONE JUST BEFORE I WAKE UP.

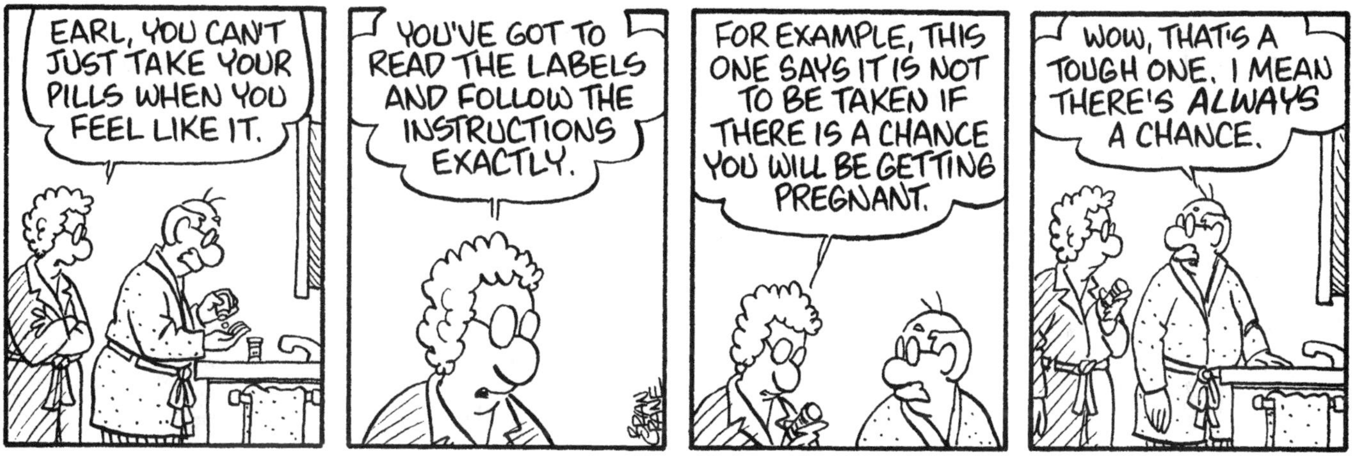
EARL, YOU CAN'T JUST TAKE YOUR PILLS WHEN YOU FEEL LIKE IT.
YOU'VE GOT TO READ THE LABELS AND FOLLOW THE INSTRUCTIONS EXACTLY.
FOR EXAMPLE, THIS ONE SAYS IT IS NOT TO BE TAKEN IF THERE IS A CHANCE YOU WILL BE GETTING PREGNANT.
WOW, THAT'S A TOUGH ONE. I MEAN THERE'S ALWAYS A CHANCE.

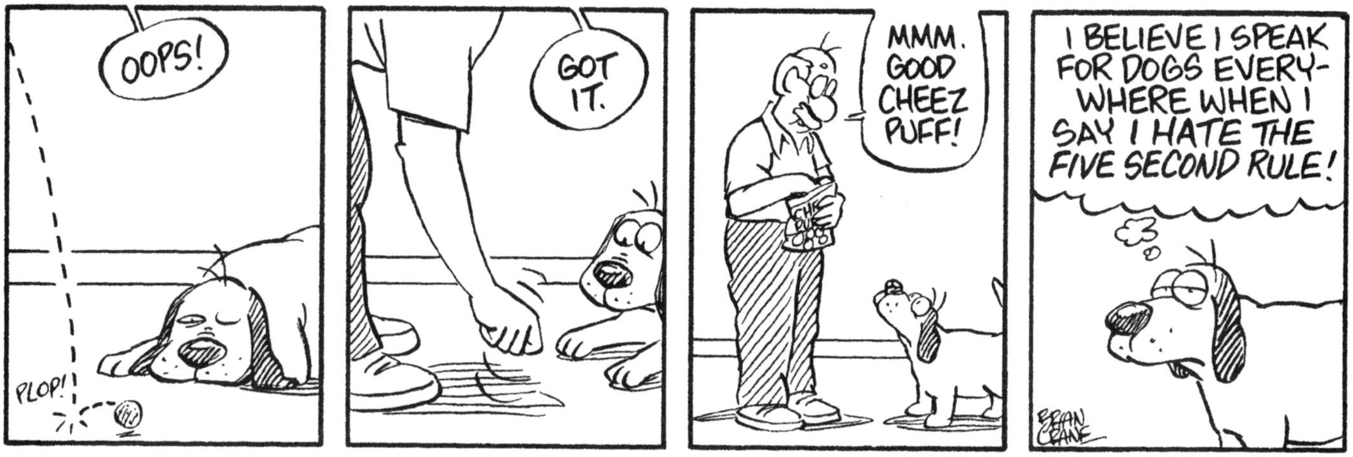
OOPS!
PLOP!
GOT IT.
MMM. GOOD CHEEZ PUFF!
I BELIEVE I SPEAK FOR DOGS EVERY-WHERE WHEN I SAY I HATE THE FIVE SECOND RULE!

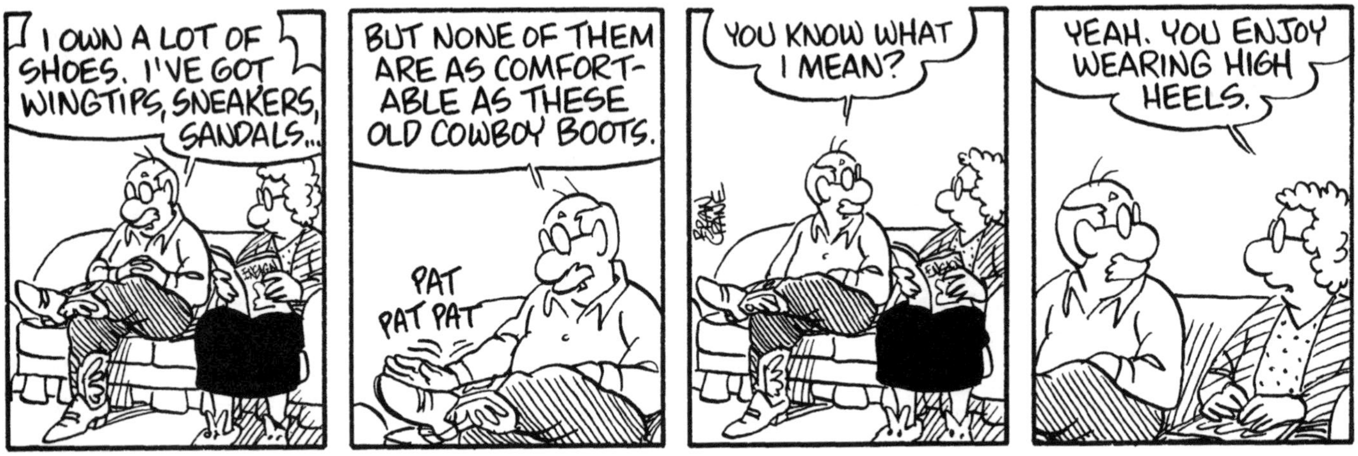
I OWN A LOT OF SHOES. I'VE GOT WINGTIPS, SNEAKERS, SANDALS...
BUT NONE OF THEM ARE AS COMFORT-ABLE AS THESE OLD COWBOY BOOTS.
PAT PAT PAT
YOU KNOW WHAT I MEAN?
YEAH. YOU ENJOY WEARING HIGH HEELS.

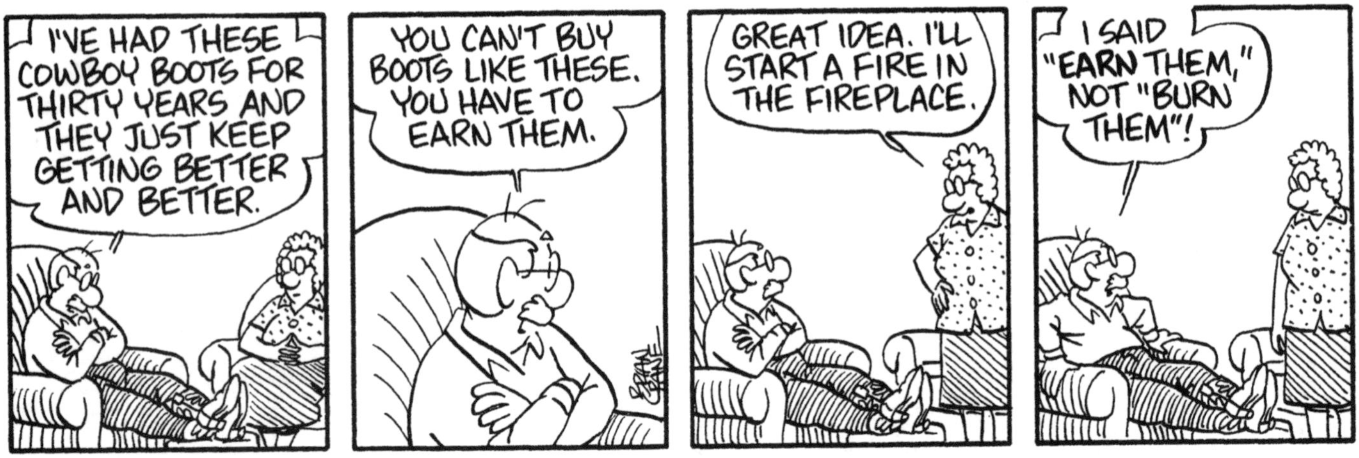
I'VE HAD THESE COWBOY BOOTS FOR THIRTY YEARS AND THEY JUST KEEP GETTING BETTER AND BETTER.
YOU CAN'T BUY BOOTS LIKE THESE. YOU HAVE TO EARN THEM.
GREAT IDEA. I'LL START A FIRE IN THE FIREPLACE.
I SAID "EARN THEM," NOT "BURN THEM"!

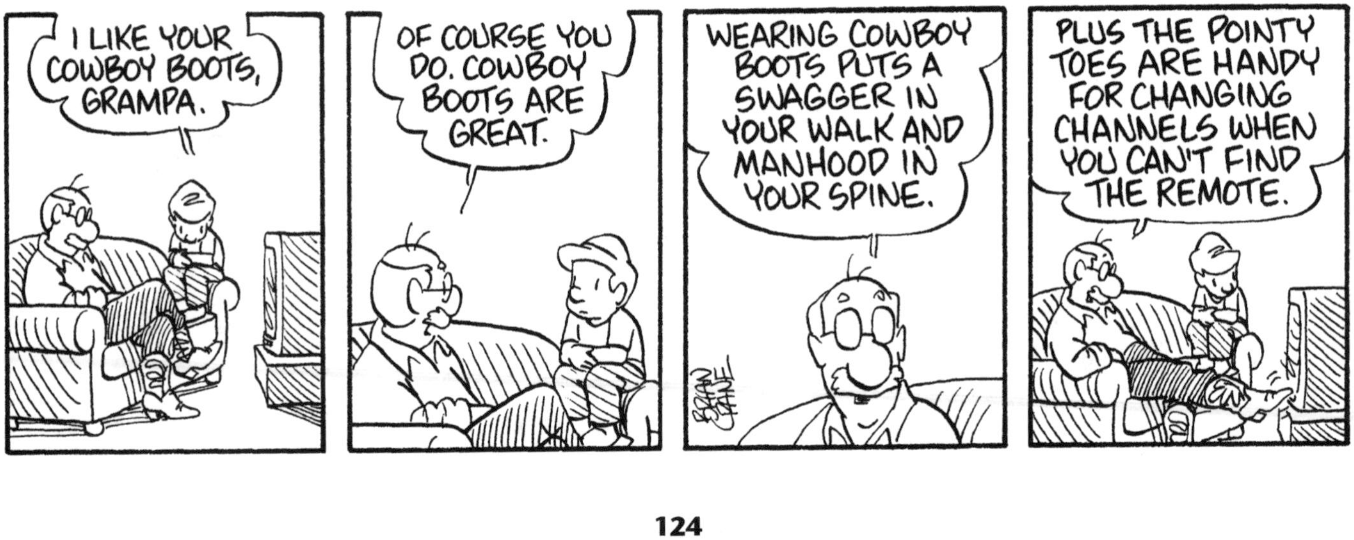
I LIKE YOUR COWBOY BOOTS, GRAMPA.
OF COURSE YOU DO. COWBOY BOOTS ARE GREAT.
WEARING COWBOY BOOTS PUTS A SWAGGER IN YOUR WALK AND MANHOOD IN YOUR SPINE.
PLUS THE POINTY TOES ARE HANDY FOR CHANGING CHANNELS WHEN YOU CAN'T FIND THE REMOTE.

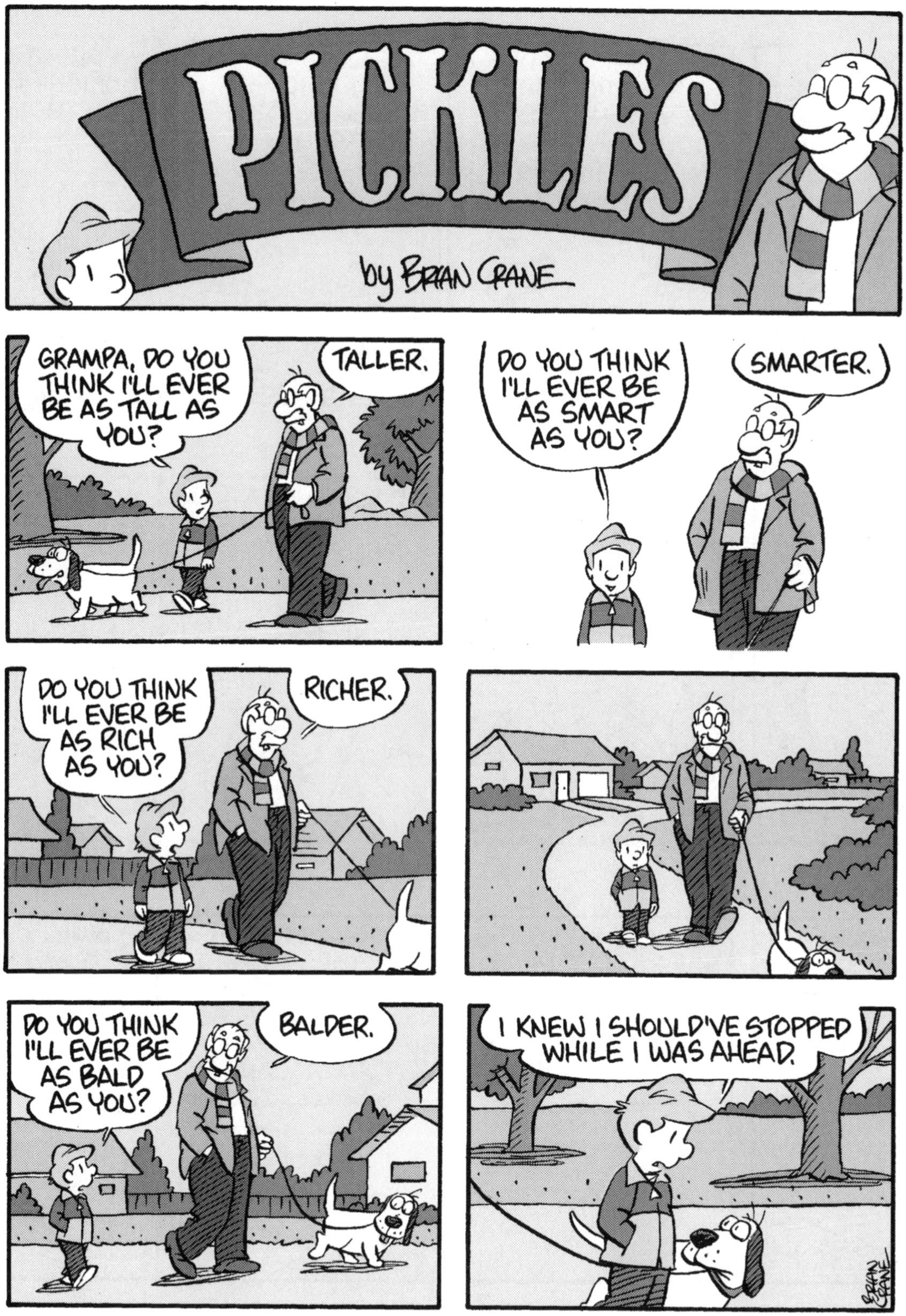
PICKLES
by BRIAN CRANE
GRAMPA, DO YOU THINK I'LL EVER BE AS TALL AS YOU?
TALLER.
DO YOU THINK I'LL EVER BE AS SMART AS YOU?
SMARTER.
DO YOU THINK I'LL EVER BE AS RICH AS YOU?
RICHER.
DO YOU THINK I'LL EVER BE AS BALD AS YOU?
BALDER.
I KNEW I SHOULD'VE STOPPED WHILE I WAS AHEAD.
BRIAN CRANE

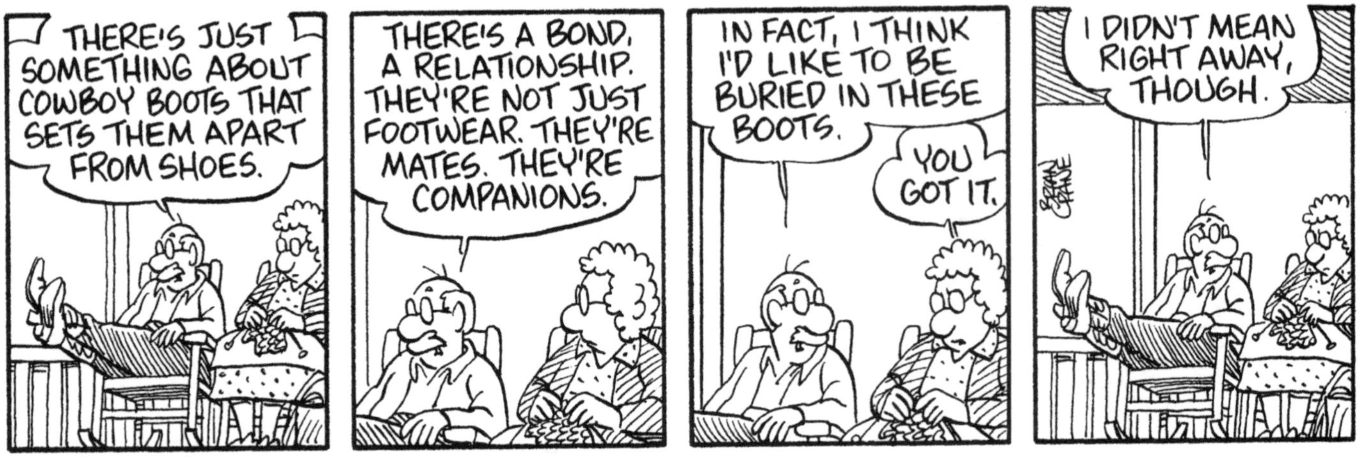
THERE'S JUST SOMETHING ABOUT COWBOY BOOTS THAT SETS THEM APART FROM SHOES.
THERE'S A BOND, A RELATIONSHIP. THEY'RE NOT JUST FOOTWEAR. THEY'RE MATES. THEY'RE COMPANIONS.
IN FACT, I THINK I'D LIKE TO BE BURIED IN THESE BOOTS.
YOU GOT IT.
I DIDN'T MEAN RIGHT AWAY, THOUGH.

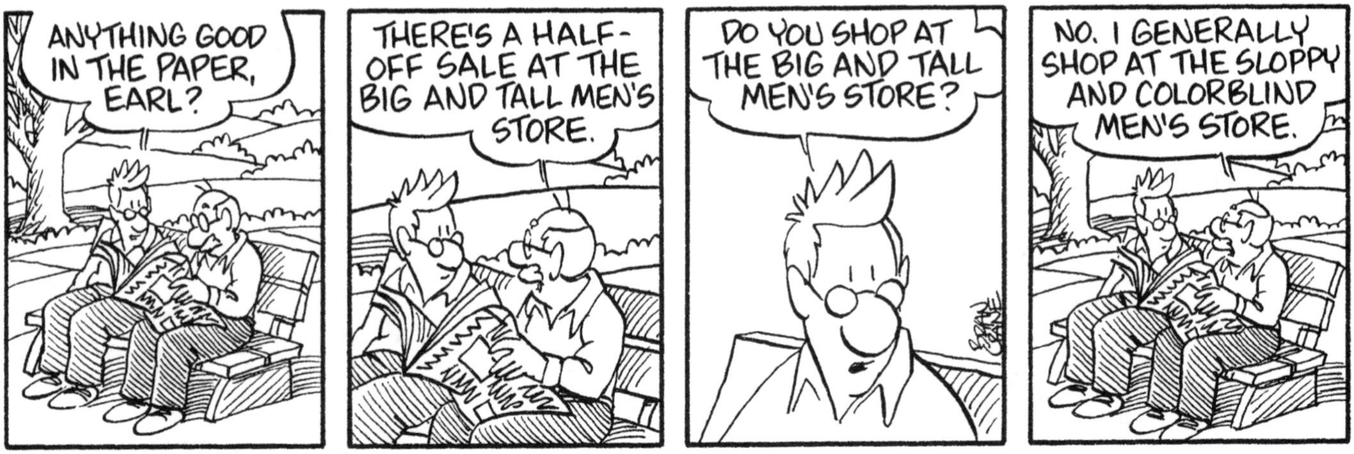
ANYTHING GOOD IN THE PAPER, EARL?
THERE'S A HALF-OFF SALE AT THE BIG AND TALL MEN'S STORE.
DO YOU SHOP AT THE BIG AND TALL MEN'S STORE?
NO. I GENERALLY SHOP AT THE SLOPPY AND COLORBLIND MEN'S STORE.

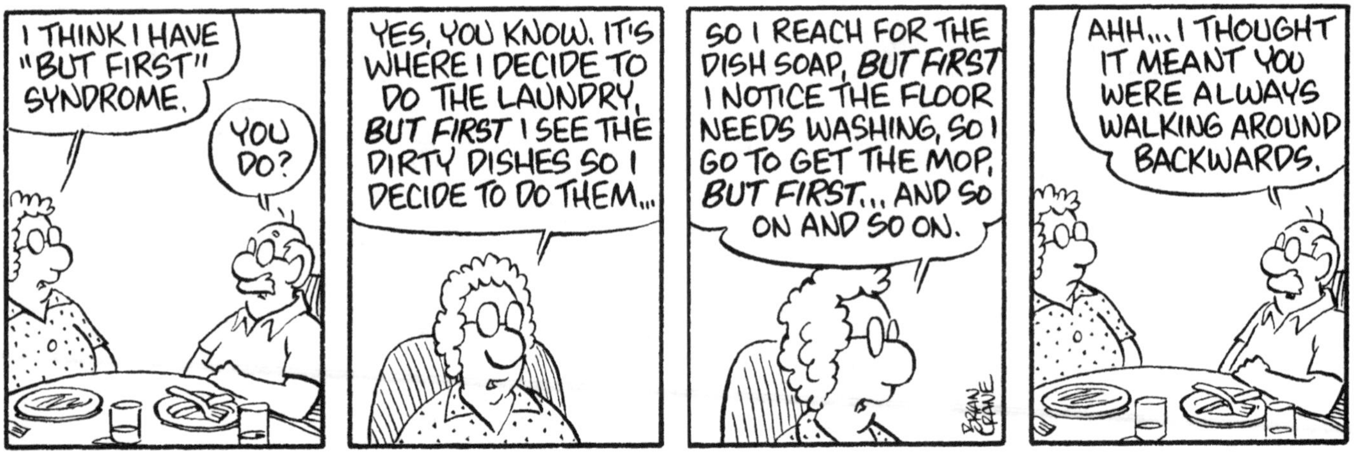
I THINK I HAVE "BUT FIRST" SYNDROME.
YOU DO?
YES, YOU KNOW. IT'S WHERE I DECIDE TO DO THE LAUNDRY, BUT FIRST I SEE THE DIRTY DISHES SO I DECIDE TO DO THEM...
SO I REACH FOR THE DISH SOAP, BUT FIRST I NOTICE THE FLOOR NEEDS WASHING, SO I GO TO GET THE MOP, BUT FIRST... AND SO ON AND SO ON.
AHH... I THOUGHT IT MEANT YOU WERE ALWAYS WALKING AROUND BACKWARDS.

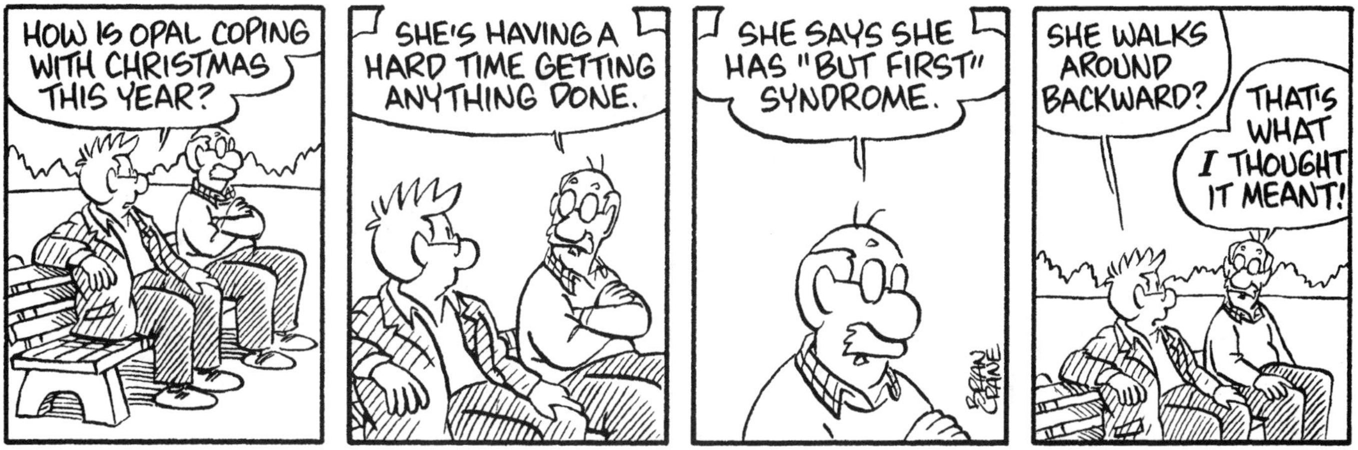
HOW IS OPAL COPING WITH CHRISTMAS THIS YEAR?
SHE'S HAVING A HARD TIME GETTING ANYTHING DONE.
SHE SAYS SHE HAS "BUT FIRST" SYNDROME.
SHE WALKS AROUND BACKWARD?
THAT'S WHAT *I* THOUGHT IT MEANT!

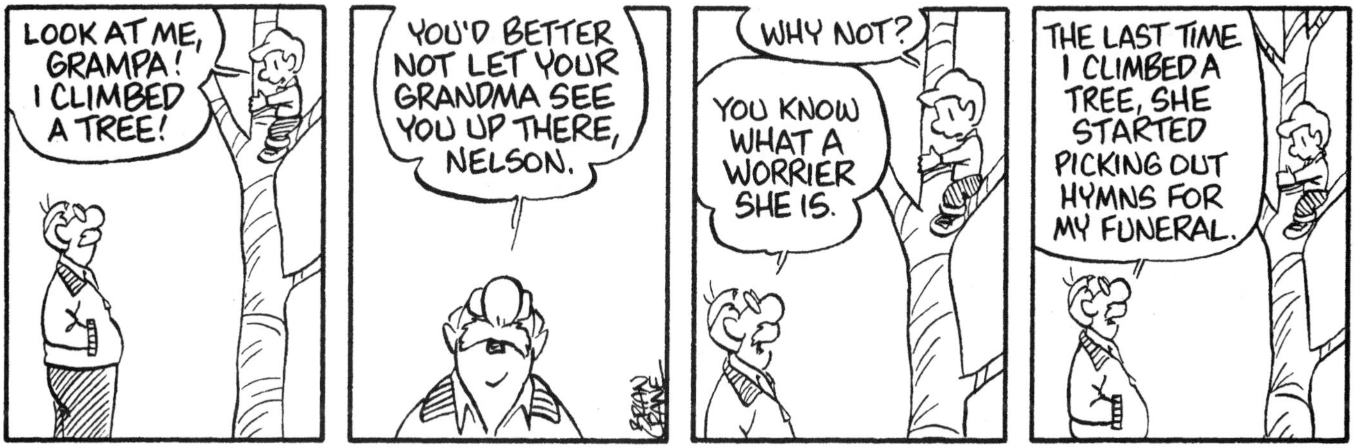
LOOK AT ME, GRAMPA! I CLIMBED A TREE!
YOU'D BETTER NOT LET YOUR GRANDMA SEE YOU UP THERE, NELSON.
WHY NOT?
YOU KNOW WHAT A WORRIER SHE IS.
THE LAST TIME I CLIMBED A TREE, SHE STARTED PICKING OUT HYMNS FOR MY FUNERAL.

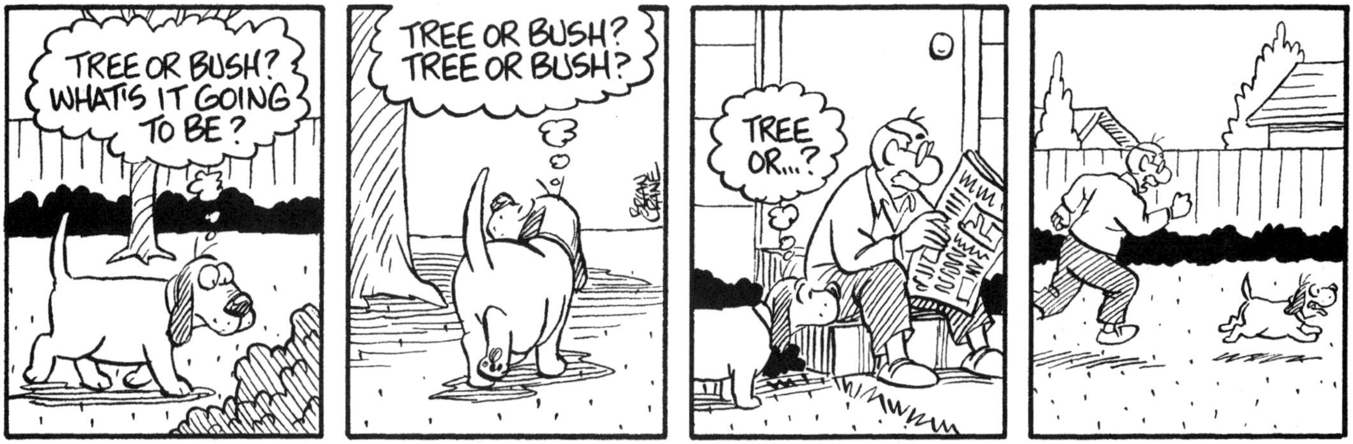
TREE OR BUSH? WHAT'S IT GOING TO BE?
TREE OR BUSH? TREE OR BUSH?
TREE OR...?

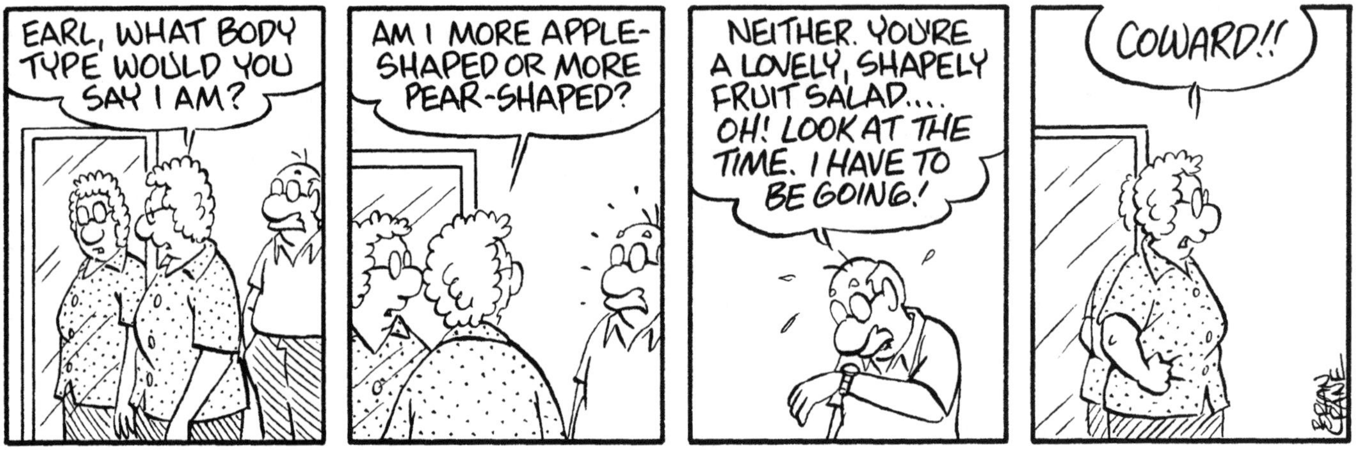
EARL, WHAT BODY TYPE WOULD YOU SAY I AM?
AM I MORE APPLE-SHAPED OR MORE PEAR-SHAPED?
NEITHER. YOU'RE A LOVELY, SHAPELY FRUIT SALAD.... OH! LOOK AT THE TIME. I HAVE TO BE GOING!
COWARD!!

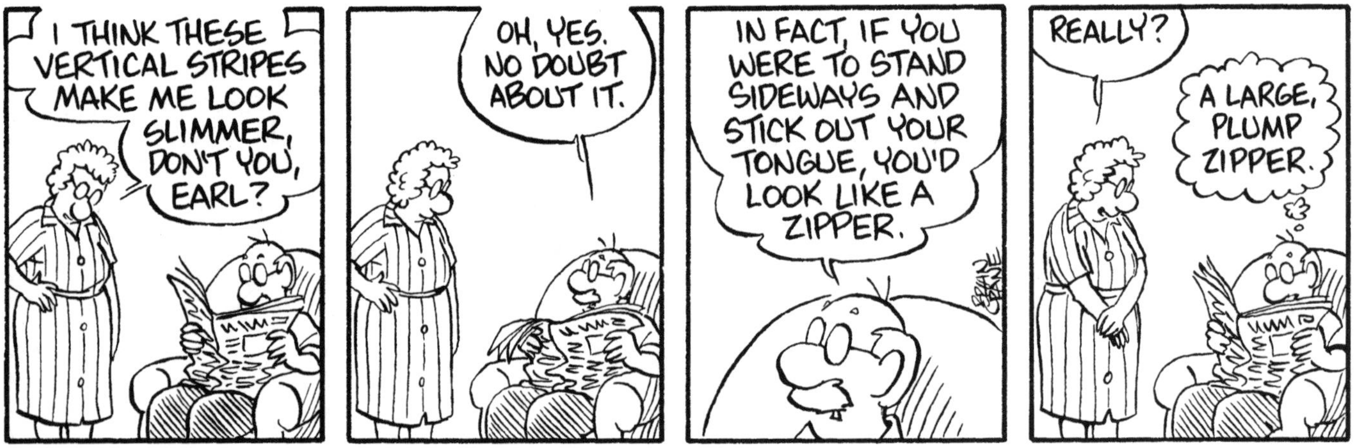
I THINK THESE VERTICAL STRIPES MAKE ME LOOK SLIMMER, DON'T YOU, EARL?
OH, YES. NO DOUBT ABOUT IT.
IN FACT, IF YOU WERE TO STAND SIDEWAYS AND STICK OUT YOUR TONGUE, YOU'D LOOK LIKE A ZIPPER.
REALLY?
A LARGE, PLUMP ZIPPER.

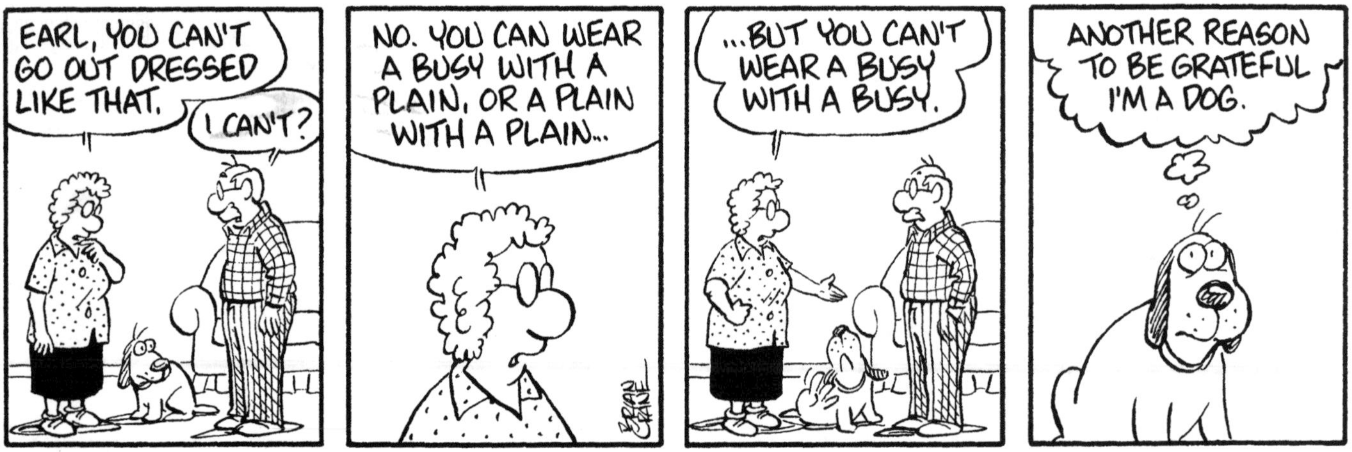
EARL, YOU CAN'T GO OUT DRESSED LIKE THAT.
I CAN'T?
NO. YOU CAN WEAR A BUSY WITH A PLAIN, OR A PLAIN WITH A PLAIN...
...BUT YOU CAN'T WEAR A BUSY WITH A BUSY.
ANOTHER REASON TO BE GRATEFUL I'M A DOG.